This book is a most welcome addition to the library of understanding that surrounds strategy and seapower. Its academic credentials are robust and its observations and deductions, I found, most helpful.

Clive Johnstone, *Rear Admiral Royal Navy, and Commander, NATO Maritime Command, Northwood*

Current trends of American 'rebalancing' from Europe and the Middle East into the Asia–Pacific, with the simultaneous challenge of conventional Western military and in particular naval capabilities under pressure, could all too easily lure the strategically untrained mind to return to Halford Mackinder's heartland theory to try to grasp the fate of European security. This would deliberately omit the importance of American seapower. In fact, the relationship between American national security and the use of its Navy as a foreign policy tool and a geostrategic instrument has too often been negated by academics, policy-makers, and even the military. This timely book offers a thorough investigation of the basic principles of American national security, naval strategy, the trajectory of US maritime power since the 1980s. It shows how US Navy strategy and its fleet evolved, and where and when it was used in support of larger national (and in some cases international) security ends.

Wolfgang Peischel, *Brigadier General, Austrian Armed Forces*

US Naval Strategy and National Security

This book examines US naval strategy and the role of American seapower over three decades, from the late 20th century to the early 21st century.

This study uses the concept of seapower as a framework to explain the military and political application of sea power and naval force for the United States of America. It addresses the context in which strategy, and in particular US naval strategy and naval power, evolves and how US naval strategy was developed and framed in the international and national security contexts. It explains what drove and what constrained US naval strategy and examines selected instances where American sea power was directed in support of US defense and security policy ends – and whether that could be tied to what a given strategy proposed. The work utilizes naval capstone documents in the framework of broader maritime conceptual and geopolitical thinking, and discusses whether these documents had lasting influences in the strategic mindset, the force structure, and other areas of American sea power. Overall, this work provides a deeper understanding of the crafting of US naval strategy since the final decade of the Cold War, its contextual and structural framework setting, and its application. To that end, the work bridges the gap between the thinking of American naval officers and planners on the one hand and academic analyses of navy strategy on the other hand. It also presents the trends in the use of naval force for foreign policy objectives and into strategy-making in the American policy context.

This book will be of much interest to students of naval power, maritime strategy, US national security, and international relations in general.

Sebastian Bruns heads the Center for Maritime Strategy & Security (CMSS) at the Institute for Security Policy, University of Kiel (ISPK). He is co-editor of the *Routledge Handbook of Naval Strategy and Security* (Routledge, 2016).

Naval Policy and History

Series Editor: Geoffrey Till

This series consists primarily of original manuscripts by research scholars in the general area of naval policy and history, without national or chronological limitations. It will from time to time also include collections of important articles as well as reprints of classic works.

US Naval Strategy and National Security

The Evolution of American Maritime Power

Sebastian Bruns

Routledge
Taylor & Francis Group

LONDON AND NEW YORK

First published 2018 by Routledge

2 Park Square, Milton Park, Abingdon, Oxfordshire OX14 4RN

52 Vanderbilt Avenue, New York, NY 10017

Routledge is an imprint of the Taylor & Francis Group, an informa business

First issued in paperback 2019

British Library Cataloguing in Publication Data
A catalogue record for this book is available from the British Library

Library of Congress Cataloging in Publication Data
Names: Bruns, Sebastian, 1982– author.
Title: US naval strategy and national security : the evolution of American maritime power / Sebastian Bruns.
Other titles: Evolution of American maritime power
Description: Abingdon, Oxon ; New York, NY : Routledge, [2018] | Series: Cass series: naval policy and history 1366–9478 | Includes bibliographical references and index.
Identifiers: LCCN 2017020529 | ISBN 9781138651739 (hardback) | ISBN 9781315624679 (ebook)
Subjects: LCSH: Naval strategy. | Sea-power. | National security–United States. | United States–History, Naval.
Classification: LCC V163 .B78 2018 | DDC 359/.030973–dc23
LC record available at https://lccn.loc.gov/2017020529

ISBN: 978-1-138-65173-9 (hbk)
ISBN: 978-0-367-87754-5 (pbk)

Typeset in Bembo
by Wearset Ltd, Boldon, Tyne and Wear

For Randy, Peter, and John.
To my parents.
And in memory of Professor Edward Keynes, PhD
(1940–2016).

Contents

Acknowledgments

This book is the thoroughly revised and extended version of my PhD dissertation at the University of Kiel, "U.S. Navy Strategy & American Sea Power from 'The Maritime Strategy' (1982–1986) to 'A Cooperative Strategy for 21st Century Seapower' (2007): Politics, Capstone Documents, and Major Naval Operations 1981–2011", 2014 (available online). I would like to thank my dear friend and colleague, Dr. Sarandis "Randy" Papadopoulos, Department of the Navy (Washington, D.C.) for his critical comments on the original draft turning it into a full-fledged book. I am indebted to Captain (USN, ret.) Peter Swartz, Center for Naval Analyses (Arlington, VA), for his wit, expertise, and ability to outsource U.S. Navy strategic research to European scholars like me. Furthermore, I want to thank Dr. John Sherwood, Naval History and Heritage Command (Washington, D.C.). The supervisors of my dissertation, Prof. Dr. Joachim Krause, Director, Institute for Security Policy Kiel University (ISPK), and the late Prof. Edward "Ed" Keynes, have also been instrumental in this endeavor. I am grateful for the support and love from my parents and family, and I thank my naval strategy colleagues in Europe and the United States who, in some form or another, supported this book through professional exchange, interviews, writings, and opening doors that otherwise might have been closed for a landlubber like me. Special thanks to Hannah Ferguson, Senior Editorial Assistant for Military, Strategic and Security Studies at my publisher, for her enduring support and patience with this book.

Acronyms and abbreviations

A2AD	Anti–Access/Area Denial
AAW	Anti–Air Warfare
ABM	Anti–Ballistic Missile
ACUS	Atlantic Council of the United States
ACT	Allied Command Transformation
AEI	American Enterprise Institute
AFB	Air Force Base
AIPAC	American–Israeli Political Action Committee
AIS	Automated Identification System
ALB	AirLand Battle
AOR	Area of Responsibility
ARG	Amphibious Ready Group
APS	African Partnership Station
ASB	Air–Sea Battle
ASuW	Anti–Surface Warfare
ASW	Anti–Submarine Warfare
ATO	Air Tasking Order
AWACS	Airborne Warning and Control System
BB	Battleship
BBAG	Battleship Action Group
BMD	Ballistic Missile Defense
BRAC	Base Realignment and Closure
BUR	Bottom–Up Review
C⁴ISR	Command, Control, Communications, Computers, Intelligence, Surveillance and Reconnaissance
CBO	Congressional Budget Office
CFR	Council on Foreign Relations
CG	Guided Missile Cruiser
CG(X)	Guided Missile Cruiser, future
CGN	Guided Missile Cruiser, Nuclear
CIA	Central Intelligence Agency
CIC	Command Information Center
CINC	Commander in Chief

CIWS	Close-In Weapon System
CJCS	Chairman Joint Chiefs of Staff
CMC	Commandant Marine Corps
CNA	Center for Naval Analyses
CNN	Cable News Network
CNO	Chief of Naval Operations
COCOM	Combatant Commander
COD	Carrier Onboard Delivery
COIN	Counterinsurgency
CONOPS	Concept of Naval Operations
CPG	Contingency Planning Guidance
CRS	Congressional Research Service
CS-21	A Cooperative Strategy for 21st Century Seapower
CSG	Carrier Strike Group
CSI	Container Security Initiative
CSIS	Center for Strategic and International Studies
CTBT	Comprehensive Test-Ban Treaty
CV	Carrier, General Purpose
CVBG	Carrier Battle Group
CVL	Light Aircraft Carrier
CVN	Carrier, Fixed Wing Aircraft, Nuclear
CVV	Aircraft Carrier, Medium Size
CVW	Carrier Air Wing
DD	Destroyer
DDG	Guided Missile Destroyer
DD(X)	Destroyer, Future
DHS	Department of Homeland Security
DOD	Department of Defense
DON	Department of the Navy
DOT	Department of Transportation
DOTMLPF	Doctrine, Organization, Training, Materiel, Leadership and Education, Personnel and Facilities
DPG	Defense Planning Guidance
DR	Disaster Relief
EBO	Effects-Based Operations
EC	European Community
EEZ	Exclusive Economic Zone
EOD	Explosive Ordnance Disposal
ESG	Expeditionary Strike Group
EU	European Union
EW	Electronic Warfare
FBI	Federal Bureau of Investigation
FF	Fast Frigate
FFC	Fleet Forces Command
FFG	Guided Missile Frigate

FGN	Federal German Navy
FOUO	For Official Use Only
FRP	Fleet Response Plan
FY	Fiscal Year
FYDP	Future Years Defense Plan
GAO	Government Accountability Office
GDP	Gross Domestic Product
GFS	Global Fleet Station
GIUK	Greenland–Iceland–United Kingdom Gap
HA	Humanitarian Assistance
HASC	House (of Representatives) Armed Services Committee
HMS	Her Majesty's Ship
HQCG	Headquarter Coast Guard
IDTC	Inter-Deployment Training Cycle
ICBM	Intercontinental Ballistic Missile
ICC	International Criminal Court
IFOR	Implementation Force
ISAF	International Security Assistance Force
ISO	In Support Of
ISPK	Institute for Security Policy at the University of Kiel
ISPS	International Ship and Port Facility Security Code
ISR	Intelligence, Surveillance, Reconnaissance
JCC(X)	Joint Command Ship, future
JCS	Joint Chiefs of Staff
JHSV	Joint High-Speed Vessel
JIATF	Joint Inter-Agency Task Force
JMSDF	Japanese Maritime Self-Defense Force
JOC	Joint Operations Concept
JSCP	Joint Strategic Capabilities Plan
JSF	Joint Strike Fighter
JSPS	Joint Strategic Planning System
KAL	Korean Airlines
LCS	Littoral Combat Ship
LEDET	Law Enforcement Detachment
LHA	Amphibious Assault Ship (General Purpose)
LHD	Amphibious Assault Ship (Multipurpose)
LPD	Amphibious Transport Dock
LPH	Amphibious Assault Ship (Helicopter)
LSD	Landing Ship, Dock
MAB	Marine Amphibious Brigade
MAF	Marine Amphibious Force
MAGTF	Marine Air-Ground Task Force
MARAD	Maritime Administration

MBA	Master in Business Administration
MCCDC	Marine Corps Combat Development Command
MCM	Mine Countermeasures
MCO	Medium Contingency Operation
MDG	Millennium Development Goals
MEU	Marine Expeditionary Unit
MIO	Maritime Interdiction Operations/Maritime Interception Operations
MNF	Multinational Force
MOOTW	Military Operations Other Than War
MPA	Maritime Patrol Aircraft
MPF (F)	Maritime Prepositioning Force (Future)
MPS	Maritime Prepositioning Ship
MRC	Medium Regional Contingency
MSC	Military Sealift Command
MSO	Maritime Security Operations
MTW	Major Theater War
MX	Missile Experimental
N00K	CNO Executive Panel
N513	OPNAV's Strategy and Concepts Branch
NAFTA	North-American Free Trade Association
NAS	Naval Air Station
NATO	North Atlantic Treaty Organization
NAVDOCCOM	Naval Doctrine Command
NDRF	National Defense Reserve Fleet
NFCPE	Naval Force Capabilities Planning Effort
NHHC	Naval History and Heritage Command
NDP	National Defense Policy
NDP	Naval Doctrine Publication
NDS	National Defense Strategy
NECC	Navy Expeditionary Combat Command
NGFS	Naval Gunfire Support
NGO	Nongovernmental Organization
NIE	National Intelligence Estimate
NM	Nautical Mile
NMD	National Missile Defense
NMS	National Military Strategy
NOC	Naval Operations Concept
NOCJO	Naval Operating Concept for Joint Operations
NPT	Non-Proliferation Treaty
NSC	National Security Council
NSD	National Security Directive
NSDD	National Security Decision Directive
NSPG	Navy Strategic Planning Guidance
NSS	National Security Strategy

NWDC	Naval Warfare Development Command
OCO	Overseas Contingency Operations
OEF	Operation Enduring Freedom
OIF	Operation Iraqi Freedom
OLA	Office of Legislative Affairs
OPA	Office of Program Appraisal
OPNAV	Office of the Chief of Naval Operations
OSD	Office of the Secretary of Defense
PDD	Presidential Decision Directive
PLAN	People's Liberation Army Navy
PLO	Palestine Liberation Organization
POM	Program Objective Memoranda
PP	Pacific Partnership
PPBS	Planning, Programming, and Budgeting System
PRM	Presidential Review Memorandum
PSI	Proliferation Security Initiative
PT	Patrol Torpedo Boat
QDR	Quadrennial Defense Review
RAS	Replenishment at Sea
RD&T	Research, Development, and Testing
RHIB	Rigid-Hull Inflatable Boat
RIMPAC	Rim of the Pacific
RMA	Revolution in Military Affairs
ROE	Rules of Engagement
RRF	Ready Reserve Force
SACEUR	Supreme Allied Commander Europe
SAG	Surface Action Group
SAM	Surface to Air Missile
SAR	Search and Rescue
SASC	Senate Armed Services Committee
SC-21	Surface Combatant for the 21st Century
SCO	Shanghai Cooperation Initiative
SDI	Strategic Defense Initiative
SEAL	Sea-Air-Land
SECDEF	Secretary of Defense
SECNAV	Secretary of the Navy
SLEP	Service Life Extension Program
SLOC	Sea Lines of Communication
SNMG	Standing NATO Maritime Group
SNMCMG	Standing NATO Mine-Countermeasures Group
SOF	Special Operations Forces
SOSUS	Sound Surveillance System
SLBM	Submarine-launched Ballistic Missile
SPS	Southern Partnership Station
SSC	Small Surface Combatant

SSN	Ship, Submersible, Nuclear
SSBN	Ship, Submersible, Ballistic Missile, Nuclear
SSG	Strategic Studies Group
SSGN	Ship, Submersible, Guided Missile, Nuclear
STANAVFORLANT	Standing Naval Force Atlantic
STANAVFORMED	Standing Naval Force Mediterranean
START	Strategic Arms Reduction Treaty
T-AH	Hospital Ship (MSC)
T-AKE	Replenishment Naval Vessel (MSC)
T-AKR	Large, Medium Speed Roll-On/Roll-Off Ships (MSC)
T-AO	Replenishment Oiler (MSC)
T-AGOS	Oceanographic Research Ship, General Ocean Surveillance (MSC)
TEU	Twenty-Foot Equivalent Unit
TLAM	Tomahawk Land-Attack Missile
TWA	Trans-World Airlines
UN	United Nations
UNCLOS	United Nations Convention on the Law of the Sea
UNITAF	United Task Force
USA	United States Army
USAF	United States Air Force
USAFRICOM	United States Africa Command
USCENTCOM	United States Central Command
USCG	United States Coast Guard
USEUCOM	United States European Command
USMC	United States Marine Corps
USN	United States Navy
USNA	United States Naval Academy
USNI	United States Naval Institute
USNORTHCOM	United States Northern Command
USNR	United States Navy Reserve
USNWC	United States Naval War College
USPACOM	United States Pacific Command
USS	United States Ship
USSOUTHCOM	United States Southern Command
USSOCOM	United States Special Operations Command
USSR	Union of Soviet Socialist Republics
USSTRATCOM	United States Strategic Command
USTRANSCOM	United States Transportation Command
VBBS	Visit, Board, Search, and Seizure
VLS	Vertical Launch System
V/STOL	Vertical and/or Short Take-off and Landing

WEU	Western European Union
WEUCONMARFOR	Western European Union Contingency Maritime Force
WMD	Weapons of Mass Destruction
WTO	World Trade Organization

1 Introduction

Seapower, strategy, and the particulars of the maritime operating environment

The U.S. Navy is ready to execute the Nation's tasks at sea, from prompt and sustained combat operations to every-day forward-presence, diplomacy and relief efforts. We operate worldwide, in space, cyberspace, and throughout the maritime domain. The United States is and will remain a maritime nation and our security and prosperity are inextricably linked to our ability to operate naval forces on, under and above the seas and oceans of the world.[1]

Research into U.S. politics and policies cannot ignore the particular role of America's sea services and the application of sea power to attain defined political and military ends. Sea power (two words), the exploitation of the opportunities of the sea, is the foundation for American hegemony. The study of the nation, U.S. influence abroad, and the underlying world view cannot be conducted without a sound appreciation for the maritime roots and the seapower (one word) status of the United States.[2] What exactly constitutes a maritime nation, and why is the United States of America one? Why is it that the U.S. Navy is such a self-esteemed maritime force?

As Robert Jervis pointed out, "Outsiders find navies especially hard to comprehend and while they are likely to enjoy photogenic rides on ships they rarely know what fleets do under everyday situations, let alone how they will operate in a crisis."[3] The central importance of the sea beyond as a source of nutrition, a place for recreation and travel, or as one of the principal determinants of the global climate, indeed the notion of sea power, therefore, often escapes the understanding of the individual and many of their political masters. Kearsley noted, "For it is through using the maritime arena as a conduit of power and as a generator of that power (exploiting the ocean's resources) that mankind has affected its own history."[4] He also pointed out that states, as the dominating agents in the global system, were the ones to exercise such power. If power is understood as attaining influence over events, then all states with access to the sea will have some form of maritime power. A navy is but one component of maritime power,[5] although it is likely the most impressive, cost-intensive, and one element begging for strategic, operational, and doctrinal excellence.

It is important to acknowledge that <u>maritime power is a relative, not an absolute concept</u>. Even the semantic terminology begs differentiation and description, for it must be clear what is meant by the various words and descriptions. As Geoff Till reminds us,

2 Flavor of Power: −Inputs −outputs

> Some of [the words analysts work with] are adjectives without nouns ('maritime', 'nautical', 'marine'), others are nouns without adjectives ('sea', 'seapower'). Sometimes there are nouns that have adjectives ('ocean/oceanic', 'navy/naval') but they tend towards greater specificity. [...] The 'power' part of the word 'seapower' itself has generated enormous attention in academic analysis of international politics. What does power actually mean? [...] Power can be either potential, or consequential – or, commonly, both! [...] It has to be seen both as an *input* and an *output*.[6]

Seeking to answer what these maritime, or more precisely naval in- and outputs are in an American context drives the academic and scientific interest of this study.

The Navy, the Marine Corps, and the Coast Guard, as the three inherently maritime and sea-going branches of the U.S. armed forces play a significant role in buttressing American foreign policy goals. They project and protect American power across the world and into some of the remotest regions of the globe. Clearly, the study of the employment of naval forces to attain foreign policy goals is more than just counting gray warship bows in a given region. Instead, it must focus on the overarching concepts of a military service and their particular relationship to the political and operational context from which they originate, and to the political goals they are meant to serve. In the political realm, such measures are often codified in strategies. Whereas the abstract art of strategy – which "seeks synergy and symmetry of objectives, concepts, and resources to increase the probability of policy success and the favorable consequences that follow from that success"[7] – has been subject to many books (particularly with the ascension of the term in virtually every field of the business and service world), there are significantly varying degrees of appreciation for the matter. More precisely, there are differing understandings of the subject altogether. In essence, strategy can mean all kinds of things to all kinds of people. Therefore, regarding the political use and application of strategy, one must be clear and concise in defining the term.

Unsurprisingly, there are a host of factors that inform, restrain, or otherwise influence security policy and corresponding strategy. These are, in no particular order, national interests, institutional checks and balances, military service interests, inter- and inner-service rivalries, grand strategic ideas, defense budgets, public opinion, domestic political dynamics and majorities, past experiences (good and bad), strategic thinking proficiency, international events and the context of the world system, military and technological developments, enduring ideas about the reasons for going to war and how to prevent it, etc. In addition, these issues often interact with each other.

The study of modern naval strategy in general and U.S. Navy strategy in particular has surprisingly attracted relatively few researchers, given the Navy's fairly prominent role in U.S. foreign and security policy. Haynes[8] and Jervis[9] argue that operations, not strategy or the strategic difference the Navy could make, became the lens by which the service and its officer corps looked at the world. The complex demands of naval operations and advanced ship and sensor technology have historically left little room in the careers of naval officers to contemplate the Navy's purpose beyond operations and the political ends to which their service (and perhaps their life) is required. When these officers ascended into the Pentagon or into positions where they were tasked to formulate strategy, they were often overwhelmed or saw little to no value in making the strategic case for the U.S. Navy altogether. This isolation negates the important role of U.S. sea power in the modern world. Conversely, modern contemporary naval strategy has attracted relatively little interest with political scientists since the heydays of Samuel Huntington and John Mearsheimer.[10]

The nature of sea power and the employment of naval force have been subject to changing political yet relatively stable geographic positions. The value of established nineteenth and twentieth century 'old-school' seapower theory need recognition and assessment. The importance of decisive battles at sea as the central determinant of victory and defeat, for example, has decreased steadily. Instead, more complex and comprehensive uses of naval forces could be observed. This complexity mandates, in turn, a coherent strategy if one wishes to use naval force successfully because "strategy now refers not only to the direct application of military force in wartime but also to the use of all aspects of national power during peacetime to deter war and win."[11]

This book provides a deeper understanding of the crafting of U.S. Navy strategy since the final decade of the Cold War, its contextual and structural framework setting, and its application. To that end, the work bridges the gap between the thinking of American naval officers and planners on the one hand and academic analyses of Navy strategy on the other hand. It also seeks to provide trends in the use of naval force for foreign policy objectives and into strategy-making in the American policy context. As such, it spans the recent history of internal U.S. Navy thought and external strategic theory.

Perhaps with a grain of salt, it must be stated that future developments and the resulting policy demands absent a crystal ball, remain somewhat speculative and often sketchy at best. After all,

> Strategy is such a plaything of technology and geopolitical shifts that one can never say with complete confidence that any particular area will always be of low strategic salience. The news headlines of the years since 1945 have been peppered with the names of unfamiliar places, about

which most people know little, but which were suddenly and often tragi-
cally thrust into importance.[12]

However, if one accepts the premise of a decline in land-centric and a rise in
maritime- or naval-centric issues in the twenty-first century, it follows that
these developments occur in an increasingly chaotic world. It also follows that
the need for sound understanding and making of strategy will be in higher
demand in the future, both in the U.S. and in its allied countries.

Outline

This study uses the concept of seapower as a framework to explain the
military and political application of sea power and naval force for the United
States of America. It will address the context in which strategy – and in particular U.S. Navy strategy and naval power – evolves. Cropsey points out that
"Wide-ranging seapower is not so much an instrument of force – although
that it is – as a condition of stable commerce, effective diplomacy, and
regional influence."[13] Using the first iterations of "The Maritime Strategy" in
the early 1980s and the publication of "A Cooperative Strategy for 21st
Century Seapower" in its revised version of 2015 as cornerstones, this study
shows how U.S. Navy strategy was developed and framed in the international
and national security contexts. It explains what drove and constrained U.S.
Navy strategy and looks at selected instances where American sea power was
directed in support of U.S. defense and security policy ends – and whether
that could be tied to what a given strategy proposed. It also discusses whether
documents had lasting influences in the strategic mindset, the force structure,
and other areas of American sea power.

First, to this end, one should discuss the theoretical foundations of seapower. Afterwards, this study embeds naval strategy in the setting of overarching U.S. policy and American grand strategy. In untangling the complex
web of a bureaucracy, the study sheds a light on who (and what) makes and
influences U.S. Navy strategy. Second, the research explains the development
of U.S. Navy strategy over the course of some three decades.

Research design and puzzle

A look at history reveals that the 1980s' versions of "The Maritime Strategy"
were the first *expressive verbis* strategic documents for the employment of naval
forces since World War II. That series of documents cannot be seen as isolated from the developments of the 1970s which substantially contributed to
their making. "The Maritime Strategy," a document that went through a
number of iterations, thus provides a unique starting point without which the
development of strategies in the decades since cannot be understood. The
objective of this survey is the study of the *strategic* development of U.S. Navy
strategy, and the broader application of sea power for U.S. national security

interests, rather than of the development of a singular *strategy*, which would require a different methodology altogether.

This book addresses the following issues as reflected by the U.S. Navy's declaratory, or published, capstone strategies. Such is the fivefold research puzzle:

- How can seapower and sea power be analyzed and understood in the American context?
- Which factors govern the utility of the Navy for U.S. foreign and security policy as a whole?
- What policies, programs, factors, and actors must be considered for each decade to arrive at a sound and highly diagnostic assessment regarding the evolution of documents and strategic concepts?
- How, where, and why was the U.S. Navy used during the decades in question? Do these selected naval operations reflect well the naval missions which strategic documents prescribed?
- What recurring themes and lessons can be drawn from three decades of Navy strategy-making and application of U.S. sea power?

It is difficult to quantify the value of sea power for national security.[14] A coherent, limiting research design founded in the spirit of the strategic studies is thus imperative. First, the timeframe is large enough to allow a coherent analysis and pattern-seeking exercise for U.S. seapower and sea power. Second, it is within the living memory of current theorists and practitioners. Source access is therefore favorable while an academic desideratum is still significant. Third, even cursory research suggests that enduring principles and conditions shape Navy strategic thinking and consecutive documents. It is thus prudent to consider a longer period of time rather than one particular strategy document or one presidential term. Fourth, and perhaps most important, the period contains reinvigorated Navy strategic statements in light of geopolitical shifts and changes, all with considerable scope and significance. This study takes the concept of seapower as a setting, explaining who (and what) makes, shapes, and factors in American sea power and, consequently, its Navy's strategy. That approach is embedded in a discussion of naval force theory, naval missions, and the particulars of the maritime domain.

Therefore, it is not a discourse analysis. Nor is it a re-telling akin to a popular history of how a certain strategy came about. Conscious of the historiography that political scientists and disciples of the strategic studies must address, this book relates pragmatically the Navy's strategies to its strategic culture and to the political, strategic, and military context at the time of publication. Spanning 35 years of U.S. Navy strategy and the employment of naval forces for various foreign and security policy means, it is also an analysis of the larger naval power theme in U.S. security policy, and the utility of naval forces as postulated in strategic documents and as underlined in selected operations.

The selection of the documents was guided by three principles:

1 A desire to pick high-level documents which reflect strategies spanning the decade, respectively, as well as institutional thought;
2 Provision of some scope and sense of where the Navy is coming from, where it found itself at certain times, and a postulation of where it was going, or where it wanted to go;
3 And finally, a workable indication of American sea power, as reflected in strategies and selected operations, for the timeframe 1981–2016. To that end, the book draws on relevant existing sources and literature, a number of partially standardized interviews,[15] and the author's own first-hand experience working for the U.S. Congress as a German Marshall Fun/ American Political Science Association Congressional Fellow.[16]

Methodology for analysis

The study uses an analytical pattern in that it concentrates on:

1 macro-level grand strategic developments;
2 domestic factors and events;
3 development of U.S. Navy strategies (taking into account technological developments);
4 the particular sea strategic concept behind such capstone documents;
5 force planning (including budgeting);
6 planned vs. actual implementation (strategically and operationally); and
7 assessments of selected strategies regarding their legacy and enduring naval power principles, in particular in light of the dialectic of strategic offense and defense on the spectrum of engagement.[17]

Using this methodology, the book takes U.S. Navy capstone documents into consideration to produce a strategic analysis. It considers only overarching, "Washington-level" documents with significant involvement of top-level officials which transport fundamental assertions about the use of American sea power (more precisely: naval power), communicate aspiration to shape the course of events, and inform the Navy, the other sea services, politics, and the larger public.[18] Given their reciprocal relationship with U.S. Navy strategy, global and regional (geo-)political situations, national security strategies and events, and technological innovations need to further inform the frame of reference.

Such a contextualizing approach serves as a pattern that allows tracking of U.S. Navy strategy development since the end of the Cold War and comprehending it as a product of the strategic *science* and the *art* of strategy.[19] There is neither a formal nor a mathematical proof that one strategy is better than another.[20] 'Successful' strategy – the adjective is problematic – thus must be measured against achieving a clearly articulated objective, the emphasis of relative superiority versus an antagonist, a faithful cost-revenue calculation, and a check of advantages and disadvantages of alternative strategies.[21] An analysis of an antagonist's or competitor's behaviors as well as of domestic politics must also be considered, where possible. Quite important is that the quality of a given strategy is dependent on the intellectual capacities of the senior political leadership.[22] In sum, the methodological challenges of strategic analysis, especially regarding the U.S. Navy, are manifold:

> Proof of a document's 'success' is impossible; too many interacting military, political, bureaucratic, economic & human factors to track; impossibility of untangling all relationships; difficulty in finding data (very sparse and unbalanced literature; difficulty in finding *accurate* data (memories can be thin reeds); precise parallels between past & present & *future* are speculative.[23]

In turn, this makes the methodology of identifying and analyzing a pattern all the more central. It should be helpful to visualize, again, the context of the subject area of interest and how it can be framed methodologically (Figure 1.1).

Limits and constraints of this study

This study, as previously noted, is in the field of political science. More precisely, it is a contribution to the sub-discipline of strategic studies. Strategic studies are less concerned with fundamental research but rather focus on

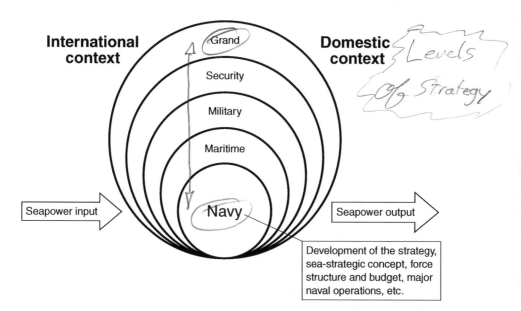

Figure 1.1 The setting of the U.S. Navy strategy.

trends and developments in a policy-prescriptive, hands-on, and operational manner. Thus, the work also acknowledges neighboring disciplines such as military history, geography, and cultural studies. Its contributions and limits follow.

First, this book must show the broad scope and application of sea power in a U.S. context to underline the role of the Navy in U.S. foreign and security policy. This is the desirable original contribution to the strategic studies.

Second, returning to the semantic problem discussed earlier, the study must define carefully what is actually meant by the term (Navy/naval/maritime) strategy. Even cursory research shows that the "U.S. Navy [is] never rigorous in its approach to policy/strategy/concepts terminology. Definitions [are] considered dull, unimportant [and] individual idiosyncratic approached abound (and change over time)."[24] The Navy has referred to its capstone documents – and in fact labeled them as – white papers, doctrines, concepts, and strategic concepts, concepts of naval operations (CONOPS), principles, missions, strategic plans, and simply strategies. Some were capitalized, others not. Some played with ellipses, others were bureaucratic acronym behemoths. Clearly, there is more in strategy than a simple branding suggests, as this study will illustrate.

Third, there must be an appreciation as part of this study as to what the original sources can supply in meaningfulness, and where they perhaps fall short in the overall assessment of sea power application and Navy success. Determining such – relative – value of one U.S. Navy document over another can be undertaken, for instance, through the prism of their alignment with national policies and Navy strategic culture, sustained convincing of political appropriators, and persuasiveness of friends, allies, and potential adversaries. Such comparisons come at a high price because a strict comparison will hardly yield more resilient results. Ultimately, only qualified general statements of a document's prevailing impact can be derived to describe emerging and lasting patterns. Therefore, the study aims at identifying recurring themes and processes in U.S. Navy strategy and strategic sea power application.

Last but not least: as an analysis of a subject with expansive U.S. national security ramifications, this study can only draw upon such material that is openly accessible at the time of writing, unclassified, or declassified. Accordingly, findings and policy recommendations of this study must be seen in light of those constraints.[25]

The use of the sea

If it holds true that "seapower is the product of an amalgam of interconnected constituents that are difficult to tease apart" and "these constituents are attributes of countries that make it easier or harder for them to be strong at sea,"[26] then it behooves to also look at these components and the actual use and usage of the sea for political purposes. The sea as a domain of defense and security is of substantial strategic importance, when one or more parties to a conflict rely on the uninhibited use of the sea lanes for transportation, provision of troops and equipment, or desire maritime resources. Command and control of the maritime arena are also of significance to deter land powers. The appreciation for one's own dependence on the uninhibited use of the sea must never be lost.[27] According to Eric Grove, one can distinguish a military, a diplomatic, and a constabulary role for the use of the maritime domain (Figure 1.2).[28]

There are three principal security-political uses of the sea. The military use includes the projection of power ashore, sea control, and sea denial. The diplomatic use includes showing of the flag and various forms of gunboat diplomacy. The constabulary use includes maintenance of sovereignty and good order, safeguarding of national resources, and peacekeeping. Navies principally have the largest role in all of these, although coast guards, state-owned civilian-crewed vessels, harbor police units, and other institutions can use the sea (in particular in a diplomatic or constabulary role) as well.[29] In any larger regional, and certainly any global struggle for power, command of the seas played a vital role.[30] The Netherlands, Spain, Portugal, and certainly Great Britain are more contemporary examples which demonstrated global political aspirations – or *Weltpolitik* – and the quest for power status goes hand-in-hand with oceanic command and the control of the seas. In all major conflicts and wars that were not exclusively fought by land powers, sea power played a role in various stages, albeit to differing degrees.[31] How does the United States, as an heir to the sea powers of the past,[32] thus stand in this line, using the sea for the roles outlined here?

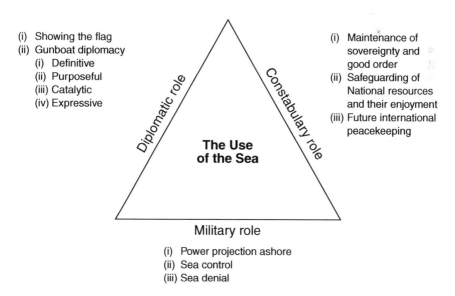

Figure 1.2 The 'use of the sea' triangle (Grove 1990: 234).

Seapower and sea power

For reasons of their physical topography and political geography, most states in most eras of their history have either displayed a clearly continental or decisively maritime imprint of their strategic posture and culture.[33]

For a state, the utilization of the sea for political purposes is an incentive for seeking prosperity and the preservation of the integrity of the sovereign (this can certainly stem from such significant dilemmas as the dependence on functioning maritime trade). A government can purposely execute maritime might to consolidate power and seek to embellish it on a grander scale. Therefore, sea power (two words) is to be understood as a functional application of power at, from, above, or across the sea. A seapower (one word) is a maritime-minded institution (a nation-state) with a given number of prerequisites to exercise sea power successfully toward larger objectives. In other words, " 'Seapower' […] is something that particular countries, or sea powers, have."[34]

The classic application of sea power is a military one.[35] The use of military might is usually for one, or a combination, of three political ends: deterrence, coercion, or defense. If military power is employed against an adversary, a state does so because it seeks to prevent that adversary from doing something (deter it), to force that adversary to change its behavior (coerce or compel it), or to protect itself against some harmful action that the adversary threatens or has taken (defend itself).[36]

Theories on sea power

The Greek philosopher Thucydides (*c*.460–*c*.395 BC) emphasized that neither sea power nor seapower could be improvised, but had to be masterfully crafted and continuously developed to serve the varying needs of a state in the different stages of peace, crisis, and war.[37] In other words, a seapower is not a disembodied concentration of armed vessels, intelligence, communication, or related competencies to launch and sustain great fleets. In fact, it resembles a living and breathing organism empowered by commerce, animated by a substantial merchant fleet, in possession of bases, and fortified by naval power.[38]

It was the U.S. naval officer Alfred Thayer Mahan, according to one of his biographers not a military strategist or navalist in any sense of the word, but rather a world politics analyst and historically minded strategy theorist,[39] who developed ideas of the principal conditions that govern the institutional seapower of nations:[40] geographic position, natural resources and climate, extent of state territory, population, and the character of the people and government. When these terms were principally maritime in nature, the likelihood for a state to claim seapower status and display a willingness to extend and defend such aspirations rose significantly. However compelling these terms are, they can only partially be supported with empirical data. It may be relatively easy to assess geographic position and conditions, and the extent of territory, on the basis of geographic (and geospatial) data. For questions of character, however, especially in a population, this is much more difficult. Seapower, according to Mahan, was thus not something that could be calculated easily using mathematical formulas.

In its functional variant, sea power means the control and influence of international trade, war at sea, and the use of naval forces as instruments of diplomacy, deterrence, and political interaction in the absence of major war.[41] Sea power as a means of exercising power, at least for a territorially constituted state, can be expressed in a formula according to Edward Wegener (1904–1981). According to Wegener, it could be expressed by the following formula:

$$\text{Seapower} = \text{Fleet} \times \text{Bases} \times \text{Maritime Thinking.}[42]$$

In relative terms

However, this equation, as Wegener was ready to admit, is only a finding of relative value. While fleet size and number of bases can be counted, maritime thinking is hardly quantifiable. Moreover, sea power as a whole is dependent on a state's political objectives, that is, what it intends to use its seapower for, as well as its geographic position. The product is therefore not to be taken as a mathematical value. Seapower is not the sum, but rather the product of the formula shown above. If one factor goes towards zero, the product is also zero.[43]

Need a bit of everything

Mahan's institutional framework for seapower has continued to be the point of departure for many theorists. According to British naval historian Eric Grove, economic strength, technological prowess, socio–political culture (factors of the first order), geographical position, dependence in terms of seaborne trade, merchant marine, shipbuilding, fish catch, offshore zone, and government policy and perception (factors of the second order) would principally affect the sea power of nations.[44] The frequent conceptual return to Mahan's thinking shows some of the enduring constants of determining sea power. Whereas the application of strategic principles to any given situation might be complex, the basics of strategy are relatively constant – a downright "Clausewitzian observation."[45,46] Along with geography, such lasting concepts provide intellectual underpinning for the military and geo-economic understandings of seapower and sea power.[47]

The application of sea power is to guarantee command of the seas, or the comprehensive control of relevant maritime areas (seas, oceans, lines of communication) for policy objectives.[48] With a proactive, offensive approach, states that seek to challenge the indivisible control of the sea shall be forced into decisive battle at sea in the sense of concentration of forces,[49] a concept based on the Swiss strategic thinker Antoine-Henri Jomini (1779–1869).[50] The idea that a superior naval battle force conducting offensive operations at sea was at the core of maritime strategy gained lasting popularity during the twentieth century.[51]

Given that complete command of the sea is impossible because of the physical nature of the oceans, and frankly unnecessary given the vast expanse of the globe, a group of French naval officers (*Jeune École*) developed a strategic theory that challenged Mahan's preconceptions. They established the more defensive concept called sea denial, or the partial disturbance of aspirations to command the seas. They advocated the use of torpedoes, mines, submarines, blockades, and targeted attacks on trading routes. Sea denial disrupted and restricted command of the seas. In marginal seas and other geographically confined areas it could even be impossible for the numerically larger, more capable navy to exercise command of the sea altogether. This approach rested on the technological innovations of the nineteenth and early twentieth centuries and signaled the evolution of classic sea power concepts. In addition, the *Jeune École* proposed raiding an opponent's commercial fleet to drain his supply and resources. Reflecting this emerging shift in thinking, command of the sea appeared to be widely anachronistic. By the 1970s it had been substituted by the more appropriate term 'sea control.' The change in terminology was a deliberate attempt to acknowledge the limitations of ocean control in an age of multi-dimensional warfare at sea. As opposed to 'command of the sea,' which insinuated total control of the seas for one's own purpose or total denial to an enemy, the new term 'sea control' pointed out the more realistically achievable control in limited areas and for limited periods of time.[52] It did not, however, address certain gray areas such as "fleets in being" (a naval force that extends control over an adjacent body of water or near seas without leaving port).

Naval forces serving as an instrument for the policy of a state must consequently be geared toward achieving political objectives, not striving for absolute dominion of the seas as an end itself. The value of military means thus should be measured in terms of their contribution to a state's grand strategy. The major foreign policy effect of sea power that rests on the ability to control (rather than command) seas in times of peace is its potential application in times of war.[53] In sum, sea control can be understood as the management of maritime lines of communication by naval means with the goal of keeping them open for one's own military and economic uses, while denying such to the enemy. It is not an absolute, but rather a relative variable in power politics. The sea, as opposed to territory ashore, cannot be conquered, occupied, or controlled in any such fashion. Whereas armies are designed and trained to control territory, navies are tasked with securing access to territory, international maritime routes, and trade.[54]

The introduction of the submarine and the aircraft in the early twentieth century and the development of nuclear weapons since the 1940s changed the nature of naval warfare and the concept of sea power as Mahan and his contemporaries defined it. World War II showcased the trend toward increasingly more joint (different branches of the military integrating) and combined (different countries' militaries increasingly working together) operations. That war also highlighted the utility of new platforms and tactics in novel naval missions, for example anti–submarine warfare (ASW). It provided the impetus for the aircraft carrier and naval aviation to replace the battleship as the capital unit of the fleets. In the age of the Cold War, which underlined the utility of naval forces on the spectrum of conflict below general (nuclear) war, it was apparent that the understanding and exercise of that sea power had to be reconsidered.[55] Against this background, the gradual supersession of Mahan's central argument of decisive battle at sea by other strategic functions below the threshold of general war became increasingly plausible and popular.

The spectrum of conflict was illustrated succinctly for "The Maritime Strategy" of the 1980s. It displayed the three generic phases of international engagement (peacetime presence, crisis response, and war) and showed the cor-relation between the probability of occurrence and the level of violence. It also marked degrees of plausible naval operations designed to support national objectives in such phases.[56] Sea power, the reasoning went, can be utilized on the whole spectrum und thus offer significant utility to policy-makers.

At the same time, the fundamentals of naval force application have remained constant, thus informing the making of strategy on how to apply sea power. Frank Uhlig has pointed out that despite the variety of conflicts that navies were engaged in during the past two centuries and the vast changes in their instruments, there is a remarkable constancy in how they go about their business. In the overwhelming majority of cases, navies have been employed for

> (1) The strategic movement of troops (and now, of armies and air forces alike); (2) The acquisition of advanced bases as close as possible to the scene of the action, by either military force or civil means; (3) the landing of armies on a hostile shore and their support then and thereafter by means of fire and logistics; (4) the blockade, and (5) the struggle for master of the local sea.[57]

[handwritten margin note: USES of the Navy]

The persistence of naval utility is noteworthy. Its relative independence from most changes in political dynamics makes it an interesting tool for statecraft. As H.P. Willmot pointed out, "Sea power is a rational instrument of state power and […] a long–term phenomenon […]."[58] This comes at a certain price, though. Pointing toward the need for a grand design and thus a distin-guished strategic approach, Colin Gray notes that, "Ships, design teams, industries, and, above all, experience cannot be improvised."[59] This in turn calls once again for a sound strategy, which in the political and military realm is usually understood as the declaratory path of how to connect ways, means, and ends with (naval) power. Such strategies must contribute to the overall goals of a state. They must inform decision–makers, preferably while offering a long–term perspective, in the political, military, and industry spheres. Pref-erably, they also convince the public because the tax-payer is ultimately the financier of such strategies and the underlying materiel in support of a funda-mental national service: survival and defense of the homeland.

It is imperative to understand strategy as an interdisciplinary approach. One must include political, economic, geographic, technological, and perhaps even sociological and psychological perspectives. Military force structure, operations, and tactics are of note as well[60] to dissolve the ritualized character of blunt force in conflicts and replace it with a higher degree of rationality.[61] While the desire for strategy is apparent, it is often nonetheless the level of the military construct that in the eyes of many decision-makers warrants the least attention. Strategy is not politically expedient, as Liotta and Lloyd cautioned.[62] Rather, it is a long-term instrument that supports shaping the future environment. In the absence of strategy, there is not a reliable direction for policy and planning. There may be several routes to the goal but enduring crises and changes along the way will be painful teachers.

According to retired U.S. Army general David Barno, the modern U.S. military is characterized by an overwhelming focus on doctrine, organization, training, leadership, materiel, personnel, and facilities weighted heavily toward the tactical level, with proportionally less investment in the operational and strategic levels. Accordingly, defense spending – both procurement and future research and development – heavily centers on tactical-level requirements. Tanks, helicopters, fighter planes, individual body armor, and assault combat ships all provide the combat power to fight and win battles at the tactical level. These are immediate demands often justified by wartime needs, but they are usually hardly rationalized by tying them to strategy.[63]

Notes

1 U.S. Navy Program Guide 2017, 3.
2 This study uses "sea power" to speak of the functional use of maritime and naval assets, whereas "seapower" describes the institutional quality.
3 Jervis, Robert, 1995, 44.
4 Kearsley, 1992, xii.
5 Rahn, 1994, 137–138.
6 Till, 2009, 20–21, emphasis in the original.
7 Yarger, 2006, 1.
8 Haynes, 2013, 7.
9 Jervis, 1995, 44.
10 Huntingon, 1954, and Mearsheimer, 1986. Notable recent publications by political scientists and IR scholars (consciously omitting historians here), indicating a reversal of this trend, include (Swiss) Larissa Forster's study, *Influence without Boots on the Ground* (2013), (Austrian) Nikolaus Scholik's *Seemacht im 21. Jahrhundert. Handbuch & Lexikon* (2015); the works of ADM (USN) ret. James Stavridis; and the forthcoming PhD dissertations by Lt. CDR (SWE N) Stefan Lundqvist (on post-Cold War maritime security changes in Western powers at Åbo Akademi University, Finland), (Austrian) Michael Haas (on U.S. naval doctrinal adaptation during the late Cold War and beyond, University of Zurich, Switzerland/University of Kiel, Germany), and (Austro-American) Jeremy Stöhs (on European navies since the end of the Cold War, University of Kiel, Germany).
11 Owens, 2007, 112.
12 Booth, 1985, 107.

13 Cropsey, 2013, 34.

14 The assessment of the relative merit of seapower has drawn intense academic interest. For a quantitative study, see Brian Crisher/Mark Souva (2012): Power At Sea: A Naval Power Dataset, 1865–2011.

15 These conversations were conducted in 2012 in Washington, D.C., Arlington, VA, Norfolk, VA and Mons, Belgium, and were graciously supported by grants of the U.S. Department of Defense/Department of the Navy (Washington, D.C.) and the *Michael-Freund-Gesellschaft* (Kiel). Moreover, in two cases interviews were also facilitated via the online communication software Skype.

16 Beyond the usual exposure to the political and politicized environment of the capital, the fellowship allowed for authoritative insights into policy-making on Capitol Hill and the Pentagon. Serving then-Representative Todd Young (a Republican Party member from Indiana, since 2017 Senator of that state), a former naval officer and member of the United State House Committee on Armed Services in the 112th Congress, the author was privileged to gain substantial experiences and insights into the 'engine room' of U.S. military and defense policy as well as to contribute/participate in policy-making processes himself. For a review of the fellowship, see Sebastian Bruns (2012).

17 This approach is inspired by Geoff Till's discussion of the setting of sea power and seapower (2009: 21).

18 Similar approach to Swartz and Duggan (2011: 16, slide 32): He cautions that CNO (Chief of Naval Operations, the U.S. Navy's highest-ranking officer) involvement and visibility should also be taken into account when choosing the capstone documents to look at. Self-descriptions, on the other hand, are often of little help, for documents of the same league have been labeled as "strategies," "concepts," "visions," "strategic plans," etc. In the face of few formal definitions on the term (some of which may even change over time, too), Swartz rightfully underscores the need for this working interpretation. It should also be noted at this time that this dissertation does not attempt to analyze unsigned and aborted draft efforts of capstone documents in-depth (for a list of examples, see Swartz and Duggan, 2011: 17, slide 34).

19 Thomas Mahnken (2010: 70) stated that, in the face of numerous strategic choices which are influenced both by people and by political realities, "[Strategy] is more an art than a science. [...] [But that] does not mean that it cannot be studies systematically. Rather, the theory of strategy consists of concepts and considerations instead of fixed laws."

20 Kugler, 2006, 86.

21 Mahnken, 2010, 69.

22 Wagener, 2010, 10–11. It should be noted that this is a difficult, if not impossible feat to measure. For illustration: just because a political or military leader in Washington, D.C. does not have a Navy background, he or she will not automatically disfavor the Navy for a lack of intellectual embrace of all things maritime. The same holds true for the other way around: a Navy background does not automatically warrant a comprehensive proposition of the sea-going services. As an instructive example, consider the presidency of James E. "Jimmy" Carter (1977–1981), a graduate of the U.S. Naval Academy (Class of 1947). As will be emphasized in the central chapters of this study, his presidency was one that is largely viewed as detrimental to the Navy. Ronald Reagan's two terms (1981–1989), on the other hand, were a period of "naval renaissance." Reagan was a U.S. Army Captain during World War II, serving on the U.S. East and West coasts, but not overseas. His background was in the acting and the advocacy business before he became a politician in the 1950s. This goes to show that personal backgrounds of stakeholders are hardly an analytical category to reckon with. Personalities and strategy-making, as much as everything else, is about context, and political and personal interplay.

23 Swartz and Duggan, 2011, 12, slide 24, emphasis in original.

24 Swartz and Duggan, 2011, 23, slide 45.
25 This book is based on the study *U.S. Navy Strategy & American Sea Power from 'The Maritime Strategy' (1982–1986) to 'A Cooperative Strategy for 21st Century Seapower' (2007): Politics, Capstone Documents and Major Naval Operations 1981–2011*, submitted as a PhD dissertation at the University of Kiel in 2014. For the purpose of this work, the manuscript has been thoroughly revised and amended for the period of 2011–2016.
26 Till, 2009, 83.
27 McDonald, 1984, 62.
28 Grove's assessment mirrors Ken Booth's analysis on the role of naval forces in foreign policy, where the latter designed a similar, albeit less ambitious triangle (Booth, 1979: 16).
29 Even non-state navies such as the Sea Tigers (the naval wing of the Liberation Tigers of Tamil Ealam during the Sri Lankan civil war), Greenpeace, and the Sea Shepherd Conservation Society (a militant marine conservation organization) utilize the roles of the sea within their means.
30 Wegener, 1974, 37.
31 Scholik, 2011, 91.
32 Potter and Nimitz (eds), 1982, xiii.
33 Gray, 1992, 2.
34 Till, 2009, 21.
35 Wegener, 1974, 25.
36 Art, 2003, 4–5.
37 Art, 2003, 15.
38 Cropsey, 2013, 168–169.
39 Schössler, 2009, 495.
40 Tangredi, 2002a, 119.
41 Tangredi, 2002a, 114.
42 Wegener, 1974, 29; Wegener, 1982, 1085–1086.
43 Duppler, 1999, 19.
44 Grove, 1990, 221–232.
45 Boorman, 2009, 92.
46 Carl von Clausewitz (1780–1831), Prussian general and military theorist, most renowned for his groundbreaking work "On War". For an introduction to his work, see Paret (1986). For a short essay on the conceptual relationship between the works of Clausewitz and Mahan, see Preuschoft (1998).
47 Tangredi, 2002a, 114.
48 Wegener, 1974, 36.
49 Crowl, 1986, 456.
50 Stahel, 2013, 40–44.
51 Till, 2009, 54.
52 Till, 2009, 145–152.
53 Wegener, 1974, 25.
54 Tangredi, 2002a, 130.
55 Hattendorf, 2004, 5.
56 Tangredi, 2002b; source: The Maritime Strategy, U.S. Naval Institute Proceedings, January 1986 supplement, 8.
57 Uhlig, Frank, 1997, 96.
58 Cited in Gray, 1994, 86.
59 Gray, Colin, 1994, 86.
60 Baylis, Wirtz, and Gray, 2010, 5.
61 Wagener, 2010, 4.
62 Liotta and Lloyd, 2005, 121.
63 Barno, 2005, 17–18.

References

Barno, David. "Challenges in Fighting a Global Insurgency." *Parameters* (Summer 2006).

Baylis, John, Witz, James, and Gray, Colin. *Strategy in the Contemporary World: An Introduction to Strategic Studies*, 3rd edition. Oxford: Oxford University Press, 2010.

Boorman, Scott. "Fundamentals of Strategy. The Legacy of Henry Eccles." *Naval War College Review*, vol. 62, no. 2 (April 2009).

Booth, Ken. *Navies and Foreign Policy*. New York: Holmes & Meier, 1979.

Booth, Ken. *Law, Force & Diplomacy at Sea*. London: George Allen and Unwin, 1985.

Bruns, Sebastian. "A Window Seat on American Politics: Reflections on the GMFUS/APSA Congressional Fellowship." *PS: Political Science & Politics 45* (2012), 343-345.

Crisher, Brian, and Souva Mark. "Power at Sea: A Naval Power Dataset, 1865–2011," working paper, Florida State University, Tallahassee, FL, 2012.

Cropsey, Seth. *Mayday. The Decline of American Naval Supremacy*. New York and London: Overlook Duckworth, 2013.

Crowl, Philipp. "Alfred Thayer Mahan: The Naval Historian." *Makers of Modern Strategy from Machiavelli to the Nuclear Age*, ed. P. Paret. Princeton, NJ: Princeton University Press, 1986.

Die Rolle der Seemacht in unserer Zeit. "*Seemacht: Eine Seekriegsgeschichte von der Antike bis zur Gegenwart*," eds. E.B. Potter and C.W. Nimitz. German edition coordinated by the Arbeitskreises für Wehrforschung von Jürgen Rohwer. Herrsching: Pawlak 1982.

Duppler, Jörg. "Seemacht, Seestrategie, Seeherrschaft." *Seemacht und Seestrategie im 19. und 20. Jahrhundert*, ed. J. Duppler. Hamburg: Mittler & Sohn (= Vorträge zur Militärgeschichte, vol. 18, distributed by the Militärgeschichtliches Forschungsamt), 1999.

Gray, Colin. *The Leverage of Sea Power: The Strategic Advantage of Navies in War*. New York: Macmillan, 1992.

Gray, Colin, *The Navy in the Post-Cold War World: The Uses and Value of Strategic Sea Power*. University Park, PA: Penn State Press, 1994.

Grove, Eric. *The Future of Sea Power*. London: Routledge, 1990.

Hattendorf, John, ed. *The Evolution of the U.S. Navy's Maritime Strategy, 1977–1986*. Newport, RI: Naval War College Press, 2004.

Haynes, Peter. *American Naval Thinking in the Post-Cold War Era: The U.S. Navy and the Emergence of a Maritime Strategy, 1989–2007*, dissertation, Naval Postgraduate School, Monterey, CA, 2013.

Jervis, Robert. "Navies, Politics, and Political Science." *Doing Naval History: Essays Towards Improvement*, ed. J. Hattendorf. Newport, RI: Naval War College Press, 1995.

Kearsley, Harold. *Maritime Power and the Twenty-First Century*. Aldershot, UK: Dartmouth, 1992.

Kugler, Richard. *Policy Analysis in National Security Affairs: New Methods for a New Era*. Washington, D.C.: NDU Press, 2006.

Liotta, P.H., and Lloyd, Richmond. "From Here to There. The Strategy and Force Planning Framework." *Naval War College Review* 58(2) (2005).

McDonald, Wesley. "Effective, Efficient Sea Power." *Sea Link. Supplement to Proceedings on the Occasion of the Politics and Sea Power Conference*, ed. U.S. Naval Institute. Annapolis, MD: NIP 1984.

Mackubin, Owens. "Commentary: Strategy and the Strategic Way of Thinking." *Naval War College Review* 60(4) (2007), 111-24.

Mahnken, Thomas. "Strategic Theory." *Strategy in the Contemporary World. An Introduction to Strategic Studies*, eds. J. Baylis/J. Wirtz/C. Gray. 3rd edition. Oxford/New York: Oxford University Press, 2010.

Paret, Peter. "Clausewitz." *Makers of Modern Strategy from Machiavelli to the Nuclear Age*, edited by P. Paret. Princeton: Princeton University Press, 1986.

Preuschoft, Olaf. "Vom Seekriege: Mahan und Clausewitz." *Marineforum*, no. 12/1998 (December 1998).

Rahn, Werner. "Germany." *Ubi Sumus? The State of Naval and Maritime History*, ed. J. Hattendorf. Newport, RI: Naval War College Press, 1994, 137–159.

Scholik, Nikolaus. *Zur geopolitisch-geostrategischen Bedeutung von Seewegen: Die Strassen von Hormuz, Malakka und die Nordwestpassage*, dissertation, University of Vienna, Vienna, Austria, 2011.

Schössler, Dietmar. *Clausewitz, Engels, Mahan. Grundrisse einer Ideengeschichte militärischen Denkens*. Münster: Lit Verlag, 2009.

Stahel, Albert. "Geostrategie und Seemacht." *Maritime Sicherheit*, eds. S. Bruns/K. Petretto/D. Petrovic. Wiesbaden: VS Verlag für Sozialwissenschaften, 2013.

Swartz, Peter, and Duggan, Karin. *U.S. Navy Capstone Strategy and Concepts: Introduction, Background and Analyses* (slideshow). Alexandria, VA: CNA, 2011.

Tangredi, Sam, ed. *"Sea Power Theory and Practice": Strategy in the Contemporary World. An Introduction to Strategic Studies*, 1st edition, eds. J. Baylis, J. Wirtz, E. Cohen, and C. Gray. Oxford, UK: Oxford University Press, 2002a, 113–136.

Tangredi, Sam. "Assessing New Missions." *Transforming America's Military*, edited by H. Binnendijk, Washington, D.C.: NDU Press, 2002b, 3-30.

Till, Geoffrey. *Seapower. A Guide for the 21st Century*. Routledge: London, 2009.

Uhlig, Frank. "The Constants of Naval Warfare." *Naval War College Review* 50(2) (March 1997).

Wagener, Martin. "Über das Wesen der Strategie." *Österreichische Militärische Zeitschrift* Nr. 4/2010 (2010).

Wegener, Edward. "Die Elemente von Seemacht und maritimer Macht." *Seemacht und Aussenpolitik*, eds. D. Mahncke, and H.-P. Schwarz. Frankfurt am Main, Germany: Metzner 1974 (= Rüstungsbeschränkungen und Sicherheit, Vol. 11).

Wegener, Edward. "Die Rolle der Seemacht in unserer Zeit." *Seemacht: Eine Seekriegsgeschichte von der Antike bis zur Gegenwart*, eds. E. B. Potter and C. W. Nimitz. German edition coordinated by the Arbeitskreises für Wehrforschung von Jürgen Rohwer. Herrsching: Pawlak, 1982, 1084-1097.

Yarger, Harry. *Strategic Theory for the 21st Century: The Little Book on Big Strategy*. Carlisle, PA: United States Army War College, 2006.

2 Strategy

Its setting

At best, strategy is only an approximate exercise. It will get the strategist somewhere near where he or she intends to go. Strategy grants a systematic approach to dealing with change, with both what should and should not stay the same. The indispensable point of departure for an endeavor as opaque and challenging as formulating strategy is the overarching national interest. Those pluralistic interests form the abstract, amalgamated bases of the foreign-policy decision-making processes. They are an ex-post category, stemming from history and national imagination, and are chaperoned by the elected government of the sovereign (when the responsibility to defend the national interests is vested in elected officials, it constitutes a primary reasoning and motivation for political action). It follows that the definition of national interests is the prerogative of the executive branch, but is subject to the 'checks and balances' of a political system of shared power.[1] For the United States, therefore, the following overarching maxims of foreign policy can be derived, recent policy shifts not withstanding:

- First, the need to prevent an attack on the American homeland is the indispensable objective for national survival;
- Second, the prevention of great-power war in Eurasia and the underlying security competition that makes these outbreaks of destabilizing violence more likely;
- Third, preservation of acceptably priced and secure supply of oil and other resources;
- Fourth, fostering of a friendly, competitive international economic order;
- Fifth, the advancement of democracy and human rights abroad in an attempt to prevent civil wars, genocide, and mass atrocities; and,
- Sixth, the protection of the environment from the adverse effects of global warming and climate change.[2]

It must be noted that there is an inherent struggle to prioritize and categorize these overarching interests against each other, and dispatch finite resources to attain these ends.[3] This process shapes how the United States makes strategy under the condition that they are, in fact, planning for uncertainty. They influence what role America seeks to play in shaping the global environment and the course of history. According to Theodore Lowi *et al.*, there have been four principal roles that the United States has played in international relations in the past. These are, in no particular order:

[handwritten: INterNAL rD Intervention]

- a Napoleonic strategy in which a powerful nation seeks to prevent aggressive actions against it by improving the internal state of affairs of a country even if that implies encouragement of a revolution in that country; *[handwritten: Super Powers united]*
- a Holy Alliance strategy of a superpower to prevent any change in the existing distribution of power among states, even if it means intervention into another country's internal affairs;
- a balance-of-power strategy, in which a concert of powers in alliances with one or more states counterbalances the behavior of other, usually more powerful nation-states; and,
- the economic expansionist role which is a grand strategy pursued by cap- *[handwritten: M.E.]* italist countries to adopt foreign policies to maximize the success of domestic corporations in their dealings with other countries.[4]

[handwritten left margin: Past U.S. Strategies]

When one connects these idealist roles with selected American security interests, it is possible to identify at least eight distinct strategies with military implications. These are

- dominion to rule the world;
- global collective security, to keep the peace everywhere;
- regional collective security, to keep the peace at some places;
- cooperative security, to reduce the occurrence of war by limiting the offensive military capabilities of states;
- containment, to hold the line against a specific aggressor state;
- isolationism, to stay out of most wars and to keep a free hand for the United States;
- offshore balancing, to keep a free hand and to cut down any emerging Eurasian hegemon; and,
- selective engagement, to do a selected number of tasks deemed critical.[5]

Domestic, foreign policy, economic, psychological, and military aspects must be considered in strategy-making as well.[6] However, states as a general rule do not have a single strategy, but rather a topical, measured system of synchronized strategies which relate to and act on one another. In accordance with the level of decision-making, contents, and scope, these sub-strategies will have complementary or conflicting military, diplomatic, or economic objectives.[7]

Democracies tend to be uneasy in the use of military force for political ends in the first place,[8] but a strategy without some sort of enforcement tool amounts to wishful thinking at best and hara-kiri at worst. Ultimately, democracies by virtue of their nature are more consensual and compromise-oriented, which often limits the velocity of decision-making. Strategy is the attempt to frame and control these processes,[9] and to hold those individuals or institutions who are engaged in them accountable. There may be global, regional, or functional strategies.[10] The ideal synthesis of these sub-strategies is a product that is very near to grand, or overarching general, strategy.[11] Liddell Hart reminds us that: "Whereas strategy is only concerned with the problem of winning military victory, grand strategy must take the longer view – for its problem is winning the peace."[12]

Security strategy is an integral part of grand strategy. It contains both a military part and a diplomatic part (recalling two of the three uses of the sea). Security strategy serves the continuous security of a state's well-being, its territorial integrity and sovereignty, the functioning of its political system, and the safety and security of its people and goods. Its goal is the applicability of military and diplomatic power in peace, crisis, and war.[13] Military strategy, "the art and science of employing the armed forces of a nation to secure the objectives of national policy by the application of force, or the threat of force,"[14] is derived from this canon. Thus, military strategy is a sub-category of security strategy, in which the branches of a military share responsibility.[15] In conjunction with diplomatic and geostrategic measures, military strategy can contribute to keeping an enemy at bay and, moreover, help attain the political objectives of armed conflict.[16] As a subset of security strategy, in peacetime military strategy prevents belligerent conflicts in the first place. If it does come to a military conflict, it seeks to reduce damage to a minimum.[17] Military strategy informs force posture, deployments, technology, and tactical actions, all for a larger political objective.

At the same time, force posture decisions, deployments, and the tactical use of force can have strategic implications.[18] Deterrence, coercion, and defense have political–military ramifications that transcend the tactical use of force. They are meant to change the political behavior of the state or non-state actor who is subject to the force. Military power can also reassure allies or coerce antagonists by dispatching troops near their territory (peacetime presence). It can be committed to punish those who commit aggression through systems of collective security and defense. It can serve as the tool for forceful interventions to prevent mass atrocities, ethnic conflicts, and genocide (humanitarian interventions). The military can also interposition itself between warring parties to keep an agreed-upon peace (peacekeeping). Intervention in civil conflicts to impose peace (peacemaking/peace enforcement) or the occupation of a territory to provide stability and seed good governance practice (nation-building) are further options. Targeted use of military force can include quick intrusion to rescue foreign nationals (rescue operations), to exact revenge for harm done (punitive operations), and highly directed use of force to prevent supplies and war materiel from reaching a destination (interdiction).

Naval forces seem particularly useful to serve these objectives. They are inherently more flexible and mobile than land or air forces, given the political context of the sea as an operating space. Their presence, and the threat of the kinetic force they could potentially leverage, can be a central contribution to achieving these ends. It follows from the relatively slow speed of deploying naval forces – a very mobile Army unit can deploy within days (depending on readiness and distance), whereas an Air Force unit can often deploy within hours – that a degree of forward presence is imperative for sustained global engagement.[19] Historically, the U.S. Navy has been forward-operating and forward-deployed from its inception, remaining in its forward-operating, forward-deployed form since the end of World War II.

Sea power can bring to bear its mobility, versatility, agility, and deterrent value ideally when it is forward-deployed rather than lingering in home port (although instances of "fleets in being" suggest certain exceptions to the rule). Thus, presence becomes a value of its own right. This holds true militarily (casualties depend on the degree of readiness, force disposition, and deployment), as well as politically in the spirit of the overarching goals. A logical chain therefore connects the large, overarching strategies and policy directives to the smallest tactical engagement. To make sense of that connection is a supreme duty of the political leadership, who must offer a compelling explanation. At the same time, military services must provide doctrine and an upward narrative to show political leaders how their tactical and operational actions have desirable strategic consequences.

Maritime and naval strategies

Putting Navy strategy (or naval) on par with maritime strategy is hazardous. The history of this semantic disarray is a long one, particularly as naval strategists have sometimes opted to use the adjectives maritime, naval, or navy – or something else altogether. Naval strategy, therefore, is best understood as that part of the American military strategy which principally draws on the contributions of the U.S. Navy to national defense and security. Naval usually also insinuates involvement of the U.S. Marine Corps. It is also part of the broader maritime (lower-case 'm') strategy (i.e., Coast Guard, seaborne trade, maritime ecology, etc.) of the nation.

With the U.S. Marine Corps' unique position in the American context (integrated with, but strategically distinct from, the Navy), there is another complicating factor at hand for the analyst concerned with precise semantics. At times, the USMC was part of a Navy/naval/maritime strategic document (i.e., the Commandant of the Marine Corps [CMC], its highest-ranking officer, would co-sponsor and co-sign a strategy). Sometimes, the Marine Corps would not partake in strategies, and on occasion even issued its own capstone documents. Therefore, use of the terms "maritime" and "naval" in the context of this study must therefore transcend too rigid semantics. In this context the use of either term signals U.S. Navy ownership in a certain capstone document, its use by the Navy alone or in conjunction with sister services and allies.

A Navy's strategy and its success are determined not only by tactical capabilities or operational tasks, but by the political context in which planning and execution occur (Grove, 1990: 159). Defense needs can only be established sensibly when measured against a threat, deciding on an acceptable level of risk, conceiving a strategy that addresses both, and building the forces that the strategy necessitates. Thus, naval strategy succeeds when the Navy complements and makes possible the execution of a coherent, overarching national security strategy.[20]

Julian Corbett (1854–1922), the noted British naval historian and strategist, warned of analytical self-restraint in discerning strategy. In his book *Some Principles on Maritime Strategy*, published in 1911, "the best theorist of his time"[21] noted:

> Naval Strategy is not a thing by itself, [...] its problems can seldom or never be solved on naval considerations alone, [...] it is only a part of maritime strategy [...] [by which we mean] the principles which govern a war in which the sea is a substantial factor. Naval strategy is but that part of it which determines the movements of the fleet when maritime strategy has determined what part the fleet must play in relation to the action of the land forces.[22]

The point of the relationship of sea power on the one hand and land power on the other hand is worth exploring. The finding that man lives on land, not at sea, is trivial. Considerably less trivial is the insight that the strategic impact of naval forces must be felt on land (Gray, 1994: 3). The value of sea power and a naval strategy must therefore be measured against what is on land. Using mobility, relatively unimpeded access, operational reach, and flexibility (all aspects inherent in leading navies), sea power, as part of a country's military and security strategy, can be compelling in crisis management and conflict resolution. It can also serve as a deterrent and contribute to limited wars. Moreover, maritime nations that bring sea power to bear can better scale their participation in conflicts and wars to a degree that continental states cannot.[23]

As Mahnken notes, "Strategy is about making war useable for political purposes. [...] It is the essential link between political objectives and military force, between ends and means."[24] In this sense, it reflects central themes of Carl von Clausewitz in that war is the continuation of politics by other means; that acts of violence in war serve a larger purpose that would be unattainable otherwise; in that a military victory may be useless if it does not serve the acquirement of a political objective.[25] Likewise, naval strategy is the operative art of orchestrating naval warfare in support of the overall effort.[26] More trenchantly, navy (or naval) strategy is the theory of using the Navy in peace, crisis, and war. In the framework of the overall grand and security strategy, it implements a nation's maritime interests. Naval strategy is therefore uniquely positioned between the political and the operational levels.[27]

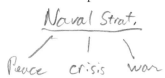

Naval missions and their implications on strategy and fleet design

In hindsight, states in general have developed six distinct ways to employ naval forces. As offensive variants, fleet-on-fleet action (or battle at sea), blockade of the enemy, and power projection/expeditionary operations can be observed. Commerce raiding (attack on commercial trade), coastal defense, and the fleet-in-being concept fall into the defensive category.[28] To frame the role U.S. naval forces could fulfill, it is instructive to take a look at the characterization of the function of modern navies. First laid out by Admiral Stansfield Turner in 1974, the "Missions of the U.S. Navy"[29] was soon adopted by many analysts as the most useful military analytical framework for roles of modern navies. These 'classic 4' missions were sea control, projection of power ashore, naval presence, and strategic deterrence. These missions, in turn, serve larger naval roles and policy objectives. Sea control and power projection have been described above; naval presence is the geographically forward deployment of naval forces to be on station for events ashore and give decision-makers the range of options to respond on the spectrum of conflict. Strategic deterrence uses sea power assets to keep an adversary from following a course of action.

The following illustration uses a slightly different metric in assigning deterrent and combative functions to sea control and power projection (Figure 2.1). It then derives specific naval function. Presence is prerequisite for these missions, although the term does not appear.

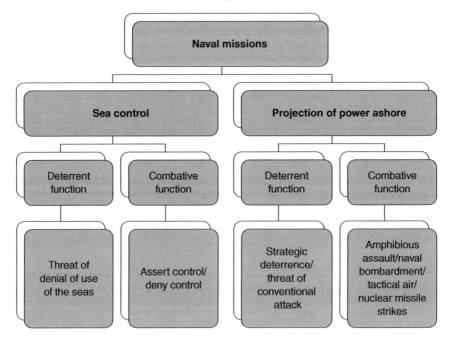

Figure 2.1 Functions of modern-day navies.[30]

Methods of sea control, as Turner outlined, include sortie control (a contemporary synonym for blockade), choke point control, open ocean operations, and local engagement through the exercise of sea control as well as forward operations to maintain and exploit the initiative.[31] Naval missions therefore serve as a suitable prism to grasp the strategic intentions of naval forces as articulated by document drafters. It follows that specific instruments (i.e., naval platforms and weapons systems) must be developed, procured, and fielded for such missions. The instruments for such endeavors are summed up in Table 2.1.

Table 2.1 explains the advantages of a balanced fleet, a popular term among naval strategists. The wider the variety of weapon systems available, the broader the operational possibilities. A properly balanced composition of weapon systems, in principle, increases naval flexibility and capacity to respond to changing or unexpected circumstances.[32] A reliance on one platform may inhibit flexibility, restrict options for the national command authority, and unbalance the fleet to become a costly niche force.

Sea control capabilities are at the heart of the naval mission set. For power projection ashore, naval presence, and strategic deterrence (the other three of Turner's 'classic 4'), a navy can utilize its sea control assets although it will be better served to field flexible warships designed for that specific purpose yet retain the capability for other missions. It is noted that the roles of navies in strategic deterrence must be divided into general, conventional deterrence – "potential adversaries are deterred, or not deterred, by demonstrations of a navy's evident ability to perform conventional maritime 'war-fighting' tasks efficiently"[33] – and nuclear (strategic) deterrence.[34] Finally, the combative function of navies also deserves detailing. One recent, durable instance of the range of power projection ashore is the British experience in the Falklands War 1982, where – perhaps with the notable exception of nuclear missile strikes – the broad spectrum of modern sea power tools was displayed.[35]

Table 2.1 Weapons systems appropriate for sea control[36]

Weapons systems Tactics:	Sortie control	Chokepoint control	Open area operations	Local defense	Forward operations[1]
Submarines	X	X	X	X	X
ASW aircraft		X	X	X	X
Fighter aircraft		X		X	X
Surveillance systems	X	X	X	X	X
Attack aircraft	X	X			X
Mines	X	X			X
Escort ships	X	X	X	X	X

Note

1 "Forward operations" was not included in the original table, but has been added here based on Till's assessment that "they [too] would require the full set of weapons systems" (Till, 1987: 65).

All of these missions describe the political function short of general war. Although naval missions have certainly evolved over time, Turner's 'classic 4' remain the lever for any serious discussion about the utility of navies. For naval planners and document drafters, these missions often provided a starting point for their concepts, ideas, and writings.[37]

The nexus of strategy, planning, and force structure

There is an indivisible, sometimes clouded, connection among the ways, the means, and the ends in policy. These quintessential components of strategy govern planning, for a given strategic document would be of little or no use if it were not speaking to *how* to achieve a proclaimed goal. Force planning (the art of structuring, budgeting, maintaining, and periodically reviving the force), thus is indispensable in any strategic deliberation and has six key variables. These are:

- national interests and objectives;
- the derived security strategy;
- the means and instruments in use;
- the risk of failure;
- the security environment; and,
- the available resources.[38]

A change in one parameter would mean modifying the other key indicators. Depending on which variable is changed, the balance of the whole effort needs adjustments in its goals, means, a reassessment of the risk of failure, or a revision of the strategy altogether.[39]

A top-down approach closely aligns with a logical strategy and force planning model. It follows a path which runs from the determination of national interests to the formulation of a national strategy and a military strategy, including components for different branches of the military. In reality, however, shifting political and economic conditions, finite resources, new and old threats, and technological advancements[40] provide for more complexity and chaos. It is thus seldom, if ever, linear. Any sound analysis of strategic and force planning processes must take into account both long-term factors and more short- and medium-term issues such as technological revolutions, a changing strategic environment, and the maritime capabilities of an opponent.[41]

Strategy remains a loop series of questions that need answers. First, which policy objectives are to be achieved ('What do we want to do?'). Second, how can the strategic execution occur ('How do we plan to do it?'). Third, an indispensable assessment of threats, vulnerabilities, opportunities, and challenges ('What are we up against?'). Fourth, unilateral or multilateral choices, alliance or coalitions or alignments, international institutions, defense forces, and other economic, political, diplomatic, and informational instruments must be weighed ('What is available to do it?'). Fifth, risks, deficiencies, unforeseen outcomes, and other cultural blinders must be considered ('What are the mismatches?'). The sixth question loops back to the first step in that it ponders strategic goals and desired or demanded end states ('Why do we want to do this?').[42]

The particulars of naval strategic culture and how they inform strategy and force employment

There is a particular strategic culture governing how one thinks about the sea as an operating space for military force. There are certain constraints, but also a number of opportunities associated with war at and war from the sea. "Naval warfare," as Bernard Brodie remarked, "differs from land warfare in the objectives aimed at, the implements used, and the characteristics of the domain on which it wages."[43] These boundaries always influence the applicability of naval power. It follows that advisors and decision-makers can formulate a wise strategy only in acquaintance with the specific opportunities (and potential shortcomings) of naval forces, thus minimizing the risk of catastrophic failure.[44]

Ship to ship = 2D
+ Aircraft/subs = 3D
+ Space/missiles = 4D
+ Electronic Warfare = 5D
+ Cyber
= 6D

Multidimensionality of the operating space

The analytically relevant space for sea power dramatically increased in complexity in the course of just over a century. Well into the 1800s, it was one-dimensional, encompassing surface warfare using oar-powered rowing boats, then sailing ships, and finally steam-powered vessels. Thanks to massive technological innovation since the early twentieth century, the space became three-dimensional owing to the advent of submarines and aviation. Later, exploration of the earth's atmosphere and space added a fourth dimension. The fifth dimension, electronic warfare (EW), has complicated the analysis.[45] With regard to the twenty-first century, cyberspace became a sixth dimension of naval warfare. Jointness and combined operational dynamics add more complexity. These developments have vastly complicated orchestrating financial, personnel, technological, and intellectual resources. Success in any one dimension is usually not very likely to win war as a whole – save perhaps for the employment of the "wild card" of the actual use of nuclear weapons fired in anger.[46]

This management consideration explains the distinct subcultures in the U.S. Navy (as much as in any other modern naval force). These subcultures, or unions, are usually the surface warfare, submarine warfare, and naval aviation careers.[47] Such early specialization usually occurs according to talent, military aspirations, socialization, and a host of other factors. Therefore, it is perhaps misleading to speak of *the* Navy as a whole. The "unions" constantly compete for budgets, promotion of flag officers to top functional/regional commands, or staff positions in the White House, Pentagon, or elsewhere.

Yet, they share a naval strategic culture that influences how members think about, and consequently appraise, their operating spaces. This culture is an amalgam of shared beliefs, values, and training regarding using military force to achieve political ends.[48] It feeds from immediate common experiences as well as a long-term overarching institutional praxis. Naval history – the academic study of war at sea, and how and why naval forces operated – becomes an important tool in conveying such experience to the officer corps, politicians, and the broader public. In other words, "naval history is far too important for naval practitioners of any generation to ignore."[49,50]

Naval forces, their oceanic environment, and the use of technology

The maritime domain differs from conditions on land in a number of ways. The physical complexity of the operating space and the forces of nature are worth noting. Wind, waves, precipitation, ice, clouds, fog, currents, temperature, or obstacles such as reefs, sandbanks, shallow waters, and confined waterways mandate a heavy dependence of naval forces on technology.[51] Mastering navigation is a central life insurance policy against the brute forces of nature. The world's physical organization influences significantly *what* navies offer to do – and *how* they do it.

The dependence on technology for survival at sea, coupled with the capabilities of the individual, can be described illustratively (in stark contrast to the way of doing business in armed forces on land) as, "The Navy mans the equipment while the Army equips the man."[52] Successful sea power rests principally on fielding and mastering sound technology to overcome the hardships and hazards of the sea. For a warship, that means staying afloat, going places, and returning home as necessary, to defend itself, serve larger policy or even strategic objectives, provide operating and rest space for its crew, and to be interoperable with other branches of the military or international partners in joint and combined operations.[53] A reliable industrial base which can provide for such an advanced system of systems is imperative if one wants to sustain forces and morale.

Points of intersection

Given the sheer tyranny of distance and the multidimensionality of the maritime domain, focal points on the high seas are coastlines and numerous choke points, straits, harbors, approaches, channels, canals, and bights. Whether natural or man-made, these hubs and bottlenecks are a prime starting point for obtaining influence through force. Collins points out that control of key straits and other natural or man-made narrows has been a basic military objective since naval warfare arose, because adversary armed forces on either side of any naval choke point may try to deny free passage to opponents.[54] The history of the twentieth century is littered with events where such bottlenecks made bold headlines. Control of sea lines of communications and choke points enables reinforcements of forces and logistical flows, whereas the control of geographic areas at sea enables the projection of power from the sea on land. Countries can be coerced or economically throttled by way of a blockade, and one's own maritime traffic and coast can be guarded against interference.[55] Choke points and sea lines can thus become a scare strategic commodity.[56] *(ie, China pushing/patrolling EEZs)*

With increasing use of the sea for commercial and political means, a larger role emerges for international law to regulate its jurisdiction. At the same time, the world's oceans are owned by the world's population (a global common), in essence an area that does not belong to a single state, but offers unique and unregulated and unrestricted access.[57] Posen emphasizes that command of the commons (the seas, air space above 15,000 feet, space, and cyberspace) is the indispensable foundation of American hegemony.

Rules of engagement govern how a navy goes about its mission at sea. There are also disadvantages to naval forces which can translate into potentially catastrophic political drawbacks. These include misinterpretation of signals, limitations of endurance, vulnerabilities, and indecisive outcomes.[58]

Jervis cautions that:

> Some technologies and tactics generate incentives to strike first. In such a situation fighting may occur even though neither side wants it: each knows that despite a mutual interest in staying at peace, attacking is much better than receiving the first blow. Because ships are small in number and relatively vulnerable, [...] navies are more prone to destabilizing dynamics of this kind than are armies. While there are cases of isolated inadvertent exchanges between land units, these rarely spread very far. But ships not only carry more national prestige, they operate in fleets and the potential for undesired escalation is very great.[59]

These issues notwithstanding, the legal context translates into the 'freedom of the seas,' which is of overarching strategic use for a global nation such as the United States. Using the freedom of the seas, the U.S. (or any other state so wishing) can routinely deploy forces across the globe to loiter at the territorial seas of a friend or competitor, survey international naval exercises, collect data and intelligence, or transit straits and canals, etc. The sea thus offers unique opportunities for a preventively tailored security and a defense policy built around crisis management and conflict prevention.[60] The control of the seas is, as previously noted, a very important power factor. Despite the United States not having ratified the United Nations Convention on the Law of the Sea (UNCLOS) to date, it has entered into American customary law and its effects are of central strategic and political importance to the U.S.

Mobility, flexibility, and scalability of naval forces

Long transits into a given theater of military operations can be a logistical nightmare for an island nation such as the United States. This problem is overcome by relying on permanent forward bases, host-nation support, or port rights in allied countries. In peacetime, crisis, and war, replenishment-at-sea (RAS) maneuvers allow extended periods on station for Navy warships; floating warehouses supply fuel, ammunition, stores, mail, and numerous other services while at sea. This allows operations in a given area for weeks (as opposed to days), with the notable exemption of nuclear-powered vessels, which are limited only by the physical and psychological endurance of the crew.

The scalability of force packages from single units to large fleets and the flexibility of naval platforms for a variety of missions vastly broaden policy options. From maritime interdiction operations to sanctions/no-fly zone enforcement, noncombatant evacuation operations, and preemptive strikes on the lower end of the spectrum to amphibious raids/assaults and full-scale strike warfare to defeat an enemy, naval forces – in principle – offer a broad and politically rationalized palette of opportunities to decision-makers.[61] Others options include support to global or regional balance of forces, surveillance and shadowing (intelligence gathering), demonstration of political will and technological innovation, sea denial (rejection of access to a certain area at sea), blockade and quarantine, "showing the flag," port visits, contributions to alliance coherence, maritime security and safeguarding from piracy and maritime terrorism, and freedom of navigation exercises.[62] Cost-intensive naval units, often delivered in only small quantities (a marked difference to the quantitatively expansive armies and air forces), must therefore be flexible enough to attend many, if not all, of these tasks successively and complementarily. A ship that serves only a single task is hardly useful (with the exception of the strategic deterrence submarines). During operations in task forces (with task groups and task units as subordinate categories), such a modular concept can be brought to full effect. U.S. Navy Admiral William Halsey, Jr. (1882–1959) compared it with a card game, stating,

> A fleet is like a hand of cards at poker or bridge. You don't see it as aces and kings and deuces. You see it as a hand, a unit. You see a fleet as a unit, not carriers, battleships and destroyers. You don't play the individual card, you play the hand.[63]

In the U.S. Navy, peacetime procedures only marginally differ from operations in conflict and war, save perhaps for the use of weapons, with accompanying risk, and the mounting tension and fear.[64] U.S. naval forces are designed to be inherently deployable and, whether in times of peace or crisis, they need to keep up a high operational tempo to overcome the inherent operational stress of being at sea.

Naval forces are a scalable and subtly tuned part of the military and policy toolbox of a state. Unlike armies and air forces, forward presence can easily be applied outside of foreign territorial waters, and withdraw with relatively little loss of political face.[65] In contrast to garrisoned, stationary forces, which may have to conquer or control territory, the advantage of naval forces is their inherently dynamic posture. At the same time, war at and from the sea must deal with the absence of geographic front lines, a vastly more complicated reconnaissance and surveillance, and nearly constant maneuverability of naval force. A ship outside of port, whether friend or foe, is hardly ever stationary. It follows that their relative mobility, flexibility, and adaptability represent a "way of life."[66] This knowledge underlines, in turn, that to make a strategic difference sea power must be tightly moored to political goals and strategic objectives.[67] Otherwise, navies risk their strategic irrelevance.

The elements of a strategic concept

The problem of formulating strategy, much less sound strategy, stems from a dilemma. On the one hand, strategy must serve as guiding principles for decision-makers. It has to be clear and concise. On the other hand, it appears illogical and outright impossible to expect from a strategy a prompt, adequate reply to any and all current and potentially emerging policy challenges. Therefore, strategy must be flexible enough to provide guidance beyond the day. The value of a written strategy thus can be constrained.[68] If the development of strategy often is a permanent process of questioning, application, and evaluation[69] – a perpetual "reality check" – the question is why does a military service, a Navy in general, and the U.S. Navy in particular need a strategy?

In 1954, noted political scientist Samuel Huntington wrote in his groundbreaking article 'National Policy and the Transoceanic Navy' that three key elements would define an armed branch of the military. According to Huntington,

> a military service may be viewed as consisting of [1] a *strategic concept* which defines the role of the service in national policy, [2] *public support* which furnishes it with the resources to perform this role, and [3] *organizational structure* which groups the resources so as to implement most effectively the strategic concept.[70]

Calling for a unifying purpose to shape and direct a military service's activities, the strategic concept should describe how, when, and where a military would protect national security. Without such a fundamental description, a military service would remain merely the sum of its people, its platforms, its traditions, and its bases. Moreover, a strategic concept provides impetus for budgetary allocation by the government and to recruit personnel, without which a military branch cannot be sustained. The resources allocated to a service, Huntington noted, are a function of the public support that the institution enjoys. The service has a responsibility to harness such support and foster an organizational culture that supports such endeavors.

> It can only do this if it possesses a strategic concept which clearly formulates its relationship to national security. [...] If a service does not posses[s] a well defined strategic concept, the public and the political leaders will be confused as to the role of the service, uncertain as to the necessity of its existence and apathetic or hostile to the claims made by the service upon the resources of society.[71]

[handwritten margin note: Vietnam war, USMC purpose mission]

Whereas these roles can be analyzed individually, one should not understand these dynamics solely as linear processes. Strategic planning is a parallel process, not a sequential one. Strategic planning and execution run on parallel tracks, often with very limited feedback and interaction between one another. It follows that by focusing on strategy as a sole determinant of naval power, the analysis must fall short. Rather, the strategy, policy, concepts, and doctrines are a determinant of national naval power, not the exclusive determinant.[72]

Makers, shapers, factors: genesis of American seapower

The United States of America and the sea power it wields are a complex and comprehensive amalgam of rational and institutional makers, shapers, and factors – as part of an "outward-looking foreign policy [...] rooted in geography, political constitution, and national character."[73] It is important to appreciate process as the key to understanding and explaining naval strategy, and ultimately how the U.S. wields naval power for national security ends. However, it does not suffice to identify and analyze ideas and concepts. To elucidate the history of naval strategy, one must move behind the ideas to consider where they came from, and how they were translated from theory into practice.[74] More than a dozen aspects could be accounted for in a comprehensive analysis of naval strategy and the historical context in which the capstone documents emerge. They concern leadership qualities and development, education, research, career backgrounds, administration particulars and procurement, budgets, etc.[75]

However, a ready template or methodology has thus far not emerged. Analysts have repeatedly attempted to grasp these complex processes and explain the determinants of naval strategy-making. The quintuplicate of "machines, men, manufacturing, management and money"[76] sums up the governing factors of the essential forces at play. Wilfried Stallmann added a sixth factor: mentality.[77] Once again, these organizational features of the Navy strategy process are difficult to weigh in their relative importance, and ultimately impossible to distinguish analytically.

Although some of these factors may be secondary in nature, their correlative value – their influence on a work-in-progress Navy strategy; reflection in tabled drafts of such documents; accurate success/failure assessment as part of a published strategy; persistence (i.e., operational reflection, and continuity in following strategies) – must be considered in the overall picture. They are not necessarily sequential in what is called the Planning, Programming, Budgeting, and Execution (PPBE) processes in the U.S. Department of Defense bureaucracy, but often parallel, converging, competing, and ultimately impossible to tease apart. It follows that the process of naval strategy-making is not mechanistic, but rather an organic dynamic. It cannot be captured easily in flow charts. In fact, it rests more on operational experience or programmatic realities (often classified, obscure, complex, and poorly articulated) than on readily definable theory. This makes the process hard to track and even harder to describe.[78] In other words, Navy strategy is an organic, intricate, non-linear, and inherently dynamic system that is methodologically challenging to analyze. If one wishes to understand why and how the Navy formulated its capstone documents the way it did, one needs to comprehend the broader grand strategy (and strategic) choices. These, in turn, were influenced by world events, domestic interests, technology, naval force employment options, and intellectual influences stemming from the idealistic strategic culture of the United States, that is, context.

Collins provided a useful illustration of the six-step planning process, fully aware that this would constitute a simplification of the dynamics.[79] According to Collins, a logical chain exists. In step 1, national interests are defined. In step 2, threats to these interests are assessed. Step 3 requires a definition of political and military objectives in the face of these threats to national interests. From this, in step 4, emerges the preferred military strategy which is influenced by domestic and foreign policies. Therefore, strategy neither emerges nor exists in a vacuum. Rather, this ultimately chaotic and overwhelming step leads, sooner or later, to realizing that means and ends are mismatched. Hence, step 5 mandates an assessment of the required resources, the available resources, and the estimated risks associated with the mismatch. Step 6, finally, leads to an appropriately revised strategy, a resource alignment, or both.

After assessments, a state concludes its ends and means are ultimately mismatched. Consequently, trade-offs and acceptable risk must be considered. Once those risks have been identified, the strategy, the resources, or both are subject to revision. Such changes can occur frequently if and when political-military priorities, threats, and policies transform. In general, the frequent and chaotic interplay and correlation between those logical steps is seldom discernible.

To comprehend continued high spending on defense and the concurrent efforts at doctrinal and strategic adjustment as well as institutional redesign, one must also look at the role of ideas – and fundamentally, to what end a military is used – as well as domestic and bureaucratic (i.e., inter-service, inter-administration, inter-governmental) politics.[80] These logical chains are often broken and obstructed.

For context, it is useful to briefly explain the functions and roles of those domestic makers and shapers of institutionalized American seapower. Given the inherent dynamics of complex bureaucracies, personal interplay, and related framework conditions, the following descriptions are only of a general nature. However, one needs to take into account the structure to arrive at a sound understanding of the shapes that U.S. Navy strategy, and the relevant developments associated therewith, can take. National security, after all, is ultimately a domestic public good.

Three generic but partly definable groups of institutional contributors to U.S. Navy strategy can be defined: makers, shapers, and factors of strategy.

- *Makers* are all those who are constitutionally obliged to "make" U.S. Navy strategy and the larger national strategy into which it links, or those who directly inform or shape such processes. The most prominent makers belong to the executive and legislative branches of government, the civilian and military bureaucracy (in particular the Department of Defense), and obviously the Navy itself.
- *Shapers* are understood as people or institutions that, bounded by constitutional obligations or driven by commercial and political interest, indirectly influence the making and execution of U.S. Navy strategy. They do not have a formal role in the making or execution of Navy strategy. Shapers can also be generic influences on Navy strategy that inform, propel, or constrain how the Navy goes about its business.
- Finally, the international context and the enduring importance of ideas are valid *factors* to be considered.

The analytical differentiations between these groups can be murky, and the criminological tracing of "Who did what when to which effect?" is difficult, if not impossible in this study. Much rests on a combination of influences, not least the assertiveness of the characters (indeed, personalities) involved. An individual strategic mindset is hard to measure, but corresponding education – e.g., PhDs in international relations or strategic studies – can serve as valuable indicators. These will play distinct roles in the succeeding chapters.

America, the seapower, is an amalgam of influences from governmental institutions, ideas, a variety of interest groups, the news media, and political movements, all of which shape the foreign policy realm[81] and transcend simplistic geo-economic determinants. The first principal starting point to lay out what "makes" American seapower is a discussion of U.S. national interests. These national interests are derived from a nation's inherent values and proclaimed rationale. The weighing of these views naturally differs and emphasis often shifts with presidential policies. Still, for the U.S. a general canon of basic and indivisible national interests can be identified. These are defense, economic, world order, and ideological interests.[82] All four groups of these will be subdivided into more comprehensible policy objectives. At the same time, policy-makers must accept certain trade-offs.

The second principal starting point for this *tour d'horizon* is the U.S. Constitution and the division of labor it postulates between the executive and the legislative branch (Table 2.2).

Ultimately, the American system of strategic planning is a pluralistic one. According to Hattendorf, four discernible levels are at work. First, high policy is established at the level of the President and modified and supported by Congress. This includes the general direction for the country, and how decision-makers spend finite resources on defined objectives. Second, the general conceptual planning for war is the responsibility of the Joint Chiefs of Staff. This group provides the military context for those high-policies needing backing. Third, the services program the force through the coordinated procurement of equipment often accompanied by statements of strategy that define the rationale for the weapons or platforms involved. It is coordinated by the Secretary of Defense (SECDEF). The Secretary gives the rationale in the division of the budget (and labor) among the branches of the military. Fourth, the preparation of operational plans is the responsibility of the various unified and specified commanders in chief. The U.S. is the only country dividing the world into geographic areas of responsibility complemented by functional military commands.[83]

These four actors in strategic planning, in other words the makers of strategy, need to be reviewed briefly for the purpose of this study.

Table 2.2 Principal foreign-policy provisions of the U.S. Constitution[84]

	Power granted to	
	President	*Congress*
War power	Commander in chief of armed forces[1]	Provide for the common defense; declare war
Treaties	Negotiate treaties	Consent to treaties, by two-thirds majority (Senate)
Appointments	Nominate high-level government officials	Confirm president's appointments (Senate)
Foreign commerce	No explicit powers, but treaty negotiation and appointment powers pertain	Explicit power "to regulate foreign commerce"
General powers	Executive power; veto	Legislative power; power of the purse; oversight and investigation

Note

1 Constitutionally, this is a congressional power (Article II, Section 2 of the Constitution, the "Commander-in-Chief clause"). The question of whether and to what extent the president has the authority to use the military absent a declaration of war by Congress is a long-standing source of debate in political and legal circles.

"Makers"

The *President* and his senior staff are the principal architects of U.S. foreign policy.[85] U.S. foreign policy is very strongly identified with the President.[86] As commander in chief, he (or she) is the head of state, head of government, and the highest-ranking commander of the U.S. military in peacetime, crisis, and war. A President's performance over the course of his term(s) is often subject to wave-like changes, and phases of strong, powerful decision-making can alternate with pursuing unrealistic policies in transition periods.[87] The President very much relies on the National Security Council (NSC), established by the National Security Act of 1947, and the National Security Advisor. The wording speaks of national security rather than foreign policy, which shows the council's limited strategic aspiration in contrast to long-term policy crafting.[88] That does not mean that the NSC could not, and would not, engage in micromanaging the Pentagon or other military issues.[89] Presidents have made use of the council and its staff to varying degrees over time, with Henry Kissinger, advisor to President Richard Nixon 1969–1974, perhaps the most illustrative case in point.

The *Congress* consists of a lower and an upper chamber, the United States House of Representatives and the United States Senate, respectively. While there is usually little in the way of disagreement over U.S. grand strategy (and, frankly, little influence on it), both legislative bodies have unique functions and rules pertaining to strategic planning outlined in Article I, Section 8, of the U.S. Constitution. The Constitution mandates that Congress shall have power to "provide and *maintain* a Navy", while it only allows the legislature to "*raise* and support Armies."[90]

This branch is particularly crucial for the Planning Programming and Budgeting System (PPBS) cycle. The PPBS links operational requirements with financial resources and points out where funds need to be steered. This cycle consists of a two-year budget plan that is brought before Congress. It rests on the so-called Future Years Defense Plan (FYDP), a six-year overview drawn from even more outward-looking documents of strategic intent. As Lowi *et al.* have remarked, "Congress's 'power of the purse' is its ultimate weapon."[91]

Military-strategic responsibility increasingly rests with the Department of Defense (DOD), the military bureaucracy, and the unified combatant commanders. Therefore, one needs to turn to the Pentagon itself, and more precisely to the *Department of the Navy* (DON), which is the governmental organizational structure for the U.S. Navy, the U.S. Marine Corps, and in wartime the U.S. Coast Guard. As §5061, Title 10 of the U.S. Code further states, the DON is composed of (1) the Office of the Secretary of the Navy, (2) the Office of the Chief of Naval Operations, (3) the Headquarters, Marine Corps (Commandant of the Marine Corps), (4) the entire operating forces, including naval aviation of the Navy and of the Marine Corps, and the reserve components of those operating forces, and (5) all field activities, headquarters, forces, bases, installations, activities, and functions under the control or supervision of the Secretary of the Navy.[92] The CMC and the CNO are the principal senior advisors to SECNAV and serve as members of the JCS.

These individuals can push or decelerate service strategies. Again, a general statement is difficult to come by and the analysis that follows will discuss the varying degrees of such senior leaders on particular strategic documents.

OPNAV has two roles. Internally, these responsibilities include the linking and coherence of parallel initiatives, the alignment of force structures, the building and maintenance of a service consensus, cohesion and esprit, the integration of warfare unions, and the focus on exercises, war games, and experimental, educational, and training efforts. Externally, OPNAV has to demonstrate that Navy leadership is thoughtful and consistent with national and joint policies, in step with or even ahead of the times, highly trustworthy for the purpose of national policies, displaying a compelling rationale for its desired new procurements, and appearing unified. Further goals include shaping and leveraging overarching (military/security/grand) strategic capstone documents.[93]

The *Unified Combatant Commanders*: the commanders of the regional or functional commands, are an integral part of the chain of command coming from the President and going to the Secretary of Defense. The Goldwater–Nichols Act reorganized and codified the role of these theater or specialized commands, essentially establishing the command structure that is largely in place today (Table 2.3).

Table 2.3 Unified and specialized commands (as of July 2016)

Name	Acronym	Estd.	HQ	Scope
African Command	USAFRICOM	2007	Stuttgart (Germany)	G
Central Command	USCENTCOM	1983	Tampa, Florida (USA)	G
European Command	USEUCOM	1947	Stuttgart (Germany)	G
Northern Command	USNORTHCOM	2002	Petterson AFB, Colorado (USA)	G
Pacific Command	USPACOM	1947	Oahu, Hawaii (USA)	G
Southern Command	USSOUTHCOM	1963	Miami, Florida (USA)	G
Special Forces Command	USSOCOM	1987	McDill AFB, Florida (USA)	F
Strategic Command	USSTRATCOM	1992	Offutt AFB, Nebraska (USA)	F
Transportation Command	USTRANSCOM	1987	Scott AFB, Illinois (USA)	F

Note
G = Geographic, F = Functional.

On balance, all of these makers:

- are instrumental to the intellectual deliberation of American seapower, for better or for worse;
- oversee (and occasionally hinder/halt) the rise of a capstone document through the echelons;
- with the assistance of their staff and independent government entities assess a document's policy repercussions, ideally both inside and outside of the United States Navy; and,
- attempt to align the processes as well as the products with overarching policy guidance and multi-faceted developments (such as technological breakthroughs, major international conflicts, manpower issues, etc.) that inform sea power practice.

They literally 'make' and drive strategy, as well as drawing on experience from the fleet, because of their designated role in the U.S. political bureaucratic system. Besides these true makers of foreign policy, there are additional influences which shape the institutional dimension of U.S. seapower, and by implication parts of Navy strategy. The 'foreign-policy establishment' is a much larger arena, including what can properly be called the shapers of foreign policy. These are a host of unofficial, informal players, and individuals who possess varying degrees of influence depending on their prestige, their reputation and socioeconomic standing, and (most importantly) the party and ideology that are dominant at a given moment.[94] The indirect shapers are other departments of the U.S. executive branch, other branches of the U.S. military (with competing interests), outside interest groups and lobbyists, the news media, and laws and courts. Often, shapers will join hands and find avenues to leverage even more influence. For example, industry representatives will work through their respective Congressman in Washington. Successful lobbying for one type of warship over another can impinge on the force structure for years while media and professional lobbyists can drive a certain agenda, be it friendly toward the Navy or not.

Finally, the debate of potent shapers of U.S. Navy strategy must include the important international context, in particular normative roots and political and military alliances.[95] Geography and alliances indicate where, when, and how U.S.-led sea power can be directed. The actual process of aligning ways, means, and ends regarding the use of military (naval) force obviously is confined to the American context (grand, military, and naval/maritime strategies are usually a sovereign function after all), but alliance and international organizational constraints must be considered.

The United States is bound in one military alliance in particular: NATO.[96] Today, NATO, as a fundamentally trans-oceanic alliance, still operates four standing naval task groups.[97] NATO naval forces were involved in embargo and strike operations in the Balkan Wars during the 1990s and operations against Libya (2011). Recently, NATO maritime operations included anti-piracy tasks

Shapers = NATO ???

at the Horn of Africa ("Operation Ocean Shield"), off the coast of Libya ("Operation Sea Guardian"), and in the Aegean Sea.[98]

A similar military bond albeit without the same trigger as the NATO treaty exists for various other U.S. defense relations, such as in the Pacific where allies like Japan and South Korea are currently concerned over an increasingly assertive and militarized Chinese foreign policy.

How the United States seeks to shape global order, and to what ends it employs its military (in particular the Navy) to attain these goals, also determines America's seapower posture. Obviously, such considerations are deeply linked to national interest and the political culture. A contemporary model proposes the theory of liberalism as a point of departure. Such a school of thought presumes that the traditional, neorealist balance-of-power politics fall short of providing sustained peace and security. The underpinning of U.S. policy in the pursuit of political goals (where applicable) are supported by military means (imperial liberalism) and/or the construction of hegemonic structures (hegemonic liberalism),[99] as well as humanitarianism. The nation's tools of influence are manifold, and the presence of military power such as forward-stationed or -deployable naval force can be a central one.

Shaping Ideals?

The visualization of national security can be traced to overarching, sometimes competing world order ideas. The analytical division into a realist-internationalist, a liberal-internationalist, a realist-isolationist, and a liberal-isolationist vision is the most compelling.[100] Such competing visions are especially compelling after fundamental changes in the international environment, where the nation ponders its future and the Navy (much like the rest of the military) has to justify its existence and relevance. The end of World War II offered much of the same knee-jerk reaction as did the end of the Cold War and the post-9/11 years. In all instances, the Navy had to justify its place in the political establishment and anticipate what framework the presidential administration would prefer to visualize American national security.

Such competing theories are the principal methods of attempting to explain U.S. foreign and security policy. If, when, and where sea power is fielded often rests on these paradigms offered by idealist, liberal, or realist convictions, world order visions, and geopolitical considerations. More fundamentally, the link among national grand strategy, national interests, and naval force is one worth exploring. In other words, the question demands knowing when, why, and how America goes to war by sea. Here, the peace-time role of naval force also factors in, with ramifications for naval presence, deployment patterns, and procurement. If a naval service cannot make its case into the national imagination or enter the visions of its political leadership, it risks looking unimaginative and self-centered. To make a strategic difference, naval strategy must be finely attuned to such demands.

Two other sets of competing visions arise about the nature of wars America conducts and the role of naval power in such conflicts. These visions are principally either countersocietal or countermilitary.[101] The former, rooted in American colonial experience, sees war as a conflict that pits one national society against another, whereas the latter stems from the European state tradition and interprets war as a clash between rival nation-states and their professional military establishments.[102] Historically, American political culture has shifted between oceanic and cis- or transoceanic visions. Whereas the former assumes that control (indeed, command) of the international commons attains political objectives, the latter assumes that war requires the destruction or occupation of the adversary's territory to achieve that purpose; the cisoceanic version puts a premium on protection of the homeland, which at least in theory assures a political stalemate. Table 2.4 shows the more practical ramifications of naval forces in the U.S. mindset. This paradigm has shaped U.S. naval thinking especially in times of strategic reorientation.

Table 2.4 Competing visions of war and their naval-strategic implications[103]

	Countersocietal	*Countermilitary*
Oceanic Vision	• Main target is enemy commerce, not its military forces • Imposing of unacceptable stalemate on an imperial aggressor • Force demands: improved intelligence and reconnaissance, space-based systems (cyber), long-range aviation, missiles, choke point control, offensive mining, forward submarine patrols, convoy escorts to defend own seaborne trade • Examples: *Jeune École*, German U-Boat fleet in World War I, II	• Sea denial, destruction of enemy fleet • Navy need not be routinely forward-deployed • Force demands: fleet to go deep into harm's way; SSN (anti-ship/anti-submarine missiles), carrier battle groups with capable air- and missile-defense escorts • Examples: Mahan (1890s), post-Vietnam period
Cis-/Transoceanic Vision	• Strategic bombing • Navy support role (Marine Corps, Army, Air Force bring war to enemy) • Enemy navy needs to be neutralized if it attempts forward operations • SLOC control • Force demands: SSBN, CVNs, amphibious lift, ASW, superior surface fleet to deter enemy (balanced fleet) • Example: early Cold War (1949–1968)	• Strategic bombing less important • Force and power projection into the littoral (carrier air strikes, amphibious landings) • Protection of allies, swift and decisive force, SLOC control, precision strikes • Navy designed and routinely dispatched forward • Force demands: carriers, cruise missiles, AAW/BMD, mobile Marine units

In theory strategy-making should directly and discernibly complement high policy in the establishment of goals and objectives for programming and war-planning. In practice, each level of strategy-making has its own demand and supply relationship, a function of the nature of the system.[104] This is a recipe for contradiction and disjunction. A strictly rational calculation of strategy is eclipsed by the practical necessity for simplification. Bureaucratic interests and a high degree of uncertainty contribute to the confusion and render logical models limited in use. Any rational calculus is forever changing against the backdrop of political events and technological developments, which alter the situation at home and on the global stage. The development of strategy and the posture of American seapower and its application of sea power is a perpetual process of questioning, application, reexamination, constant adjustment, and reevaluation.

Notes

1 Maull, 2006, 64–65.
2 Art, 2003, 7.
3 Art, 2003, 47.
4 Lowi *et al.*, 2010: 697–698.
5 Art, 2003, 82.
6 Ruge, 1960, 424–425.
7 Wagener, 2010, 6.
8 Gray, 1994, 61.
9 Boorman, 2009, 93.
10 Kugler, 2006, 66–69.
11 But, as Michael Gerson noted in the opening remarks of a CNA-sponsored conference on seapower in Washington, D.C.'s Army-Navy Club on 4 August 2011, "Grand Strategy is not always great strategy."
12 Hart, 1967, 322.
13 Wagener, 2010, 6.
14 Oxford Dictionary of the U.S. Military, 2002, 274.
15 Wagener, 2010, 6.
16 Kugler, 2006, 102.
17 Stallmann, 2000, 1–2.
18 Art, 2003, 5.
19 Fischbock, 1982, 2.
20 Cropsey, 2013, 16.
21 McDougall, 2011, 32.
22 Corbett, 1911, 9–11.
23 Till, 2009, 60. The argument between continental and maritime strategists has a rich history and repeatedly stirred controversies in academia. If one follows the deliberations of early twentieth-century geopolitical thinkers such as Harold Mackinder or Karl Haushofer, world politics is first and foremost the struggle for continental domination over the Eurasian heartland (the 'world island' in Mackinder's words). Hegemonic policies across the sea, they asserted, was doomed to fail from the beginning (McDougall, 2011: 31). However, a look into history will qualify that argument. The courses of World Wars I and II were decisively changed after the United States was drawn into the conflict (1917, 1941). Massive economic and materiel support for allies, successful battles at sea (e.g., Midway 1942), colossal amphibious landings (e.g., Normandy 1944), and the

prevalence of commercial shipping in the Battle of the Atlantic (1941–1943) are visible reminders of what sea power if directed properly can accomplish. This goes to show that decisions in epochal military struggles could be forced from the sea by seapowers (Duppler, 1999: 13–14). The final decision, obviously, occurred on land because continental powers either collapsed because of internal struggles or because a massive use of force was directed against the land-wards center of gravity by the antagonists (Gray, 1994: 8). For more on the seapower/maritime versus land power/continental argument, see Sheehan (2010: 52–54).

24 Mahnken, 2010, 69.
25 Sheehan, 2010, 49.
26 Duppler, 1999, 16. Wegener, 1974, 28.
27 Duppler, 1999, 17.
28 According to the Oxford Dictionary of the U.S. Military (2002: 145), a fleet-in-being is "a fleet that avoids decisive action, but, because of its strength and location, causes opposing forces to locate nearby, and so reduce the number of opposing units available for operations elsewhere." A fleet-in-being strategy was employed by the German High Sea's Fleet during World War I.
29 Turner, 1974, reprinted in Hattendorf, 2004, 31–52.
30 Alford, 1980, 66, reprinted in Till, 1987: 53; see also Kearsley, 1992, 9.
31 Till, 1987, 59–63.
32 Till, 1987, 65.
33 Till, 1987, 92.
34 Strategic deterrence by U.S. Navy submarines armed with nuclear-tipped missiles as the naval leg of the U.S. nuclear triad exploits the maritime domain and fields advanced technology. For the purpose of this study, the strategic nuclear deterrence use of the sea is outside of the core interest of the analysis. The SSBN's special role in the naval strategic context is symbolized best by U.S. nuclear weapons being subject to the jurisdiction of a specialized functional military command, the U.S. Strategic Command, commanded separately from conventional naval forces.
35 Even more than 35 years after it was fought, the Falklands War still warrants deeper study in the context of naval warfare and strategy. It was a conflict of many "firsts" (first modern A2/AD war, first successful attack of a nuclear hunter/killer submarine against a major enemy surface combatant, operational debut of the V/STOL Harrier aircraft, an illustration of the Royal Navy's new Invincible-class aircraft carrier in combat action, etc.) and a major expeditionary joint operation. Although the conflict dynamics must be understood by its historical background, the lessons of the war hold continuous relevance. The official Navy report (DON, 1983) is also worthwhile, and the best lessons-learned study remains Cordesman/Wagner (1991: 238–401). Two books instrumental to the course of the conflict are the memoirs of the British South Atlantic naval task force commander (Woodward/Robinson, 2012) and the authoritative military history account (Middlebrook, 2001). For Royal Navy submarines, see Hennessy and Kinks, *The Silent Deep. The Royal Navy Submarine Service since 1945*. London. Allen Lane 2015, ch. 7.
36 USNI, 1975, 9, cited in Till, 1987: 65.
37 For a concise overview of these naval missions with a focus on the evolution in light of twenty-first century security challenges, see Forster (2013: 25–49).
38 Bartlett, Holman, and Somes, 1995, 114–126.
39 Fitschen, 2007, 19–20.
40 Lloyd, 1997, 3; Stallmann, 2000, 8; George and Bennet, 2005, 276.
41 Till, 1999, 242.
42 Liotta and Lloyd, 2005, 122.
43 Cited in Barnett, 2009, 44.

44 (Strategic) Failure also has effects on learning. Armies and navies hardly ever learn from success (Gray, 1994: 23), and may thus fall victim to planning for the last, rather than the next conflict. As a matter of fact, Gray noted that "painful experience provides excellent education" (ibid: 43).

45 Gray described the five dimensions of naval warfare as surface, sub-surface, aviation, EW, and nuclear weapons (1994: 132–133).

46 Gray, 1994, 135.

47 It should be noted that the U.S. Marine Corps is part of the surface and aviation communities, because of its unique position within the Department of the Navy. Its roles in modern combat and war-fighting (infantry, counterinsurgency, *et al.*) furthermore shape the self-image of the USMC. Interestingly, a subculture for EW, cyberspace, or nuclear weapons has not (yet) taken shape.

48 Barnett, 2009, 9.

49 Grove, 1992, 189.

50 For further discussion of the subject, see Jervis (1995).

51 See also Gary E. Weir, *An Ocean in Common: American Naval Officers, Scientists, and the Ocean Environment.* College Stations, TX. Texas A&M Press: 2001.

52 Barnett, 2009, 17.

53 See also Gary E. Weir (ed.), *You Cannot Surge Trust. Combined Naval Operations of the Royal Australian Navy, Canadian Navy, Royal Navy, and the United States Navy, 1991–2003.* Washington, D.C. USGPO: 2013.

54 Collins, 1998, 57.

55 Fischbock, 1982, 1. Maritime trade and seaborne commerce increasingly dominate prosperity and global economic development, and are consequently a good worth safeguarding in times of peace, conflict, and war. Often, these sea lines are compared with land-based routes. In contrast to highways or railway lines, however, fixed and clearly marked routes are unusual at sea – save for harbors, choke points, approaches, and roadsteads.

56 Nincic, 2002.

57 Posen, 2003.

58 Forster, 2013, 15–17.

59 Jervis, 1995, 43.

60 Feldt, 2003, 25.

61 USNWC, 2011, 39.

62 Hofmann, 1983, 137–139.

63 Cited in Barnett, 2009, 79.

64 Barnett, 2009, 41.

65 Hofmann, 1983, 144.

66 Barnett, 2009, 64–66.

67 Gray, 1994, 11.

68 Wagener, 2010, 2.

69 Hattendorf, 2004, 2.

70 Huntington, 1954, emphasis by the author.

71 Huntington, 1954.

72 Swartz, 2011, 46, slides 91–92. CAPT (USN) John Byron, in a 1987 USNI Proceedings article, noted four determinants, namely strategy, resource input, force structure, and technology. Each drives and is driven by the other three (Swartz, 2011: 46).

73 Cropsey, 2013, 85.

74 Rosenberg, 1993, 145.

75 Rosenberg, 1993, 150–152.

76 Sumida and Rosenberg, 1995.

77 Stallmann, 2000, 259.

78 Rosenberg, 1993, 174.

79 Collins, 2002, 6.
80 Goldman and Arquilla, 1999, 11.
81 Lowi *et al.*, 2010, 680.
82 Bindra, 2005, 7.
83 Hattendorf, 2004, 1.
84 Based on Lowi *et al.* 2010, 684.
85 Lowi *et al.*, 2010, 680–681. Sirakov, 2012.
86 The actual power of the presidency as a person or as an institution is among the favorite subjects of researchers who focus on the political system of the United States. For an overview of the debate and literature on the subject, see Hastedt (2012: 151–152). One of the key standard discussions of Presidential powers is Neustadt (1991).
87 Hastedt, 2012, 156.
88 Hacke, 2005, 32. On the role and history of the National Security Council, see Rothkopf (2005), Auger (2012), and Horlohe (2012).
89 For a very recent example of a Secretary venting about these incursions into Pentagon responsibilities, see Gates (2014: 352, 452, 553, 586–588).
90 U.S. Constitution, Art I, Sec. 8, emphasis added.
91 Lowi *et al.*, 2010, 684. A study on the Congressional role in American naval power and strategy would be highly desirable.
92 It also includes the U.S. Coast Guard if it operates under the command and jurisdiction of DOD/DON by Presidential or Congressional direction in times of national emergency. The last such occasion was World War II. In peacetime, the Coast Guard's governmental structure was the Department of Transportation (DOT), but since 2003 this has been the newly formed Department of Homeland Security (DHS).
93 Swartz, 2011, 85, slides 169–170.
94 Lowi *et al.*, 2010, 685.
95 Varwick and Hecht, 2012.
96 On European influence on U.S. foreign policy, see Risse-Kappen (1995).
97 Standing NATO Maritime Groups 1 and 2 (which evolved from standing NATO naval forces in the Atlantic, activated in 1968, and the Mediterranean, activated in 1992) and Standing NATO Mine Countermeasure Groups 1 and 2 (activated under different names in 1973 and 1999, respectively) train and operate together. U.S. Navy units are participating regularly in these exercises, providing a visible commitment to the alliance.
98 A study on the relationship between NATO and the U.S. Navy would be desirable. For starters, see Peter Swartz, *Evolution of U.S. Navy Roles in NATO: Always an Important Part of a Larger Whole*, Draft Paper, Arlington: Center for Naval Analyses, 2004 (unpublished), and Felix Seidler, *Maritime Herausforderungen der NATO. Strategische Auswirkungen und Effektivität des Handels.* Frankfurt: Peter Lang, 2015.
99 Krause, 2009, 91.
100 Rhodes, 1999, 18.
101 Rhodes, 1999, 21–25.
102 These ideas have long-standing naval roots. See Dirk Bönker, *Militarism in a Global Age. Naval Ambitions in Germany and the United States before World War I*, Ithaca/London, Cornell University Press: 2012.
103 Rhodes, 1999, 23–25.
104 Hattendorf, 2004, 1–2.

References

Alford, Jonathan, ed. *Sea Power and Influence: Old Issues and New Challenges*. Farnborough, UK: Gower, 1980.

Auger, Vincent. "The National Security Council." *Routledge Handbook of American Foreign Policy*, eds. S. Hook and C. Jones. New York/London: Routledge, 2012.

Barnett, Roger. *Navy Strategic Culture: Why the Navy Thinks Differently*. Annapolis, MD: Naval Institute Press (NIP), 2009.

Bartlett, Henry, Holman, Paul, and Somes, Timothy. "The Art of Strategy and Force Planning." *Naval War College Review* 48(1) (January 1995).

Bindra, Sukhwant Singh. *US Foreign Policy Process*. New Delhi: Deep & Deep, 2005.

Bönker, Dirk. *Militarism in a Global Age. Naval Ambitions in Germany and the United States before World War I*. Ithaca /London, Cornell University Press: 2012

Boorman, Scott. "Fundamentals of Strategy. The Legacy of Henry Eccles." *Naval War College Review* 62(2) (April 2009).

Collins, John. *Military Geography for Professionals and the Public*. Washington, D.C.: Brassey's, 1998.

Collins, John. *Military Strategy: Principles, Practices, and Historical Perspectives*. Washington, D.C.: Brassey's, 2002.

Corbett, Julian. *Some Principles of Maritime Strategy*. Mineola, NY: Dover, 1911.

Cordesman, Anthony, and Wagner, Abraham. *The Lessons of Modern War, Volume III: The Afghan and Falklands Conflicts*. Boulder, CO, and San Francisco: Westview Press, 1991.

Cropsey, Seth. *Mayday. The Decline of American Naval Supremacy*. New York and London: Overlook Duckworth, 2013.

Department of the Navy, Office of Program Appraisal. "Lessons of the Falklands. Summary Report, February 1983." Washington, DC: DON, 1983.

Duppler, Jörg. "Seemacht, Seestrategie, Seeherrschaft." *Seemacht und Seestrategie im b19. und 20. Jahrhundert*, ed. J. Duppler. Hamburg: Mittler & Sohn (= Vorträge zur Militärgeschichte, vol. 18, distributed by the Militärgeschichtliches Forschungsamt), 1999, 13–20.

Feldt, Lutz. "Zukunftsperspektiven der Deutschen Marine." *Europäische Sicherheit 9/2003* (2003).

Fischbock, Martin. "Die Funktion von Seestreitkräften in einem gewandelten technologischen Umfeld," thesis, University of Kiel, Kiel, Germany, 1982.

Fitschen, Patrick. *Die Transformation der US-Streitkräfte: Die Neuausrichtung der Streitkräfte der Vereinigten Staaten zwischen 2001 und 2006*. Frankfurt am Main, Germany: Peter Lang (= Analysen zur Sicherheitspolitik, Vol. 1, Distributed by the Institut für Sicherheitspolitik an der Christian-Albrechts-Universität zu Kiel), 2007.

Forster, Larissa. *Influence without Boots on the Ground: Seaborne Crisis Response*. Newport, RI: Naval War College Press, 2013.

Gates, Robert. *Duty: Memoirs of a Secretary at War*. New York, London: Random House, 2014.

George, Alexander, and Bennett, Andrew. *Case Studies and Theory Development in the Social Sciences*. Cambridge/London: MIT Press, 2005.

Goldman, Emily, and Arquilla, John. "Structure, Agency, and Choice. Toward a Theory and Practice of Grand Strategy." *The Politics of Strategic Adjustment. Ideas, Institutions, and Interests*, eds. P. Trubowitz/E. Goldman/E. Rhodes. New York: Columbia University Press, 1999.

Gray, Colin. *The Navy in the Post-Cold War World: The Uses and Value of Strategic Sea Power.* University Park, PA: Penn State Press, 1994.

Grove, Eric."The Utility of History to Modern Navies." *Military History and the Military Profession*, eds. D. Charters, M. Milner, and J.B. Wilson. Westport, CT/London: Praeger, 1992.

Hacke, Christian. *Zur Weltmacht verdammt. Die amerikanische Außenpolitik von J.F. Kennedy bis G.W. Bush.* 3. Auflage, aktualisierte Neuausgabe, München: Ullstein, 2005.

Hart, Liddell. *Strategy.* 2nd, revised edition, London: Faber & Faber, 1967.

Hastedt, Glenn. "The Presidency." *The Routledge Handbook of American Foreign Policy*, eds. S. Hook and C. Jones. New York/London: Routledge, 2012.

Hattendorf, John, ed. *The Evolution of the U.S. Navy's Maritime Strategy, 1977–1986.* Newport, RI: Naval War College Press, 2004.

Hofmann, Wilfried. "Die Rolle von Seestreitkräften in der Aussenpolitik." *Der Einsatz von Seestreitkräften im Dienst der Auswärtigen Politik*, ed. Deutsches Marine Institute. Herford: Mittler 1983 (= Schriftenreihe des Deutschen Marine Instituts, Vol. 3), 137–145.

Horlohe, Thomas. "Nationaler Sicherheitsrat." *Die Außenpolitik der USA. Theorie, Prozesse, Politikfelder, Regionen*, ed. S. Koschut and M.-S. Kutz. Opladen/Toronto: Barbara Budrich, 2012.

Huntington, Samuel. "National Policy and the Transoceanic Navy." *U.S. Naval Institute Proceedings* 80(5) (May 1954).

Jervis, Robert. "Navies, Politics, and Political Science." *Doing Naval History: Essays Towards Improvement*, ed. J. Hattendorf. Newport, RI: Naval War College Press, 1995.

Kearsley, Harold. *Maritime Power and the Twenty-First Century.* Aldershot, UK: Dartmouth, 1992.

Krause, Joachim. "Liberaler Imperialismus und imperialer Liberalismus als Erklärungsansätze amerikanischer Aussenpolitik." *Zeitschrift für Aussen- und Sicherheitspolitik* 1(1) (2009).

Kugler, Richard. *Policy Analysis in National Security Affairs: New Methods for a New Era.* Washington, D.C.: NDU Press, 2006.

Liotta, P.H., and Lloyd, Richmond. "From Here to There. The Strategy and Force Planning Framework." *Naval War College Review* 58(2) (2005).

Lloyd, Richmond. "Strategy and Force Planning Framework." *Strategy and Force Planning*, edited by the Naval War College. 2nd edition, Newport: Naval War College Press, 1997.

Lowi, Theodore, Ginsberg, Benjamin, Shepsle, Kenneth, *et al. American Government. Power and Purpose.* 11th edition, New York, NY: Norton, 2010.

McDougall, Walter. "History and Strategies. Grand, Maritime, American." *American Grand Strategy and Seapower Conference Report*, ed, M. Gerson and A. Lawler Russel. Alexandria, VA: CNA, 2011.

Mahnken, Thomas. "Strategic Theory." *Strategy in the Contemporary World. An Introduction to Strategic Studies*, edited by J. Baylis/J. Wirtz/C. Gray. 3rd edition. Oxford/New York: Oxford University Press, 2010.

Maull, Hanns W. "Nationale Interessen! Aber was sind sie?" *Internationale Politik* 10 (2006).

Middlebrook, Martin. *The Falklands War, 1982.* London: Penguin, 2001.

Neustadt, Richard. *Presidential Power and the Modern Presidents: The Politics of Leadership from Roosevelt to Reagan.* New York, NY: Free Press, 1991.

Nincic, Donna. "Sea Lane Security and U.S. Maritime Trade: Chokepoints as Scarce Resources." *Globalization and Maritime Power*, ed. S. Tangredi. Washington, D.C: NDU Press, 2002.

The Oxford Essential Dictionary of the U.S. Military. New York, NY: Oxford University Press, 2002.

Posen, Barry. "Command of the Commons. The Military Foundation of U.S. Hegemony." *International Security* 28(1) (Summer 2003), 5–46.

Rhodes, Edward. "'… From the Sea' and Back Again: Naval Power in the Second American Century." *Naval War College Review* 52(2) (April 1999).

Risse-Kappen, Thomas. *Cooperation among Democracies. The European Influence on U.S. Foreign Policy*. Princeton, NJ: Princeton University Press, 1995.

Rosenberg, David. "The Realities of Modern Naval Strategy." *Mahan Is Not Enough: The Proceedings of a Conference on the Works of Sir Julian Corbett and Admiral Sir Hugh Richmond*, eds. J. Goldrick and J. Hattendorf. Newport, RI: Naval War College Press, 1993.

Rothkopf, David. *Running the World. The Inside Story of the National Security Council and the Architects of American Power*. New York, NY: Public Affairs, 2005.

Ruge, Friedrich. "Strategie. Versuch einer Definition (1960)." *Erleben – Lernen – Weitergeben." Friedrich Ruge (1894–1985)*, edited by J. Hillmann. Bochum: Dr. Winkler 2005 (= Kleine Schriften zur Militär- und Marinegeschichte, Band 10).

Seidler, Felix. *Maritime Herausforderung der NATO. Strategische Auswirkungen und die Effektivität des Handelns*. Frankfurt et al.: Peter Lang, 2015.

Sheehan, Michael. "The Evolution of Modern Warfare." *Strategy in the Contemporary World: An Introduction to Strategic Studies*, 3rd edition, eds. J. Baylis, J. Wirtz, and C. Gray. Oxford, UK, and New York: Oxford University Press, 2010.

Sirakov, David. "Präsident." *Die Außenpolitik der USA. Theorie, Prozesse, Politikfelder, Regionen*, eds. S. Koschut, M.-S. Kutz. Opladen/Toronto: Barbara Budrich, 2012.

Stallmann, Wilfried. *Die maritime Strategie der USA nach 1945: Entwicklung, Einflussgrößen und Auswirkungen auf das atlantische Bündnis*. Dissertation, University of Kiel, Germany, 2000.

Sumida, Jon, and Rosenberg, David. "Machines, Men, Manufacturing, Management and Money: The Study of Navies as Complex Organizations and the Transformation of Twentieth Century Naval History." *Doing Naval History. Essays towards Improvement*, ed. J. Hattendorf. Newport, RI: Naval War College Press, 1995.

Swartz, Peter. *Evolution of U.S. Navy Roles in NATO: Always an Important Part of a Larger Whole*, Draft Paper, Arlington: Center for Naval Analyses, 2004 (unpublished manuscript).

Swartz, Peter, and Duggan, Karin. *U.S. Navy Capstone Strategy and Concepts: Introduction, Background and Analyses* (slideshow). Alexandria, VA: CNA, 2011.

Till, Geoffrey. *Modern Sea Power*. London: Brassey's Defence Publishers, 1987.

Till, Geoffrey. "Die Ursprünge des maritimen Verhaltens der Großmächte: Die Zeit des Kal-ten Kriegs und die Jahre danach." *Seemacht und Seestrategie im 19. und 20. Jahrhundert*, ed. J. Duppler. Hamburg: Mittler & Sohn 1999 (= Vorträge zur Militärgeschichte, Volume 18, distributed by the Militärgeschichtliches Forschungsamt), 241–264.

Till, Geoffrey. *Seapower. A Guide for the 21st Century*, 2nd edition. London: Routledge, 2009.

Turner, Stansfield. "Missions of the U.S. Navy." *Naval War College Review* 26(5) (September 1974): 2–17 (modified version in *U.S. Naval Institute Proceedings*, vol. 100, no. 12 [December 1974]: 18–24).

U.S. Naval War College. "Navy Roles, Functions, Capabilities, Limitations. Power Point Presentation held at U.S. Army Staff Officer Course C-306, Ft. Belvoir, Virginia." Newport, RI: U.S. Naval War College, 2011.

Varwick, Johannes, and Tobias Hecht. "Internationale Organisationen." *Die Außenpolitik der USA. Theorie, Prozesse, Politikfelder, Regionen*, eds. S. Koschut/M.-S. Kutz. Opladen/Toronto: Barbara Budrich, 2012.

Wagener, Martin. "Über das Wesen der Strategie." *Österreichische Militärische Zeitschrift Nr. 4/2010* (2010).

Wegener, Edward. "Die Elemente von Seemacht und maritimer Macht." *Seemacht und Aussenpolitik*, eds. D. Mahncke, and H.-P. Schwarz. Frankfurt am Main, Germany: Metzner 1974 (= Rüstungsbeschränkungen und Sicherheit, Vol. 11).

Weir, Gary E. *An Ocean in Common: American Naval Officers, Scientists, and the Ocean Environment*. College Stations, TX. Texas A&M Press, 2001.

Weir, Gary E (ed.), *You Cannot Surge Trust. Combined Naval Operations of the Royal Australian Navy, Canadian Navy, Royal Navy, and the United States Navy, 1991–2003*. Washington, D.C. USGPO, 2013.

Woodward, Sandy, and Robinson, Patrick. *One-Hundred Days. The Memoirs of the Falklands Battle Group Commander*. London: Harper, 2012.

3 Prelude

1945–1980, a "naval baisse?"

Describing the 1980s as a gleaming 'naval re-birth' implies that there must have been a great deal of agony and sluggishness prior, in French parlor, a 'naval baisse.' It is instructive to look at the development of the U.S. Navy prior to the 1980s, in particular in the Cold War and the 1970s.[1] The U.S. Navy came out of World War II as a large force resting on battleships and aircraft carriers. In conjunction with allies, the U.S. Navy had developed and brought to bear a variety of sea power measures. These ranged from sea control, efficient anti-submarine and anti-surface warfare, large-scale amphibious landings, carrier aviation, to naval gun-fire support, and others. A massive military and commercial shipbuilding program sustained the allied efforts and provided the embattled allied war economies. Allied forces were supplied with men and materiel courtesy of U.S. maritime power. The war began with a shock on the morning of December 7, 1941 with the Japanese attack on the U.S. naval base in Pearl Harbor (Hawaii), and ended for U.S. sea power on a high note with the Japanese capitulation on the deck of the battleship *Missouri* (BB 63) in Tokyo harbor on September 2, 1945. However, the Navy soon found itself in stormy political weather. In September 1945, a month after the nuclear bombing of Hiroshima and Nagasaki forced Japan to surrender (at the moment of the Navy's apotheosis), Navy Secretary James Forrestal appeared before the House Committee on Naval Affairs and asked, 'Why should we maintain any Navy after this war?' Absent a maritime enemy, and with air-atomic warfare the apparent mode of the future, the Navy did not have a post-war mission.[2]

The Soviet Union, the principal foreseeable antagonist, was a continental land power almost straight from a textbook, and did not possess an offensive naval fleet.[3] The advent of nuclear weapons – the Soviet Union's first testing of a weapon in 1949 ended the U.S. monopoly on them – in its cynical Dr. Strangelovian sense lured many strategists to assume that nuclear delivery platforms and a small conventional standing army, not a globally engaged military controlling the seas, were the wave of the future. The next war, in all likelihood, was bound to be quick, escalatory, nuclear, and ultimately devastating. In other words, strategic thinking was nuclear thinking. That limited the Navy's purpose to little more than transport of reinforcements. The prospect of all-out nuclear war degraded sea power.

Organizationally, strategically, and perhaps even intellectually, the Navy was ill-prepared for the post-war strategic landscape. Instead, it found itself fighting bureaucratic domestic wars. The reorganization of the national security apparatus through the creation of the Department of Defense (through the National Security Act of 1947, as later amended)[4] robbed the Navy of considerable bureaucratic clout and established the U.S. Air Force as a serious competitor for resources, political influence, and a major role in the coming war.[5] The Navy, as all services, was also subject to extensive demobilization from its wartime posture. This was significantly in the interest of Congress, which proclaimed that, as Baer pointed out, "the United States had command of the sea and was in no danger of losing it."[6]

In an era of nuclear warfare, other uses of a Navy in limited warfare and power projection – two classic sea power measures, after all – were in little demand. However, the conditions under which defense policy operated soon changed. In April 1950, a joint group from the Department of State and the Department of Defense issued a directive that changed the U.S. outlook on the world. National Security Council memo #68 (NSC-68)[7] called for an assertive, staunch anti-Soviet policy worldwide, coupled with substantial investments in defense. Although the message did not put the Navy in a significantly more favorable position, it implied a larger utility of American sea power in the emerging postwar order and a strategy of containment of Soviet Russia.

Five World War II and post-war developments helped buttress the U.S. grand strategy of containment in the maritime realm, which later became known as combat-credible forward presence. First, the wartime creation and use of fast carrier task forces to attack and destroy critical targets ashore and at sea; second, the wartime creation and use of Navy-Marine Corps amphibious task forces to assault defended forward beaches; third, the late-war creation and use of mobile afloat logistic support forces to refuel and replenish forward warships far forward, while under way, even in combat; fourth, the development of air-delivered nuclear bombs as the most lethal and important weapons in the American arsenal; and fifth, the 1949 U.S. Navy decision to develop the attack submarine as a principal forward ASW weapon system.[8]

The decision to send the *Missouri* (BB 63) to Turkey in 1946 signaled early American commitment to the volatile states in the East Mediterranean littorals in the face of Communist inroads. The U.S.-led United Nations force to intervene in the Korean War between 1950 and 1953 relied substantially on naval assets such as battleships, carriers, and amphibious assaults. The Navy sought to bring to bear the advantages inherent to its force: mobility, readiness, flexibility, and power-projection ashore. Its instruments were more discriminating than what the Air Force and the supporters of nuclear war proposed. Other limited conflicts of the time seemed to vindicate that position and underscore the Navy's role and the view the service held of itself.

The Suez Crisis of 1956 underlined the troublesome constellation in the Middle East as a hot proxy conflict between East and West, and it gave a role to sea power. An Israeli drive toward the Suez Canal was backed by British and French naval forces, but the Soviet Union was drawn into the conflict on the side of Arab nationalists. The intervention of President Dwight D. Eisenhower halted the escalatory path and eventually defused a crisis which severely curtailed British and French power and prestige.[9] Two years after Suez, the U.S. intervention in Lebanon in 1958 rested on the capabilities of the decade-old, forward-based U.S. Sixth Fleet in the Mediterranean Sea. The Suez crisis and the U.S. intervention in the Levant also turned out to be a significant motivation for the Soviet Union to acquire more offensive sea power capabilities under Admiral Sergey Gorshkov.

The Cuban Missile Crisis in October 1962, which put Soviet missiles on the U.S. doorstep, was eventually defused by a naval quarantine (a type of naval blockade) around the Communist-ruled Caribbean island, driving home the value of measured political and military responses, particular by American sea power.[10] Consequently, the doctrine of massive retaliation (a general nuclear war strategy devised in the mid-1950s) was superseded by a doctrine of flexible response by the late 1960s. U.S.-led sea control supported the containment of the Soviet Union by surrounding it with forward-based forces and covering the seas in between.[11] Whereas the grand and military strategies against the Soviet Union were codified, the U.S. Navy failed to publish its thinking in written, publicly concise, and declaratory fashion. That left the Navy dependent on the global political fever chart, domestic political opinion, and the general budget share that the service could obtain. The Navy's narrative atrophied because it was not explained what exact strategic importance the Navy had in the overall design of U.S. foreign and security policy.[12]

Meanwhile, new platforms such as the *Forrestal*-class aircraft carrier, the development of sea-launched missiles capable of carrying nuclear warheads, and the feasibility of nuclear propulsion for surface warships and submarines gave the Navy longer, state-of-the art legs. This shaped the Navy's *raison d'être* but came at further cost to its strategic mindset and its military-intellectual capabilities. The promises of technology eclipsed the need to think about the political ends of naval warfare. Admiral Hyman G. Rickover, the father of the nuclear navy, established a power base outside of service control.[13] Until his forced retirement in 1982, Rickover went on a comprehensive campaign to establish and maintain a nuclear Navy. Although each warfare community (surface, subsurface, aviation) wrestled for support and influence, winning support for nuclear-powered ships significantly drove the Navy's narrative.

In the next major crisis, the Vietnam War (1964–1973), U.S. sea control remained largely uncontested, and consequently the Navy very much focused on strike warfare against shore targets. Sustained carrier strike warfare, naval gunfire support, coastal and riverine operations, counterinsurgency, and late in the war the mining of North Vietnamese ports drove USN involvement in Vietnam. This came at the expense of Navy sea control capabilities.[14] In Washington, the Defense Reorganization Act of 1958 had given increasing operational and force-structure planning oversight to the Secretary of Defense at the expense of all service chiefs including the CNO. By 1967, Secretary of Defense Robert McNamara's style of management frustrated many who saw a Navy's value in more than just riverine and coastal small-boat operations, carrier air strikes against an elusive enemy, and junior partnership to the other branches of the U.S. military, but they lacked arguments against seemingly compelling statistics from the Pentagon leadership. It did not help that President Lyndon B. Johnson micro-managed significant U.S. military issues in Vietnam, and that the Army, Marine Corps, and Air Force had shouldered considerably more costs and losses in Southeast Asia. The Navy found itself between a rock and a hard place.

Vietnam was the limited war the Navy had talked about when it had rationalized its force-structure and training as contrast to the popular nuclear-war scenarios. Against a coastal country, major tactical firepower could be brought to bear, and the use of attack aircraft carriers and bombers for shore bombing did vindicate parts of the force structure. Ultimately, however, the Navy was much less prepared for other dimensions of limited war, such as small-unit actions to attain coastal control, riverine patrols, and counterinsurgency. The emphasis of carrier air strikes also came at the expense of understanding and practicing the value of sea control in the age of the flexible military response strategy.[15]

In July 1969, President Richard Nixon, in an address on the Pacific island of Guam, sought a way out of the unwinnable war in Southeast Asia. In what became known as the Nixon Doctrine,[16] the President went on record underlining that the U.S. would keep its treaty and alliance commitments. It would also continue to offer nuclear deterrence to support its allies, but unlike in Vietnam, the U.S. would stay out of what it saw as regional Asian wars. To support the Nixon Doctrine, an ocean strategy based on a deterrent force of missile submarines and a general-purpose fleet was formulated. The latter would permit the Navy to control selected sea areas, project power abroad, and maintain a naval presence where desirable, albeit with a much smaller force.[17]

The Navy now faced three major challenges. It tilted internally toward some missions at the expense of others and lacked the intellectual verve of a broad, comprehensive understanding and application of sea power; it was at a disadvantage in the budgetary competition with the other services which had borne the brunt of Vietnam; and in the face of financial austerity under Nixon, it had to rely on and utilize an increasingly aging and shrinking fleet of a large number of different ship and aircraft types. Dramatic social and demographic dynamics in desegregating the Navy and transitioning to an all-volunteer force (reflecting changes in U.S. society) put an additional burden on the service.[18] The Navy's public image for effectiveness was further rocked by such catastrophes as the deadly blaze aboard the aircraft carrier *Forrestal* (CV 59).[19]

To add insult to injury, just as the United States wandered deeper and deeper into the Vietnamese quagmire and the Navy faced its internal problems, the Soviet Navy aspired to emerge as a formidable naval challenger on the high seas. Moscow sought to augment its coastal defense forces (which had relied on diesel submarines and light surface units) with more capable ships, thus reflecting broader geopolitical claims and significant strategic ambitions for a blue-water navy.[20]

At the time of withdrawal from Vietnam, the U.S. Navy had intellectually and conceptually maneuvered itself into a corner and was not able to stand up to a sea-control challenger. As an institution, the Navy had adhered to power-projection and reliance on attrition strikes from the sea against a foreign shore. This came at the cost of neglecting the sea control mission, undercutting the general purpose fleet. Concurrently, the discourse concentrated on naval platforms, not the missions. Fortuitously, the introduction of nuclear-powered ballistic submarines (SSBN) had freed the aircraft carriers from their nuclear role and provided an impetus for revitalized thinking on what could be achieved with these (and other) ships in the first place.

At the same time, a reemergence of conventional war concepts provided a new thrust for Navy thinking and planning. A Sino-Soviet political split signaled the potential for inner-Communist bloc rifts and provided leverage for U.S. strategy. The defense drawdown by the United Kingdom (including the Royal Navy) from east of Suez highlighted an important transfer of presence requirements to the U.S. and its Navy.[21] Decolonization since World War II had multiplied the number of countries worldwide, some victims of violent civil wars which became sites for proxy superpower conflict. In parallel, world maritime trade experienced growth, despite the first in a row of oil price shocks, as still more first-world countries emerged as economic powers since 1945.[22]

This is not to say that the nuclear, bipolar world ceased to dominate world affairs; in fact, just as the superpowers negotiated the Non-Proliferation Treaty (NPT), other countries (India, South Africa, and Pakistan) aspired to join the exclusive "nuclear club." Such thinking emphasized conventional force, even in the age of nuclear warfare, as the weapon of choice. Ironically, opposing (and roughly equal) nuclear forces diminished in their political value, while conventional balances became more important in their relation to nuclear equilibrium, especially deterrence, and incremental escalation. Détente, the easing of the Cold War begun under Richard Nixon and continued under his successor Gerald Ford, temporarily replaced the containment approach toward the Soviet Union. However, direct Soviet-American conflict was always a possibility, as the naval confrontation during the Yom Kippur War (1973) readily demonstrated.[23]

The Navy needed to reinvigorate its offensive strategic thinking rather than simply support defensive considerations. To that end, five major efforts to codify Navy thought emerged during the 1970s: These were "Project SIXTY" (1970), "Missions of the U.S. Navy" (1974), "Strategic Concepts of the U.S. Navy" (1975–1978), "Sea Plan 2000" (1978), and "The Future of U.S. Sea Power" (1979). The selection of the commander of the U.S. brown-water naval forces in Vietnam, Admiral Elmo "Bud" Zumwalt, as Chief of Naval Operations is therefore not without a timely sense of irony. A hands-on personality, Zumwalt was "determined to right the balance and give the Navy a full-service doctrine and a full-service force" (Baer, 1994: 393). That approach included the designation of the Strategic Concepts Branch (OP-603) and the CNO Executive Panel (OP-00K), specific offices within OPNAV to foster and institutionalize strategic development.

"Project SIXTY"[24] (a planning memorandum, the CNO's favored vehicle to distribute his views in the navy) was signed by Zumwalt in 1970. It was a self-described assessment and sought to spell out a direction for the Navy. Strategic deterrence, sea control, power projection, and maritime presence were articulated as the principal ordered tasks of the U.S. Navy for American national security.[25] The memorandum proposed to shape the future fleet along the lines of a "hi-low mix" of expensive capital ships for power projection (specifically new carriers and some submarines) and more affordable, smaller, low-value sea control combatants.[26]

"Missions of the U.S. Navy," drafted and signed by Vice Admiral Stansfield Turner (then President of the Naval War College), was published four years later.[27] It elaborated on the preceding document and outlined four distinct naval missions: power projection, sea control, naval presence, and strategic deterrence. Those were the 'classic 4,' which fundamentally focused the Navy's roles in U.S. foreign and security policy. Turner's paper illustrated the relationship of missions and tactics, created new vocabulary, and underlined the focus on the Soviet Union, thus providing lasting intellectual legacy for the Navy officer corps in the decades to come. The advent of new platforms and technologies and the introduction of the Harpoon anti-ship missile in the 1970s provided a further influx of capabilities, especially for surface warfare, to support a broader mission and mindset.[28] However, the national leadership in the early and mid-1970s was not very interested in power projection or sea control. Consequently, the services did not even need to consider their role in the next war and the political ends of their contributions to national defense. The Navy (much like the Marine Corps, the Army, and the Air Force) continued to think about itself in isolation and focused on how to fight, not why.

For the time being, senior leaders in Washington were consumed by domestic post-Watergate and post-Vietnam agendas, which added to overall strategic uncertainty. Successive administrations under Richard Nixon, Gerald Ford, and Jimmy Carter reduced the Navy's role in national war plans, with the notable exception of further investing in the nuclear ballistic missile submarines now used for strategic deterrence. Presidents followed a policy that hoped to drive strategic decisions through a combination of cost-control measures, diplomacy with the Soviet Union, a hope for arms-control agreements, and a rejection of limited armed conflicts like Vietnam.[29]

One of the palpable effects of this was a significant drop in force levels. Old ships were retired *en block* and scrapped without suitable replacements. Congressional austerity, a senior political leadership that invested in things other than the Navy, and the high inflation rate which drove up unit cost further limited ship-procurement. Consequently, the Navy battle force consistently stayed behind the force level goals articulated by its leaders. Fleet size dropped from 769 ships in 1970 to just 512 in 1975. It reached a contemporary all-time low of 464 in 1977.[30] This quantitative attrition of American sea power was met with intellectual erosion of sound naval strategic thinking; Admiral Rickover's nuclear ideology went so deeply into the service's educational and operational structure that it left little room for thought exercises (and writings) on more traditional naval missions and how these in turn should shape strategy.[31]

In the face of a worn-out and ever-shrinking fleet, Admiral James L. Holloway (CNO from 1974 to 1978) provided a new focus on long-range planning, including calling for prospective ship levels from 500 to 800 warships.[32] To Holloway, sea control and power projection were not to be ranked or prioritized. Instead, they depended on one another.[33] A qualitatively and quantitatively robust and more capable naval force would be needed – not least because the momentous Red Fleet exercises Okean-70 (1970) and Okean-75 (1975) drove home to many the extent of Soviet naval armament and their adoption of a global offensive maritime strategy.[34] The emergence of a Soviet blue-water navy sparked increasing attention on Moscow's naval doctrine, strategy, and operations. That analysis surprisingly indicated that the Soviet Union assigned a much higher priority to defending the Soviet homeland and its strategic SSBN reserve. A Battle-of-the-Atlantic-style campaign against allied sea lines of communication, which had loomed large in Western strategic minds, was considered less likely.[35] This insight yielded one of the central tenets of "The Maritime Strategy" a decade later, namely configuring its forces and thrust to engage the SSBN, not to guard Atlantic SLOCs.

Very prominently, the concept of swinging the U.S. Navy from the Pacific to the European theater in times of crisis and war gained some notoriety. The Navy operated under what was known as the 1.5-war assumption, or providing enough forces to respond to one contingency in Europe and have the on-station Pacific forces 'swing' to the European theater if deemed necessary (or the other way around). It was entirely plausible that U.S. interests in one area would be abandoned if the need arose to transfer forces to the other theater. In times of conflict and crises, this choice could have disastrous consequences, both militarily and politically.

The Navy instead wanted to give intellectual support to the concept of keeping a two-ocean force ready and available should superpower war (contrary to the conviction of the senior leadership) not be confined to the Central European front. In practice, however, the 'swing strategy' remained the official doctrine, regardless of how fraught with geostrategic challenges and how filled with intellectual shortsightedness it was. National strategy had largely dismissed the Pacific, and consequently the Navy did not receive sufficient guidance for that theater. Why, indeed, should there be a two-ocean navy when the national grand strategy did not favor global maritime power projection in a general war with the Soviet Union in the first place? Contrary to most assumptions in Washington, to the Navy a Pacific campaign would not have been a half-war, but rather part of a two-ocean war with the Soviet Union, for which the Navy was ill-prepared. Toward the end of the 1970s, the gap between internal Navy thinking and the naval part of the national defense policy as outlined in the Carter administration's Presidential Review Memorandum-10 (PRM-10) widened.[36] Critics such as the political scientist and military strategist Edward Luttwak blasted the administration and the Navy publicly for failing to come up with a coherent and consistent maritime strategy.[37]

Secretary of the Navy Graham Claytor and Undersecretary of the Navy James Woolsey took it upon themselves to produce "Sea Plan 2000," a study done with the consent and by direction of the Secretary of Defense.[38] A mid-1977 working group's effort from the Navy Secretariat, rather than OPNAV, the document underlined how naval forces could be decisive in crises and war with the Soviet Union by maintaining stability through forward deployments and the perception of naval power; by containing crises through their inherent capability to affect outcomes ashore and lasting superiority at sea versus the Red Fleet; and by deterring global war through the protection of sea lines of communication, reinforcement of allies, keeping pressure against the Soviet Union, while hedging against further possible contingencies.[39] It also suggested three different force level options aimed at maintaining "a balanced fleet as national insurance" (Ryan, 1981: 130). This standard aimed to turn around force level declines and reflected that despite the U.S. industrial base' capabilities, warships could not be churned out from the shipyards overnight.

At the same time, "Project Sea Strike," a complimentary effort aimed at taking on the Soviet military at sea, originated with Admiral Thomas Hayward during his time as Commander, U.S. Seventh Fleet.[40] Hayward wanted to place the Pacific Fleet within a global naval strategy to be used in the event of war with the Soviet Union. In his mind, the command needed to develop an offensive plan, if only for political flexibility, not just keep the defensive one that it already had. Ultimately, such offensive-minded ideas would serve to hedge against the impractical reflex to swing forces from the Pacific to another theater. Scholar John Hattendorf pointed out that "[…] By using Sea Strike as a threat to the Soviet Union, Pacific Fleet planners argued that U.S. naval forces in the Pacific could make a strategic difference by preventing the move of Soviet forces to Europe."[41] Together with re-discovering its naval mission roots, the Navy now proposed thinking about the larger political context, to extend deterrence beyond Europe and the Atlantic, and began to emancipate itself from the burdens of the past. Those in Washington, however, were not quite ready to support this.

Hayward soon succeeded Holloway as CNO, serving from 1978 to 1982. In congressional hearings on Capitol Hill, Hayward criticized the civilian planning in the Department of Defense and how it diametrically opposed naval planning. To Congress, the administration, and the public, he sought to explain the need for an offensive Navy with a global aspiration. Hayward suggested a naval force reliant on technological superiority and carrier aviation offensively addressing Soviet claims to power. If possible, the Soviet Navy should not have the luxury of maintaining sanctuaries for its conventional and nuclear deterrence maritime assets. In theory, this offered a compelling narrative for a large, strong, and global Navy.[42] However, Hayward soon learned that convincing political leaders is often more of a marathon than a 100-yard dash. A global maritime thinking did not fare well with President Carter and his Secretary of Defense, Harold Brown. The administration continued to direct resources toward meeting the Red Army on the ground in Europe, not at sea. A maritime strategy was superseded by that continental commitment and the focus shifted away from the Pacific (as the Navy underlined) to Central Europe (where the Army and the Air Force led the charge). The two-ocean Navy concept was not maintained further. By all indications, the Navy was closer to being reduced to a one-ocean force than growing into a two-ocean navy.

For the time being, the colliding ideas in Washington over the role and direction of the U.S. Navy could not be resolved, although Carter (a U.S. Naval Academy graduate, after all) did not fully dismiss a Navy's role. To him, the main task remained sea control and Third World contingencies. The President actively debated the future U.S. Navy. Carter, for example, supported a smaller, conventionally powered carrier earmarked for peacetime presence missions (dubbed the CVV) during 1978/1979. He encountered the fierce opposition of those who lobbied for further nuclear-powered *Nimitz*-class large aircraft carriers. These platforms were the most capable in the world. They were designed for global operations and general war against the Soviet Union, and supporters insisted that power projection and sea control for the Navy were mutually accommodating and indivisible.[43] A distant blockade of the Soviet Union was floated as an alternative by the supporters of the Carter policies, but that move never gained much traction.[44] Eventually, the Navy was able to lobby Congress successfully for the inclusion of CVN 71 (the future USS *Theodore Roosevelt*) into the budget for fiscal year 1980. The point was made that without a sufficient number of CVNs, the Navy feared that it would be reduced to convoy escorts and ASW.[45] As such, "Sea Strike" and "Sea Plan 2000" were the Navy's codified attempts at pushing back the defense policy of the Carter administration (and scuttling the CVV in the process). The main point of the Navy's argument was that the Central Front could not be seen isolated from the European flanks such as the Mediterranean and the Norwegian Sea. What was more, emphasizing a

NATO-Warsaw Pact war in Germany with a severely constrained role for naval forces, in the minds of Navy advocates, risked national survival.

Linking policy objectives to war-fighting capabilities again became the essence of strategic thinking and a competitive narrative. Admiral Hayward quite masterfully nourished this renaissance within the Navy in the face of a militarily hesitant, human-rights-policies-heavy Carter administration that clearly preferred continental over maritime thinking.[46] In the minds of Navy leaders, they needed to offer a compelling idea which could overcome the established strategy based on a battle between ground forces and supporting air forces in Germany (which, to most Navy people, was not even strategy, but rather a logistics exercise and a question of 'Who could get there first?').[47]

These developments occurred against the background of geopolitical events appearing to give the Soviet Union and its allies a leg up in the bipolar world conflict.[48] In December 1979, the Soviets invaded Afghanistan, coming within striking distance of the warm water ports of the Indian Ocean. A little farther to the West, the fall of the U.S.-supported Shah in Iran to the Mullah regime in January 1979 replaced one authoritarian regime with another, albeit one staunchly anti-American. The kidnapping of U.S. embassy personnel on 4 November 1979 yielded the Teheran hostage crisis. It lasted a full 444 days, and a U.S. military operation to free the captives ("Operation Eagle Claw") resulted in catastrophic failure.[49] In a sweeping recognition of the strategic interests of the United States in the Persian Gulf region, Jimmy Carter proclaimed a new policy during his State of the Union address in January 1980.[50] The president announced the prospective use of force if vital U.S. Indian Ocean/Persian Gulf interests were impaired by a Soviet takeover. The presence of two carrier strike groups during the crisis signaled the merits of a continuous, combat-credible forward naval presence in the region going beyond the Indian Ocean island of Diego Garcia (recently leased from the British), and a token force based in Bahrain. However, there were simply no assets available for a three-ocean Navy that was needed to convincingly buttress the Carter Doctrine. In other words, and certainly not limited to the Indian Ocean, Carter essentially began naval armament without wanting to pay for it.[51]

After one term, Carter was voted out of office in the November 1980 general election. The Navy had learned the hard way that

> as any other agent of government, [it] is the instrument of national policy, its junior partner in every regard, and to disassociate itself from the broad national position is to disassociate itself from the source of its purpose and its strength.[52]

Yet, the Navy's rearguard battles set the stage for a reinvigoration of strategic naval thinking that formed the roots of "The Maritime Strategy." Both as a process and a capstone document (or, more fittingly, a series of documents), "The Maritime Strategy" is a product of its 1970s context.

"Horizontal escalation,"[53] or the (asymmetric)[54] use of naval forces outside of the narrow North Atlantic context prescribed by the Carter administration, ought to be appraised as the central intellectual driver of "The Maritime Strategy" under Reagan. Although burdened with a significant risk – what if the Soviet Union and the Warsaw Pact member states would also attempt to escalate horizontally? – such an innovative approach, developed by naval thought leaders unfettered by the lean geostrategic and fiscal environment at the time, was the "chief originality of the [M]aritime strategy."[55] Still, this feat and the wide-ranging consequences it had a couple of years later could hardly have been possible without the *naval baisse* environment that much of the 1970s U.S. political leadership exhibited.

Notes

1 For an overview of the U.S. Navy history and its capabilities from the founding to the early Cold War, see for example Love (1992a), Rose (2006a,b), and Symonds (2006). It is important to note that the history of capstone documents as a broad category can be traced back to roots of the U.S. Navy. The Navy always had some form of capstone document, of varying proficiency and quality, since its inception in 1775 (see Swartz, 2011b: 47–58, slides 94–115 for a list), but none of the quantity and quality that emerged with "The Maritime Strategy" and the follow-on capstone documents.

2 Baer, 1994, 275. See also Schmidt-Skipiol, 1992, 4.

3 See George Kennan, alias X, (1947). The famed essay "The Sources of Soviet Conduct" established the basis for the American policy of containing the Soviet Union using sea control as the glue that tied the United States to its European and Far East allies.

4 For the National Security Act (1947), as amended through Public Law 110–53 (August 3, 2007), see Library of Congress (2007).

5 The argument between the Navy and the Air Force came to a head in the controversy over resource allocation towards a new supercarrier, the planned *United States* (CVA 58). Only three days after the keel of the massive new warship was laid, construction was abandoned on the grounds that the money would be better invested in long-range B-36 bombers. This preservation of carrier aviation became known as 'Revolt of the Admirals,' "and in these terms, the National Security Act of 1947 was a Navy victory. It denied the Air Force the control of naval aviation. The Navy could keep direct control of its carrier-based and land-based aircraft [...]" (Baer, 1994: 291). For an account, see Jeffrey Barlow, *Revolt of the Admirals. The Fight for Naval Aviation 1945–1950*, Washington, D.C.: Naval Historical Center, 1995. See also Jeffrey Barlow, *From Hot War to Cold. The U.S. Navy and National Security Affairs, 1945–1955*. Palo Alto: Stanford University Press 2009.

6 Baer, 1994, 278.

7 The original report was made available by the Truman Library: National Security Council (1950).

8 Swartz, 2014, 2–3.

9 For a discussion of the events and the strategic ramifications of the Suez Crisis, see Kyle (2011).

10 For a history of events, see Munton and Welch (2011). For the U.S. Navy's perspective on the Cuban Missile Crisis, see Utz (1993).

11 Baer, 1994, 335.

12 Schmidt-Skipiol, 1992, 5.

13 Francis Duncan, *Rickover: The Struggle for Excellence*. Annapolis, U.S. Naval Institute Press, 2011.
14 Nichols and Tillman, 1987; Sherwood, 2004; Marolda *et al.*, 2013.
15 Baer, 1994, 392–393.
16 For an analysis of the Nixon Doctrine, see Litwak (1986). The text of the speech can be found in Nixon (1969).
17 Ryan, 1981, 66.
18 For accounts, see for example Sherwood (2007) and Freeman (2009).
19 134 people lost their lives in the July 1967 catastrophe at sea. For an account, see Freeman (2004).
20 Willy Brandt, German chancellor 1969–1974, rather joyfully recounted a discussion of the naval build-up with his visiting guest of honor, Soviet leader Leonid Brezhnev. The Russian remarked that in terms of submarine armament, the U.S. domination in the subsurface domain would not last long, for the Soviet Union would "bake a new submarine every week" – an image that the General Secretary accentuated for the amused Chancellor Brandt by forming the hands like kids do when they "bake" things playing in a sandbox (Brandt, 1989: 210).
21 For discussions of the drawdown of the Royal Navy in the second half of the twentieth century, see Grove (2005: 213–263) and Redford and Grove (2014).
22 A key enabler for the post-war economic growth was the Bretton-Woods monetary management system established in 1944 to codify and govern financial and commercial relations among the world's major industrial states in the mid-twentieth century. The agreement was toppled in 1971 after the U.S. unilaterally withdrew from the system. For more on the economic expansion after World War II, see Crafts and Toniolo (1996) and Rosenberg (2002).
23 In response to the coordinated Syrian–Egyptian attack on Israel, there was considerable confusion in Washington on the best way forward. Admiral Thomas Moorer, CJCS, sided with Henry Kissinger and James Schlesinger on maintaining a careful support of Israel which sought to avoid torpedoing the post-war situation and U.S. relations with the Arab world. Accordingly, the U.S. Sixth Fleet maintained a rather dispersed position. A task force around the carrier *John F. Kennedy* (CV 67) stood at Gibraltar, and another task force around the carrier *Independence* (CV 62) took position just south of Crete. ADM Daniel Murphy, Commander Sixth Fleet, was flabbergasted. It was not until the Soviet Navy surged more than 100 Russian naval vessels in support of Egypt and Syria that the U.S. hesitantly changed its position to also include U.S. provision of supplies to Israel and a direct maritime presence in the Eastern tip of the Mediterranean (Love, 1992a: 653–658).
24 The document is reprinted in Hattendorf (2007: 1–30).
25 The paper emphasized sea control over maritime power projection. The former, in the Vietnam years, had been neglected and Admiral Zumwalt sought to address the sea control backlog without ceding power projection capabilities.

> Zumwalt preferred the term *sea control* to Mahan's *control of the sea*, the latter implying total use or total denial. Such extreme measures were neither possible nor necessary in the 1970s. *Sea control* connoted all the Navy need realistically aim for: use of a limited area for a limited time.
>
> (Baer, 1994: 404, emphasis in original)

26 Although the report called for four classes of ships meant to meet the Soviets at sea, only one was put into service, the *Oliver Hazard Perry* (FFG 7 etc.) patrol frigates. A second, more ambitious low-end class designated as a 17,000-ton, 25-knot sea control ship priced at the fraction of that of a nuclear aircraft carrier and equipped with helicopters and V/STOL (vertical/short-takeoff-and-landing) airplanes never saw the light of day (Baer, 1994: 405).

27 Turner, 1974.

28 Some of the new capabilities introduced in the 1970s were the two naval command platforms of the *Mount Whitney*-class (LCC 19/20), P-3C maritime patrol aircraft, A-6E 'Intruder' and EA-6B EW jets, the Mk 48 torpedo, the RH-53D AMCM helicopter, carrier-launched F-14 'Tomcat' AAW jets, the first of the *Nimitz*-class nuclear-propelled aircraft carriers (CVN 68 etc.), *Spruance*-class (DD 968) destroyers, *Los Angeles*-class (SSN 668) attack submarines, *Tarawa*-class (LHA-X) amphibious ships, and the above-mentioned *Perry*-class frigates. Operationally, the advent of satellite technology and the concept of battle groups centered around nuclear aircraft carriers (CVBG) marked major changes (Swartz 2011d: 6, slide 6). Additionally, the AEGIS integrated shipboard weapons system was developed. Applying computers, radars, and missiles, the system creates a defense umbrella for surface warships by automatically detecting, tracking, and countering anti-ship weapons. See also Malcom Muir, *Black Shoes and Blue Water: Surface Warfare in the United States Navy, 1945–1975.* Washington, D.C., USGPO, 1995.

29 Baer, 1994, 411.

30 Hattendorf, 2004, xiv–xv.

31 Mark R. Hagerott, *Commanding Men and Machines. Admiralship, Technology, and Ideology in the 20th Century US Navy.* PhD dissertation, University of Maryland. College Park, MD 2008.

32 Hattendorf, 2004, 7–8.

33 Schmidt-Skipiol, 1992, 6.

34 On U.S. thinking about the Soviet Navy 1967–1981, see Hattendorf (2004: 23–36).

35 Center for Naval Analyses, 1992, 48. See also Owen Coté, *The Third Battle. Innovation in the U.S. Navy's Silent Cold War Struggle with Soviet Submarines.* Newport. Naval War College Press, 2003.

36 The White House, 1977.

37 Hattendorf, 2004, 13.

38 The Navy was upset with the Carter Administration's national security review (Presidential Review Memo 10) and its output (Presidential Directive 18), in which the Navy participated but wound up not being listened to very much. Claytor and Woolsey got the Deputy Secretary of Defense (Woolsey) to formally request Claytor to do a Navy Force Planning Study, which became "Sea Plan 2000," and which was then formally delivered by Claytor to Secretary of Defense Harold Brown – and only then distributed more widely through the Navy and Defense community (Peter Swartz, e-mail to author, July 22, 2014). The document "Sea Plan 2000" is reprinted in Hattendorf (2007: 103–124).

39 Hattendorf, 2004, 15. Swartz, 2011a, 6, slides 11–12.

40 Hattendorf, 2004, 17–20.

41 Hattendorf, 2004, 18–19.

42 The 1978 hearings introduced the term 'naval supremacy' into the political discussion. This superiority reflected the strategic interests of the Navy as an organization to mitigate risk and uncertainty in the face of continuing Soviet naval assertiveness. It was designed to be a qualitative, unilateral supremacy over the Red Fleet, without having to rely on allies to attain such supremacy (Rudolf, 1990: 173). In contrast, these contributions were specifically encouraged in the 1979 "The Future of U.S. Sea Power" document authored by Admiral Hayward (reprinted in Hattendorf, 2004: 125–134).

43 On the carrier debate and the stakes it entailed, see Ryan (1981: 104–119).

44 Rudolf, 1990, 161.

45 Love, 1992b, 674.

46 On the Carter administration's disarmament efforts, fleet posture policies, and the role of Congress in debating these issues, see Rudolf's comprehensive chapter (1990: 146–240).

47 As Rear Admiral (ret.) James Stark recounts (interview 2012, 00:00:45–00:01:30), "There was no deception, there was no political dimension to it; the Navy wanted to put more of that in [the debate]."

48 On context for the U.S. Navy in the world and its capstone strategies and concepts 1971–1980, see Swartz's slides (2011d).

49 Crist, 2012, 31–32. For an on-scene account of the operation by one of the commanders, see Kyle (1990).

50 For an analysis of this new grand strategic component, see Crist (2012: 33–48). For the text of the speech, see Carter (1980).

51 Love, 1992b, 700. On the U.S. Navy's shift to the Indian Ocean, see Ryan (1981: 153–166).

52 Baer, 1994, 415.

53 See Joshua M. Epstein, Horizontal Escalation. Sour Notes of a Recurrent Theme, in: Steven E. Miller/Stephen van Evera (eds.), *Naval Strategy and National Security. An International Security Reader.* Princeton, NJ. Princeton University Press, 1988, 102–114, and Michael MccGwire, Naval Power and Soviet Global Strategy, in: Steven E. Miller/Stephen van Evera (eds.), Naval Strategy and National Security. An International Security Reader. Princeton, NJ. Princeton University Press, 1988, 115–170.

54 As noted Cold War historian and strategist John Lewis Gaddis characterized it, symmetrical responses mean reacting to threats to the balance of power at the same place, time, and level of the original provocation. Asymmetrical response, on the contrary, involves shifting the location or nature of one's reaction onto terrain better suited to the application of one's strength against the opponent's weakness, thus gaining a significant degree of initiative (John Lewis Gaddis, "Containment: Its Past and Future," *International Security*, Vol. 5, No. 4, Spring 1981, 80).

55 Randy Papadopoulos, e-mail to author, January 16, 2017.

References

Baer, George. *One Hundred Years of Seapower: The U.S. Navy 1890–1990.* Stanford, CA: Stanford University Press, 1994.

Barlow, Jeffrey. *From Hot War to Cold. The U.S. Navy and National Security Affairs, 1945–1955.* Paolo Alto, CA: Stanford University Press, 2009.

Barlow, Jeffrey. *Revolt of the Admirals: The Fight for Naval Aviation 1945–1950.* Washington, D.C.: Naval Historical Center, 1995.

Brandt, Willy. *Erinnerungen.* Ullstein: Berlin, 1989 (Lizenzausgabe des SPIEGEL-Verlags, 2006/2007: Hamburg).

Carter, James E. "The State of the Union Address Delivered before a Joint Session of the Congress, 23 January." 1980.

Center for Naval Analyses. *1991–1992 Biennial Report. Fifty Years of Naval Analysis.* Alexandria, VA: Center for Naval Analyses (CNA), 1992.

Coté, Owen. *The Third Battle. Innovation in the U.S. Navy's Silent Cold War Struggle with Soviet Submarines.* Newport, RI, Naval War College Press, 2003.

Crafts, Nicholas, and Gianni Toniolo (eds.). *Economic Growth in Europe after 1945.* Cambridge: Cambridge University Press, 1996.

Crist, David. *The Twilight War: The Secret History of America's Thirty-Year Conflict with Iran.* New York: Penguin Press, 2012.

Duncan, Francis. *Rickover: The Struggle for Excellence.* Annapolis, MD, NIP, 2011.

Epstein, Joshua M. "Horizontal Escalation. Sour Notes of a Recurrent Theme," Naval *Strategy and National Security. An International Security Reader.* eds. Steven E. Miller and Stephen van Evera, Princeton, NJ. Princeton University Press, 1988.

Freeman, Gregory. *Sailors to the End. The Deadly Fire on USS* Forrestal *and the Heroes Who Fought It.* New York, NY: William Morrow Paperbacks, 2004.

Freeman, Gregory. *Troubled Water: Race, Mutiny, and Bravery on the USS* Kitty Hawk. New York, NY: Macmillan, 2009.

Gaddis, John Lewis. "Containment: Its Past and Future," *International Security* 5(4) (Spring 1981).

Grove, Eric. The *Royal Navy since 1815. A New Short History.* Basingstoke: Palgrave Macmillan, 2005.

Hattendorf, John, ed. *The Evolution of the U.S. Navy's Maritime Strategy, 1977–1986.* Newport, RI: Naval War College Press, 2004

Hattendorf, John, ed. *U.S. Naval Strategy in the 1970s.* Newport, RI: Naval War College Press, 2007.

Kennan, George (alias "X"). "The Sources of Soviet Conduct," *Foreign Affairs* 25(4), July 1947 (1947).

Kyle, John. *The Guts to Try: The Untold Story of the Iran Hostage Rescue Mission by the On-scene Desert Commander.* New York, NY: Orion Crow Publishing, 1990.

Kyle, Keith. *Suez. Britain's End of Empire in the Middle East.* London: I.B. Tauris, 2011.

Library of Congress. "National Security Act of 1947 as amended July 3, 2007." Washington, D.C.: Library of Congress, 2014.

Litwak, Robert. *Détente and the Nixon Doctrine: American Foreign Policy and the Pursuit of Stability, 1969–1976.* Cambridge: Cambridge University Press, 1986.

Love, Robert. *History of the U.S. Navy, Volume I: 1775–1941.* Mechanicsburg, PA: Stackpole, 1992a.

Love, Robert. *History of the U.S. Navy, Volume II: 1942–1991.* Mechanicsburg, PA: Stackpole, 1992b.

Marolda, Edward, Doyle, Sandy, and Sherwood, John. *Nixon's Trident: Naval Power in South East Asia, 1968–1972.* Washington, D.C.: NHHC, 2013.

Muir, Malcom. *Black Shoes and Blue Water: Surface Warfare in the United States Navy, 1945–1975.* Washington, D.C., USGPO, 1995.

Munton, Don, and Welch, David. *The Cuban Missile Crisis. A Concise History.* 2nd edition. Oxford: Oxford University Press, 2011.

National Security Council. "A Report to the National Security Council–NSC 68, April 12, 1950. President's Secretary's File, Truman Papers." Independence, MO: Truman Library, 2014.

Nichols, John, and Tillman, Barrett. *On Yankee Station: The Naval Air War over Vietnam.* Annapolis, MD: NIP, 1987.

Nixon, Richard. "274 – Informal Remarks in Guam with Newsmen, 25 July 1969." Santa Barbara, CA: The American Presidency Project, 1969.

Redford, Duncan, and Grove, Philip. *The Royal Navy. A History since 1900.* London: I.B. Tauris, 2014.

Rose, Lisle. *Power at Sea, Vol. 1. The Age of Navalism, 1890–1918.* Columbia, MO: University of Missouri Press, 2006a.

Rose, Lisle. *Power at Sea, Vol. 2. The Breaking Storm, 1919–1945.* Columbia, MO: University of Missouri Press, 2006b.

Rosenberg, Samuel. *American Economic Development since 1945: Growth, Decline and Rejuvenation.* Basingstoke: Palgrave Macmillan, 2002.

Rudolf, Peter. *Amerikanische Seemachtpolitik und maritime Rüstungskontrolle unter Carter und Reagan.* Frankfurt am Main, Germany: Campus, 1990.

Ryan, Paul. *First Line of Defense: The U.S. Navy Since 1945*. Stanford, CA: Hoover Institution Press, 1981.

Schmidt-Skipiol, Joachim. *Die "Maritime Strategy" der Vereinigten Staaten von Amerika nach 1945*. Unpublished paper for 32. Historisch-Taktische Tagung der Flotte, 1992.

Sherwood, John. *Afterburner. Naval Aviators and the Vietnam War*. New York, NY: New York University Press, 2004.

Sherwood, John. *Black Sailor, White Navy. Racial Unrest in the Fleet During the Vietnam Era*. New York, NY: NYU Press, 2007.

Stark, James, Rear Admiral United States Navy (retired). Washington Navy Yard, Washington, D.C., September 5, 2012, 01 hr 41 min.

Swartz, Peter. *A Short History of the U.S. Navy in the Cold War (1945–1990): Strategy and Operations* (unpublished draft paper, Alexandria, VA, 2014).

Swartz, Peter, and Duggan, Karin. *U.S. Navy Capstone Strategy and Concepts: Introduction, Background and Analyses* (slideshow). Alexandria, VA: CNA, 2011a.

Swartz, Peter, and Duggan, Karin. *The U.S. Navy in the World (1970–2010): Context for U.S. Navy Capstone Strategies and Concepts, Volume II* (slideshow). Alexandria, VA: CNA, 2011b.

Swartz, Peter, and Duggan, Karin. *The U.S. Navy in the World (1970–1980): Context for U.S. Navy Capstone Strategies and Concepts* (slideshow). Alexandria, VA: CNA, 2011c.

Swartz, Peter, and Duggan, Karin. *U.S. Navy Capstone Strategy and Concepts (1970–2010): A Brief Summary* (slideshow). Alexandria, VA: CNA, 2011d.

Symonds, Craig. *Decision at Sea: Five Naval Battles that Shaped American History*. New York: Oxford University Press, 2006.

Turner, Stansfield. "Missions of the U.S. Navy." Naval *War College Review* 26(5) (September 1974): 2–17 (modified version in *U.S. Naval Institute Proceedings*, vol. 100, no. 12 [December 1974]: 18–24).

Utz, Curtis. *Cordon of Steel. The U.S. Navy and the Cuban Missile Crisis* (= The U.S. Navy in the Modern World, No. 1, ed. by Edward Marolda). Washington, D.C.: Naval Historical Center, 1993.

The White House. "Presidential Review Memorandum/NSC-10. 18 February 1977." Washington, D.C.: The White House, 1977.

4 A "naval renaissance"[1] through "The Maritime Strategy" (1981–1989)

Similar to changing currents and tides or the 'bull and bear' phases of stock markets, strategic culture and strategic implementation also undergo periodic ups and downs, which in turn decisively affect the role of sea power, the genesis of capstone documents, and their respective political and military implementation. The 1980s was such a high time, especially during the decade's turbulent early years.

U.S. Navy strategy 1981–1989: the macro-level

Global trends and challengers to U.S. security

The Soviet Union appeared to come out of the 1970s on a high note, having acquired visible influence and access worldwide. The build-up of its blue-water navy and its challenge to the United States were symbolically best illustrated by the Soviet's utilization of the former U.S. naval bases in Cam Ranh and Da Nang (Vietnam). The communist naval build-up resulted in a quantitative, but not necessarily qualitative dynamic upper hand at sea vis-à-vis the United States early in the decade. The Red Fleet's global aspirations were visibly underlined by the large Okean-80 naval exercise (1980). The introduction of new warships such as the *Akula*-class attack submarines first commissioned in 1984 – which could not be detected reliably by the U.S.-maintained SOSUS system – drove home the point of global Soviet blue-water intentions.[2]

The impression of a stable, powerful, even prosperous Soviet Union would turn around within just a few years. The West watched a stunning stagnation in Soviet Russia and a rapid succession of leaders in the Kremlin. Leonid Brezhnev, in office since 1964, died in 1982. He was succeeded by the ailing Yuri Andropov, who passed away in 1984. Then, Konstantin Chernenko governed little over a year before dying in 1985. His successor, in turn, was the young and assertive Mikhail Gorbachev. Under his reign, the tight grip of the Soviet Union on its Warsaw Pact alliance loosened imperceptibly.[3] The continuous unraveling of Communist leadership led to the end of the Cold War in 1989. But in the early and mid-1980s, nuclear-underwritten stalemate seemed destined to stay. The bipolar world order – not to be confused with the medical condition, but perhaps often with similar symptoms – was a hallmark of superpower relations. While the Cold War deepened at the beginning of the 1980s, major arms limitations inroads contained and then reduced the number of nuclear weapons in the second half of the decade.[4]

On balance, the constellation of parallel Cold War and lower-level inter- and intrastate competition continued to dominate international affairs. In Europe, the process of political integration continued to deepen with the integration of the European Community (EC). NATO, founded in 1949 as Europe's insurance policy against the Soviet Union and its Warsaw Pact, remained in place. In response to the introduction of SS-20 nuclear-tipped missiles in Eastern Europe, a dual-track decision was agreed upon. Moscow's failure to withdraw its SS-20 missiles from the Central front resulted in a coordinated NATO decision to upgrade and expand its own arsenal of theater (as opposed to intercontinental) nuclear weaponry, consisting of Pershing II and ground-launched cruise missiles. In Europe, this step could only be marshaled against substantial domestic protest, especially in West Germany. In 1983, movies like "The Day After" (about the world after a nuclear war) and "War Games" (about the threat of nuclear escalation between the United States and the Soviet Union), as well as German singer Nena's hit record "99 Luftballons" ("99 Red Balloons" in its Anglo-American variant, about a mass release of balloons which triggers inadvertent nuclear war) had considerable impact on, and were a deep-felt expression of, public opinion in opposition to NATO's double track decision.

In the ongoing context of the Cold War, the Soviet Union remained the central challenger to American security. In response, the U.S. fielded a more assertive foreign policy, a stronger commitment to national defense, more confrontational rhetoric, and offensive security strategies.[5] By extension, some states like Libya continued to challenge regional (rather than grand strategic) U.S. security interests. In the 1980s, the United States sought to hedge against being drawn too openly into proxy wars (like Angola or Nicaragua). It only engaged militarily with substantial ground troops if it was assured of a clear mission success (e.g., in Grenada 1983 and Panama 1989). This underlined the value of naval forces as a foreign policy tool. In principle, sea power provided more nuanced but open options in peacetime, crisis, and war when ground forces were not available or other means appeared to be too risky.

Conflicts, crisis, and wars

Soviet offensive military, diplomatic, and economic outreach had tied together separate locations of strategic American interest, namely the Middle East (with close ally Israel and access to natural resources) and the West Pacific (a forward U.S. naval hub). Those who had turned away from the costs and responsibilities of armed interventions in the years after the conclusion of the Vietnam War were shocked by a series of American humiliations by antagonist powers. The embassy seizure in Teheran in November 1979, the introduction of Soviet naval ships to recently forsaken Vietnamese bases (providing distant reach into a critical maritime arena), and the invasion of Afghanistan which threatened a Soviet grab for the Indian Ocean region (including access to its maritime and energy supply lines) contributed to conveying that American power and influence was waning.[6]

Consequently, the public perception of the military's readiness and its capabilities suffered a blow. Since the conclusion of the Vietnam War, there had been a marked American skepticism and sometimes even outright unwillingness to engage militarily. The impression that even limited commando operations by Special Forces could not be marshaled successfully added to America's crisis of self-confidence.[7] The Middle East at the time continued to be in grave turmoil. Iran and Iraq fought a war against one another, 1980–1988. Israel's air force raided Iraq's nuclear plant at Osirak in June 1981. In the meantime, Egypt consolidated a new leadership under Hosni Mubarak after his predecessor Anwar El Sadat, an advocate of reconciliation with Israel, was assassinated on October 6, 1981.

In the South Atlantic, the Falklands War from April to June 1982 occupied the minds of politicians and militaries in the West and the East alike.[8] Although the United States was not a warring party in this conflict, it quickly sided with the U.K.[9] The war between Great Britain and Argentina over the South Atlantic islands was an instrumental example of modern warfare at (and more so from the) sea. Its lessons included the roles and values of smaller and larger warships, aircraft performance, anti-ship missile use, submarine operations, ship survivability, logistics, and more. Consequently, the Department of the Navy commissioned its own review that was submitted in 1983, outlining the lessons the United States could draw from that South Atlantic war.[10] In the context of the Cold War, and thus perhaps most importantly to the U.S.,

> the effect of the Falklands War was far greater than simply the retaking of the islands. It greatly improved the credibility of NATO's deterrence in demonstrating the willingness of a Western democracy to fight for principle, and its skill in doing so.[11,12]

1983 was a very tense year in the U.S.-Soviet conflict, prompting superpower tensions to the brink of serious and direct war. On October 25, U.S. Marine Corps, Navy SEALs, and Army forces invaded the Caribbean island of Grenada. Operation Urgent Fury was designed to oust the Socialist government on the island.[13] U.S. forces' involvement in the Lebanese Civil War also escalated that year: two suicide attacks on the American embassy and the Marine Corps barracks in Beirut caused a large number of casualties, prompting U.S. withdrawal a few months later.[14] During the transitions at the top leadership position of the USSR, the Reagan administration continued its strictly anti-communist rhetoric. In parallel, arrangements were made for the deployment of new MX intercontinental ballistic missiles, and a Strategic Defense Initiative (SDI) was proclaimed. Amid renewed tensions, a South Korean 747 jet was shot down on September 1, over the Sakhalin Peninsula.[15] Three weeks later, on September 26, a Soviet early-warning installation erroneously detected a U.S. nuclear missile launch. The Russian officer of the guard decided to override his orders, based on his knowledge of previous false alarms – thus sparing the world a retaliatory Soviet nuclear strike at the U.S. heartland and resulting global nuclear war.[16]

During the first half of November, NATO conducted its "Able Archer" military staff exercise. The Soviet Union, by all accounts, considered this exercise to be a thinly disguised veil for an imminent decapitating nuclear first-strike of the alliance against the Warsaw Pact and increased the readiness of its forces. In the fall of 1983, the world was closer to nuclear war than at any other time of the Cold War,[17] with the possible exception of the Cuban Missile Crisis of 1962. Fortunately, tensions leveled and then decreased slightly after 1983.

In the middle of managing the superpower confrontation, Libyan dictator Muammar Gaddafi continued to be a secondary, but very persistent nuisance in international affairs. Sponsors of international terrorism prompted the United States to retaliate repeatedly.[18] And in 1989, Central America once again became the site of a U.S. military intervention, this time in Panama. Throughout the decade in the Caribbean region, a "War on Drugs" also consumed many intergovernmental resources. The U.S. Navy began to be tasked with a supporting role in the attempt to curtail drug shipments from South America to the markets in the United States (practicing its low-intensity conflict-resolution skills in counter-narcotics operations in the process).[19]

Personalities, domestic conditions, and national security strategies

Presidents, secretaries, and policy/strategy leaders[20]

Ronald Reagan succeeded Jimmy Carter in the White House in 1981. Reagan had already campaigned for the Republican Party ticket four years earlier, only to lose the presidential primaries to then-incumbent Gerald Ford. In 1976, a controversial CBO study about the role of the Navy and future battle-force levels had diverted considerable public attention to the question of military force levels.[21] The Republican Party platform had taken this discussion into the primaries that year. Reagan was therefore no stranger to the concept of a large Navy. In 1980, with foreign policy issues high on the election agenda and President Carter attacked as a weak American leader, the focus in the primaries and the general election in 1980 again turned to the future size of the military. The 600-ship Navy theme tracked strongly with audiences during the campaign.[22]

The new president sought a tougher stance against the Soviet Union, as amplified by his support for the controversial Strategic Defense Initiative and a more aggressive rhetoric.[23] He reversed his course notably toward the end of his first term and took a significantly less confrontational public stance going into 1984 and his re-election campaign.[24] As his Secretary of Defense, Reagan chose Casper "Cap" Weinberger (in office from 1981 to 1987). During a speech in Washington, D.C., on November 28, 1984, Weinberger stated six conditions under which U.S. military forces would enter a conflict. This doctrine was informed by the post-Vietnam reluctance to commit military power in limited wars, and influenced by the U.S. interventions in Grenada and Lebanon in the year before. For Secretary Weinberger, the U.S. should only assign military forces when its vital interests or those of allies were at stake. If combat forces were deployed, they should be sized accordingly and committed to defined political and military objectives. The relationship between objectives and the forces committed should be continually reassessed and adjusted if necessary, beginning with the exploration of whether a conflict was in the American national interest at all. Consistent support of the American people and their elected leaders in the legislative and executive branches was also a prerequisite. In any case, the Secretary proclaimed, the commitment of U.S. forces to combat should be a last resort.[25]

As Secretary of State, Reagan picked Alexander Haig, a retired four-star Army general, graduate of the Naval and the Army War Colleges, and former SACEUR (1974–1979). After a tumultuous 18 months in office (which included international foreign policy crises in the Falklands and in Lebanon), Haig – who frequently clashed with Secretary of Defense Weinberger – resigned over disagreements with administration policies.[26] His successor was the loyal George P. Shultz, who remained in office until 1989. Shultz efficiently managed the foreign policy challenges of the time and he was among the first to advocate a more cordial approach to the Soviet Union from March 1985.

Over at the Pentagon, John Lehman was sworn into office as Secretary of the Navy early in 1981. Lehman quickly ascended as the face and public voice of "The Maritime Strategy."[27] He saw himself as the Navy's chief executive officer:

> The best CNOs have provided real leadership and good professional advice to the president, but never have they operated as chief executive officers. When the Secretary of the Navy does not run the Navy, the Navy simply is not run.[28]

Lehman's get-go attitude, youth, and media-savvy personality made him a star in Washington. He provided the necessary top cover and climate where ideas of an offensive, forward Navy which provided the Commander in Chief with multiple opportunities on the spectrum for peacetime engagement, crisis, and war could blossom. As "The Maritime Strategy" was disseminated,

Lehman had to increasingly cede control of the process to the Navy Staff's OP-603 office, and the wider Navy, who fleshed out its details.[29]

Admiral Thomas Hayward, CNO until 1982, oversaw the transition from Carter to Reagan. Hayward had created the Strategic Studies Group (SSG) at the Naval War College, which became one of the key influences on "The Maritime Strategy." Traditionally, the Navy's service chiefs are usually appointed for a single term of four years (with the notable exception of Admiral Arleigh Burke, CNO 1955–1961) and so it would be up to the incoming admiral to assess the changing circumstances and steer the Navy forward. As an administrative rather than an operational leader, Navy strategy and strategic documents are among the prime activities for CNOs. In 1982, Admiral James Watkins, Hayward's deputy, became CNO. He was the first member of the submariners' union to rise to that position since Admiral Chester Nimitz. Watkins provided continuity from the Hayward era. "The Maritime Strategy" was then further developed by Watkins' flag officers and their staffs between 1982 and 1984. Watkins was succeeded in 1986 as CNO by Admiral Carlisle Trost, another submariner who embraced "The Maritime Strategy" (Trost participated in the development of "The Maritime Strategy" in some previous posts). Trost's term was characterized by the rapidly changing nature of global political conditions and a significant number of transitions in the Reagan administration. Trost in turn was succeeded by Admiral Frank Kelso (1990–1994), the third consecutive submariner to head the Navy leadership. In Admiral William Crowe Jr., yet another submariner, the Navy also provided the Chairman of the Joint Chiefs of Staff from 1985 to 1990. The influence of the military in the executive branch rose during the Reagan administration, with a rising budgetary tide lifting all services' boats. The Navy, both its uniformed and civilian leadership, sought to capitalize on this environment, looking to push back the civilian and scholarly control of military (and by implication of naval/maritime) strategy using systems analysis tools that dated back to the tenure of Secretary McNamara.[30]

In Congress, the Republicans held a majority of Senate seats during Reagan's first term, but lost it to the Democrats in the 1984 election. The House of Representatives was under Democratic control over the whole decade. Although working with a divided government, Reagan's policies during his first term fared reasonably well on the Hill, largely because of the persuasive and aggressive lobbying of Lehman and powerful allies in the committee chair seats. Even without these political multipliers, Congress was generally sympathetic toward the Navy, because the discussion had shifted from certain budget items like expensive aircraft carriers or nuclear submarines to the overall rationale of the Navy in U.S. national security. Additionally, the increase in defense money benefited many states and districts with defense-related industry or military bases. In fact, Lehman's strategic home-porting initiative, underwritten as a force dispersal action to hedge against a massed Soviet attack, multiplied the number of naval stations throughout the country, thus potentially providing thousands of jobs and revenue dollars to more states and municipalities.

Domestic conditions

The Reagan administration steadily increased its defense budget (Figure 4.1). A persistent national security consensus and a more assertive foreign policy buttressed that policy.

Selected U.S. national security policies, doctrines, and capstone documents

By 1980, détente between the superpowers had ended. The U.S. continued its overarching grand strategic path of attempting to contain the sprawl of Soviet influence worldwide. But the trauma of the Vietnam War loomed large in the American psyche, and world events suggested a downturn in U.S. power that even the Carter Doctrine could not decelerate significantly. The Reagan administration, in turn, spoke out against the Soviet Union, buttressing its rhetoric with potent and controversial policies.

The first major national capstone document, National Security Decision Directive (NSDD) 32, appeared on May 20, 1982. It stated the overarching security policy goals of the United States as deterring a military attack by the Soviet Union and its allies, against the U.S. and its allies; strengthening of U.S. influence globally through existing alliances and coalitions; containing and reversing Soviet military presence worldwide; neutralizing non-military efforts by the Soviet Union; pursuing long-term liberalization of the Soviet

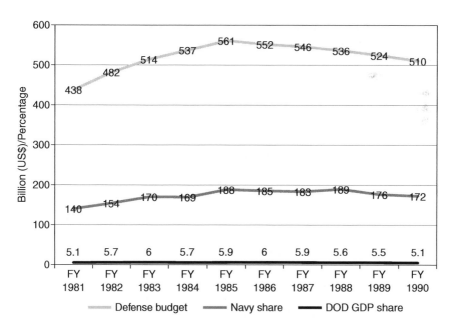

Figure 4.1 U.S. Defense Budget FY 1981–1990, in FY 12 billion US-$; GDP share in % (Swartz, 2011a: 10, slide 20 and 15, slide 29).

bloc; strengthening the U.S. military; assuring America access to foreign markets and resources, as well as access to oceans and space;[31] nonproliferation of nuclear weapons; encouraging the provision of development aid by the U.S. and its allies to the Third World; and the promotion of a well-functioning international economic system.[32]

Reagan's address to the nation on March 28, 1983 was another milestone in his administration's national security policies, laying out the rationale for the Strategic Defense Initiative (SDI). Despite its tremendous costs and doubtful viability, Reagan supported this ground- and space-based system designed to destroy incoming ICBMs. To his critics, the high-tech "Star Wars" program signaled a grave waste of resources; to some in the Soviet Union and even in Europe, SDI signaled that the U.S. was beginning to plan a limited, first-strike nuclear war by evading mutual assured destruction.[33] The U.S. Navy would ultimately assume a role in a significantly smaller version of SDI.

On the lower end of the conflict spectrum, U.S. support of anti-communist governments and insurgencies increased. The Reagan Doctrine attempted to destabilize Soviet proxies through material aid and training for insurgents and rebels in countries such as El Salvador, Nicaragua, Angola, Cambodia, and Mozambique. In Afghanistan, the U.S. supported the Mujahidin in their war against the Soviet invaders.

Most of these programs were shrouded in secrecy, so one revelation made headlines and sent the Reagan administration into its most serious domestic crisis. In the Iran–Contra affair, it was revealed that Contra rebels in Nicaragua were supported with revenues of weapon sales to Iran. These in turn were designated to free American hostages from the hands of Shiite militias in Lebanon. Iran, which demanded more weapons, humiliated the Reagan administration as it had previously treated the Carter government.[34] The Iran-Contra conspiracy came to a head in July 1987, when National Security Council staffer Colonel Oliver North, USMC, was summoned to testify before Congress on the scandal. North was indicted in 1988 (and Reagan barely avoided an impeachment). By then, an exodus of seasoned hardliner national security decision-makers already had begun. CIA director William Casey passed away, and National Security Advisor John Poindexter (a retired Vice Admiral), presidential speechwriter Pat Buchanan, and Secretary of Defense Weinberger left the administration in the course of 1987.[35] National Security Advisor Frank Carlucci became Secretary of Defense and General Colin Powell followed in Carlucci's position.

On the bureaucratic side, the Goldwater-Nichols Act of October 1986 was the most important congressional intervention in DOD bureaucracy since the creation of the Department in 1947. It mandated increasing focus and emphasis on joint strategy, planning, and operations in the military realm. More so, it mandated annual presidential reports on national security strategy, and it triggered a flood of new publications on 'jointness.' Crucially, it reinforced these steps by altering officer careers in all services The Navy was skeptical of such deep integration, which it perceived as irreversible. The most visible and perhaps far-reaching organizational change in the 1980s was the standing up of new combatant commands.[36] Henceforth, the nation's naval forces would be far more tightly integrated into joint concepts and operations, in spite of the unique nature of the maritime environment and of warfare at and from the sea.[37]

The Reagan administration rushed out its first National Security Strategy (NSS) in January 1987, soon after Goldwater–Nichols was signed into law. This NSS was thus "prepared in a very limited period of time and reflected the intent to document only current strategic thinking. [...] Taken as a whole, of course the document portrayed a comprehensive strategic approach toward the Soviet Union,"[38] but it did not integrate strategy across regions of U.S. strategic interest. Its January 1988 follow-up document came at a time of increasing fiscal deficits. It attempted to formulate a comprehensive and integrated national security strategy, for example elevating economic elements of national power into the calculation.

Reagan's successor George H.W. Bush submitted his first NSS in March 1990. The rapidly changing geopolitical landscape in Eastern Europe greatly complicated delivering a visionary administration statement of ways–means–ends causality on time. The original Goldwater-Nichols legislation had implicitly assumed a fairly stable state in the international environment, with the yearly report articulating incremental changes to both perceptions of and responses to that environment.[39] In an increasingly uncertain environment, the NSS therefore appeared over a year later than planned. The central formal document by which the President and the Secretary of Defense were advised on military matters was the National Military Strategy, compiled by the CJCS. Its classified 1989 version submitted by Admiral Crowe included chapters on national military objectives and national military strategy and an appraisal of U.S. defense policy and intelligence. It looked at fiscal constraints on force levels, and evaluated risks to U.S. national interests. The capstone document still focused on the Cold War and the Soviet Union, emphasizing the military value of alliances such as NATO while highlighting forward-deployed forces.[40] Such was the lay of the land in the 1980s when the Navy sought to use the momentum provided by the Reagan administration and its policies to present its case vocally for a coherent strategy.

Developing and promulgating USN strategy 1981–1989

Evolution

When Reagan was sworn in as President in January 1981, the Navy was on an upward swing and the seeds for what would become "The Maritime Strategy" had long been planted.[41] The Reagan administration's policies and people provided the top cover and much-desired fertilizer. According to Lehman, "The Maritime Strategy" rested on eight principles. First, it was derived from and depended on the overall national security strategy established by the President. Second, that national strategy provided the Department of the Navy with maritime tasks such as controlling international crises, deterring war, sea control, access, support of land battles, and attack at the source. Those tasks – third – required maritime superiority, which in turn – fourth – required a disciplined maritime strategy (as the art of distributing and applying military means to fulfill policy ends). That strategy was imperative for relating and conforming Navy and Marine Corps planning, programming, budgeting, and research and development efforts. The document also reoriented ship, aircraft, and weapons system design plans as well as personnel and training policies. Fifth, the strategy had to be based on a realistic threat assessment. Sixth, it needed to be global, not sequential as a land campaign. Seventh, it needed to fully integrate U.S. and free world forces, including Air Force, Coast Guard, and the Army. And finally, the strategy needed to be a forward one.[42]

The actual document has its roots in a workshop on Soviet naval intelligence convened in 1981. At least eight larger iterations of various length and scope were produced, both in classified and after 1986 in unclassified versions. The vetting process itself obviously produced numerous drafts and versions. Table 4.1 gives an overview of the documents and their principal drafters.

The broad spectrum of contemporary media outlets was utilized, ranging from (classified) briefings to public versions and discussions in journal articles, illustrated professional magazine exposures, and books. Even a VHS video was produced to distribute "The Maritime Strategy" to all ships in the fleet.[43] The characters of the strategies were always those of a work in progress.[44] There was never one single manuscript, but rather a plethora of documents. Accordingly, parallel efforts were under way to continuously improve and operationalize "The Maritime Strategy." A consolidation of existing thinking rather than a vision, "The Maritime Strategy" aspired to be an "explanation of use of current forces. [It] told a story; provided a narrative."[45] As a comprehensive concept, it included peacetime forward-deployed heavy attack carriers forces for offensive operations in a global war, and as a national power instrument for regional crises intervention (it was not simply a war plan against the Soviet Union) it was so convincing that inner-administration disagreement focused merely on its semantics, that is whether the United States should aspire to 'naval supremacy' or 'naval superiority.'[46]

Besides referring to numerous national overarching strategic guidance documents, U.S. laws, memoranda of understanding with sister services, joint documents, and allied capstone documents, the authors of "The Maritime Strategy" could draw from a vast number of contemporary contextual publications. Examples included earlier documents such as Project SIXTY (1970) and Sea Plan 2000 (1978). Beginning in 1981, a host of public statements in speeches, testimony, and articles by John Lehman and other individuals, official reports, the output of the Strategic Studies Group, a flow of intelligence

Table 4.1 Main 1980s USN capstone documents (Swartz, 2011a: 24–26, slides 48–52; 2011b: 69, slide 138)

Name	Status/format	Year	Principle drafters
The Maritime Strategy	Secret briefing	1982	CDR Spence Johnson, LCDR Stan Weeks
The Maritime Strategy	Secret publication	1984	CAPT Roger Barnett, CDR Peter Swartz
Amphibious Warfare Strategy	Secret publication	1985	CAPT Larry Seaquist, Col Phil Harrington (USMC)
The Maritime Strategy	Secret publication, revision	1985	CAPT Larry Seaquist, CDR Wood Parker
The Maritime Strategy	Unclassified booklet (*Proceedings*)	1986	CAPT Linton Brooks, CDR Robbie Harris, Maj Hugh O'Donnell (USMC), Dr. Harvey Sichermann, CAPT Peter Swartz, Fred Rainbow (U.S. Naval Institute Proceedings professional magazine)
"Looking Beyond the Maritime Strategy"	Unclassified article	1987	CNO staff
The Maritime Strategy	Secret publication, revision	1989	CDR Mitch Brown

accounts about the Soviet Navy,[47] and other papers helped to explain how all the pieces of the Navy fit together.[48] As the strategy emerged, it was tested repeatedly by the fleet in large-scale and smaller exercises.[49] The academic discussion of just what kind of strategy "The Maritime Strategy" really was, or even if it was a by-the-book strategy at all, is ultimately futile:

> To the developers of the Maritime Strategy in OP-603 […], and to the thinkers at the Naval War College, the Maritime Strategy was intended to reflect – and to drive – *all* aspects of naval policy. It was at once the Navy's declaratory strategy, budget strategy, employment strategy, and programming strategy.[50]

These carefully crafted moves hardened the strategy and elevated it in the public political and military discourse. They reflected Navy institutional thinking and made it accessible to wider audiences.

The writing process then was truly "organic."[51] Extensive socialization of the briefing material (among those who had access) allowed interactions, both critical and supportive.[52] In the spring of 1984, the classified document was ready for CNO Watkins's signature. Various briefings and shorter articles followed, and in 1986 an unclassified version was published as a supplement to the U.S. Naval Institute's professional journal, *Proceedings*.[53] A number of semi–official writings and unofficial publications from outside, which escorted the conceptual processes of writing and re-writing the strategy, emerged concurrently.[54]

Strategic concept

The central innovations of "The Maritime Strategy" were its dedicated offensive approach and the three distinctive stages of naval force employment in peaceful presence, crisis response, and global conventional war. Rather than sticking to the more defensive notions of naval force employment of previous decades, it sought to charge against the Soviet Union in peacetime to broaden the conflict. This required forward-deployed and forward-based assets. In addition, the strategy sought to exploit Russia's unfavorable geographic position and posture as a land power. To the planners, this warranted a closer look at the global choke points. Control of man-made or natural narrows where commercial and military shipping has to pass, was a key strategic enabler for the thrust against any assertive Soviet naval claims. Choke point control therefore kept Soviet naval forces from exercising sea control, while dispersing their forces, controlling sea lines of communication, and supporting American ground troops and allies.[55]

As opposed to the proponents of preparing for the European central front scenario for the next war, where tactical nuclear weapons would likely be used in the very early stages of the conflict,[56] the maritime strategists in their war games chiefly emphasized conventional forces and a globalized approach. The authors of "The Maritime Strategy" reasoned that by keeping the conflict nonnuclear (i.e., escalating horizontally rather than vertically), the United States' geographic, military, economic, and political advantages (all of which are key components of sea power) could favorably underpin Washington's grand strategy and provide for a higher likelihood of prevailing in the conflict. It was expected that a prolonged conventional war would wear out the Soviet Union's planned economy and authoritarian regime.[57]

A further major impetus to the intellectual formation of the strategy was the realization that Soviet military doctrine had undergone a significant change itself. Like the West, the Soviet Union had also become somewhat acquainted with the demands of the Cold War. Consequently, the USSR toned down the idea of an offensive, global nuclear war against the United States and its allies. Instead, Moscow focused on obtaining control of Europe. In the Soviet view, this would be facilitated by deterring a U.S. nuclear attack using assets like its SS–20 missiles and the submarine ballistic missile reserve. A defensive strategy was designed to protect that fleet in the hope of essentially safeguarding that deterrent. It was on these assumptions that U.S. Navy planners re-energized their offensive ideas. If the navies of the United States and its NATO allies could overcome Soviet defenses, they could put at risk the Soviets' strategic reserve. If they destroyed submarines before the submarines sailed into the open ocean, they could better assure the safety of NATO shipping. If they conducted amphibious campaigns on Europe's flanks in support of a ground war to hold or regain Europe, they would bring to a general war a great maritime asset.[58]

In a protracted conventional war, the need for secure SLOCs would dramatically rise as European allies would expend their depots and war-fighting platforms in battles of attrition. Containing and attacking the Soviet subsurface capabilities at their bastions, consequently, could be a prime enabler for U.S. sea control, thus securing and defending the maritime highways for NATO.

In the Pacific, far away from the Central Front occupying many NATO allies' minds, things stood somewhat differently.[59] The Navy rejected the notion of the Carter years that war would be confined to one theater, most likely Europe. That was the principal reason why the service never really warmed to the force posture earmarked for the Pacific. In the meantime, the Soviet Pacific Fleet benefited disproportionally from the USSR's naval build-up, focusing on the Sea of Okhotsk, the Kuril Islands, and two large naval bases as staging points. The Soviet Navy fielded SSBNs, V/STOL carriers, heavy cruisers, and amphibious assets. It routinely and substantially engaged in naval diplomacy and show-of-force missions in the Pacific and Indian Ocean regions. It could also threaten the sea lines of communication in the West Pacific, and shadow U.S. naval movements in the Pacific.

In the days of the 'swing strategy,' the Pacific would have been largely deserted, with grave strategic and political ramifications for the United States. Now, an offensive in the Pacific as first devised in "Sea Strike" would – given the right number of ships and suitable doctrinal guidance – bind Soviet forces. These would then be unavailable to be employed against NATO flanks, the Persian Gulf, Asia, or to threaten sea lines of communication. An American offensive based principally on carrier battle groups would capitalize on the Western advantageous geography and forces against weaker and less geographically favored Soviet forces.[60]

Fundamentally, the Navy sought to make a deliberate strategic difference by enhancing deterrence, controlling escalation, solidifying the Western alliance, influencing neutral states, defending the U.S., supporting land campaigns, limiting Moscow's options, and increasing Soviet uncertainties. Throughout, "The Maritime Strategy" promised to help gain the initiative and provide both a strong deterrence and create a favorable termination of hostilities.[61]

Consequently, "The Maritime Strategy" was a farewell to the 'swing strategy' of the Carter years and the smaller fleet that came with it. Instead, it advocated an offensively focused fleet composed around carriers and a host of smaller platforms. "The Maritime Strategy" saw itself not just as the war plan against the Soviet Union, but aspired to be the coordinated narrative for peace, crises, war, and war termination. In other words, it explained the Navy's reasoning in war-fighting and in what was dubbed the "violent peace."[62] As such, it connected the defense at the place of aggression to the opening of new fronts and "linked symmetric with geographic-asymmetric reactions"[63] mediated by a larger force structure.

In the strategy, the Navy's and the Marine Corps' missions were intimately connected. Instead of separately going their own ways in sea control, power projection, or intervention, the two sister services were placed into wide-ranging, synthetic categories: peaceful presence, crisis response, and global conventional war. More precisely, surface warfare, ASW, AAW, EW, and strike warfare were considered in a globalized manner instead from a limited Navy/Marine Corps or even a 'warfare union' perspective. "The Maritime Strategy" was also broad in scope, attempting to show how all the players – U.S. home and forward-deployed forces, U.S. Navy, sealift and preposition-ing forces, Marine Corps, Coast Guard, Army, Air Force, allied/friendly navies, and perceived neutrals such as China – might play.[64] Quite signifi-cantly, "The Maritime Strategy" postulated in its 1985 version that "naval forces *prevent major global war* through controlling crises and containing limited wars."[65]

This is not to dismiss vocal critics of the Navy's effort. On the contrary, there were substantial camps of individuals and groups who lobbied against "The Maritime Strategy." Critics attacked the Navy's assumption about the nature of a general war, its assessment of likely Soviet actions in such a war, the disconnection to national political objectives, and the notion of offensive operations. These controversies fueled the general debate in the public and professional realm, which in turn gave the Navy a chance to make its case.[66] In response, the Navy was willing to admit certain realities right away. It was certainly true that the defeat of the Soviet Union at sea would not guarantee a successful defense of NATO, but it was also true – and more important – that the loss of its supremacy at sea would guarantee the alliance's defeat.[67]

The critics aligned along a few broad strands. The first and most fierce charge related superficially to the general defense budget. The Navy's plan of action, so the argument went, absorbed money that could well go into Army and Air Force at the Central Front in Germany to provide deterrence and war-fighting capabilities where the Cold War could predictably turn hot soonest. Supporters of this notion often included former Carter administra-tion officials (such as former Undersecretary of Defense Robert Komer).[68] Behind such an approach stood the clash of the two schools of thought, of maritime vs. continental strategists which underwent a renaissance during the 1980s.[69] Those critics often failed to acknowledge that the Navy fully knew "The Maritime Strategy" was merely the oceangoing component of national military strategy, and that U.S. success still relied on a complementary land component, as well. The Navy understood that the Russian center of gravity lay at land, not at sea.

A second line of thought sought to attack the aircraft carrier. This stance reflected earlier debates about that capital class of ships during the Carter and Truman administrations.[70] Again, the carrier as a platform was not ruled out altogether. Instead, critics suggested looking (again) at an inexpensive, some-what smaller, conventionally powered version to employ the Navy for a distant blockade of the Soviet Union.[71] The large-deck carrier critics proved unable to drive home their point. Navy proponents could even invoke Pres-ident Carter as a crown witness who did not oppose the nuclear carrier program after he had at first vetoed one ship during his presidency. And this time, the Navy made the case against its carrier critics that in fact both were in need: the large carrier Navy would be suitable for power projection against the Soviet Union, while smaller sea–control platforms would serve the U.S. well in Third World interventions.[72] In other words, the Reagan administra-tion sought both, big carriers for the economy–of–scale effect and small-deck vessels (LHA/LPH/LHD) as a supplement.[73] The Navy's view of the argu-ment was summed up by Swartz as,

> The Soviets may be the main enemy, Europe may be the central piece of geography in the global balance and the ground and air battle on the Central Front may be the main event, but it is not the only event.[74]

The third line of argument was less strategically founded. It simply accused the Navy of putting forward a shipbuilding and ship-financing strategy. The slogan of the 600-ship Navy appeared arbitrary (it was not) and unrelated to the needs of national security (it was not), and critics advocated spending that money on any other program or budget item. It does hold true that Lehman used "The Maritime Strategy" to sell the President, Congress, and the Amer-ican people on the 600-ship goal with which the Navy was not unhappy.[75]

The fourth group included the operational challengers who questioned the viability of the main features of "The Maritime Strategy." Why should the relative safety of practiced nuclear and conventional deterrence be discarded in favor of an aggressive, untested naval offensive action?[76] To these critics, the Navy's argument of a low likelihood of a Soviet anti–CVBG campaign seemed flawed. Critics pointed out that in sound traditional military planning, one's own force and action should not be shaped by the intentions, but by the capabilities of the enemy – and the Soviet Navy did have tactical nuclear capabilities.[77]

A related fifth and very important strand questioned the Navy's underlying assertion it could keep the conflict with the Soviet Union conventional at all. Escalation control lay at the heart of "The Maritime Strategy" even though commentators had warned of inadvertent nuclear confrontation, stating that a nuclear exchange between the Soviet Union and the United States could be its unintended consequence by the seemingly conscious decision to fight a conventional war.[78] In fact, the dynamics of the nuclear age could spell dia-metrically opposing effects to what planners envisioned, namely that escala-tory pressures simply overruled any conventional war plans that policy-makers harbored. NATO's Northern flank was at a special risk of being the stage for nuclear escalation because U.S. naval operations (forward operations of attack submarines, offensive carrier battle group operations in the Barents and Norwegian Seas, and a NATO naval counterattack in defense of Norway) all occurred in proximity to the Soviet ballistic missile submarines stationed in Murmansk. "The Maritime Strategy" significantly raised the risk that potential belligerents were willing to run to guard their own strategic forces. The fine academic distinction between defensive and offensive acts was hardly fully assessable at sea or in the fog of war.[79] Nuclear war at sea was certainly a possibility that needed to be taken into account. Accidents at sea (caused by routine covert operations in the vicinity of the opponent's territorial waters or major naval assets, harassment for tactical military purposes, routine monitoring, or other brazen conduct), the attractiveness of ships as nuclear targets, the launch autonomy of naval commanders (especially on submarines where the order was not physical or technical, but doctrinal [recall here the Navy's aversion against doctrine] and thus dependent on personnel and discipline), and U.S. and Soviet general doctrine for conduct of nuclear war all provided enough potential to trigger atomic warfare at sea.[80]

Often overlooked, the authors of "The Maritime Strategy" included a vital list of uncertainties at the end of their work.[81] "The Maritime Strategy" simply needed to hedge against the incalculable aspects of the subject, especially where conflict might occur. It was downright speculative if, where, and how Soviet aggression could lead to war, and NATO, the U.S. military, and the branches of the military were seldom followers of the same school. The view that war between the United States and the Soviet Union could be triggered in Southwest Asia (not the Pacific, the North Atlantic, or Central Europe) had some subscribers, not least because of the schizophrenic position in which the Navy found itself. In the 1980s, the Navy's surface and air operations focused heavily on that region while U.S. Navy planners zeroed in on NATO areas and the West Pacific, and the submariners concentrated on the Arctic.[82] Correspondingly, to hedge against such uncertainties, naval force structural planning had to be coordinated into "The Maritime Strategy."

Force structure

When Ronald Reagan took office, forward–hub deployments continued to shape force posture, procurement, and shipbuilding. By 1980, the Soviet Navy habitually challenged U.S. sea control in the Sixth Fleet area of responsibility; a dramatic change from the more hypothetical threats that triggered its establishment in 1947. The standing Soviet presence in the Mediterranean and its routine challenges of U.S. Navy ships and planes required a more focused support of the force in the Mediterranean. The increasing demands of an emerging permanent Middle East force, although not concurrently reflected in shipbuilding plans, also influenced force structure. Several older warships, technologically outdated and often operationally worn, were decommissioned or placed into the reserve fleet during the 1970s.[83] Technological innovation and comprehensive computerization increasingly shaped the force and its assets.[84] The naval ascent, both qualitatively and quantitatively, intensified over the decade, resting on both the legacy fleet and new additions to the force.[85] Figure 4.2 shows the size of the Navy against postulated force level goals.

It must be noted that the goal of fielding 600 warships was never achieved. This pertains to the particulars of naval force planning and building, that is the substantial amount of resources to be invested over a long period of time for a relatively small number of units.[86] It also suggests that the 600-ship Navy as proposed was more of a sensible baseline rather than a strictly enforced (and perhaps sensibly unenforceable) force level goal.[87]

In fact, the number dovetailed with and was driven by Lehman's political message of combat-credible forward naval presence. Mandated to organize, train, and equip, the Navy – or Lehman, the public face of the Navy's efforts – gave Congress and the President a detailed strategy. To carry out that strategy, the narrative continued, 600 warships were needed, precisely the same number already under discussion during earlier force level debates. Affordability – specifically the claim to save costs by procuring two aircraft carriers in one single fiscal year, twice – was also a major selling point to Congress. To the public, the ambitious yet relatively rational force level goal, linked to strategy seemed to integrate well into the policies of the Reagan

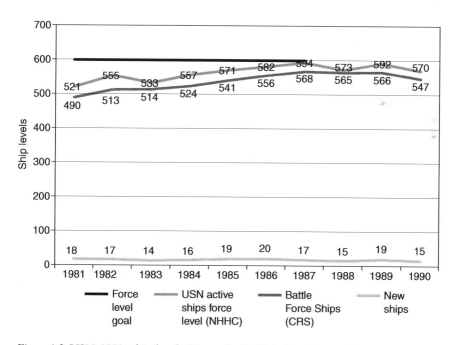

Figure 4.2 USN 1980s ship levels (Hattendorf, 2008: 12, Swartz, 2011a: 16, slide 31 & 2011b: 29–30, slides 58–60).[88] The 600-ship baseline was dropped towards the end of the decade pending formal review of force level goals.

administration. It also provided a sense of good stewardship of the public's resources.[89]

The 600-ship Navy plan proposed 15 carrier battle groups (CVBG) including 16 carrier air wings (CVW), four surface action groups centered around reactivated battleships (BBAG/SAG) of the *Iowa*-class, 100 nuclear-powered attack submarines (SSN) plus ballistic missile submarines, and suitable amphibious lift for Marine Corps elements (a Marine Amphibious Force [MAF] and a slightly smaller Marine Amphibious Brigade [MAB]). It was also to include between 100 and 110 frigates, 31 mine-countermeasure vessels (MCM), and support ships to match.[90] These numbers remained deliberately squishy to reflect uncertainties in budgeting and procurement, although some elements were publicly developed further.

The 600-ship Navy was purposely carrier-centric, which is less surprising when one considers the prominent role these large platforms played in the posture of U.S. sea power since the early 1940s. Moreover, Lehman, the architect of the plan, was a reserve naval aviator with a degree of appreciation for that particular platform – and a bias. The battle group concept was developed to put to sea powerful force packages: CVBGs would consist of two (optionally nuclear-powered) cruisers, four guided-missile destroyers, and the same number of guided-missile frigates. The carriers, the center piece of the proposed plan, would be conventionally- and nuclear-powered platforms of the *Midway*-, *Forrestal*-, *Kitty Hawk*-, *Enterprise*-, and *Nimitz*-classes.[91] *Theodore Roosevelt* (CVN 71) was authorized during the Carter years (FY80) and joined the fleet in 1986; *Abraham Lincoln* (CVN 72) and *George Washington* (CVN 73) were both included in the FY 83 budget, joining the fleet in 1986 and 1989, respectively. *John C. Stennis* (CVN 74) and *Harry S. Truman* (CVN 75) were included in the FY 88 budget, but did not join the fleet until 1995/1998.[92] To obtain congressional acceptance of the massive national investments into two carriers in one budget year was a master stroke. Congress, which "needs to know the broad flow of events, not minute details,"[93] adopted the general sense of naval power as the prime underpinning of American security. The remaining question became 'how much' would be enough.

The surface action groups each consisted of one battleship, a cruiser, a quartet of destroyers, and the same number of guided-missile frigates. The four *Iowa*-class battleships built in the 1940s and in action during World War II, Korea, and Vietnam, were previously seen as outdated for most late-Cold War naval missions. They appeared to be outmoded and given their large crew size were relatively cost-ineffective. But the return of these behemoths – at a fraction of the cost for a new warship of comparable size – demonstrated two things. The Soviet Union, from 1980 on, added their own Kirov-class nuclear-powered battle cruiser as powerful surface combatants. As such, the battleships of the *Iowa*-class were their match, but also a determined symbol of naval diplomacy. Second, they were an operational addition much sought-after by the U.S. Marine Corps and war-planners alike. The Marines valued the precious battleship's firepower which provided naval gunfire support ashore. To modify them, several wide-ranging changes to design, armament, and weaponry were discussed. Innovations implemented on board the *Iowas* (otherwise anachronisms in the computer age) included modern communications equipment, close-in weapons systems (CIWS) for self-defense, and Tomahawk cruise missiles.[94] After all, in the words of the Secretary of the Navy,

> the new naval mission was to demonstrate to the Soviet Union every day that the U.S. Navy and its allies would have the capability to defeat the Soviet navy and to strike hard into the Soviets' heartland if they ever attacked a member of NATO.[95]

President Reagan was sold on the merits of such measures by Lehman and others. "The Maritime Strategy" action officers managed to insert parts of emerging rationale into his speeches. Consequently, in his address on the occasion of the re-commissioning of the *New Jersey* (BB 62) on December 28, 1982, Reagan noted the United States was a naval power dependent on trans-oceanic trade. To the president, it followed that naval power was needed to guarantee the freedom of the seas beyond choke points. To counter the land-based Soviet Union, whose naval build-up was characterized as illegitimate for defense needs, this required U.S. maritime superiority.[96]

The 600-ship Navy rested principally on a mix of new ships and legacy platforms modified to compose a large and sustainable force. The 31 ships of the 8,000-ton *Spruance*-class destroyers (DD 963 through DD 997) were the backbone of the late Cold War surface Navy.[97] Additionally, the 5,600-ton *Farragut*-class guided missile destroyers (DDG 37 through DDG 46) and the 4,600-ton *Charles F. Adams*-class guided missile destroyers (DDG 2 through DDG 24) were as valuable to the 1980s Navy as the 7,800-ton *Leahy*-class guided missile cruisers (CG 16 through CG 24) and its sister ships, the 8,000-ton *Belknap*-class (CG 26 through CG 34) guided missile cruisers. Of note were nine nuclear-powered surface warships, a legacy of Admiral Rickover until he was forced to retire by Lehman in January 1982. The 15,000-ton *Long Beach* (CGN 9), 9,100-ton *Bainbridge* (CGN 25), the slightly smaller 8,700-ton *Truxton* (CGN 35), and the 11,700-ton guided missile cruisers of the *Virginia*-class (CGN 38 through CGN 41) plus two 10,000-ton cruisers (*California*-class) were powerful, large, and expensive assets to the Navy's arsenal. On the lower end, the conventionally powered 2,600-ton *Garcia*-class frigates (FF 1040 through FF 1051), the numerous 4,200-ton *Knox*-class frigates (FF 1052 through FF 1097), and the *Oliver Hazard Perry*-class 4,100-ton newcomer guided missile frigates (FFG 7 through FFG 61) served as the workhorses of the Navy.[98]

The *Perry*-class frigates actually began joining the fleet in the late 1970s. The Reagan administration thus was able to easily continue and expand procurement of these vessels, rather than having to have completely new designs developed. True, new designs joined the fleet in the 1980s as well, complementing the legacy ships. These and the additions from the 1970s increasingly changed the mindset of the Navy. New and more capable platforms such as the *Spruance*-class allowed for a larger tactical and operational flexibility. As operational commanders rotated back into shore billets in Washington, they took with them the knowledge of the expanded versatility and often included it in their strategic thinking and planning. This was a textbook case of a "bottom-up" change in naval thinking: new weapons demanded an original operational culture and, along the way, amplified fresh thinking about naval power.

One of the most notable new additions to the Navy's fleet was the 9,600 ton, Aegis-equipped guided-missile cruisers of the *Ticonderoga*-class (CG 47 through CG 73).[99] Originally based on a *Spruance*-class destroyer hull, the ship's capabilities were far-ranging, featuring the typical Mk-41 VLS for missile employment. Helicopters, long a mainstay aboard Navy ships, were a natural addition and also increased the vessel's operational flexibility. Four guided-missile destroyers of the 9,800 ton *Kidd*-class (DDG 993 through DDG 996), originally slated for the Shah's Iranian navy and based on the *Spruances*, also joined the U.S. fleet. Toward the end of the decade, preparations were made to procure the next-generation destroyer, named after the lead ship *Arleigh Burke* (DDG 51 class, still in production to date).[100]

Below the surface, the 17,000 ton *Ohio*-class nuclear-propelled ballistic missile submarines (SSBN 726 through SSBN 746) began joining the fleet (*Ohio* was commissioned in 1981). The Trident II C-4 SLBM greatly extended the range of its predecessors to some 4,000 miles. The 6,900-ton *Los Angeles*-class nuclear-powered fast attack submarines (SSN 668 through SSN 773), of which a total of 62 were procured, provided the U.S. with another powerful tool in the maritime domain against the Soviet Navy. The Los Angeles boats joined the established 4,600-ton submarines of the *Sturgeon*-class (SSN 637 through SSN 687) to buttress the operational ideas of "The Maritime Strategy."[101] Arrangements were made for an improved *Los Angeles*-class SSN, as well as the larger *Seawolf* attack submarine (SSN 21), meant to be the main submarine platform well into the twenty-first century. Massive cost overruns meant that only three of the originally planned 29 *Seawolfs* were ever procured.

In the amphibious component, the first of eventually eight *Wasp*-class small carriers (LHD 1 through LHD 8) came online. Developed as a direct successor to the *Tarawa*-class (LHA 1 through LHA 5), they joined the legacy fleet of *Raleigh*- and *Austin*-class amphibious transport docks (LPD 1 through LPD 15) and *Thomaston*- and *Anchorage*-class dock landing ships (LSD 28 through LSD 40). A modern equivalent, the 15,800-ton *Whidbey Island*-class (LSD 41 through LSD 48) entered the fleet from 1985 onwards.[102]

Augmenting the 600-ship Navy was a variety of auxiliaries. To recapitalize its MCM fleet, the U.S. Navy procured the *Avenger*-class boats (MCM 1 through MCM 15). New ocean surveillance ships (T-AGOS 1 through

T-AGOS 18), 25 maritime prepositioning ships (MPS), and 116 ships in the reserve supported the forward-deployed, offensive-minded strategy.[103] Military sealift program assets (U.S. government-owned fleets of prepositioning and fast sealift ships subject to CINC demand and JCS adjudication[104] included the *Algol*-class[105] fast sealift vessels (T-AKR 287 through T-AKR 294)[106] and fleet oiler replenishment ships of the *Henry J. Kaiser*-class (T-AO 187 through T-AO 204).[107] The Navy also welcomed two *Mercy*-class hospital ships (T-AH 19/20), both of which used converted commercial tanker hulls. These unarmed ships, painted white and marked by an oversized red cross, have assisted in numerous humanitarian assistance missions and disaster relief since then.

Regarding naval aviation, the fleet saw some major changes as well. Aircraft deliveries remained at a high rate, with the operational availability rate averaging 71 percent from 1980 to 1988. The P-2 Neptune maritime patrol/ ASW aircraft, the F-4 Phantom II fighter-bomber, the A-7 Corsair II attack jet, and the F-8 Crusader jet were retired. New P-3C Maritime Patrol Aircraft (MPA), F/A-18 C/D Hornet multi-role aircraft, and MH-53E Sea Dragon and SH-60 Seahawk multi-mission helicopters were incorporated into the fleet. Improved F-14B Tomcats continued to be procured in great numbers; A-6 Intruder attack and EA-6B Prowler electronic countermeasures aircraft took center stage. Total aircraft numbers are given in Figure 4.3.

Additionally, U.S. allied navies were not dormant in the 1980s, often recapitalizing and modernizing their own fleets to reflect operational experiences and political demands, and NATO nations' commitment to devote 3 percent

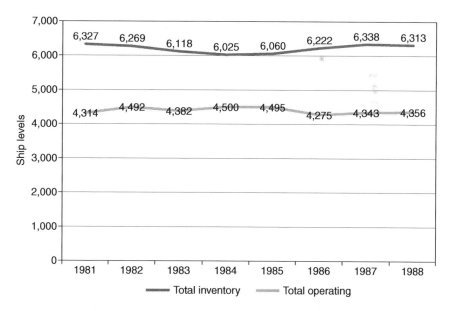

Figure 4.3 Inventory of U.S. Navy aircraft, 1981–1988; this OPNAV study was discontinued by 1989.[108]

of their economy to defense expenditures. These allies often provided the lower-end or niche capabilities within NATO, while the United States was able to focus on the more costly high-end assets. "The Maritime Strategy" was parsed so that the integration of allies could be facilitated.

The U.S. Navy's fleet force structure throughout the decade is presented in Table 4.2.

Strategic and operational implementation: planned vs. actual

At the beginning of the 1980s and throughout most of the decade, the confrontation with the Soviet Union shaped conceptual thinking. The U.S./ USSR maritime balance, according to a Department of Defense presentation, is given in Table 4.3.

Hence, fundamental asymmetries prevailed between the two nations, their sea power assets, and their respective sea-strategic concepts. While the U.S. and the Soviet Union often came very close – literally bumping into each other at times in the Mediterranean and the Black Sea – other real-time contingencies dominated the operational action and expertise of the 1980s Navy.[109]

Major U.S. naval operations[110]

The thrust of "The Maritime Strategy" was potentially useful in the overarching objective of deterring (and, if must be, defeating) the Soviet Union as

Table 4.2 U.S. Navy active ship force levels, 1981–1989 (Navy History and Heritage Command, 2011)

Date	9/81	9/82	9/83	9/84	9/85	9/86	9/87	9/88	9/89
Battleships	0	0	1	2	2	3	3	3	4
Carriers	12	13	13	13	13	14	14	14	14
Cruisers	27	27	28	29	30	32	36	38	40
Destroyers	91	89	71	69	69	69	69	69	68
Frigates	78	86	95	103	110	113	115	107	100
Submarines	87	96	98	98	100	101	102	100	99
SSBNs	34	33	34	35	37	39	37	37	26
Command ships[1]	4	4	4	4	4	4	4	4	4
Mine warfare	25	25	21	21	21	21	22	22	23
Patrol	1	4	6	6	6	6	6	6	6
Amphibious	61	61	59	57	58	58	59	59	61
Auxiliary	101	117	103	120	121	123	127	114	137
Surface total	196	202	195	203	211	217	223	217	212
Total active	521	555	533	557	571	583	594	573	592

Note

1 Command ships are large purposely built or converted military vessels designed to embark a fleet commander. They are equipped with command and control facilities, office space, and accommodation for the admiral and his/her staff.

Table 4.3 U.S./USSR maritime balance[111]

Factor	U.S.	Soviet Union
Geography	• Open access to oceans • Long distance to allies	• Constrained access to oceans • Short distances to allies
Missions	• Sea control/power projection	• Sea denial/peripheral sea control
Offensive capability	• Few large ships • Sea-based aviation • Attack submarines • Amphibious forces	• Many small shops • Land-based naval air force • Anti-ship missile system • Attack submarines
Defensive capability	• Marginal AAW capability • ASW • Air cover	• Marginal AAW capability • Inadequate ASW • Inadequate sea-based air
Sustained operations	• Excellent under way replenishment • Worldwide base structure	• Limited under way replenishment • Limited overseas base system
Technology	• Major advantage – offensive and defensive technology	• Anti-ship missiles and surface ocean surveillance
Experience	• Extensive exercises • Volunteer force • Wartime experience	• Limited at-sea time • Manning by conscripts

it was for lesser contingencies. It was also a strategy that could be executed with available forces; it was a real-time strategy.[112]

> It was my firm view that conflict with the USSR was a low probability event … although we often found ourselves (USN) involved in 'crisis response' events possibly sparked by the USSR via its proxies. That said, the fleet was designed for a fight with the Soviets and our responses to various non-Soviet 'crises' were handled as 'lesser included' events, i.e., with the forces (fleet) designed to fight the Soviets.[113]

On balance, the Navy and the Marine Corps responded to 47 individual crises during the 1980s, many more than the Army and the Air Force did.[114] The following is a discussion of three selected U.S. naval operations of the decade. Keeping in mind the particular nature of a forward-deployed fleet (the force was not kept in a U.S. port until problems arose but rather maintains a permanent forward presence in areas of interest), the following paragraph illustrates some of the 'real-world' engagements for the service.

Lebanon (1982–1984)

Occupying the U.S. operational focus in the first third of the decade was the civil war in Lebanon, a country ravaged by turmoil and armed conflict for years. After the 1982 Israel– PLO war in Lebanon, a Western multinational force remained in Beirut to deter the outbreak of further hostilities. Israel, Syria, Lebanon, and the Palestinian Liberation Organization (PLO), and Iran wrestled for influence as fractional strife continued to fuel the violent unrest.[115] The Soviet Union did not appreciate the Western military presence in one of its premier areas of interest and influence.[116] In 1982, 800 U.S. Marines were stationed in Beirut as part of a multinational peacekeeping force. They were quickly caught in the middle of the murky conflict. The deteriorating security situation was not properly reflected in more appropriate rules of engagement. Shortcomings in intelligence collection and contradictions in the chains of command severely diluted the U.S. effort to remain outside of the raging civil war.[117] A more coercive, active U.S. military intervention from the sea remained undone because the high-value warships could have been at risk from terrorist attacks and close-in weapons if they loitered too close to shore.

Ultimately, fear of mission creep – an epitome of the Vietnam syndrome – led to an overly cautious political attitude in Washington, with disastrous results on the ground by 1983. On April 18, an explosion at the U.S. embassy in the Lebanese capital claimed the lives of 63 (17 of whom were Americans), and on October 23, the detonation of a truck-borne bomb at the Marine Corps barracks killed 241 U.S. servicemen.[118] In the meantime, the recently reactivated battleship *New Jersey* (BB 62) had arrived off the Levantine coast. However, retaliatory strikes were not conducted until December after aircraft from the carriers *Independence* (CV 62) and *John F. Kennedy* (CV 67) had engaged Syrian-controlled surface-to-air missile positions, and the U.S. Navy lost planes and pilots.[119] The New Jersey's guns were more heavily used in February of 1984, when the decision to withdraw the remaining U.S. Marines from Lebanon was flanked by a massive, but hardly strategically useful barrage of the battleship's 16-inch shells at enemy positions in the Bekaa Valley east of Beirut.[120] This engagement was the most intense shore bombardment since the Korean War (in which the *New Jersey*, incidentally, took part).

The U.S. Navy's engagement in Lebanon revealed flaws in the uniformed chain of command, the policy objectives of the mission, and the uninspired tactics of naval aviators, which eventually caused the catastrophic U.S. score sheet.[121] For the time being, the Reagan doctrine goal – to sustain American influence in regions of strategic interests – appeared to be under severe pressure.[122]

Libya (1981–1989)

Libya was another key contender for attention during 1980s U.S. naval operations. For over a decade, the Libyan government under Muammar Gaddafi presented a key foreign-policy challenge to the United States, not the least because Gaddafi was staunchly anti-Israel and a ruthless, aggressive dictator.[123] He was also assumed to be developing weapons of mass destruction.

The Gulf of Sidra, a large body of international water hugged by the Libyan coastline, was declared subject to extensive Libyan claims of sovereignty. To uphold the right of free maritime passage and prevent a creeping Libyan entry into customary law, President Reagan in August of 1981 authorized freedom of navigation (FON) exercises that would cross the self-proclaimed Libyan "line of death." To the U.S., that action had both a legal and an operational connotation because the Gulf of Sidra was the only place in the Mediterranean that was free of any major sea lanes or airways. For decades, the U.S. Sixth Fleet had depended on it for periodic live-fire exercises.[124] In the process of the operation, which included the carriers *Forrestal* (CV 59) and *Nimitz* (CVN 68), two of the Libyan Air Force aircraft that sought to intercept the U.S. force were shot down by Navy fighters.[125]

U.S. forces repeatedly clashed with the Libyan military between 1981 and 1989, but the largest military engagements occurred in 1986.[126] In response to hijackings of commercial airliners and the ocean liner *Achille Lauro*, and the bombings of the Rome and Vienna airports in 1985, Gaddafi was accused as the mastermind and financier of these perpetrations. From January through March 1986, the U.S. Navy used its routine challenges of unlawful Libyan territorial claims to mount large-scale naval exercises. On its third incursion, a large force – consisting of the three aircraft carriers *Coral Sea* (CV 43), *Saratoga* (CV 60), *America* (CV 66), the guided–missile cruisers *Ticonderoga* (CG 47) and *Yorktown* (CG 48), and "122 other American warships"[127] – under the command of Admiral Frank Kelso (later CNO) sought to draw out Libyan forces. This resulted in a high attrition of the inferior green–water Libyan Navy and a demonstration of defense capabilities against surface to air missiles (SAM). This operation, although showing fewer problems than encountered in Lebanon a few years earlier, also showed the limits of the Reagan doctrine in counter–terrorism operations. In early April, just weeks after the clash, state-sponsored terrorist attacks on the "La Belle" discotheque in West-Berlin (a club frequented by U.S. service members, two of whom were among the three dead) and a TWA flight en route from Rome to Athens (killing four Americans) could be traced to the Libyan regime's brazen attempt to profit from what was seen as American hesitancy.

In a joint Air Force-Navy retaliatory strike on April 15, 1986 codenamed "Operation Eldorado Canyon," the U.S. launched a large-scale attack on Libyan shore targets in Tripoli and Benghazi. It utilized naval assets on station in the Sixth Fleet AOR and Air Force elements based in the U.K., which participated despite the need for a concerted refueling effort and a detour around Gibraltar (France had declined the U.S. over-flight rights for this operation). The operations in the Gulf of Sidra in 1986 marked the first operational employment of Aegis-equipped guided-missile cruisers and destroyers[128] and by-and-large discouraged Gaddafi from further acts of terrorism.[129] Lehman's gleaming conclusion in his memoirs spells out,

It was precisely those ships, aircraft, and weapons that had been ridiculed during the early 1980s by the antinaval reformers in Congress and their academic camp followers that performed so brilliantly: the aegis cruiser, the F-14, the F-18, the A-6, the F-111, the Harm antiradiation missile, and the Harpoon antiship missile. [...] Another obvious and strong lesson was the destruction of the myth of interservice rivalry.[130]

If anything, the Gulf of Sidra clashes underlined that, when provoked, the Reagan administration took a much tougher stance against regional challenges in comparison with President Carter. At the time, the United States (after Reagan's policy reversal) and the Soviet Union (under newly elected president Gorbachev) circumspectly approached each other. Comparably minor skirmishes such as U.S. operations against Libya demonstrated the strategically vital position of naval strength from which Reagan could negotiate.[131]

Persian Gulf (1987/1988)

The third large U.S. naval operation of the 1980s took place in the Persian Gulf, the Strait of Hormuz, and the Arabian Sea. Those bodies of water had been elevated to major strategic importance since the promulgation of the Carter doctrine. The Iran-Iraq War, which consumed much of the decade for the belligerents, began when Iraqi ruler Saddam Hussein expedited an increasingly aggressive foreign policy to control more oil reserves in the Middle East.[132] In addition to the land fighting, warfare also included attacks on shipping in the Gulf. Control of regional sea lines along with destruction of enemy merchant ships (and those of its allies) and the protection of oil export assets became key objectives in Iraq's strategy and operations.

Since Iraq owned few maritime or naval assets that were worth attacking, Iran responded by targeting ships trading with Bagdad's allies in the Persian Gulf, principally Kuwait. Seventy-one merchant ships were attacked in 1984 alone, compared with 48 in the first three years of the war.[133] Two years later, Iraq stepped up its air attacks on tankers serving Iran and Iranian oil-exporting facilities. At this point, U.S. interests and those of her allies were increasingly at risk, although Washington had officially remained neutral, only gradually tilting toward the Iraqis, and the Iran–Contra affair notwithstanding.[134]

In the fall of 1986, the government of Kuwait sought help from the international community. Its tanker fleet was affected disproportionally by the Iranian attempts to curtail oil revenue supports for Iraq's war efforts.[135] Utilizing the provisions of international law and the terms of trade of commercial shipping, freighters were reflagged with the U.S. ensign and escorted by allied warships. The U.S. was reluctant at first to provide such support.[136] In "Operation Earnest Will," up to 30 U.S. Navy warships patrolled the Arabian Sea, with periodical incursions of cruisers, destroyer, and frigates through the Strait of Hormuz to provide escort service through the mine-infested narrow maritime highway. All the while, command and control problems impaired sea power action at this critical interface of two U.S. regional commands (U.S. CENTCOM and U.S. PACOM).[137] Overcoming problems with MCM capabilities and equipment governed daily operations.[138]

In 1987 and 1988, the naval action escalated. First, on May 17, 1987, the guided-missile frigate *Stark* (FFG 31) was hit by two Exocet air-to-surface missiles from an Iraqi jet, which mistook the American vessel for an Iranian warship. Thirty-seven U.S. sailors were killed, but damage control efforts were successful in keeping the five-year old ship from sinking. In addition, the Navy – tasked with preventing the actual distribution of Iranian mines rather than having to find and clear them once they had been laid – repeatedly clashed with Iranian forces in the following months. On April 14, 1988, the *Stark*'s sister ship *Samuel B. Roberts* (FFG 58) struck a mine.[139] The resulting explosion injured ten sailors, and on April 18 the U.S. retaliated against Iranian command and control platforms with "Operation Praying Mantis" (Love, 1992b: 787–790). Surface ships and carrier-based aircraft obliterated two oil platforms used by the Iranian military as command and control posts. In this battle, U.S. naval forces sank or damaged half of Iran's operational navy.[140] But it took a tragic incident for Iran to agree to a ceasefire proposal negotiated by the United Nations. On July 3, 1988, the guided-missile cruiser *Vincennes* (CG 49) mistakenly shot down Iran Air flight 655, killing 290 passenger and crew aboard the Airbus A-300.[141]

Politically, "the United States' stand in the Gulf during 1987–1988 erased the negative images resulting from the failed Iranian rescue mission and withdrawal from Lebanon,"[142] and the U.S. Navy reduced its forces in theater down to just five warships patrolling in the Gulf by the summer of 1990.[143]

On balance, the 1980s witnessed growing U.S. involvement in the Mediterranean, the Middle East, and Southwest Asia. The conflicts generated by turmoil in Libya, Lebanon, and Iran kept the Navy quite busy. Containing the spillover-effects from these lesser-included events dominated U.S. response in both the Mediterranean and the Persian Gulf/ Indian Ocean areas. However, this level of activity did not preclude the forward-deployed forces from also pursuing more traditional Cold War missions of deterrence and surveillance against the Soviets in the thrust of "The Maritime Strategy."[144] In fact, it was the combination of such efforts and events that characterized American naval power in support of national security for the 1980s.

Relationships to allies

To the authors of "The Maritime Strategy," the inclusion of allies was very important.[145] NATO member states were particularly crucial, although fundamentally the Navy's effort was obviously one that carried American national interests, not necessarily that of America's allies. Again, the benefits of a non-static document rather than that of a cast-in-stone doctrine are obvious for the diplomacy part of the Navy's effort.

However, "The Maritime Strategy" sent a mixed message to European leaders, signaling that the U.S. was willing and able to fight in the North Atlantic and the Pacific, but it was unclear how these two theaters were connected strategically. The underlying, permanent uncertainty about the stakes at which the United States would be willing to commit to the defense of Europe did not go away.[146] Concurrently, leaders may have worried that escalation in the Pacific would trigger a hot war over Berlin and in the Central Front. In addition, the Navy's conviction that "The Maritime Strategy" could keep any global war non-nuclear risked undermining a key pillar in NATO's flexible response strategy: if Western strategists emphasized in their public (and private) pronouncements that armed conflict would remain conventional, the Soviet Union might feel encouraged believing that it could easily avoid nuclear punishment for any conventional aggression.[147]

NATO at the time was considered as heavily nuclear- and Germany-centric, and too dominated by the battle doctrine at the Central Front in Hesse and Bavaria.[148] It followed that the Navy's narrative was to emphasize theaters of war against the Warsaw Pact that lay at the flanks, or even outside of NATO area. On the Southern flanks, the littoral states of the Mediterranean Sea needed to be reassured of the salience of "The Maritime Strategy." The Mediterranean had been the site of repeated U.S.–Soviet naval confrontations and it was the operating area for Moscow's forward-based forces, which sought to counter-balance the U.S. Sixth Fleet's assets. Turkey and Greece, two key NATO allies, held a geo-strategically important position. On the Northern flanks, the "The Maritime Strategy" was reasonably attractive to allies such as Norway: the country would have been "on the wrong side of the barrier"[149] had a GIUK[150] distant blockade strategy prevailed. On the other hand, Norway was at risk of being drawn into a U.S.-Soviet conflict first, and held little interest in an escalating naval strategy.[151]

Politically, European leaders in the 1980s were often very much concerned about arms control, often vocally supported by large public demonstrations and peace movements. "The Maritime Strategy" neglected this issue.[152] Although naval arms limitations are inherently difficult,[153] the Soviet Union repeatedly proposed them. Whether this was a practical proposal or a political maneuver, those attempts ultimately did not lead anywhere.[154]

To test "The Maritime Strategy" at sea (and to quell allied concerns about operating forward), a number of large U.S./NATO exercises were conducted in the context of "The Maritime Strategy." Examples included Ocean Safari and Northern Wedding exercises in 1981, where operations in the North Atlantic remained undetected by the Soviets for four days.[155] In Fleet-Ex 83, three aircraft carriers operated in the North Pacific, significantly contributing to Soviet nervousness in 1983. Ocean Safari 85 ran from August to September 1985 and included convoys crossing the Atlantic and hugging the European coast from Iceland to Portugal. More than 150 warships, among them the battleship *Iowa* (BB 61) and the *Saratoga* (CV 60), *Enterprise* (CVN 65), and *America* (CV 66) CVBGs, participated in this sweeping demonstration of

NATO naval power. Teamwork 88 was the largest multinational exercise in the decade. Held in the summer of 1988, it simulated operations in the Norwegian fjords.[156] On the far side of the world in the Pacific, PacEx 89 was a massive naval exercise that drew out aircraft carriers, battleships, and numerous other warships. Allied navies from Canada, Japan, and the Republic of Korea routinely trained there with the U.S. Navy, in the Rim of the Pacific (RIMPAC) exercise first held in 1975; Japan joined in 1980. As "The Maritime Strategy" had laid out, these exercises signaled to the Soviets that if they attacked NATO in Europe, "they could have expected us to be coming at them in the Pacific."[157]

Assessment: a strategic sea power renaissance, 1981–1989

"The Maritime Strategy" capstone documents of the 1980s, "a tumultuous period for sea power theory,"[158] represented a dedicated re-focus of the nexus of national and naval interests.[159] As Geoff Till has pointed out, the maritime posture of the Cold War United States was largely dominated by three decision-making processes, namely, the checks and balances between the President and Congress, the state of relations between the services, and the relations between the different 'unions' within the Navy itself.[160] "The Maritime Strategy" utilized executive/legislative branch synergies and overcame inter-service and inter-warfare union competition for the time being. These three parallel successes (otherwise often highly unlikely to be achieved concurrently) made "The Maritime Strategy" a Cold War success. For the administration, as Lehman wrote in his memoires, it was one of the rare opportunities to hit the ground running.

> The President had specifically called for maritime superiority in his principal national security campaign speech in Chicago in March 1980, and the six-hundred-ship objective was a plank in the Republican platform. The Secretary of Defense offered strong intellectual support, and the Senate and House Armed Services Committees were equally committed.[161]

A post-World War II naval depression had cumulated in the 1970s, when the inability to articulate the Navy's strategic role in national politics, diminishing budgetary resources, an ageing and ever-shrinking fleet, the Vietnam War legacy, and the Soviet naval challenge on the high seas threatened the future of the service. The Navy was unable to develop and implement a suitable strategy. Attempts to recapitalize the fleet lacked direction and political support. During the anti-naval early Presidency of Jimmy Carter, the discrepancy between the political ideas of the administration and the ideas of the Navy reached a highpoint[162] which was hard to overcome.

In the 1980s, CNOs Hayward and Watkins in conjunction with Secretary Lehman managed to turn around the disorientation on the use of force that prevailed in the 1970s by tying together main elements of offensive U.S. Navy thinking into a comprehensive and easily understood narrative. None of these individuals accepted the gunboat diplomacy and spotty escort duties that CNO Zumwalt and Presidents Nixon and Carter had cherished. Most importantly, they did not accept any naval strategy that was based on an unbuilt ship such as the CVV concept.[163] The goal of a 600-ship Navy, an arbitrary number, served a political purpose of signaling the intent to pursue a global and proactive U.S. sea power role. The Navy's strategic missions were in place before the goal of 600 ships in the inventory was informal national policy, and not the other way around as vocal critic Robert Komer would have it.[164] These ideas lay dormant until the external and internal conditions were such that they could be awakened. The 600-ship Navy therefore dovetailed "The Maritime Strategy," although it was a convenient vehicle to bolster the intellectual work of the Navy with clear numbers also beneficial to the defense industry. More than the simple and often scrutinized game of counting ships, "The Maritime Strategy" must therefore also be assessed for the deed it performed for the Navy and the nation as an intellectual exercise and for verbalizing a force-structure goal.

"The Maritime Strategy" connected the naval missions of power projection and sea control by building a forward naval force.[165] For the moment, this eclipsed the ballast of prevalent air power doctrine, massive retaliation, the threat of nuclear annihilation, and sharply limited understandings of sea control with which the Navy had been burdened. Now, the Navy was able to obtain the initiative in strategically communicating a causal ways-means-ends relationship, employing the constituents of functional and institutional maritime power, and explaining to the senior policy-makers that they could exploit naval flexibility and mobility for larger national ends.

The Navy's compelling strategic narrative tracked with the White House, Capitol Hill, the Pentagon, allies, and the public. "The Maritime Strategy" was also very much aligned with the strategic culture of the Navy. It boosted the service's confidence to engage in discussion, by arguing for build-up of naval forces of all types and by aligning with national defense policies.[166] Its offensive nature projected power to the flanks of Europe. It integrated naval aviation to help discourage a Soviet drive westward, and to destroy Soviet attack submarines, thereby guarding the oceanic sea lines of communication. That move exposed the Soviet strategic ballistic missile submarine fleet in its bastions. Seth Cropsey, Deputy Undersecretary of the Navy for the Reagan and the Bush administration, exuberantly summed up the effects of "The Maritime Strategy" as follows:

> This strategy was disputed, criticized, and disparaged. It proved immensely successful. It offered a coherent and sensible raison d'être that took full advantage of all the Navy Department's capabilities. The new maritime strategy undertook missions that supported the other military services and advanced the United States' interest in opposing U.S.

strengths to Soviet weaknesses for the purpose of achieving strategic advantage over the Soviet Union. It was comprehensible, capable of being articulated, and inseparable from the navy's successful effort to increase the fleet from its forty-year nadir of 464 combatants to nearly six hundred ships in less than a decade.[167]

How effective and successful "The Maritime Strategy" really was remains challenging to qualify. Stallmann, for example, remains outspokenly skeptical about the possible success of conventional U.S. forces (a) disabling 300 Soviet submarines, (b) securing the SLOCs in the Pacific and the Atlantic, (c) advancing into the area within reach of land-based naval aviation to attack military bases, and (d) influencing potential events at the Central Front by way of an amphibious landing.[168] While never tested by a World War III with the Soviet Union, it did not succeed in a broad reformulating of the Reagan administration's national policy and strategy to match the innovations proposed by "The Maritime Strategy."[169] In addition, some of the assertions of "The Maritime Strategy" must be questioned. Its conviction that global war with the Soviet Union would remain conventional may appear convincing in hindsight given the extensive reforms under Gorbachev from 1985, but it was a deliberate bet that – given events such as in 1983 – amounted to brinkmanship.

"The Maritime Strategy" that appeared in the January 1986 issue of *Proceedings* "lurked in embryo of 'Sea Plan 2000' of 1978."[170] It was driven by the Navy's conviction that it could contribute more to making a strategic difference in the next war than by adhering to the defensive sea control and maritime highway safeguarding that the Carter administration foresaw. That last was a role in which "the U.S. Navy was disinclined to confine its strategic ambitions to the role of a maritime railroad company."[171] It was Admiral Holloway's opposition to Carter's swing strategy which helped pave the way; successive CNOs embraced Holloway's views. The edge that the Soviet Union seemed to gain as it strove to become a full-spectrum blue-water navy was countered by building more U.S. warships and by adopting an offensive wartime strategy that would allow the U.S. to seize the initiative early in a great-power war.[172] "The Maritime Strategy" of the 1980s attempted to draw both from Mahan (stressing the decisive war-fighting and political capabilities of navies) and from Huntington (providing a purpose and the needed resources to the Navy for national defense) to formulate a sound, explanatory narrative. The document also accurately reflected the *Zeitgeist* of the early 1980s.[173]

Without a naval strategic *baisse*, there could not have been a naval *renaissance*. Using this characterization more pointedly, one could therefore speak of a naval *strategic* renaissance, which played out under the Reagan administration's agenda. After all, the Navy embraced established missions, concepts, and practices already on the shelf rather than inventing something completely new.[174] Additionally, from the 1960s the Navy began fielding the ships and aircraft that formed the backbone of "The Maritime Strategy." "The Maritime Strategy," logical under the Reagan administration, was a process that built on restoring a sound narrative passed from Hayward to Watkins and Lehman. The first Reagan administration's defense plans helped overcome previous uncertainties, lending the budgetary and intellectual vigor allowing "The Maritime Strategy" to unfold. To the public, the actual conflicts and missions that occupied the Navy in the 1980s bore little resemblance to the high-end global plans of "The Maritime Strategy."

The Navy ended the 1980s with considerably higher morale and consensus on its rationale than it had entered the decade. There was upbeat triumphalism as the Warsaw Pact unraveled. The Navy was reasonably confident in its strategy- and policy-making abilities (not least because their capstone document retained the same name and format) and its operational and tactical competence. It displayed confidence in the modernity of its systems and the fleet-deployment strategy and fleet readiness.[175] The strategy's accomplishment was not so much caused by radical, new ideas; instead, "The Maritime Strategy" succeeded in clearly articulating where naval ideas should fit into the broader national military strategy and the more detailed plans and operations of regional commanders. Equally significant was that the strategy provided a lucid target for planning and decisions on force structure.[176] Additionally, the public image and support of the Navy rose through the roof, which further boosted service cohesion and morale.[177]

For the moment, these positive aspects were larger than some other dawning concerns.[178] Immediate problems such as leveling ship numbers toward the end of the 1980s, the still unsatisfactory state of ASW and MCM platforms and capabilities, and the April 19, 1989 turret explosion on the *Iowa* (BB 61), which killed 47 sailors, paired with broader challenges. The Navy lost its Goldwater-Nicholls battles against centralization and the momentum of "The Maritime Strategy" slowed down considerably towards the end of the decade as officers rotated to other billets. The White House was not enthusiastic about fully replacing its grand strategic posture of deterrence and newfound caution with an offensive Navy as relations with the Soviet Union thawed. The Reagan administration was also occupied fighting for its own political survival in the wake of the Iran-Contra affair.

Therefore, the "The Maritime Strategy" should not be confused with a maritime grand strategy; as a service strategy, it was subordinate to the continental grand strategy of preventing domination of the Eurasian landmass by an adverse or hostile power.[179] The Navy had anticipated it could validate major acquisitions for an offensive carrier and submarine fleet, and that it did. It could also reasonably hope that, after debate, a new national strategy for a global maritime war would emerge, a strategy in which this offensive force would be the main naval component. That did not happen. The legacy of "The Maritime Strategy" is, therefore, that of a sound and timely revival of the Navy's strategic thinking and articulate purposefulness. It was not the Navy's attempt to capitalize on budget and zero-sum game theories versus the other branches of the military. It was not simply a ship- and technology-procurement strategy. After all, Luttwark pointed out that the political effectiveness of navies is governed by the political context, not the tactical capabilities.[180] However, the Navy, in the words of CNO Watkins, was seen "singing from the same sheet of music"[181] and "The Maritime Strategy" served as the songbook. Additionally, as much as it was an offensive military strategy and a Navy narrative, "The Maritime Strategy" was therefore a self-sustaining, offensive bureaucratic measure for the service, Congress, the White House, and the American people.

The international context shifted dramatically between 1989 and 1991, essentially nullifying the business model on which "The Maritime Strategy" rested. It once again raised the question 'What do we need a Navy for?' After "the Navy's Cold War zenith,"[182] American sea power for the 1990s would have to be reconsidered.

Notes

1 Hartmann 1990; see also Rudolf (1990: 241–362) for a similar characterization.

2 On the rise of the Soviet Union as a major naval power, see e.g., Ryan (1981: 135–152), Potter and Nimitz (1982: 1016–1043). On the state of Soviet naval strategy and programs through the 1990s as of late 1982 from the U.S. intelligence community, see the unclassified, insightful national intelligence estimate (NIE 11–15–82/D), reprinted in Hattendorf (2004: 101–182).

3 Poland for instance was the first country under Moscow's umbrella to allow independent labor unions. A few years earlier in 1981, the same country had installed martial rule to fend off domestic turmoil in the hope of preventing a Soviet intervention on the template of the Red Army's incursion into Czechoslovakia in 1968.

4 Peter Rudolf noted that Ronald Reagan put an end to talks about conventional arms limitations at sea, something which the Carter administration had carefully started; instead, Reagan focused exclusively on nuclear arms control efforts (1990: 241). The Navy did not seem particularly invested in arms control at all.

5 Keller, 2008, 105–131.

6 Baer, 1994, 426–427.

7 To maritime strategists such as retired Vice Admiral Lyons, "[John] Lehman's favorite fleet admiral" (Swartz, 1996: 94), Islamic Anti-American fundamentalism has its roots in the U.S. inability and unwillingness to act swiftly and decisively in the face of aggression in Teheran. The American withdrawal from Lebanon after the Marine Corps Barracks bombing in 1983 and the attack on the U.S. embassy in 1984, in his view, encouraged the notion that once U.S. casualties had to be taken into consideration, the political power base for American interventions would crumble and U.S. forces would withdraw, a key idea on which al-Qaida built its own strategy. Lyons lobbied unsuccessfully to retaliate against Iran in 1979/1980 and against Hezbollah in Lebanon in 1983/1984 (Lyons interview, 2012: 00:35:00–00:46:20).

8 To British naval historian Eric Grove, the war was the "most notable naval event of the decade and the most significant traditional, fleet vs. fleet battle in the post-war era" (Grove, 1990: 159). It is important to note that this war was an inner-system and not a U.S.-Soviet proxy conflict.

9 In a presentation at the "Falklands War – 30 Years On" conference in Portsmouth (U.K.) on May 19, 2012 and in subsequent statements, Lehman revealed

that the United States made preparations to deploy the U.S. Navy's helicopter carrier *Iwo Jima* (LPH 2) should one of the Royal Navy's aircraft carriers be lost (see also Lehman, 2012).

10 For the report, see DON/OPA (1983).

11 Lehman, 2001, 283.

12 For Falklands War analyses, see in particular Sandy Woodward (with Patrick Robinson), *One Hundred Days. The Memoirs of the Falklands Battle Group Commander*, London, Harper Press 2012; Martin Middlebrook, *The Falklands War*, Barnsley, Pen & Sword 2012; Peter Hennessy and James Kinks, *The Silent Deep. The Royal Navy Submarine Service since 1945*, London, Penguin Books, 388–459.

13 John Lehman blasted the Grenada operation for the near total lack of intelligence, a lack of interoperability between the land and sea forces of the U.S., and the exceptionally high attrition rate of helicopters (Lehman, 2001: 289–296). Still, the military operation met its objective.

14 Hammel, 2005, 285–420.

15 KAL flight 007 bound for Seoul had digressed from its designated route because of a navigational error. In consequence, it violated Soviet airspace (twice). It was shot down by Soviet interceptor jets, which may have mistaken the airliner for a U.S. intelligence gathering plane patrolling outside Russian airspace at the same time. All passengers aboard the commercial airliner, among them a sitting U.S. Congressman, were killed.

16 Hoffmann, 1999, A19.

17 Schild, 2013, 190.

18 Lehman, 2001, 350–360.

19 Thompson, 1999, 1–28.

20 In line with Hattendorf (2004: 1), with the addition of Congress to the discussion (see also introduction to this study).

21 Love, 1992b, 678–688. That paper analyzed three force levels: 600 ships assembled mainly around 14 aircraft carrier groups, 500 ships grouped around 12 carriers, and 400 vessels clustered around 10 carriers. The study was criticized for weighing sea control tasks versus power projection against the Soviet Union, rather than having the Navy do both (see also Rudolf, 1990: 113–114).

22 Lehman, 2001, 100–101.

23 In an address on March 8, 1983, the President called the Soviet Union an "evil empire" (Reagan, 1983). In a much-less confrontational June 12, 1987 speech in front of the Brandenburg Gate in Berlin, with reference to the iconic nature of the speech's site he appealed to Soviet General-Secretary Gorbachev to "open this gate, tear down this wall" (Reagan, 1987).

24 Schild, 2013, 191–202.

25 Weinberger, 1984. Weinberger's successor was Frank Carlucci, who had served the Reagan administration in various positions and oversaw the last two years of the Reagan administration (1987–1989). His impact on foreign policy was limited compared with Weinberger. When George Bush Sr. became President of the United States in 1989, Richard "Dick" Cheney was nominated as Secretary of Defense (1989–1993).

26 His relatively short time in office, his military career, and his policy management isolated him from any serious influence on "The Maritime Strategy." For an account of his one and a half years in office in his own words, see Haig (1984).

27 Swartz (1996: 118) recalls that

Lehman repeated the same themes over and over again in his speeches, rather than jumping from topic to topic. He made himself, the U.S. Navy, and the Maritime Strategy synonymous in the public, Capitol Hill, and much of the Pentagon mind.

28 Lehmann, 2001: 105.
29 Thanks to his energetic way of handling his exceptionally long tenure as Secretary of the Navy, Lehman quickly eclipsed the legacies of his Carter-era bureaucrat predecessors Graham Claytor (1977–1979) and Edward Hidalgo (1979–1981). Lehman successors also stood in his shadow, and Jim Webb (1987–1988), William Ball (1988–1989), and Lawrence Garrett, III. (1990–1992) consequently only had short terms with little lasting influence. It should be cautioned that there were (and probably are still today) as many fans of Lehman ("The right man at the right time" [Rudolf, 1990: 244]) as there are cautious critics ("There was more to the Maritime Strategy than John Lehman" [Swartz, 1996: 95]). Lehman was a key figure in "The Maritime Strategy," but by far not the only driver.
30 Rudolf (1990: 243) suggests that the leadership of the Pentagon was brought off-balance by the Navy Department's assertiveness in the 1980s. In the view of that author, Secretary of Defense Weinberger was in a particularly unfortunate position. Rudolf attests to a lack of security-policy expertise and describes him as much less versed than his predecessor Harold Brown.
31 Space gained increasing prominence in the military and political spheres in the 1980s. It served both as an operating space for satellites and weaponry, as SDI promised, and as a frontier for American destiny as the Space Shuttle program readily demonstrated (damped only by the explosion of the Challenger space shuttle on January 28, 1986).
32 The White House, 1982, 1–2.
33 Schild, 2013, 155–161.
34 Hacke, 2005, 373.
35 Bierling, 2003, 183.
36 Swartz, 2011b, 26, slide 52.
37 Swartz, 2014, 18.
38 Snider, 1995, 7.
39 Snider, 1995, 8.
40 Meinhart, 2012, 84.
41 For a discussion of the period 1945–1955, see Palmer (1988). Representative accounts on the origins of "The Maritime Strategy" and the underlying assumptions also by Barnett (1989) and Gray (1990). Swartz (2011b: 32, slide 64) notes that the Navy "had benefited from increased visibility during [the] last years of Carter Administration (late 1979–1981): utility of CVBGs, ARGs, sealift, preposition ships [was] recognized and funded."
42 Lehman, 2001, 121–137.
43 "Maritime Strategy: Global Maritime Elements of U.S. Military Strategy," https://youtu.be/xQTFtveAZQQ.
44 There are at least three strands, combining a total of 24 threads of possible explanatory patterns pertaining to the analytical genesis of Navy strategy. These include a rational strand, "like they teach you at staff college and the junior service college courses. How 'the book' says you make Strategy, or at least how you should" (Swartz, 1996: 16); an organization strand, "like they teach you at the Kennedy School and the senior War College courses. How Pentagon and fleet insiders say you 'really' make Strategy" (ibid: 17); and a personality strand, "like you read in the newspapers and memoirs and see in the movies: How the participants say they and their colleagues actually made Strategy." (ibid.) Swartz, the political scientist and military staff action officer for "The Maritime Strategy", goes on to note that

I was one of the twisters of the 24 threads. These threads did not flow to us on neat conveyor belts, neatly twisted into three strands. Rather, they often arrived all tangled in balls and knots. Sometimes they were thrown at us. [...] Other times they were just rolled over, underhand. We had to do lots of untying and untangling. [...] Other times we had to go looking for them as they flowed elsewhere [...]. Then we had to reroute them over to our desks and lay them together to form the line we were making.

(Ibid.: 15)

This realization, of course, goes back to the challenges of discerning the analysis of naval strategy from a political science point of view discussed in the first chapters of this book.

45 Swartz, 2011a, 5, slide 10.
46 Rudolf, 1990: 249–251, Love, 1992b: 708.
47 For a representative open-source analysis, see Ford and Rosenberg (2005). The Soviet Union was not idly standing on the sidelines of the intelligence business, as the exposure of the Walker family spy ring in the U.S. demonstrated. U.S. Navy Chief Warrant Officer John Walker and his associates provided information about the U.S. Navy to the Moscow from 1965 to 1985 – resulting in "the Navy's biggest betrayal" (Prados, 2010).
48 For a comprehensive list of contemporary publications, see Swartz (2011a: 16–21, slides 31–42).
49 See section 8.6.3 for details. See also interview with Admiral (ret.) Lyons (2012, 00:20:00–00:30:00).
50 Swartz, 1996: 55, emphasis in original.
51 Swartz, 2011a: 22–27, slides 44–54.
52 Of note is an unofficial 'Navy Study Group' convened in the Washington, D.C.-area between 1983 and 1985 by Commander Jim Stark, a graduate of The Fletcher School of Law and Diplomacy at Tufts University, a Massachusetts graduate school focusing on international affairs and attracting a number of U.S. Navy officers as their students. This outside forum to discuss and influence naval strategy has, in various iterations and under different conveners, survived until today.
53 See Watkins (1986). This is the document that is often referred to as *the* "Maritime Strategy."
54 For a comprehensive list of these, see Swartz (2011a: 28–29, 31, slides 55–57 and 61), and Swartz' annotated bibliography on the accompanying debates in Hattendorf (2004: 185–277).
55 Collins, 2002, 58.
56 Such a scenario unfolds in Tom Clancy's novel "Red Storm Rising," first published in 1986. The story, based on actual contingency plans and a commercial wargame, follows a NATO-Warsaw Pact war which begins in Southwest Asia. As the conflict broadens, violent battles in Central Germany and naval campaigns in the North Atlantic and Barents Sea eventually turn the tide for the U.S. and its allies.
57 That, in turn, did not exclude the Navy's forgoing of nuclear options. Improved SLBM type Poseidon and Trident I formed the submarine leg of the nuclear deterrence triad (with ICBM and strategic bombers as the other two legs). At any time, in any circumstance, the Navy was to be prepared to act more or less along a continuum of violence whose levels ranged from display to nuclear war (Baer, 1994: 432). The use of nuclear weapons in naval warfare has limited plausibility. They were only suitable in a general nuclear war, which would severely curtail the relevance of naval forces in the first place. Its only objective during the Cold War, therefore, was deterrence. They did so by carrier- or submarine-launched missiles (Grove, 1990: 92).
58 Baer, 1994: 421.

59 See Edward Marolda, *Ready Seapower. A History of the U.S. Seventh Fleet*. Washington, D.C. Naval History and Heritage Command, 2012; Narushige Michishita, Peter M. Swartz and David F. Winkler, *Lessons of the Cold War in the Pacific: U.S. Maritime Strategy, Crisis Prevention, and Japan's Role*. Washington, D.C. Wilson Center: 2016.

60 Baer, 1994: 425.

61 Hattendorf and Swartz, 2008: 192.

62 Cable, 1989.

63 Rudolf, 1990: 254.

64 Swartz, 2011a: 34, slide 67.

65 Swartz, 2011a: 34, slide 68, emphasis in original.

66 Critique was stated in various forums such as Congressional hearings and in academic journals. For a worthwhile dispute, see Brooks (1986) and Mearsheimer (1986) in an issue of *International Security*.

67 Lehman, 2001: 188.

68 "The guy that everyone in the Navy loved to hate" (Captain (ret.) Robbie Harris interview, 2012, 00:39:10–00:39:30).

69 On representative musings about the continental vs. maritime debate, see Dunn and Staudenmaier (1984), Komer (1984), and Barnett (1987).

70 The same arguments are made today for *Forrestal*-class and *United States* (CVA 58) cancelled in the late 1940s: "The only thing that has changed is the names of some countries we invade, the hull number of the ship, and the name of the ship" (Scott Truver interview 2012, 00:18:20–00:18:50).

71 Rudolf, 1990: 306.

72 Rudolf, 1990: 272.

73 Grove, 1990: 127–128.

74 Swartz, 1996: 27.

75 Bill Keller, "The Navy's Brash Leader," *New York Times*, December 15, 1985.

76 The 'love affair' with nuclear deterrence points to a fundamental and inherently American struggle (Rudolf, 1990: 117): throughout its history, the United States has often oscillated among engagement, reluctance, and disengagement in world affairs. During the Cold War, the United States embraced its role as the leader of the West. The nuclear bomb and its associated deterrence value vaguely promised a cold, but stable balance. In other words, it was a weapon to end all wars. As history showed, local wars were still the case, but the dreaded global World War III did not start.

77 Rudolf, 1990: 296–297.

78 Posen, 1982: 29.

79 Ibid.: 31–34.

80 Ball, 1985: 3–4.

81 Hattendorf, 2008: 193–199.

82 Swartz, 2011b: 35, slide 69.

83 Examples include the *Gearing*-, *Fletcher*- and *Allen-M-Sumner*-class destroyers, the *Iowa*-class battleships, World-War-II escort carriers, and old cruisers.

84 For a basic discussion of modern U.S. and allied warship design, technology, sensors, and armament from a contemporary perspective, including sectional drawings of warship classes of the U.S. Navy since the end of World War II, see Silverstone, 2009.

85 For an analysis on the relationship of "The Maritime Strategy" and fleet design from an interactive point of view that goes beyond operations research and systems analysis, see Friedman, 1987.

86 From inclusion into the defense budget to keel-laying to rollout, the procurement of a nuclear-powered aircraft carrier usually takes anywhere from three to seven years, not including sea trials and shakedown. The timeline for smaller

units such as conventionally driven cruisers, destroyers, and frigates is similarly arduous. This is a marked contrast to procurements for the Army and the Air Force, where large quantities of material can be fielded comparably rapidly to achieve substantial economy-of-scale effects in RD&T and procurement.

87 In March 1982, the Congressional Budget Office issued a report which studied four options to arrive at 600 ships. Option I would attain these goals by 1992, which meant the ships would have to be endorsed and authorized no later than 1988. This was most likely the shortest period of time in which the Navy's objective could be reached. Congress could decide to accomplish the same goals, but over a longer time. Hence, Option II would expand the authorization period from six to ten years, with authorizations extending through FY 1992 and force goals substantially achieved by 1996. Option III would be a lower cost-alternative version of producing fewer ships, but one in which the kinds of warships procured would all be of the same types contained in current Navy plans. It would result in a substantially smaller fleet than Options I and II. Option IV would bring in some ship types not contained in Navy plans. It would attain numerical force levels comparable with the Navy goals at a lower cost than Options I or II (Globalsecurity. org, 2011). The report is Congressional Budget Office (1982), Building a 600-ship Navy: Cost, Timing, and Alternative Approaches. CBO: Washington, D.C. Correspondingly the same institution studied the manpower demands for a 600-ship Navy in Congressional Budget Office (1983), Manpower for a 600-ship Navy: Costs and Policy Alternatives. CBO: Washington, D.C.

88 The Congressional Research Service and the Naval History and Heritage Command apply slightly different metrics to the determination of ship inventory/ fleet size.

89 On Lehman's narrative, see Swartz's reflections (Swartz interview, 2012, 01:45:15–01:51:10). Swartz was Lehman's "Maritime Strategy" action officer from 1984.

90 Swartz, 2011b: 31, slide 61

91 The advanced, significantly improved versions of the 90,000-ton carriers are also sometimes called the *Theodore-Roosevelt*-subclass.

92 To arrive at the large number of carriers available for strike groups, some legacy platforms received service-life extension programs (SLEP) and extensive modernization in the 1980s. The decision to continue the procurement of the enhanced *Nimitz*-class carriers occurred on the basis of extensive advocacy studies by the Navy on future carrier platforms. According to one participant, no less than 43 different versions (including operational analysis) were considered at one point or another, including V/STOL, tactical and support variants, and even conversions of *Spruance*-class destroyer hulls into low-end aircraft carriers (Scott Truver interview, 2012: 00:10:40–00:15:00).

93 James Stark, interview 2012: 00:28:13–00:28:46.

94 The major technological innovations that were mature in the 1980s included the Aegis integrated naval combat system, of which the Mk-41-Vertical Launching System (VLS) was derived; the Tomahawk cruise missile, in its various versions (it gave the Navy an independent strike quality); the Harpoon ASuW missile; and the RIM-7 Sea Sparrow anti-ship/-missile missile. The 1980s contained a number of incidents such as the Falklands War Exocet attacks on British warships and the 1987/1988 missile threat for U.S. Navy ships in the Persian Gulf, which both displayed the opportunities and shortcomings of naval missiles and their respective command systems. For a detailed overview of U.S. Navy weapons systems, see Terzibaschitsch (2001).

95 Lehman, 2012.

96 Reagan, 1982.

97 Terzibaschitsch, 2002: 49–54.

98 Terzibaschitsch, 2002: 55–58 The U.S. Navy had expurgated its inventory by 1980 of old World War II and first-generation ships, paying off whole classes such as the *Forrest Sherman*-type destroyers and the three *Albany*-class guided missile cruisers (Silverstone, 2009: 70–71, 41–42).

99 The Aegis system is a totally integrated shipboard weapon system that combines computers, radars, and missiles to establish a defense umbrella for surface shipping. They system is capable of automatically detecting, tacking, and destroying airborne, seaborne, and land-launched weapons (*The Oxford Essential Dictionary of the U.S. Military*, 2002: 5).

100 Terzibaschitsch, 2002: 39–46

101 Submarines have a significant value in ASuW and against surface ships, but limited to impossible AAW capabilities. Enemy action or technological malfunctions can quickly become unit kills. Command and control limitations for submerged boats remain an operational challenge. They are also impractical for naval diplomacy. In short, submarines are useful for sea denial and strategic deterrence, but not for sea control (Grove, 1990: 132–134).

102 Terzibaschitsch, 2002: 82–97, Silverstone, 2007: 98–105.

103 Reserve forces were augmented as well. On the Ready Reserve Force (RRF) and its sister institution, the National Defense Reserve Fleet (NDRF), see Terzibaschitsch, 2002: 146–174. Since 1976, the RRF supports the rapid worldwide deployment of U.S. military forces. As a key element of strategic sealift, it primarily supports transport of Army and Marine Corps unit equipment, combat support equipment, and initial resupply during the surge period before commercial ships can be marshaled. They fall under the jurisdiction of the Maritime Administration (MARAD), management of which is overseen by DOD and DOT.

104 Swartz, 2011b: 53, slides 105–106

105 The U.S. shipping company Sea-Land Service, Inc. – now owned by Maersk – had tried to introduce [these] speedier vessels in the 1970s with SL-7 ships. They had a top speed of 33 knots, but their fuel bills wiped out any [commercial] advantage. They were soon sold to the U.S. Navy, which has more money or braver accountants.

(Rose George, Ninety Percent of Everything. Inside Shipping, the Invisible Industry that puts Clothes on your Back, Gas in your Car, and Food on Your Plate. New York, NY. Picador, 2013, 64)

106 Terzibaschitsch, 2002: 175–176.

107 Terzibaschitsch, 2002: 113–117.

108 Cited in Hattendorf, 2008: 13.

109 David F. Winkler, *Cold War at Sea. High Seas Confrontations between the United States and the Soviet Union*. Annapolis, MD. Naval Institute Press, 2000.

110 Major naval operations understood as the sustained commitment of forces engaged in expeditionary operations against a shore or a fleet. On the problem of analytical definitions, see Vego (2008: 7–39).

111 Adapted from Ryan, 1981: 182.

112 Hattendorf and Swartz, 2008: 140.

113 Robbie Harris, e-mail to author, January 27, 2014.

114 Baer, 1994: 446.

115 Hartmann, 1990: 231–234; Lehman, 2001: 302–303.

116 Lehman, 2001: 303.

117 Ibid.: 304–310.

118 A parallel attack on the French compound at Beirut at few moments later killed 58 French soldiers. Six civilians were also among the dead that day.

119   See Lehman (2001: 319–331) for an account.

120   Love, 1992b: 746.

121   Lehman, 2001: 330. These lessons learned significantly contributed to the changes in all three areas that Lehman sought to implement in the coming months and years, such as seeking innovations in naval aviation (Love, 1992a: 744–745).

122   Love, 1992b: 747.

123   President Reagan labeled him the "mad dog of the Middle East" (The President's News Conference, April 9, 1986, The American Presidency Project, www.presidency.ucsb.edu/ws/?pid=37105).

124   Lehman, 2001: 351.

125   Siegel, 1991: 43.

126   Love, 1992b: 755–768.

127   Lehman, 2001: 356.

128   Lehman, 2001: 174.

129   With the notable exception of the bombing of New York City-bound PanAm flight 103 over Lockerbie, Scotland, on December 21, 1988. Two-hundred and seventy passengers, crew, and people on the ground were killed.

130   Lehmann, 2001: 360.

131   Mirroring one of the first uses of naval force during the Reagan years, yet another Gulf of Sidra incident between U.S. jets and Libyan interceptors occurred in January 1989. Four F-14 Tomcats from *John F. Kennedy* (CV 67) engaged and shot down two MiG-23 airplanes (Love, 1992b: 768).

132   For a chronology of events, see Pemsel (2006: 1264–1270).

133   Schneller, 2007: 13.

134   Love, 1992b: 773.

135   Crist, 2012: 160–164.

136   According to Schneller the request was also addressed to the United Kingdom, China, and the Soviet Union. "It was the specter of the Soviets using the escort mission to project power into the region that finally precipitated U.S. government action" (2007: 14–15). As Love points out (1992b: 774),

> American strategy was about to be transfigured by Kuwait's diplomacy. Instead of having to fight its way to the Gulf, the Red Navy was now being invited to appear at the artery of Europe's oil supplies under the aegis of a multinational policing effort, a prospect that especially horrified [Casper] Weinberger.

When the U.S. attempted to involve NATO powers in the defense of shipping in the Gulf, the member states coldly declined because they did not seek to entangle the alliance outside of Europe. It took attacks on European-flagged commercial shipping to reverse that course partially.

137   On the problems encountered through clashes between "type A" personalities, see Love (1992b: 780–781).

138   Schneller, 2007: 16–18. "The Maritime Strategy" called for both the Atlantic and Pacific fleets to advance into well-mined Soviet waters, and so Congress was asked to authorize the construction of *Avenger*-class minesweepers in 1982 (Love, 1992b: 783) (eventually, 14 of these mine countermeasure ships were commissioned by 1994). Mines threatened to erode the otherwise high confidence of Navy planners to put all of the service's assets into harm's way.

139   See Bradley Peniston, *No Higher Honor. Saving the USS* Samuel B. Roberts *in the Persian Gulf.* Annapolis, MD. Naval Institute Press, 2006.

140   Schneller, 2007: 19.

141   Love, 1992b: 791–793.

142   Schneller, 2007: 19.

143   Ibid.: 19.

144 Cobble *et al.*, 2005: 28.
145 Swartz (1996: 48) recounts that

> press and commentators in allied countries, especially Australia, often were (or acted) shocked when they heard their country was tied in to USN maritime Strategy, which to them meant Lehman's wild ride to the Kola [Peninsula, S.B.] and nuclear provocation and escalation.

For an early push-back, see Desmond Wettern's interview/article with John Lehman (1984).
146 For a comprehensive review of "The Maritime Strategy" from a European perspective, see (Captain, Royal Navy) Gretton (1989).
147 Posen, 1982: 29.
148 Swartz, 1996: 27.
149 Baer, 1994: 433.
150 Greenland–Iceland–United Kingdom "gap."
151 Rudolf, 1990: 310. Weickhardt (1988) provides a concise discussion of the maritime and continental ramifications in the Barents Sea/Northern flank setting.
152 Swartz critically reflected the absence of arms control from "The Maritime Strategy" stating that the authors of the document understood such measures to be part of the general onslaught against the Navy by Central front advocates and supporters of détente (Swartz interview, 2012, 01:07:45–01:09:15). For a representative discussion on the arms control implications of "The Maritime Strategy," see Stefanick (1986).
153 Grove, 1990: 154.
154 Rudolf, 1990: 380–383.
155 Admiral "Ace" Lyons, who would later rise to Deputy CNO and Commander, U.S. Pacific Fleet, had commanded that exercise. He introduced new operational orders and attributed the fact that the Soviets could not find his ships using old cypher material (as it was proven four years later when the Walker spy ring was broken, there was indeed a leak and the Soviets were reading U.S. Navy communications) (Lyons interview, 2012, 00:18:00–00:21:15).
156 For a representative earlier discussion of the operational ramifications of "The Maritime Strategy" (in Northern European waters), see (VADM) Mustin (written while deployed aboard USS *America*) (1986). See also Eric Grove, *Battle for the Fjords*. Annapolis, MD. Naval Institute Press, 1991.
157 Lehman, 2001: 364.
158 Tangredi, 2002a: 125.
159 Barnett, 2009: 90.
160 Till, 1999: 252–253.
161 Lehman, 2001: 115.
162 Stallmann, 2000: 169.
163 Baer, 1994: 430.
164 Robert Komer in an interview with Peter F. Kroegh on the TV show "American Interests" (November 29, 1986).
165 It also added sealift as third component of U.S. seapower and it was flanked by the introduction of fitting platforms into the fleet (Grove, 1990: 98).
166 Swartz, 2011a: 45, slides 89–90.
167 Cropsey, 2013: 97.
168 Stallmann, 2000: 213–214.
169 Although President Reagan never signed "The Maritime Strategy," it was in line with his way of handling the presidency. He mentioned it in some speeches, which was enough as far as most of the Navy was concerned. In fact, Reagan's relative non-involvement in naval issues was a contrast to President Carter, and perhaps provided the right amount of breathing-space for the seapower ideas to

take shape. "The Maritime Strategy" dovetailed the national security directives. If it ever sought to influence and decisively shape overarching national security strategies, it failed – overtaken by the course of world events, hampered internally by transitions in high offices (and subsequent agenda-changes) and the fact that it never aspired to be such a vision.

170 Gray, 1995: 202.
171 Gray, 1995, 202.
172 Love, 1992: 716.
173 As has been pointed out before, seapower is not only a military concept to control events at sea. Moreover, it serves to influence events ashore. It controls international trade and commerce. The use of naval force in wars is subject to certain opportunities (and some limitations). Navies are instruments of diplomacy, deterrence, and political influence in situations below hot conflict (Tangredi, 2002b: 114).
174 Owens, 1999: 167.
175 Swartz, 2011b: 96, slide 192.
176 Weeks, 1992: 30.
177 After all, some of the most iconic popular culture products of the decade have a dedicated Navy component. Examples include the 1986 blockbuster movie "Top Gun" about heroic naval aviation training, starring Tom Cruise, Val Kilmer, and the score of Giorgio Moroder; Tom Clancy's debut novel "The Hunt for Red October," first published by Naval Institute Press in 1984 and subsequently turned into a successful movie (1990) starring Alec Baldwin and Sean Connery; and the 1989 hit song "If I Could Turn Back Time" by Cher, which featured a jubilant music video (the major artistic and marketing platform of the 1980s) filmed aboard the battleship *Missouri* (Bruns, 2010).
178 For a stern warning about the future of "The Maritime Strategy" from an end-of-decade perspective, see O'Rourke, 1988. The author cautions that the Navy should address the critics of the strategy or risk turning into a lucrative target for Congress and the other branches of the military, esp. in budget terms.
179 Owens, 1993: 11.
180 Cited in Grove, 1990: 159.
181 Cited in Baer, 1994: 432.
182 Haynes, 2013: 42.

References

Baer, George. *One Hundred Years of Seapower. The U.S. Navy 1890–1990*. Stanford, CA: Stanford University Press, 1994.

Ball, Desmond. "Nuclear War at Sea." *International Security* 10 (3) (1985).

Barnett, Roger. *Navy Strategic Culture: Why the Navy Thinks Differently*. Annapolis, MD: Naval Institute Press (NIP), 2009.

Barnett, Roger. "The Maritime-Continental Debate Isn't Over." *U.S. Naval Institute Proceedings* 113(6) (June 1987).

Barnett, Roger. "The Origins of the US Maritime Strategy (Part II)." *Naval Forces* 10(5) (1989): 58–60, 62.

Bierling, Stephan. *Geschichte der amerikanischen Außenpolitik. Von 1917 bis zur Gegenwart*. München: C.H. Beck, 2003.

Brooks, Linton. "Naval Power and National Security: The Case for the Maritime Strategy." *International Security* 11(2) (1986): 58–88.

Bruns, Sebastian. "Zwischen Top Gun und Homer Simpson: Die US-Navy und die Populärkultur." *MarineForum* 10/2010 (2010): 51–53.

Cable, James. *Navies in Violent Peace*. Basingstoke, UK: Palgrave Macmillan, 1989.

Cobble, Eugene, Gaffrey, H.H., and Gorenburg, Dmitry. *For the Record: All U.S. Forces' Responses to Situations, 1970–2000 (with Additions Covering 2000–2003)*. Alexandria, VA: CNA, 2005.

Collins, John. .*Military Strategy: Principles, Practices, and Historical Perspectives*. Washington, D.C.: Brassey's, 2002.

Congressional Budget Office. *Building a 600-Ship Navy: Cost, Timing, and Alternative Approaches*. Washington, D.C.:GPO, 1982.

Congressional Budget Office. *Manpower for a 600-Ship Navy: Costs and Policy Alternatives*. Washington, D.C.:GPO, 1983.

Crist, David. *The Twilight War: The Secret History of America's Thirty-Year Conflict with Iran*. New York: Penguin Press, 2012.

Cropsey, Seth. *Mayday. The Decline of American Naval Supremacy*. New York and London: Overlook Duckworth, 2013.

Department of the Navy, Office of Program Appraisal (DON/OPA). "Lessons of the Falklands. Summary Report, February 1983." Washington, D.C.: DON, 1983.

Dunn, Keith, and Staudenmaier, William. *Strategic Implications of the Continental-Maritime Debate*, Washington, D.C.: Center for Strategic and International Studies, 1984.

Ford, Christopher, and Rosenberg, David. "The Naval Intelligence Underpinnings of Reagan's Maritime Strategy." *The Journal of Strategic Studies* 28(2) (2005): 379–409.

Friedman, Norman, "The Maritime Strategy and the Design of the U.S. Fleet." *Comparative Strategy* 6(4) (1987): 415–435.

George, Rose. *Ninety Percent of Everything. Inside Shipping, the Invisible Industry that puts Clothes on your Back, Gas in your Car, and Food on Your Plate*. New York, NY. Picador, 2013.

Globalsecurity.org (ed.). "Surface Warfare Shipbuilding." 2011. www.globalsecurity. org/military/systems/ship/scn-surface.htm.

Gray, Colin."The Maritime Strategy is Not New." *U.S. Naval Institute Proceedings*, 116(1) (1990).

Gray, Colin. "Sea Power for Containment: The U.S. Navy in the Cold War." *Navies & Global Defense. Theories and Strategy*, eds. K. Nelson and E.J. Errington. Westport, CT: Praeger, 1995, 181–207.

Gretton, M.P. "The American Maritime Strategy: European Perspectives and Implications," *Royal United Services Institute for Defence Studies Journal* 134(1) (1989).

Grove, Eric. *The Future of Sea Power*. London: Routledge, 1990.

Hacke, Christian. *Zur Weltmacht verdammt. Die amerikanische Außenpolitik von J.F. Kennedy bis G.W. Bush*. 3. Auflage, aktualisierte Neuausgabe, München: Ullstein, 2005.

Haig, Alexander. *Caveat. Realism, Reagan, and Foreign Policy*. New York, NY: Scribd, 1984.

Hammel, Eric. *The Marines in Beirut, August 1982-February 1984*. Minneapolis, MI: Zenith Press, 2005.

Harris, Robbie, Captain United States Navy (retired). Via Skype from Kiel, 18 October 2012, 01hr 38min.*

Hartmann, Frederic. *Naval Renaissance: The U.S. Navy in the 1980's*. Annapolis, MD: NIP, 1990.

Hattendorf, John, ed. *The Evolution of the U.S. Navy's Maritime Strategy, 1977–1986*. Newport, RI: Naval War College Press, 2004.

Hattendorf, John, and Swartz, Peter, eds. *U.S. Naval Strategy in the 1980s*. Newport, RI: Naval War College Press, 2008.

Haynes, Peter. *American Naval Thinking in the Post-Cold War Era: The U.S. Navy and the Emergence of a Maritime Strategy, 1989–2007* (dissertation, Naval Postgraduate School, Monterey, CA, 2013.

Hennessy, Peter, and Kinks, James. *The Silent Deep. The Royal Navy Submarine Service since 1945*. London, Penguin Books, 2015.

Hoffmann, David. "Shattered Shield: 'I had a funny feeling in my gut,'" *Washington Post*, February 10, 1999.

Keller, Patrick. *Neokonservatismus und amerikanische Außenpolitik. Ideen, Krieg und Strategie von Ronald Reagan bis George W. Bush*. Paderborn: Schöningh, 2008.

Komer, Robert. *Maritime Strategy or Coalition Defense?* Lanham, MD: Rowman & Littlefield, 1984.

Komer, Robert. "A Conversation on U.S. Maritime Strategy with Peter Kroegh on 'The American Interest.'" 1986.

Lehman, John. *Command of the Seas*. 2nd ed. Annapolis, MD: NIP, 2001.

Lehman, John. "Reflections on the Special Relationship." *Naval History Magazine*, 26(5) (October 2012).

Love, Robert. *History of the U.S. Navy, Volume I: 1775–1941*. Mechanicsburg, PA: Stackpole, 1992a.

Love, Robert. *History of the U.S. Navy, Volume II: 1942–1991*. Mechanicsburg, PA: Stackpole, 1992b.

Lyons, Jim "Ace," Vice Admiral United States Navy (retired). Washington, D.C., September 21, 2012, 01 hr 28 min.

Marolda, Edward. *Ready Seapower. A History of the U.S. Seventh Fleet*. Washington, D.C.: NHHC, 2012.

Mearsheimer, John. "A Strategic Misstep: The Maritime Strategy and the Deterrence in Europe." *International Security* 11(2) (1986).

Meinhart, Richard. "National Military Strategies: A Historical Perspective, 1990 to 2012." *U.S. Army War College Guide to National Security Issues, Volume II. National Security Policy and Strategy*, 5th edition, ed. B. Bartholomees. U.S. Army War College: Carlisle, PA, 2012

Michishita, Narushige, Swartz, Peter M., and Winkler, David F. *Lessons of the Cold War in the Pacific: U.S. Maritime Strategy, Crisis Prevention, and Japan's Role*. Washington, D.C. Wilson Center, 2016.

Middlebrook, Martin. *The Falklands War, 1982*. London: Penguin, 2001.

O'Rourke, Ronald. "The Maritime Strategy and the Next Decade." *U.S. Naval Institute Proceedings* 114(4) (April 1988): 34–8.

Owens, Mackubin. "Toward a Maritime Grand Strategy: Paradigm for a New Security Environment." *Strategic Review (Spring 1993)* (1993): 7–19.

Owens, Mackubin "U.S. Maritime Strategy and the Cold War." *Mysteries of the Cold War*, ed. S. Cimbala. Aldershot, UK: Asghate 1999.

The Oxford Essential Dictionary of the U.S. Military. New York, NY: Oxford University Press, 2002.

Palmer, Michael. *Origins of the Maritime Strategy: American Naval Strategy in the First Postwar Decade*. Washington, D.C.: Naval Historical Center, 1988.

Pemsel, Helmut. *Seeherrschaft (III). Seekriege und Seepolitik von 1914 bis 2006*. Wien/Graz, Austria: Neuer Wissenschaftlicher Verlag/Köhler 2006 (= Weltgeschichte der Seefahrt, Vol. 7).

Peniston, Bradley. *No Higher Honor. Saving the USS* Samuel B. Roberts *in the Persian Gulf.* Annapolis, MD. NIP, 2006.

Potter, E.B., and Nimitz, Chester. "Die Sowjet-Union wird Seemacht." *Seemacht. Eine Seekriegsgeschichte von der Antike bis zur Gegenwart,* eds. E.B. Potter/C.W. Nimitz. Deutsche Fassung herausgegeben im Auftrag des Arbeitskreises für Wehrforschung von Jürgen Rohwer. Herrsching: Pawlak, 1982.

Prados, John. "The Navy's Biggest Betrayal." *Naval History* 24(3) (May 2010).

Reagan, Ronald. "Remarks at the Annual Convention of the National Association of Evangelicals in Orlando, Florida, 8 March 1983." 1983.

Reagan, Ronald. "Remarks on East-West Relations at the Brandenburg Gate in West-Berlin, 12 June 1987." 1987.

Reagan, Ronald. "Remarks at the Recommissioning Ceremony for the U.S.S. *New Jersey* in Long Beach, California. 28 December 1982." 1982.

Rudolf, Peter. *Amerikanische Seemachtpolitik und maritime Rüstungskontrolle unter Carter und Reagan.* Frankfurt am Main, Germany: Campus, 1990.

Ryan, Paul. *First Line of Defense: The U.S. Navy Since 1945.* Stanford, CA: Hoover Institution Press, 1981.

Schild, Georg. *1983. Das gefährlichste Jahr des Kalten Krieges.* Paderborn *et al.*: Schöningh, 2013.

Schneller, Robert. *Anchor of Resolve: A History of U.S. Naval Force Central Command/ Fifth Fleet.* Washington, D.C.: NHHC, 2007.

Siegel, Adam. *The Use of Naval Forces in the Post-War Era: U.S. Navy and U.S. Marine Corps Crisis Response Activity, 1946–1990.* Alexandria, VA: CNA, 1991.

Silverstone, Paul. *The Navy of the Nuclear Age, 1947–2007.* London: Routledge 2009 (The U.S. Navy Warship Series, vol. 5).

Snider, Don. The *National Security Strategy. Documenting Strategic Vision.* 2nd edition. Carlisle, PA: Strategic Studies Institute, 1995.

Stallmann, Wilfried. *Die maritime Strategie der USA nach 1945: Entwicklung, Einflussgrößen und Auswirkungen auf das atlantische Bündnis.* Dissertation, University of Kiel, Germany, 2000.

Stark, James, Rear Admiral United States Navy (retired). Washington Navy Yard, Washington, D.C., September 5, 2012, 01 hr 41 min.

Stefanick, Tom. "America's Maritime Strategy–The Arms Control Implications." *Arms Control Today* 16(9) (September 1986).

Swartz, Peter, Captain United States Navy (retired). Washington Navy Yard, Washington, D.C., September 7, 2012, 03 hr 27 min.

Swartz, Peter. *The Maritime Strategy of the 1980s: Threads, Strands and Line* (dissertation draft, Alexandria, VA, 1996).

Swartz, Peter. *A Short History of the U.S. Navy in the Cold War (1945–1990): Strategy and Operations* (unpublished draft paper, Alexandria, VA, 2014).

Swartz, Peter, and Duggan, Karin. *The U.S. Navy in the World (1981–1990): Context for U.S. Navy Capstone Strategies and Concepts* (slideshow). Alexandria, VA: CNA, 2011a.

Swartz, Peter, and Duggan, Karin. *U.S. Navy Capstone Strategies and Concepts (1981–1990): Strategy, Policy, Concept, and Vision Documents* (slideshow). Alexandria, VA: CNA, 2011b.

Tangredi, Sam, ed. *Globalization and Maritime Power.* Washington, D.C.: NDU Press, 2002a.

Tangredi, Sam, ed ."*Sea Power Theory and Practice*": Strategy in the Contemporary World. *An Introduction to Strategic Studies*, 1st edition, eds. J. Baylis, J. Wirtz, E. Cohen, and C. Gray. Oxford, UK: Oxford University Press 2002b.

Terzibaschitsch, Stefan. *Kampfsysteme der U.S. Navy: Waffen und Elektronik auf amerikanischen Kriegsschiffen.* Hamburg, Germany: Koehler, 2001.

Terzibaschitsch, Stefan. *Die Schiffe der U.S. Navy.* Hamburg, Germany: Koehler, 2002.

Till, Geoffrey. "Die Ursprünge des maritimen Verhaltens der Großmächte: Die Zeit des Kalten Kriegs und die Jahre danach." *Seemacht und Seestrategie im 19. und 20. Jahrhundert,* ed. J. Duppler. Hamburg: Mittler & Sohn 1999 (= Vorträge zur Militärgeschichte, Volume 18, distributed by the Militärgeschichtliches Forschungsamt), 241–264.

Thompson, Leroy. Naval *Operations in Support of the U.S. Counterdrug Policy.* Carlisle, PA: U.S. Army War College, 1999.

Truver, Scott. Washington Navy Yard, Washington, D.C., September 10, 2012, 01 hr 50 min.

Vego, Milan. *Major Naval Operations.* Newport, RI: Naval War College Press, 2008.

Watkins, James. "The Maritime Strategy." *U.S. Naval Institute Proceedings* 112(1) (January 1986).

Weeks, Stan. "Crafting a New Maritime Strategy." *U.S. Naval Institute Proceedings,* 118(1) (January 1992): 30–7.

Weickhardt, George. "U.S. Maritime Strategy and Continental Options." *Strategic Review* 16(4) (April 1988).

Wettern, Desmond. "US Naval Strategy. Problems of Allies—and Enemies." *Navy International* 89(8) (August 1984).

The White House. "National Security Decision Directive Number 32, National Security Strategy." Washington, D.C.: The White House, 1982.

Winkler, David F. *Cold War at Sea. High Seas Confrontations between the United States and the Soviet Union.* Annapolis, MD. NIP, 2000.

Woodward, Sandy, and Robinson, Patrick. *One-Hundred Days. The Memoirs of the Falklands Battle Group Commander.* London: Harper, 2012.

5 Managing strategic change and embracing a new world order (1989–2001)

The powerful images of the fall of the Berlin Wall on November 9, 1989 hold their place as an iconic and peaceful transition of the twentieth century. The rapid and revolutionary disintegration of the East German regime triggered a process that quickly led to Germany's unification. Conquest of the symbol of the Iron Curtain notwithstanding, the end of superpower conflict was a process that began much earlier than 1989. Likewise, it did not end that night in Berlin, but perhaps more precisely with the formal dissolution of the Soviet Union on December 26, 1991.[1]

These political events had historic military and geostrategic ramifications. The U.S. Navy suddenly neither a peer naval competitor nor a superior maritime adversary; further, a credible naval adversary could not be discerned in the foreseeable future.[2] Other real-world events – some associated, others unconnected to the unraveling of the Soviet empire – continued to demand the attention of senior policy and military decision-makers. For the U.S. Navy, the lasting relevance and indeed growing importance of sea power under the American umbrella in the emerging post-Cold War world order needed fresh assessment. These results needed to be channeled and transformed into applicable capstone documents which reflected the increasing consolidation of the defense establishment into a growing joint and efficiency-driven system, but it was far from clear what that would look like.

In the past – during the World Wars and the late Cold War – enemy submarines, surface, and naval aviation (even if they resumed the form of defensive and partial sea control only) threatened the survival of U.S. military and commercial shipping, access, and political influence in times of crises. By implication, American power was potentially inhibited. The U.S. Navy therefore had for decades invested considerable financial and intellectual resources into a force designed to meet and also rise above that naval threat. When the Soviet Union faded away from the world stage, it took with it the powerful blue-water navy that Moscow had maintained. Most of the niche-capability Warsaw Pact naval assets, principally directed against American and allied ships, submarines, and aircraft, went with it. Consequently, U.S. Navy leaders almost immediately faced hard questions in Washington as to what its role and functions were in the future against less maritime capable yet politically assertive targets.

At the core of the debate was the question of just how much the future development of naval forces would cost.[3] Once again, the Navy was tasked with verbalizing an institutional expectation about what the next war would look like and how it would be won by a significant contribution of American sea power. The Navy needed to unify for a multi-front campaign against Congress, the White House, and the other branches of the military. Mindful of Huntington's 1954 warning that a military service needed a strategic concept in order to make sense to itself and to the public, successive Navy declaratory capstone documents went about seeking to explain the broad purpose for American security and the future development of the service.

Prelude

On August 2, 1990, President George Bush, Sr., gave a much-noticed speech in Aspen, Colorado. His address focused on emerging new geopolitical conditions and reflected the president's desire to drastically re-shape U.S. military posture. Acknowledging that the danger of a Soviet-led invasion of Western Europe was remote with Warsaw Pact forces in a rapid decline and withdrawal, Bush proclaimed that it mattered how the U.S. reshaped its forces so that they could still exercise forward presence, crisis response, and surge capability. The president warned against cuts across the board and challenged his audience to conceptualize the future force.[4]

In other words, the president called for a makeover of the U.S. military (a top-down approach designed to leave no stone unturned). At the time, the military, especially the USN, maintained a peacetime forward presence in Europe, the Pacific, the Mediterranean, and the Persian Gulf. It was designed for crisis response and surge ability. It retained an edge in developing and fielding advanced weapon technology.

Although the country continued to hedge against a potential renaissance of Soviet-style large-scale conflict, the President announced a comprehensive restructuring of its all-volunteer forces over a period of five years. Bush's speech came at a very peculiar time. On the same day he spoke in the Rocky Mountain resort town, halfway around the world Iraq invaded its neighbor Kuwait. That was precisely the sort of regional contingency, unrelated to the U.S.-Soviet relationship but affecting U.S. national interests that Bush had described as a consequential national security issue in the post-Cold War era. Within days, the U.S. decided to deploy troops to the Persian Gulf to guard Saudi-Arabia against continued Iraqi military aggression, then to expel Saddam Hussein's troops from oil-rich Kuwait. Seeking the imprimatur of the international community, the administration also deliberately involved the United Nations.[5] Bush's Aspen speech signaled the dawn of a new decade, and the events of that day – Bush's rhetoric, his ideas on restructuring the military, and the Iraqi aggression against Kuwait – set a defining tone for the early 1990s.

In an address before a joint session of Congress on September 11, 1990, the President underscored his thinking using the notion of an emerging "New World Order."[6] He lobbied heavily for his course of action in the Persian Gulf region, one viewing the U.S. Navy once more engaged in Middle East waters. Strategically the Navy, whose highest-ranking officer, the CNO, in May 1990 had still defended "The Maritime Strategy" of the 1980s, stood before the idea's wreckage. Just as the president outlined a drastically different "New World Order," the Navy declared to the public (and itself) that its policy was "Steady as she goes". Haynes unapologetically concludes that, "'The Maritime Strategy' was too tainted and too rooted in the past to be of much use in an environment in which only self-proclaimed 'new' ideas could be assured a hearing."[7]

U.S. Navy strategy 1989–2001: the macro level

At the outset of the first post–Cold War decade, precisely because the antagonist was gone, the U.S. Navy was not necessarily out of business. With the end of the Cold War, the perpetual threat of quick, decisive global nuclear war, and mutually assured destruction had receded.[8] It was replaced by a more regional nuclear threat and the world suddenly looked much different.[9] Colin Gray notes that,

> [t]he demise of one of the superpowers eliminate[d] for a while the most nominally persuasive of threats to the strategic utility of sea power: the peril of a war so brief and destructive that sea power's enabling action would be short-circuited.[10]

In other words, naval forces could now be more important than ever because they offered a variety of missions beyond pure ship-on-ship combat or nuclear deterrence. As Lundesgaard points out, it is the naval forces' "ability to exploit the international commons, their mobility and their status as symbols of power that make them useful for anything from diplomatic missions to a full-scale naval battle between peer competitors."[11] The demise of the Soviet Union brought a "unipolar moment"[12] opening a window of opportunity for the politically triumphant U.S. to remake the post–Cold War order. Small-scale contingencies would become more important than ever.[13]

The fundamental change of an ocean without a rival eventually forced the U.S. Navy to undertake a significant strategic alteration in its culture and outlook. It was a rare moment of "top-down" revolution brought about by a systemic shift making obsolete many of the convictions it held dear. While shifting geopolitics creates new policy challenges and potentially new military adversaries, twentieth-century navies remained technology-based, manpower, and capital-intensive organizations which could not be transformed quickly, and whose basic employment requires a great deal of time and effort to master.[14] The question became how to reorient the service.

The new threefold challenge, therefore, consisted of (a) the short-term goal of assessing how rapidly the old Cold War military threats were declining to draw down forces rationally, (b) the medium-term test of assessing the residual military threat and crafting an overarching policy to address it, and (c) the long-term task of defining what manner of military threat might force the U.S. to reconstitute all or some part of the military-industrial base it was planning to disassemble.[15] At the same time, it was by no means clear what this unraveling world order would look like: a "clash of civilizations," (as Samuel Huntington outlined in 1993), the "end of history" (as Francis Fukuyama suggested in 1989), or a murky, undistinguishable mixture of different futures?

Global trends and challengers to U.S. security

The bipolar order of the Cold War was replaced by a consolidating and increasingly economically interdependent system that had emerged slowly over the past decades and now integrated fiercely. As CNO Trost noted in an article, "Global economic interdependence is a fact of life."[16] This proclaimed condition yielded an increasingly tightly knit community of market economies. Presumably, nations from the former Second and Third World (the Warsaw Pact and the non-aligned developing nations, respectively) were freed from the shackles of their history. They could improve their societies and economies with better competitiveness and a larger degree of assimilation in global markets. As a dominant economic world power, the United States could embrace the increasing globalization of goods and services.[17]

From the moral high ground after "winning" the Cold War, to the U.S. it appeared that advancement of democratic systems would benefit everyone. This was first outlined by the support of the Bush administration for democratization processes in Eastern Europe after the end of the Soviet Union. Later, under President Bill Clinton, this post-containment policy was expanded. The new strategy was coined in a speech that Anthony Lake (Clinton's National Security Advisor) gave on September 21, 1993 in Washington, D.C. In his remarks titled "From Containment to Enlargement," Lake outlined four aspects of the emerging U.S. grand strategy: the strengthening of the community of large market democracies, the help and support for new democracies and market economies, the countering of aggressive states hostile to democracy and markets, and pursuing a humanitarian agenda that anchored the liberalist market ideas in regions of concern. Lake cautioned that this should be done pragmatically and carefully, and to include NATO.[18]

As a symbol of the prospects and promises of globalization, maritime trade grew. The triumph of the 20-foot equivalent unit (TEU) shipping container enabled the increasingly economic usage of the seas for just-in-time transport and delivery. The growth in maritime trade underlined the indispensable economic dimension of sea power: maritime highways, which often passed through choke points, require sustained investments in their safety and security. According to this line of thinking, safe and stable conditions ashore enable the security of adjacent shipping lanes. Consequently, the protection of sea lines of communication (Mahan's classic notion) was broadened and redefined, outlining an old, but potentially vastly expanded field of activity for naval forces. Globalization of goods and services, in other words, also offered a flip side: the globalization of challengers and dangers no longer confined to a particular country or military pact.

Overseas, a 1991 *coup d'état* in the USSR, still under the Soviet Red Star, attempted to displace Mikhail Gorbachev. His eventual successor Boris Yeltsin fended off a constitutional crisis in 1993 and engaged in desperate attempts to halt the disintegration of the country, for example, by military intervention in Chechnya (1994). These changes did not alter the Navy's challenges.

The dissolution of the Soviet Union posed the immediate risk of transferring nuclear weapons and related material from the newly independent former Soviet republics back to Moscow, to dismantle them on-site, and to contain proliferation of radioactive material and other Soviet legacy technology to rogue states. These states – Iran, Iraq, North Korea, Libya, Syria, Sudan, or Afghanistan – kept the United States busy throughout the decade. Some of these countries had benefited from Soviet economic and military support throughout the Cold War, for example diesel-electric coastal submarines, capable missile boats, mines, or anti-ship rockets. On the high end, more and more countries acquired ballistic missile capabilities; the People's Republic of China, North Korea, Iran, India, and Pakistan come to mind.[19] In East Asia, China slowly emerged as a maritime player in the region, at first expanding its small coastal defense fleet to a more blue-water oriented offshore navy. Maritime incidents throughout the decade in the South China Sea and the Taiwan Strait signaled Beijing's growing assertiveness. In 1998, under a cover-up, it acquired the derelict Soviet aircraft carrier *Varyag* to underline its quest for maritime reach.

Absent a significant threat to U.S. (and indeed, global) survival, a spotlight turned on emerging civil wars, some of which had smoldered for the duration of the Cold War. Terrorism, organized crime, and climate change gained in importance as national security concerns. Natural disasters and related famines, refugee waves, and other humanitarian catastrophes often provided an impetus for U.S./Western consideration and involvement. Organized crime infiltrated many parts of societies around the world, and modern piracy (chiefly in Southeast Asia around the Strait of Malacca for the time being) slowly moved into focus. Although the 1980s had seen a significant rise in the number and quality of terrorist acts, the 1990s featured some lethal incidents as well.[20] The terrorist network Al-Qaida emerged as a major facilitator of attacks against U.S. targets. It stood behind the 1993 bombing of the World Trade Center in New York. Five years later, two nearly simultaneous explosions directed against the U.S. embassies in Kenya and Tanzania on August 7, 1998 killed 224 and wounded more than 4,000 others. Finally, on October

12, 2000, at 11:18 a.m. in the Yemeni port of Aden, suicide bombers detonated an explosive-laden boat directly against the port side of the guided-missile destroyer *Cole* (DDG 67). The resulting blast tore a large hole in the ship's hull, killed 17 sailors, and wounded 37 others.[21]

In summary, with the threat of nuclear annihilation as a factor in national survival gone, grand strategy was increasingly defined in a broad and comprehensive sense. The territorial perception of security and resulting way of warfare were eclipsed by a more diffuse, elusive, and transnational nature of events and threats.

Conflicts, crises, and wars

The major conflicts, crises, and wars of the decade reflected such challenges. The U.S. intervention in Panama in December 1989, in the shadows of the geostrategic events in progress in Central and Eastern Europe, was a relatively minor incursion.[22] It was a different case with the Gulf War. "Operation Desert Shield," mounted after the Iraqi invasion of Kuwait on August 2, 1990, and "Operation Desert Storm" (the offensive action from January 1991 to expel Saddam Hussein's force from the sheikdom in accordance with United Nations resolutions and as a part of an allied coalition effort) were the first larger post-Cold War military operations. The Gulf War had obvious strategic ramifications. It featured clear regional aggression and incursion by a rogue power into a neighbor's territory; it occurred in a world region of supreme strategic interest regarding resources; and former Cold War adversaries and a reunited Germany participated (to various degrees) on the same allied side.

In another expedition to buttress the "New World Order," U.S. troops were ordered into Somalia in 1992 to contain a civil war, which broke out after the demission of Somali dictator Mohamed Siad Barre in 1991. The images of human suffering on the Horn of Africa were picked up by international media, generated public interest and concern, and eventually triggered a series of U.N.-led operations. Images of U.S. Marines wading ashore in Somalia unopposed were widespread, but at the same time created a mounting expectation for an equally smooth and swift military operation. As the events unfolded, this was not the case. In what became known as the Battle of Mogadishu, U.S. and allied forces fought Somali militia particularly viciously on October 3 and 4, 1993. The operation – a tactical draw but a strategic U.S. defeat of the kind that the United States had not witnessed since the Vietnam Tet Offensive (1968) – was aborted. The gruesome media coverage of fallen American soldiers being dragged through the streets of Mogadishu unsettled the American public.[23] This contributed to the U.S. decision not to intervene in the equally bloody genocide in Rwanda in 1994, where ethnic Hutus murdered hundreds of thousands of ethnic Tutsis. American inability to contain the Somali civil war shaped the global perception of U.S. military capabilities and informed skepticism regarding the American political will to accept casualties. Not unlike the U.S. policy after the Beirut barracks bombing of 1983, such perception can empower an adversary's opinions and policies to undermine American leadership. In the harsh assessment of Haynes, Somalia was therefore nothing less than "a fiasco, a geopolitical knockdown, and a nightmare for Clinton."[24]

The new president inherited a number of regional crises when he took office in January 1993, including Somalia. Bill Clinton's activist foreign policy sought to reframe the understanding of and approach to security and national defense. Consequently, American military engagement in the armed conflicts of the decade remained selective and heterogeneous at best. The 1990s, in essence, witnessed a series of crises and smaller (but often protracted) wars. None of them occurred against a global challenger to fundamental U.S. security interests. Each crisis therefore had assessment on its own merits by American policy and strategic leaders. Clinton came into office focused on the economy and not necessarily on international security. In principle, he was an inward-looking, domestic president who relied on advisors to make and shape foreign policy. The emerging global security environment was outlined comprehensively in an article by Secretary of Defense Les Aspin in the February 1993 issue of "The Officer" Magazine. The list, reprinted in a work by two Chinese authors[25] is characterized by its remarkable foresight (although the aspects of the strategic environment naturally were broad). To date, it provides the basis for many discussions on contemporary national security challenges. The changes in the geopolitical environment were so fundamental they necessitated a fresh look at the threats they produced and, in turn, their implications for the use of U.S. military force. Aspin's observations implied nothing less than a fundamentally challenging strategic environment and military mindset (Table 5.1).

This was the context U.S. leaders confronted in the early 1990s. Some of these aspects were amplified over the decade while others receded in importance and impact.

Personalities, domestic conditions, and national security strategies

Presidents, secretaries, and policy/strategy leaders

President George Bush Senior, 41st President of the United States, oscillated between more assertive grand strategic aspirations of a new world order and the immediate task at hand: managing the post-Cold War transition.[26] As his secretary of defense, Bush chose Richard ("Dick") Cheney, who had come to Washington in 1969 on an American Political Science Association fellowship. He was a Washington insider and, by all accounts, a hardliner. Cheney, a former congressman and staffer in the Nixon and Ford White House administrations, oversaw the re-setting of the course and posture of U.S. defense policy after the end of the Cold War. As secretary of state, Bush

Table 5.1 Old and new security environment[27]

1. In regard to the geopolitical environment

Old security environment	New security environment
Bipolar (rigid)	Multipolar (complex)
Predictable	Uncertain
Communism	Nationalism and religious extremism
U.S. the number one Western power	U.S. only the number one military power
Permanent alliances	Temporary alliances
A paralyzed United Nations	A dynamic United Nations

2. In regard to threats faced by the U.S.

Old security environment	New security environment
Single (Soviet)	Diverse
Threat to U.S. survival	Threat to U.S. interests
Clear	Unclear
Deterrable	Non-deterrable
Europe-centered	Other regions
High risk of escalation	Little risk of escalation
Use of strategic nuclear weapons	Terrorist using nuclear weapons
Overt	Covert

3. In regard to the use of military force

Old security environment	New security environment
Attrition warfare	Decisive attacks on key targets
War by proxy	Direct reinforcement
Reliance primarily on high technology	Integrated use of high, medium, and low technology
Forward deployed	Power projection
Forward based	Home based
Host nation support	Reliance on own strength

nominated James Baker (1989–1992) who was later succeeded by Lawrence Eagleburger (1992–1993). Baker, a reserve Marine, was instrumental in leading State Department support of German reunification, management of the Soviet Union's disintegration, and the Gulf War. The military coalition in that war would have been unattainable without his diligence.[28] His successor Eagleburger (the only career diplomat to advance to the top of the State Department) had a considerably shorter track record. The disintegration of Yugoslavia dominated his time in office.

In the Pentagon, the national security team was complemented by Secretary of the Navy Henry L. Garrett. Less vocal about strategic matters than the CNO, Garrett resigned in June 1992 after three years in office following an investigation of the "Tailhook '91" scandal.[29] The scandal unseated the

Navy's strategic culture. It fueled internal distortions and prompted social changes that affected the service throughout the remainder of the decade. Garrett's (acting) successor for the remainder of the Bush Sr. presidency (1992–1993) was Sean O'Keefe, a former Congressional staffer and Pentagon analyst. Service secretaries and CNOs throughout the 1990s spent a considerable time righting the public image and internal well-being of the Navy after "Tailhook," but the scandal became emblematic for a hollowed-out, morally discredited, and macho military service in disarray.[30]

Admiral Frank Kelso III was appointed as Chief of Naval Operations, following the more strategically versed Carlisle Trost. Kelso served as CNO from June 1990 to April 1994, was the third submariner in a row in the position, and was a product of early career-specialization under Admiral Rickover. He had participated in developing and testing "The Maritime Strategy" as a flag officer. In one of his previous commands, the U.S. Sixth Fleet, he oversaw combat operations against Libya in 1986. Kelso was an honest and pragmatic but hardly an ambitious leader. His major task was to unambiguously transition the service to a post-Cold War design. In his view, that called for new policies, but not a whole new strategy.

The most important strategic leader of the Bush years in the military realm was arguably General Colin Powell (USA), Chairman of the Joint Chiefs of Staff. By utilizing the provisions laid out in the Goldwater-Nichols Act, the general was turning the Pentagon's decision-making process on its head. To hedge against coming post-Cold War draw-downs and budget cuts, Powell decisively changed the process by which U.S. strategy was determined. Instead of global conflict with the Soviet Union, the emerging security to-do list included now a stronger emphasis of presence, crisis response, and regional (limited) conflict missions for the military. This was a far-reaching shift, flanked by a notable desire in Congress to obtain reduced spending on a considerably smaller military – a "peace dividend." This amounted to a force and strategy determined by the Congressional budget instead of the other way around. Aware of the legislative branch's desires, Powell attempted to retain the existing institutional balance between the armed services and to avoid an indiscriminate dilution of rational strategic objectives. In such a strategic and diplomatic approach, Powell clearly outshone the service chiefs and secretaries.[31] He utilized the power granted to him as the principal military advisor to the President, and aimed to provide integrated, joint strategic direction of his own (he lacked faith that presidential guidance or service planning would be effective in downscaling U.S. defense posture rationally). The price for his approach was that seemingly non-integrated service concepts such as "The Maritime Strategy" were dropped in favor of strategic planning from the Joint Staff.

The 1992 presidential elections brought William J. "Bill" Clinton into the White House, signaling a generational change in the American presidency. As his running mate, Clinton selected Senator Albert "Al" Gore of Tennessee. Gore had been a soldier in Vietnam and had some expertise in foreign affairs (and unsuccessfully ran for President in 1988 and again in 2000). The Clinton administration replaced containment of the Soviet Union with a strategy of enlargement and political-economic engagement built on the idea that mutually connected, prospering nations would not aspire to regional hegemony and become threats or challenges to the U.S. Clinton's first national security strategy linked national and global prosperity with geostrategic values of market-based democracy.[32]

This hardly altruistic approach broadened and strengthened existing alliances such as NATO, while retaining American leadership and military contingency planning in nuclear and conventional terms. It included opening new avenues of cooperation with countries around the world (such as NATO's Partnership for Peace [PfP] with Central-Eastern Europe) and in the near neighborhood, such as the trilateral North American Free Trade Agreement (NAFTA) among Canada, the United States, and Mexico (1994). Clinton's approach also pointed to the concept of military intervention on humanitarian grounds, should American values demand so.[33]

As his Secretary of Defense, Clinton selected Les Aspin, a Representative from Wisconsin and former chairman of the House Committee on Armed Services (HASC). Aspin faced a number of daunting military policy challenges after he joined the administration, including the role of women and homosexuals in the military, the posture of the force, the size of the defense budget, and the perennial closing of military bases throughout the country and abroad. The Navy anxiously awaited the results of Aspin's decisions. In his confirmation hearing before the Senate Armed Services Committee (SASC) on January 15, 1993, he stated that U.S. naval forces

> should be sized and shaped not only for armed conflict, but also for the many other important tasks we call upon them to do. Forward presence is certainly a key ingredient, along with such missions as peacekeeping, humanitarian assistance, deterrence and crisis control.[34]

Aspin faced growing pressure during the foreign policy crises of 1993, cumulating in the embarrassing defeat of U.S. forces in the Battle of Mogadishu. He stepped down after just one year at the helm of the Department of Defense.

His successor was William Perry, an experienced businessman and defense policy insider, who served from 1994 to 1997. His idea of a preventive defense sought to avert threats from emerging in the first place, but if that failed, to deter and if need be to fight decisively using military force. Geographically, this pulled the military forward. Like his predecessors, Perry was confronted with a host of post-Cold War crises abroad as well as on the home front. Increasingly frustrated with the Republican-controlled House of Representatives, after Clinton's reelection, Perry was succeeded by William Cohen, an experienced Republican Senator from Maine who stayed until 2001. As Secretary of Defense, Cohen had to deal with the Kosovo War, cruise missile strikes against Iraq, the U.S. embassy bombings in Africa, and the terrorist attack on the destroyer USS *Cole* in Yemen. Clinton's Department of State was led by Warren Christopher during the first term (1993–1997) and Madeleine Albright, the first female U.S. Secretary of State, from 1997 to 2001. Christopher, a lawyer from California who had served the Johnson and Carter administrations, managed the broad, diffuse challenges that the United States faced in the early 1990s. Albright held a PhD in Political Science from Columbia University and had previously served as U.S. ambassador to the United Nations. Her experience in international diplomacy endeared her to Clinton. The Balkans and Iraq remained focal points of her time in office.[35]

From 1993 to 1998, the Navy Department was headed by Secretary of the Navy John H. Dalton. A businessman with a five-year career on active duty in the Navy as a nuclear submarine officer, Dalton came into public office just as the Navy was recovering from the fallout of the "Tailhook" scandal. For the remainder of his service, he concentrated on managing that embarrassment. He also dealt with issues arising from the further integration of women into the Navy (Bowman, 1998). His immediate focus on smoothing and integrating the service culture is emblematic of Dalton's unwillingness to engage in a larger strategic vision. He left the office after five years, a long period for a Secretary of the Navy, and was replaced by Richard Danzig, his Undersecretary of the Navy. Danzig was driven to achieve more synergies and *corps d'esprit* in the Navy and the Marine Corps while modernizing the force and conceptualizing how to influence events on shore.[36]

To achieve these goals, Danzig, a more energetic strategist than his predecessor, adopted an increasingly activist, bi-partisan approach to strengthening the Navy. He stayed on for the remainder of Clinton's second presidential term.

Despite such continuity in the civilian leadership of the department, the top military management was in dire straits. CNO Kelso, who was active on the capstone documents for the service but mismanaged the "Tailhook" fallout, left office in April 1994. He was replaced by Admiral Jeremy "Mike" Boorda, who was selected to restore the Navy's public image, rebuild service morale, and reestablish good relations with Congress.[37] Boorda was the first enlisted sailor to rise through the enlisted ranks and become CNO. A surface warfare officer, he enjoyed good standing as a "Sailors' Sailor," and his operational record with NATO Mediterranean operations let him stand out as unique and practically tested. His relationship to the top Navy brass (especially Naval Academy graduates and aviators) was less stellar because of Boorda's background and his sweeping handling of the "Tailhook" affair.[38] Personally, this CNO took much criticism over his wearing of valor insignia on combat medals from service during the Vietnam War. On May 16, 1996, after just two years in office, Boorda killed himself in his Washington Navy Yard residence, partly over those allegations.[39] His suicide at age 56 shocked the nation. The Navy now had to deal with yet another addition to the agonizing series of scandals and embarrassments. It would be up to Boorda's successors to steer the service into calmer waters and restore public, inner-service, and Congressional confidence.

Admiral Jay Johnson, a naval aviator, was selected to straighten the Navy's course. Johnson largely shied away from publishing major declaratory strategies. Instead, he focused on implementing the "… From the Sea" (1992) and "Forward … From the Sea" (1994) capstone documents his predecessors had issued. To restore the Navy's edge, he also directed efforts to develop the next generation of warships, aircraft, and information systems. He improved the quality of life and work in the Navy by directing changes in the inter-deployment training cycle (the period of time between deployments), trimming at-sea time, and taking steps to reduce wear and tear on equipment. He optimized procedures throughout the bureaucracy of the service so that sailors could spend more time ashore with families and enjoy increasing benefits in pay, health care, and housing.[40]

Increasingly inward-looking to calm service culture and reassure Congress, CNOs did little to infringe on the turf of the CJCS. Over the course of the 1990s, the Chairman was always a U.S. Army general. Powell, John Shalikash-vili, and Hugh Shelton oversaw a period in which the joint staff became deeply involved in defense-planning and strategy-making. The Navy seemingly lost its ability and the informal responsibility to master its own strategic fate to fellow military men and to civilians. Congressional influence on strategy-making and defense-planning rose considerably, most prominently displayed by the mandate to submit a Quadrennial Defense Review (QDR) beginning in 1997. That report sought to verbalize for Capitol Hill (since 1994 Republican-controlled) what the Pentagon and the services were planning.

Domestic conditions

The industrial and defense sector in the U.S. consolidated in the 1990s. This was related to the restructuring of the military and budgetary reduction. The Bush Sr. administration and in particular the Clinton administration reduced overall government spending on defense. The military budget dropped significantly from its Cold War heights, although the Navy was able to retain its roughly one-third of the share among the services. Figure 5.1 outlines the declining defense expenditures in absolute and relative terms.

Of the multitude of defense companies, through mergers, acquisitions, and bankruptcies, by 2000 only five larger firms remained (Lockheed Martin, General Dynamics, Raytheon, Northrop-Grumman, and Boeing). Affecting defense as well were several rounds of base realignment and closures (BRAC), signaling the withdrawal of the military from some parts of the country. In the states affected, this added to an overall dismal public image with which the Navy had to cope.

A series of bad press incidents plagued the service at the time, too. Beginning with the turret explosion aboard the battleship *Iowa* (BB 61) in 1989, an

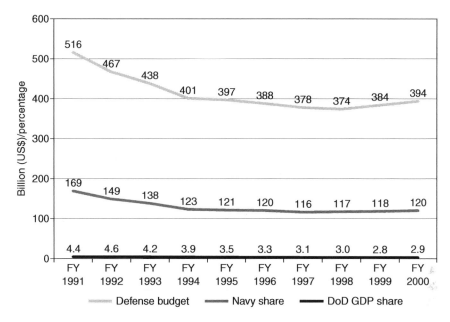

Figure 5.1 1990s U.S. Defense Budget, FY 1991–2000, Navy share in FY 12 billion US-$; GDP DoD share in %.[41]

FBI anti-corruption investigation involving Department of the Navy and defense industry individuals, lawsuits over the cancelled McDonnell Douglas A-12 carrier stealth bomber in the early 1990s, the "Tailhook" scandal and the following investigations (the Navy lost some 15 percent of its flag officers because of demotions and forced retirements), a cheating scandal at the U.S. Naval Academy in 1994, and Boorda's suicide in 1996 cumulated to paint the Navy in a devastating state. All these affected Navy morale, retention, and public standing. This was terrifying to a service proud of its traditions, its heritage, and its gallantry.[42] The problems contributed to the impression that the Navy neither had the integrity nor the vision to serve as a key tool for U.S. foreign and security policy ends.

Selected U.S. national security policies, doctrines, and capstone documents

The "long 1990s" saw an endless stream of national security policy revisions, doctrinal documents, and capstone strategies. As the world order was redefined, successive administrations and their policy and military leaders attempted to grasp the imminent changes and frame America's post-Cold War role. Trying to plan for the future occurred amidst real-world defense and national security developments. These documents naturally were the product of a vetted, interagency process. As such, they were carefully crafted, but often only resembled a low, bland, common denominator. The tight schedule between national security strategies – after staff produced one document, they immediately began work on next – put immense pressure on authors and robbed the creation of new, ground-breaking insights and ways-means-ends causalities to influence public and political discourse.[43]

In addition, the joint staff was also very active in producing series of documents: National Military Strategies in 1992, 1995, and 1997; East Asia reports in 1990, 1992, 1995, and 1998; and joint doctrinal publications like "Joint Vision 2010" (1996) and "Joint Vision 2020" (2000). The Pentagon still submitted its own annual Defense Department reports. The Contingency Planning Guidance (CPG) – written by the Secretary of Defense, approved by the President, for the Chairman of the Joint Chiefs of Staff – sought to tie together the guidance given in NSS and the Defense Planning Guidance (DPG). In turn, the CPG served as the principal source document for the Joint Strategic Capabilities Plan (JSCP). Finally, periodic analyses such as the National Intelligence Council's Global Trends Report 2010 (November 1997) and Global Trends Report 2015 (December 2000) added to this alphabet soup of documents. A few of them still stand out from this bouquet, that is, from the perspective of this study and consequently deserve discussion in more detail. These are, in chronological order, the 1991 Base Force Report, the 1993 Bottom-Up Review, and the 1997 Quadrennial Defense Review (QDR).[44]

Soon after the fall of the Berlin Wall, CJCS General Powell and his staff produced a concept entitled the Base Force, and developed in the 1992 National Military Strategy.[45] It was to replace the global containment strategy whose objective was fading. The NMS advocated a more nuanced focus for the emerging threats of the post–Cold War world, including a distinct regional and surge focus. The growing federal deficit also demanded action by military planners. From a congressional perspective, it was the hope for a 'peace dividend,' rerouting funds from defense to social welfare programs. This made budget cuts attractive. Accordingly (and partly to push back across-the-board un-strategic cuts), the Base Force called for substantial financial and manpower reductions while retraining a sensible base. To offset capability gaps and leverage efficiencies, the report also emphasized more honest drives for jointness.[46]

The report provided a floor for future planning. Its objective was to outline the minimum force needed to execute the new U.S. strategy, meet obligations stemming from enduring national security needs, and preserve American interests in the changing world. It also hoped to retain some capabilities should a resurgent Soviet Union again challenge the U.S. and the West (which at the time seemed like a distant, but still possible outcome). The Base Force outlined four elements of U.S. defense strategy, namely strategic deterrence, forward presence, crisis response, and the ability to reconstitute the U.S. military quickly. Rather than focusing on the ultimately unpredictable future engagements specifically (thereby dismissing a threat-based strategy), the report used a capabilities-based analysis to arrive at the defined, balanced base force.[47] The report persisted as the force structure concept for the remainder of the Bush administration. Its underlying principles were voiced by General Powell (dubbed the "Powell Doctrine") building on the principles laid out in the Weinberger Doctrine a few years earlier, including clear provisions on the U.S. use of military force.

The Bottom-Up Review (BUR) of 1993, directed by Secretary of Defense Aspin, was the second major force structure review, just a couple of years into the decade and written for the new Democratic administration.[48] While the report can be explained partially by the incoming administration's desire to distance itself from the work of its predecessors, it also points toward the high level of uncertainty cloaking 1990s' defense planning. Sensible strategic planning in the face of uncertainty was in higher demand than ever. The Bottom-Up Review was even more assertive and wide-reaching in terms of force and budget reduction, proposing cuts of up to one-third, thereby surpassing the Base Force's 25 percent reductions. In addition, this review's most serious shortcoming from the Navy's perspective was its downplaying of the capability of U.S. naval forces to shape the strategic environment through forward presence. Instead, Secretary Aspin's approach was explicitly threat-based.[49] Importantly, the BUR preempted Clinton's first national security strategy of 1994, calling for an increasing operations tempo and a higher deployment rate by a significantly smaller military. In setting the political and rhetorical stage for U.S. participation in multilateral operations, it signaled the intent to increase burden-sharing among allies and drive efficiencies, or in other words: "to do more with less."

The Bottom-Up Review cautioned that in strategic planning, external threats were important but needed to be compared with the nation's resources. It noted four overarching priorities for the U.S., namely, (1) defeating aggressors in major regional contingencies (MRC); (2) deterring regional conflict and provision of stability in areas of strategic interest; (3) conducting of small-scale interventions (peacekeeping, peace enforcement, humanitarian assistance, and disaster relief); and, (4) deterring attacks against the U.S., its forces, or its allies by WMD.[50] The document further assumed that U.S. forces would need to be designed so these four tasks could be achieved abroad. To that end, it used a two major regional contingency (MRC) force-sizing metric. In other words, it called for forces of a quantity and quality to engage decisively in two major regional conflicts in parallel (e.g., North Korea and the Persian Gulf). In addition, the report incorporated and measured demand for smaller-scale conflicts or crises needing U.S. forces, overseas presence (i.e., U.S. military forces conducting regular peacetime operations), and deterrence of attacks with weapons of mass destruction, either against U.S. territory or forces, or on U.S. allies.[51]

The U.S. military would continue to be tasked with addressing the spectrum of conflict across all these categories, making post-Cold War peacetime operations and crisis response a busy, but – so it was hoped – relatively manageable task.[52] The central struggle for planners would be to balance the war-fighting capabilities of the force on the one hand with the peacetime presence requirements, as mandated by the report, on the other. When the Bottom-Up Review was implemented, it occurred to leaders that military deployments and engagements as well as political commitments were "from a historical perspective, more frequent, larger, and of longer duration than had been seen in the past."[53] This feature reflected the Clinton administration failure to prioritize its use of the U.S. military, instead employing it as an active and often indiscriminate foreign policy tool. These lesser contingencies took a toll on the force and almost equaled the stress of one MRC. That was one principal reason why during the second half of the presidency, Clinton went from a more interventionist approach to instead economizing the military use solely to win wars. A careful global engagement was once again replaced by a regional war prism as the overriding planning metric. In addition, the ambitious promotion of democracy and market economy slowed considerably, for instance with Russia and China.[54] Finally, Clinton needed to concentrate on domestic issues, not least his impeachment in 1998/1999.

The third major capstone document of the decade came in 1997 with the Congressionally mandated Quadrennial Defense Review (QDR).[55] One of its major motivations was to balance the defense program needs with budgetary provisions and to strengthen the role of the legislature. Central to this approach was to offset one of the key problems that had developed during the previous years, namely, the migration of funds from modernization accounts to the funding of ongoing operations. Given how important continuous modernization of military assets is including research, development, testing, and evaluation, especially for ships with their long build times this was especially crucial. In the 1990s, more and more costly advanced weapons, sensors, and command and control systems moved into place, a process widely known as transformation. The QDR replaced the MRC model with the 2-Major-Theater-Wars (MTW) force-sizing metric, which recognized an adversary's asymmetric means in warfare, and emphasized peacetime engagement and smaller-scale contingencies (SSC) to build stability. Nevertheless, military end strength decreased.[56]

These three national strategic capstone documents (Base Force, Bottom-Up Review, and Quadrennial Defense Review) underlined the broad consequences that changes in global circumstances and different administrations can have on military planning. In addition to the tectonic political and geostrategic rifts, the overarching capstone documents of the 1990s were increasingly informed and influenced by technology-based war-fighting concepts sometimes perceived as revolutionary.

Developing and promulgating USN strategy 1989–2001

While "The Maritime Strategy" was a series of documents under one name and one large geostrategic naval concept, the 1990s was not afforded such luxury by the Navy. Accordingly, rather than discussing the evolution of the documents and the sea-strategic concepts behind them, this chapter will present each document's genesis and evolution followed by the analysis of its strategic scope. A synopsis at the end of this chapter will point out aspects of continuity and change.

The April 1990 issue of *Proceedings*, the U.S. Naval Institute's professional magazine, featured a strikingly candid illustration taking direct aim at the 'steady as she goes' mentality of some in the navy leadership. The photograph showed a print copy of "The Maritime Strategy" being consumed by flames.[57] As the 1980s' capstone document of American sea power went up in smoke, it signaled the opportunity for a fresh start. This do-over resulted in several attempts by the Navy leadership to promulgate core thinking about the role of naval power in this new world.[58] In the process, however, the Navy's message diluted. New capstone documents did not address a naval way of thinking about the political ends of war. Instead, they increasingly limited themselves to *how* the Navy would fight the next war. With little in the way of major threats or peer competitors on the horizon, the defense establishment was hard pressed to argue why a large, balanced Navy was necessary in the first place. Two successive presidential administrations did not help to push back such concerns. The service's strategies were no longer comprehended as how to make a strategic difference akin to "The Maritime Strategy," but rather as simple war plans and justifications for its force structure (Table 5.2). Operations dominated.

These capstone documents also struggled with a secondary rationale, namely, providing the Navy internally with a sense of cohesion which "The Maritime Strategy" had achieved. Initially, U.S. Navy expectations for its post-Cold War role were relatively far-reaching and widely optimistic. The Navy leadership viewed its political and operational postures and the way it did business as highly adaptable to the aftermath of the superpower conflict. It could be reasonably confident that by all indications (and providing an unchanging if not larger share of the budget) it would be a very, if not the most relevant force in the future security environment.[59] This amounted to political wishful thinking on its part. The Navy misjudged the persuasive power in the face of geostrategic shifts, public expectations toward post-Cold

Table 5.2 Main 1990s USN capstone documents[60]

Name	Self-titled format	Year	Status
The Way Ahead	Vision	1991	Unclassified
The Navy Policy Book	Policy	1992	Unclassified
… From the Sea	Vision	1992	Unclassified
Naval Warfare (NDP 1)	Doctrine	1994	Unclassified
Forward… From the Sea	Strategic concept	1994	Unclassified
Navy Operational Concept	Operational concept	1997	Unclassified
Anytime, Anywhere	Vision	1997	Unclassified
Navy Strategic Planning	Strategic planning	1999	Secret
Guidance	guidance	2000	Unclassified

War peace and serenity, its own lackluster ability to innovate and change institutionally, and two successive administrations which shied away from verbalizing strategic visions. Consequently, no single crisis or challenge that the U.S. faced in the 1990s proved compelling enough to threaten U.S. national survival. The role of the military in general, and naval power in particular, to address these threats was disconnected from the definition of American interests. The Navy was eventually unable to drive home to Congress and the American public the need to keep up a large force, as useful and sound as their arguments for a balanced fleet may have sounded to itself.

The Way Ahead (1991)/The Navy Policy Book (1992)

Evolution

The 1991 document drew significantly from an informal working group of Navy Department staff officers who met regularly to discuss Navy and Marine Corps issues.[61] Parallel to a few non-starting formal efforts, an informal association of Navy and Marine Corps officers – self-titled as the "Ancient Mariners" (consisting of OPNAV and outside staff) – took it upon themselves to come up with a new concept to address the changing world. Concepts briefed there were consequently tested and expanded and "thus, this early developmental work became an ancestor to the series of statements that were soon to follow."[62] One of these was "The Way Ahead," published as an article in the April 1991 issue of *Proceedings* magazine. Signed by Secretary of the Navy Garrett, CNO Kelso, and the Commandant of the Marine Corps, General Alfred Gray, it provided overarching bureaucratic and intellectual clout without fully discarding "The Maritime Strategy" (which many admirals still held dear) in the process. Despite the momentous geopolitical shift of 1989–1991, neither CNO Trost nor his successor Frank Kelso asked for a formal replacement of "The Maritime Strategy." Hedging against a resurgent Soviet Union remained an objective because it was unclear what the next steps for Moscow's decaying empire would look like.

"The Way Ahead" identified three challenges for the Navy Department. These were finding efficiencies and the cost-effectiveness of the industrial base, the force size (in light of a foreseeable adverse fiscal situation), and the shape and size of the twenty-first century Navy.[63] Navy leaders at the time were indifferent to a really comprehensive new maritime strategy, whereas mid-level naval strategists – strategically thinking staff officers with tours in the OP-603 branch and experience in the fleet – saw the need for an ambitious post-Cold War document almost immediately.[64] To Kelso, cost-effectiveness was more desirable than a grand-strategic marching direction for the Navy. For this reason the CNO lobbied heavily to publish "The Navy Policy Book," a 1992 medium-length internal U.S. Navy booklet whose audience was the officer corps and the enlisted ranks of the Navy. Kelso saw it as a complementary work to "The Way Ahead" and "The Maritime

Strategy" (which was officially shelved). With this trio of publications as an intellectual foundation, Kelso sought to implement business–world inspired, but frowned-upon "Total Quality Leadership" principles in the Navy.[65] The Policy Book's *en passant* mention of the USMC and the clear lack of an ambitious way-means-ends correlation contributed to its limited influence and, consequently, it was never updated or repeated.

Strategic concept

"The Way Ahead," as noted above, drew on catalytic ideas and themes discussed by the informal D.C.-based Navy group in 1990. Their ideas included the Navy–Marine Corps' understanding of themselves as enablers for follow-on operations and a decisive crisis response capability by their forward presence and expeditionary nature. The piece also discarded one of Mahan's most sacred principles, postulating that the U.S. Navy's future lay in supporting the land battle, not exclusively the conduct of war at sea (although ASW and AAW were to be maintained to shield against future capable sea-going adversaries).[66] Those concerns were motivated principally by the U.S. experience of the Gulf War, notwithstanding that the conflict left the Navy somewhat marginalized in the actual fight.

The Base Force study call for a fleet of 450 Navy ships served as the definite bottom line for the Navy's deliberations. The Base Force aligned U.S. military objectives along four principles: deterrence, forward presence, crisis response, and force reconstitution. The Navy heavily focused on the first three. "The Way Ahead" called for sea-based strategic forces for nuclear deterrence, surge forces designed to react rapidly to any crisis, coordinated forward-deployed expeditionary forces with comprehensive logistic, medical, and repair support, and a sea-based maritime prepositioned force.[67] It also emphasized humanitarian assistance, nation-building, security assistance, peacekeeping, counter-narcotic/-terrorism/-insurgency operations, and crisis response.[68] Sea control, the traditional U.S. naval mission, was only mentioned in passing. This reflected a Navy sentiment that control of the sea, at least in the open ocean, would be uncontested in the near- and mid-term. Amid criticism of its lack of prioritization and perception that the Navy's ideas were not radical enough, "The Way Ahead" by all accounts had negligible influence and impact.

... From the Sea (1992)

Evolution

"... From the Sea" was the work of subsequent working groups, using a standardized OP-603 strategy brief as a basis for continuous refinement between October 1991 and March 1992.[69] With memories of the Gulf War fresh on their minds, the Center for Naval Analyses hosted a project called the Naval Force Capabilities Planning Effort (NFCPE). The NFCPE brought seasoned naval officers together with civilian academics, Congressional staffers, and people from the think tank community.[70] The goal was to exert upward pressure. The group sought to position the Navy and the Marine Corps in national strategic plans and provide long-range perspective for mid- and long-term national security threats. Using a historical case study, the participants assessed the future environment and the Navy's role in it. Using what became known as the "Manthorpe Curve," a graph by Captain William H.J. Manthorpe, it showed that historically, the period between the end of one global hegemonic power and the rise of another was roughly 20 years. In other words, the next challenger would materialize around 2011, and if it were not a resurgent Soviet Union, it would be a Eurasian power, or coalition of states. Independent of that cycle, a second dynamic connected a continuous, low level of conflict (i.e., limited wars) that drew in larger powers. Extrapolating from the wars in Korea (1950–1953), Vietnam (1965–1975), and the Gulf War (1990–1991), Manthorpe calculated that crisis interval to be 15 years. That gave the U.S. roughly until 2005. The study concluded that the U.S. had some time until the next global threat emerged. For the time being, it was at liberty to concentrate on the-rest-of-the-world threats.[71]

How these challenges were to be addressed remained more controversial. Warfare area specialists brought forward differing arguments, underlining a platform or operating area's particular relevance. Analysis of past Navy/ Marine Corps crisis response had shown that even in a volatile, Cold War bipolar environment, American sea power had overwhelmingly been applied to counter land-based threats, not for the decisive battle at sea. Historically, in this it had been more Corbett than Mahan. This was surprising even to seasoned naval officers, given that "The Maritime Strategy" had focused extensively on the global at-sea struggle against the Soviet Union. For their work, the authors from the NFCPE utilized that revelation. It was relatively safe to assume that the trend for sea power to influence events ashore, driven by geopolitical developments and policy decisions in Washington, D.C., was likely to continue and even deepen. By consensus, they argued that regional wars and the related instability they conveyed, rather than great-power competition, was the most pressing problem for the United States.

In the course of spring and summer 1992, "… From the Sea" was further sharpened by extensive, multi-person reiterations to turn it from an internal paper into a publication and, according to Vice Admiral Leighton Smith, to make sure people on the Hill understood it.[72] The drafts were unclassified and designated "For official use only" (FOUO) to broaden the eventual audience as much as possible. Thus, it was not only an internal paper for the Navy, but an attempt also to gain national political attention in the White House and on Capitol Hill. Contributors included flag and staff officers as well as contractors, but the recurring themes of forward presence and power projection remained. With the new Secretary of the Navy Sean O'Keefe as a co-signer, "…From the Sea" was pushed out in the November 1992 issue of *Proceedings* magazine and the Marine Corps' counterpart, the *Marine Corps Gazette*.[73]

In "... From the Sea," the Navy and the Marine Corps sought to present themselves as having understood and principally embraced the defense policies of the Bush administration. It is remarkable how timely the publication was, given the Presidential election of the same month. However, it was equally driven by the need to at least get something out by Election Day. Consequently, the naval services made certain unsigned copies of "... From the Sea" circulated after Clinton's inauguration.[74] The Navy wanted the publication to grab people's attention just like the Air Force's "Global Reach, Global Power" pamphlet (1990) had. Thus, it needed presentation in an attractive (although somewhat budget-consuming) format.[75] The January 1993 version, the third and final edition of "... From the Sea," reiterated the themes of the original drafts. The Navy now had a white paper with glossy pictures and illustrations positioning it in the policy community. Although the selection of illustrations conveys the impression that the Navy consisted of surface and naval aviation mostly (submarine images do not appear until well into the brochure), "... From the Sea" tracked. It remained the Navy's primary post-Cold War strategic and comprehensive approach for the rest of the decade.[76]

Strategic concept

The working group that drafted "... From the Sea" emphasized the value of command of the sea (absent a peer-competitor, the broader 'command of the sea' became popular again, often used in conjunction with the narrower 'sea control') as the indivisible basis for protection of U.S. citizens and territory. Forward, sea-based operations to guard U.S. interests and promote commitment abroad were the logical consequence. Additionally, command of the sea was described as the basis for deterrence, power projection, and crisis response. All of these were long-standing constants in the U.S. Navy's mission mindset.

This effort energized the Navy's thinking. Instead of reactively describing what the Navy would do different from the Air Force or the Army, the authors of "... From the Sea" sought to lay out the unique capabilities of their service. This narrative related naval purpose to warfighting as well as to broader American diplomatic and economic interests. Although naval force structure is primarily structured for war, the group asserted, holding and using command of the sea could very well influence events ashore at any time. The authors concluded that naval forces must, therefore, conduct geographically forward-deployed operations and focus increasingly on the coast and littoral areas instead of the high seas.[77]

While global sea control did not seem to be an issue for the Navy any more, local and regional sea control in confined and shallow waters (straits, canals, or the littoral regions) were elevated to higher strategic importance.

Consequently, "... From the Sea" focused on strike and power projection (underlining for example the use of the Tomahawk missile for surface and land attack). It deemphasized ASW and blue-water engagements, which primarily served to win and exercise sea control against peer enemy forces.[78]

Still, the final version of "... From the Sea" contained no fewer than six maritime capabilities: powerful presence, strategic deterrence, sea control, extended crisis response, power projection from the sea, and provision of sealift. It later cited four traditional operational means (forward deployment, crisis response, strategic deterrence, and sealift) to which it affixed another four required key operational capabilities (command, control, and surveillance, battle space dominance, power projection, and force sustainment).[79] "... From the Sea" did not mention a particular country as a specific threat, but the context of its publication showed clearly that the Gulf War was a template. It also raised the role of the Marine Corps to equality with the Navy, something that critics dismissed as showing the undue influence of the USMC. To them, traditional and more comprehensive naval tasks on the high seas were unjustifiably overshadowed by the less significant effect-ashore faction.

Admittedly, the document displayed a much broader focus on political viability in Washington than on operational salience. When Clinton's defense policy agenda took shape, forward presence and peacetime crisis response in "... From the Sea" were deemphasized: they were seen as lacking traction with the new decision-makers. In essence, they were costly diversions from what the incoming administration perceived as a need to field a downsized, less aggressive, and less ambitious American military posture worldwide. To the Navy, "... From the Sea" offered a sharpening of its outlook on the world. To policy-makers, the strategic concepts it offered tracked with their general outlook on the world.

Naval Warfare (NDP 1) (1994)

Evolution

Among the tasks proposed by "... From the Sea", restructuring the Navy to carry out the new strategy was a high priority. This included the establishment of a new Naval Doctrine Command (NAVDOCCOM) in Norfolk (Virginia), home to the Navy's largest fleet installations (and largest naval bases of the world). To support the concepts laid out in "... From the Sea," the new command rolled out its first publication in 1994.[80] NDP 1 "Naval Warfare" attempted to provide a guideline account of official operational Navy behavior. It also responded to the prevalent "jointness and joint doctrinal frenzy"[81] amidst the implementation of Goldwater–Nichols and the impact of post-Gulf War success. With NDP 1, the Navy sought to find a vehicle to explain itself and what it did to other military branches where doctrine (and the appreciation for doctrine) constituted elementary parts of the strategic culture. Therefore, NDP 1 used a format similar to that of the joint publications. This displayed that the Navy really wanted to arrive at a more coherent and joint articulation. It also conveyed that it understood the diction and the dynamics of the modern military.

This capstone document during the tenure of CNO Frank Kelso was entirely drafted and published at NAVDOCCOM [or NDC]. It was a deliberately different approach from the bureaucratic power politics in the Pentagon and in Washington. Additionally, NDP 1 did not seek outside contractors as advisors and its writing process forfeited early-on participation of the Naval War College. NDP 1 also illustrated, as much as how the preceding three capstone documents did, Kelso's limited strategic aspirations. In the face of General Powell's accumulated power as CJCS, Admiral Kelso did not think he was responsible for much more than equipping, training, and organizing the force.

Admiral Kelso's perspective was that his job, like that of OPNAV, was to focus on the means. The White House, OSD, and now the Chairman of the Joint Chiefs of Staff determined the ends. The CINCs and their naval component commanders determined the ways. In the CNO's view, strategy – the relating and orchestration of ways, means, and political ends – was someone else's responsibility.[82]

Strategic concept

NDP 1 was the fourth (and final) capstone document signed by CNO Kelso. The Navy's somewhat uneasy relationship with doctrine (in contrast to other branches of the military), the problematic relationship between the Navy and the Marine Corps, and the eventually incomplete roster of publications notwithstanding, NDP 1 laid out naval objectives to advance the broad lines of maneuver over attrition warfare. It used examples from naval history to convey its key ideas and "its purpose was to explain the inherent nature of the enduring principles of naval force and to translate the vision and strategy of '… From the Sea' into doctrinal reality."[83] In citing Admiral Turner's four missions of 1974 (sea control, projection of power ashore, naval presence, and strategic deterrence), NDP 1 subsumed established roles of naval forces and also spoke to general principles of war.[84] Those were not new by any means; they were simply restated as the underlying objectives those conducting naval warfare needed to keep in mind. More importantly, NDP 1 listed a number of principles and mission-sets that previously had not been featured as prominently, including naval operations other than war.[85] As such, NDP 1 offered some potential, but it was too broad in scope and widely seen as a product that led nowhere. To its critics, it was a diluted, goalless paper emanating from a command in Norfolk, not Washington. It did not seem to be informed by any measurable input from major makers and shapers of American seapower, and NDP 1 was eventually eclipsed by rival documents, "… From the Sea" (1992) and "Forward … From the Sea" (1994).

Forward ... From the Sea (1994)

Evolution

Admiral Boorda, previously serving as Commander in Chief Allied Forces Southern Europe and as Commander in Chief, U.S. Naval Forces Europe, was an officer uniquely experienced in conducting the real-world naval operations (the Yugoslav civil war) after the collapse of the Soviet Union. Just months after Boorda's ascension to the Navy's highest billet, the December 1994 edition of *Proceedings* featured "Forward ... From the Sea."[86] This strategic concept article had already appeared in the *Marine Corps Gazette* two months earlier and was published as a stand-alone 12-page booklet as well. "Forward ... From the Sea" originated in N513, the Strategy and Concepts Branch of the Navy Department. Its publication did not mean "... From the Sea" was outdated, but the Navy looked to capitalize on the momentum brought about by the change in the White House. This indicates the higher political intent of "Forward ... From the Sea." In addition to serving as a yardstick of the incoming CNO, the document provided a testimonial of naval strategic thinking to the new (Clinton-administration) Secretary of Defense Perry and Secretary of the Navy Dalton. "Forward ... From the Sea" was, therefore, designed to enable a Democratic imprint on a previous, Republican-signed strategy.[87]

As mentioned, the Clinton administration had conducted the "Bottom-Up Review" of the Defense Department in 1993 and the President published his "National Security Strategy of Engagement and Enlargement" in 1994. The military services needed to align with these documents and reflect overarching demands to make their national case. In particular, the Navy sought to link force structure changes (the 1993 review) to forward presence demands (the 1994 NSS). The service wanted to demonstrate that it understood both force structure consequences and policy demands of the new era.[88] With "Forward ... From the Sea", Navy planners attempted to deliver a political response.

With this fifth Navy-only capstone document in just four years (not counting related documents and aborted efforts), the service had been incredibly busy continuously portraying itself to the post-Cold War senior political leadership. To the defense establishment and the bureaucracy – the Joint Staff, the National Security Council, and the Secretary of Defense – as well as the public and on Capitol Hill, this amounted to the equivalent of a capstone document feeding frenzy, and the naval case was deemed unviable. The Navy was also increasingly blindsided by the seemingly consistent jointness crowds. It was difficult and downright foolish to justify ad-hoc single-service thinking and planning in the increasingly joint, coordinated, and integrated force. For a service proud of its uniqueness and whose strategic culture was deeply rooted in the past, this promised to be a monumental challenge.[89]

Even here, the Air Force and Army strategic cultures and operational validations confronted the Navy with a headwind. The Gulf War had seemingly validated the Army's AirLand Battle concept and the Air Force's strategic bombing doctrines. One academic press even reprinted an Army doctrine manual. Whether the Navy liked it or not, the forces of the time worked against it, leaving it unable to think more conceptually about its role in national defense.

Strategic concept

"Forward ... From the Sea" restructured and expanded the strategic concepts of "... From the Sea". It postulated power projection from sea on land, sea control, maritime supremacy, strategic sealift, and strategic deterrence as key enduring naval roles. That echoed the mission sets that Admiral Stansfield Turner postulated in the 1970s (which John Lehman and others in the 1980s reiterated). "Forward ... From the Sea" then added another enduring and fundamental function: naval presence. This notion of being-on-scene globally complemented the emphasis on countering regional threats. Its organizing construct, in a clear nod to "The Maritime Strategy" absent in most other post-Cold War Navy capstone documents, emphasized the continuum nature of forward operations. These ranged from peacetime presence to crisis response to regional conflict, with a merely academic distinction between phases, not necessarily operational or even strategic ones. Forward-deployed (permanent or rotating) naval forces were hailed as a well-suited instrument of U.S. foreign policy to buttress American grand and military strategy, regardless of circumstances.

These presence requirements would have consequences for Navy force structure that needed to be addressed. It was simply not enough to rely on stand-off strike capabilities such as the Tomahawk missile alone. Instead, by implication the Navy wanted and needed a balanced fleet that featured both (and more of), high-end and low-end capabilities. Such a force mix could in turn only be exploited if the Navy actually was forward-deployed. Presence fulfilled the regional commanders' requirements and provided a reason for the large fleet. The service realized that there was an opportunity created by the Bottom-Up Review needing transformation into one benefiting the Navy. Nevertheless, "Forward ... From the Sea" differed from "From the Sea" in several respects. It had a global perspective, not a regional, littoral, tactical, or overly expeditionary focus like its predecessor.[90] Terms such as "broad oceans," "transoceanic," and "highways of the seas" conveyed a global per-spective that had been absent in "... From the Sea."[91]

Unfortunately for the Navy, what began as an attempt to flesh out some concepts and improve "... From the Sea," had the contrary effect. "Forward ... From the Sea" clouded many of the achievements that "...From the Sea" already had provided. As Captain (ret.) Joe Bouchard recalls,

> '... From the Sea' was a very important document. They got it right. It really had significant impact on the Navy. Significant change in direction.

'Forward … From the Sea' was a waste of time – there was nothing new in it. And in fact, it was regressive. It eliminated some of the bold thought that '… From the Sea' showed and tried to do more to preserve the Navy's classic way of operating – in that sense, it went backward.[92]

At the same time, the Navy opened itself up to criticism from Congress and its sister services. In particular, 'presence' was attacked. Its diplomatic and military effects were hard to quantify, and naval forces, so the critics argued, were designed, sized, and budgeted for war-fighting requirements, not peace-time engagement. It looked too much like the Navy's Cold War way of doing business with others. Some thinkers cautioned that the Navy would be first in line for force level cuts if politics mandated a scaling-back of presence missions, whereas regional challengers fielding anti-access and area-denial capabilities (such as sowing mines and maintaining diesel-electric submarines) could inhibit forward U.S. Navy presence. The Navy's label "combat-credible forward presence" challenged some strategic convictions of the other military services: the Air Force considered its firepower more robust than that of the Navy. The Army hailed boots on the ground as the probable tool of influence. The Marine Corps could easily misinterpret the strong Navy role in the new capstone document as a step back from "… From the Sea," and did. This infighting underscored that the military services battled continu-ously for resources and national attention. In addition, the warfare unions themselves were individually attempting to reverse the downsizing since the end of the Cold War, with the submariners arguing for more boats, the naval aviators for air wings for 15 carriers, and the surface warfare community pro-ducing a goal of 360–380 surface combatants (cruisers, destroyers, and frig-ates). This beauty contest hardly served the overall goal of the Navy as a whole, to do better in the budgetary processes and present itself as the nation's Swiss army knife for national security. Consequently, the impact of such wish lists remained minimal at best.

Navy Operational Concept (1997)

Evolution

The Navy Operational Concept[93] was published as a consequence of the Navy and the Marine Corps' inability to overcome their operational differ-ences. These substantial frictions (rooted in the Corps' strategic culture and its perception of "Forward … From the Sea") came to a head in the mid-1990s when developing a new concept to operationalize "Forward … From the Sea." The first such attempts in 1995/1996 proposed a Navy-Marine Corps Naval Operations Concept (naval = Navy and Marine Corps). It was intended to serve as a connector between the "… From the Sea" and "Forward … From the Sea" capstone documents, providing methodology and a modus operandi into which the NDP series fed. Ferocious struggles between competing commands and individuals led the Navy, which sought to emphasize blue-water, high-seas capabilities much to the Corps's disdain, to abort this common plan in the course of 1996. In parallel, the CNO Executive Panel (N00K) headed by Captain Ed Smith drafted another white paper with the name "2020 Vision," a companion piece for a "Navy Long Range Planning Objectives" memorandum that was scheduled to be signed later in 1996.[94]

When Admiral Jeremy Boorda took his life in May 1996 amidst public allegations over his display of two Vietnam War service medals, these efforts halted. Admiral Jay Johnson, Boorda's successor as CNO, struck a markedly calmer tone during his tenure. He discarded his predecessor's two draft strategic planning documents.[95] His indifference to the idea of a missile-carrying arsenal ship scuttled that idea, too. Aviator Johnson, "not a visionary or an innovator" (ibid.: 177), instructed N513 (OPNAV's Strategy and Concepts branch) under Commander Joe Bouchard to start over and draft a Navy-only operational concept. It was designed to provide guidance for programmers in OPNAV's N8 branch, support training, and help finalize tactics, techniques, and procedures. Working together with Vice Admiral Art Cebrowski of the Space, Information Warfare, and Command and Control (N6) branch, the term 'network-centric warfare' was introduced into the discourse. A single-service Navy (not naval) Operational Concept was the result. It was not intended to replace "Forward ... From the Sea," but rather to be a complementary document. It was rolled out in January 1997, signed by Admiral Johnson, and distributed via e-mail, the internet, and later in *Sea Power*, the professional magazine of the Navy League (a civilian, non-profit military organization). Reflecting the general sentiment toward it and the document's style, its lead author conceded "It was less ambitious, but it worked" in providing a conceptual, programmatic underpinning for the Navy's range of activities.[96]

Strategic concept

The Navy Operational Concept recognized that "... From the Sea" and "Forward ... From the Sea" continued to drive the U.S. Navy's destiny. In limiting its own level of ambition and scope, the document merely pointed out that naval force could have a decisive role in small-scale contingencies and could be integral to bigger joint campaigns. In addition, the concept underscored that the Navy also saw its role in post-conflict situations too, for example to secure withdrawal of troops or to control sanctions regimes. The Navy Operational Concept therefore presented two interconnected ideas. Naval operational maneuver (an idea lobbied by Captain Bouchard, and advocated by analyst Wayne Hughes at Naval Postgraduate School) and speed of command (Vice Admiral Cebrowski's brainchild). Both were keen to invigorate network-centric warfare (a doctrine translating the information advantage of superior technology into an operational advantage). This approach required investment in advanced weapons, sensors, and platforms, and a naval force large enough and equipped to cater to the demands on the whole six-phase spectrum of conflict. The NOC was notably silent of naval missions. As an operational document, it deliberately shied away from discussing the larger strategic effects of naval force.

Anytime, Anywhere (1997)

Evolution

Just six months after the NOC, 1997 saw the second of three capstone documents produced under CNO Johnson. But in the meantime, two key policy documents had been interposed. The first congressionally mandated QDR and an updated NMS were released in May of that year. For "Anytime, Anywhere," which appeared in the November issue of *Proceedings* magazine,[97] the CNO Executive Panel staff (N00K) (specifically Captains Ed Smith and Robby Harris) took the helm in drafting it. The ad-hoc working group undertook an effort to move the Navy's focus away from over-emphasizing presence, therefore stressing kinetic and war-fighting measures. This was especially crucial against the backdrop of the QDR's stated goal of a U.S. Navy force level goal of between 305 and 310 ships. With ever-declining budgets and single-digit procurement of new Navy ships per year, the service needed to underline its capabilities on the higher end of the conflict spectrum to rationalize itself to Congress and the American people. However, the short four-page statement did not gain traction, mostly because it did not align very well with a national defense policy that increasingly emphasized non-military approaches. The self-proclaimed decisive role for U.S. naval forces in conflict was not validated in later campaigns such as the Kosovo War (1999). In essence, its "catchy title had more influence than [its] content."[98]

Strategic concept

"Anytime, Anywhere" showed remarkable continuity with its predecessors "… From the Sea," "Forward … From the Sea," and the "Navy Operations Concept." "Anytime, Anywhere" focused on deterring conflict and shaping the conflict environment. It attempted to bolster the Navy's role with a focus on more taxing missions. Instead of concentrating too heavily on presence, the paper emphasized power projection, sea control, and war-fighting as the service's chief strategic and contributions to political ends. These were traditional Navy missions, principally again echoing Admiral Turner's position. Littoral warfare, deterrence, the enabling capability of naval forces, sealift, and the Marine Corps were only mentioned in passing.

This reflected the drifting apart of the Marine Corps' and the Navy's strategic approaches and operational realities. Concurrently, the Marine Corps developed what became known as the "three-block war" description for the demands of modern conflict. In military operations other than war (MOOTW), the modern soldier needed to be trained and equipped to sequentially and even simultaneously conduct war-fighting, peacekeeping, and humanitarian operations, all within the range of three city blocks. This recognition was not simply a metaphor; it reflected the Marine Corps' operational experiences of the previous decade, matching CMC Krulak's emphasis on non-lethal force. The Marines embraced these new challenges and the realities of the 1990s settled in the minds of the USMC planners.[99] At the same time, the Navy – with "Anytime, Anywhere" – conceptually went back to the 1970s. While this was a markedly different approach in comparison with the Marines, the Navy also positioned itself against the Air Force and seeming promise of the Revolution in Military Affairs.[100]

Navy Strategic Planning Guidance (1999/2000)

Evolution

The final set of documents for Admiral Johnson's tenure as CNO, and the last for the decade, came in 1999 and 2000. The Navy Strategic Planning Guidance (NSPG) documents were a set of two rather voluminous publications (the 1999 document had 55 pages, the 2000 one 90).[101] Both were drafted in OPNAV N51 under Rear Admiral Joseph Sestak, who had already been deeply involved in "Forward...From the Sea". He and his staff utilized several earlier, abortive strategy drafts circulating in OPNAV. The NSPG represented the attempt for a continuous, cyclical update attuned to geo-strategic and world environment changes, joint planning, and the QDR (the next of which was scheduled for 2001). In addition, it was intended as a link to the Planning, Programming, and Budgeting System (PPBS). As such, it would provide a long-term and truly strategic planning basis instead of one that simply looked to fulfill CINC demands for forces.

The 2000 version discussed the incipient process of globalization and the ascent of regional challengers to U.S. security and maritime access to key regions of the world. In keeping with the Manthorpe curve, it foresaw that a peer competitor would not arise before 2020. Until then, the fleet was to hedge against land-based rogue actors and their militaries. NSPG 2000 underlined the Navy's purpose to be maritime power projection, explaining a means–ways–ends causality for the use of naval force. Significantly, it also proposed an innovative institutional process for addressing long-term strategic planning objectives, thus making true strategic planning worthy of the name. The new format and the new vocabulary ended after the second go-around, although it was to be republished annually. It became another failure to institutionalize format, and the long document lacked traction with the Secretary of the Navy, Richard Danzig. Additionally, key figures in OPNAV and the CNO would soon move on from their respective postings. Admiral Vern Clark, a surface warfare officer, became the new CNO in July 2000 and immediately introduced new priorities. That Presidential election year, it was particularly uncertain what the next four years would look like.

Strategic concept

The "Navy Strategic Planning Guidance" documents were framed by Clinton National Security doctrine favoring selective U.S. military engagement[102] and the anticipation of a new administration after the upcoming November 2000 general election. In addition, the NSPG was published in the middle of the four-year cycle of the Quadrennial Defense Reviews. The QDR 1997 experiences had been absorbed and the QDR 2001 loomed. These factors explain why the capstone documents were largely directed internally and intended to convey that the Navy understood its place in time. At the same point, unclassified versions of the NSPG 1999/2000 spent considerable time developing a new organizational framework for the core-strategic relationship among ways, means, and ends. Maritime power projection to execute it became the overarching strategic imperative of naval forces. The naval means were forward presence and knowledge superiority. The ways were control of the battlespace (a newly introduced term), battlespace attack, and battlespace sustainment. The four ends were: regional stability, deterrence, timely crisis response, and war fighting and winning.[103]

The documents provided a wealth of ideas tying together established and novel missions (including homeland defense, information operations, maritime interception operations, counter-terrorism and counter-drug tasks, and humanitarian operations), identified rogue states and non-state actors as threats, made specific reference to the (rapidly evolving) process of globalization, emphasized the need for cooperation with other government and non-governmental security actors, and framed the Navy as an enabling force that focused on the littorals and beyond.[104] The price for such an ambitious and comprehensive strategic document was its voluminous size and its lack of priorities, rendering it useless in the minds of many decision-makers. Such shortcomings were emblematic of many 1990s Navy capstone documents in their limited sustainability and shared sense of disorientation.

Table 5.3 provides an overview of the 1990s' sea-strategic missions – or core capabilities – these documents declared. It lists the strategies and, where applicable, the missions they (in their own words) foresaw for employment of U.S. sea power to attain strategic ends.

For comparison: "The Maritime Strategy" envisioned only three primary missions. These were sea control, power projection, and sealift (two of them among Turner's 'classic 4').

On balance, the process of writing strategy between 1989 and 2001 was not nearly as organic as the one in the previous decade. Perhaps one should not have expected it to be. The evolution of U.S. Navy capstone documents in the 1990s resembled a number of persistent trial-and-error processes. Key to understanding these was a sense of continuity despite changing geostrategic

Table 5.3 1990s Capstone documents and Navy sea-strategic concepts[105]

Name	Year	Missions identified
The Way Ahead	1991	
The Navy Policy Book	1992	20 characteristics of naval operations including sea control, projection of power, naval presence, strategic deterrence ("classic 4" from ADM Turner 1974)
… From the Sea	1992	Six capabilities ("classic 4", crises, sealift)
Naval Warfare (NDP 1)	1994	10 characteristics of "what we do," including "classic 4"
Forward … From the Sea	1994	Five fundamental and enduring roles ("classic 4" and sealift)
Navy Operational Concept	1997	
Anytime, Anywhere	1997	Four broad missions ("classic 4" expanded): sea and area control, power projection, presence, deterrence (sea control as the prerequisite)
Navy Strategic Planning Guidance	1999/2000	10-part multilevel model, including "classic 4" missions

circumstances, alternating presidential administrations and leadership styles, rapid technological advancements, and shifting budgetary priorities. The strategic-planning efforts were also complicated by intra-Navy rifts, inter-service rivalries, public backlash at Navy scandals, and a shrinking force. Individuals and organizations worked together or separately to create ideas. To policy-makers, however, these lacked the coherence and thrust crucial for political deliberations in Washington. The Navy worked increasingly hard to shed its Cold War thinking and posture, but had difficulties in keeping up with the pace Air Force and Army thought. Both of these services were fortunate in displaying their capabilities and how they made a strategic difference during the crises of the 1990s, something the Navy could not realistically claim.

Force structure[106]

The U.S. Navy came out of the Cold War with a large fleet of almost 600 ships and a global strategy resting on the division of the world into distinct areas of responsibility along the lines of the world oceans. In the 1990s, joint-ness, integration, and new command structures increasingly subordinated Navy prerogatives. The Base Force proposal of 1990 curbed any expectations that the high ship number would be politically viable in the aftermath of the

Soviet Union's break-up. The Navy, as much as the other branches of the military, would have to cut back. It meant reducing the fleet from 540 to 451 ships, the size of the fleet in 1977, and the number of carriers from 15 to 12.[107] The number of the desired force was eventually reduced even further to 416 ships. The Base Force study calculated a basic need for 55–80 SSN, 12 aircraft carriers (conventional/nuclear powered), about 150 surface combatants, and 51 amphibious ships.[108] CNO Trost continued to advocate a large high-end fleet, stating that,

> Survival […] requires advanced electronics and weapon systems and does not allow the luxury of 'low-mix' platforms. The 'hi-tech,' advanced military capability of the world's nations is underscored by the British experience in the South Atlantic [Falklands War, in particular Royal Navy losses to Exocet missiles, S.B.] and our own in the Persian Gulf [the Exocet missile attack on *Stark*, S.B.].[109]

To the Navy, the Cold War tactic of relying on prophecies of advanced technology and associated concepts remained the most promising route in the budgetary process.[110] The Navy's capstone document "… From the Sea" (1992) rested on this predisposition (although the feeling was it did not fully justify the force the Navy really wanted). The Bottom-Up Review (1993) was the first to state the obvious, namely, the disappearance of the Soviet Union as a threat. More important (and unlike the Base Force study), the Bottom-Up Review promised unequal cuts among the services to meet projected defense budget savings, inflation-adjusted, of up to 40 percent. The Bottom-Up Review slashed the military by a third (the Base Force had cut only a quarter) and especially cut into funds and materiel for expeditionary operations at a time when the military's overseas missions skyrocketed. The Navy disproportionally bore that burden.

The tally of the BUR – the self-acclaimed "comprehensive review of the nation's defense strategy, force structure, modernization, infrastructure, and foundations"[111] – recommended 346 ships, among which were just 45–55 SSN, 11 carriers (plus one in reserve), roughly 124 surface combatants, and 36 amphibious vessels (a disappointing low total in the eyes of many). The 1997 QDR, the third major force structure review, had implicitly accepted that downsizing. The Navy provided a rationale for 50–55 SSN, 11 carriers (plus one in reserve), 116 surface combatants, and 36 amphibious vessels.[112] The Navy's force level goal eventually tallied 305, later adjusted to 310, ships, merely half the number that Secretary Lehman and others had lobbied for just over a decade earlier.

Throughout the 1990s, the size of the Navy was driven by the rotational needs of a 2.5 carrier presence globally – one in the Persian Gulf, one in the Western Pacific, and a half (that is, half a year in aggregate) in the Mediterranean, signaling the changed geostrategic focus of the Navy after the Cold War era.[113] The Mediterranean, absent a Soviet squadron (or other challenger of its kind) to stir up the region, rapidly lost geopolitical relevance to most strategic planners, even if the Balkan wars of the 1990s showed the utility of having strong naval forces and at least one aircraft carrier for crisis response. The regional war prism (North Korea, Iraq) was the prevailing metric and mandated a stronger, consistent, carrier-augmented presence in both the Persian Gulf and the Western Pacific. Traditionally thinking more globally than many civilian strategists, the Navy began to emphasize the Pacific and the Indian Ocean long before the term "Pivot to Asia" or 'rebalancing to Asia' even entered public discourse. At the same time, the focus on military operations other than war (MOOTW) intensified.[114]

Figure 5.2 shows the various U.S. Navy force level goals and the actual numbers. Again, the CRS and the NHHC use slightly different metrics to arrive at their respective fleet tallies.

Figure 5.2 illustrates that force level goals, with the exception of the last couple of years in the decade, were lower than the actual Navy inventory. In other words, the Navy had more ships than the political planners granted it or wanted to pay for. Table 5.4 breaks down the total numbers of the inventory.

Two distinct challenges arose for the Navy. First, it needed to balance high-end capabilities with demand for low-intensity conflict prevention. Conceptually, the Navy moved faster into the littorals than it could field corresponding technology to work in them. Second, the Navy did not give up on the blue-water focus. Therefore, it needed to modernize its assets

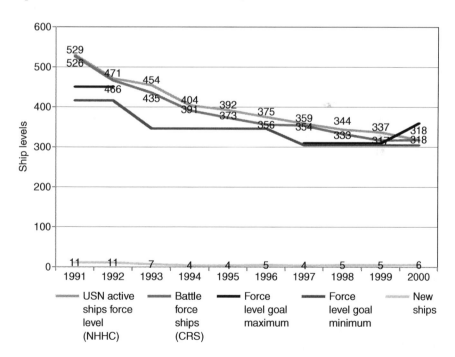

Figure 5.2 USN 1990s ship levels[115]; the Base Force and the QDR did not postulate a single number as a force goal but rather opted for a 'landing zone' quantity.

Table 5.4 U.S. Navy active ship force levels, 1990–2000[116]

Date	9/90	9/91	9/92	9/93	9/94	9/95	9/96	9/97	9/98	9/99	9/00
Battleships	4	1	–	–	–	–	–	–	–	–	–
Carriers	13	15	14	13	12	12	12	12	12	12	12
Cruisers	43	47	49	52	35	32	31	30	29	27	27
Destroyers	57	47	40	37	41	47	51	56	50	52	54
Frigates	99	93	67	59	51	49	43	42	38	37	35
Submarines	93	87	85	88	88	83	79	73	65	57	56
SSBNs	33	34	30	22	18	16	17	18	18	18	18
Command ships	4	4	4	4	4	4	4	4	4	4	–
Mine warfare	22	22	16	15	16	18	18	18	18	18	18
Patrol	6	6	6	2	7	12	13	13	13	13	–
Amphibious	59	61	58	52	38	39	40	41	40	41	41
Auxiliary	137	112	102	110	94	80	67	52	57	57	57
Surface total	203	188	156	148	127	128	123	122	109	106	128
Total active	570	529	471	454	404	392	375	359	344	337	318

accordingly, also presenting an old-vs.-new dichotomy. Against the background of the pricey revolution in military affairs (RMA) and shrinking, ever-finite military budgets, this spelled hard choices for the Navy.

The cost-and-manpower-intensive *Iowa*-class battleships were retired, but only some of their capabilities would be replaced by modern ships. With the behemoths of World War II also went a ll ships whose major Cold War task was fleet air defense.[117] On occasion, this included relatively new ships that still had some time available to serve the Navy. All nine nuclear-powered cruisers (CGN) and the *Leahy*- and *Belknap*-classes were decommissioned; the *Ticonderoga*-class remained as the only type in service and an indispensable asset to the fleet. Another Aegis-capable addition to the fleet in the 1990s was the 9,000-ton guided missile destroyer of the *Arleigh-Burke*-class (DDG 51 etc.), today's backbone of the U.S. Navy surface fleet (and numerically largest destroyer class worldwide). These destroyers, much like the larger cruisers, were equipped with VLS launch tubes to carry cruise and air defense missiles. The most dramatic shift occurred in the mission area of ASW operations and programs. A wide-ranging dismantling of Cold War ASW capabilities stripped the Navy of whole classes of ships. For example, all 46 *Knox*-class frigates were decommissioned. The *Spruance* and *Kidd*-class destroyers and ocean surveillance ships of the T-AGOS-type were eased out, and the SOSUS array was shut down. The numbers of attack submarines, *Perry*-class frigates, maritime patrol aircraft (P-3C), carrier-based ASW planes (i.e., S-3 Viking), and helicopters (i.e., SH-3 Sea King) were cut considerably.[118]

The decade was also characterized by transformative technology. Ballistic missile defense (BMD) research, development, and testing began in earnest. Widespread use of personal computers, cell phones, and networks dramatically changed the way the Navy did business. In terms of tactics, visit/board/search/seizure (VBSS) capabilities were increasingly developed and tested for maritime security operations. Capable software supported the use of precision guided munitions, a revolutionary aspect first demonstrated to a broader audience during the Gulf War. The Tomahawk cruise missile became the premier standoff weapon against distant, mid-range, and tactical targets. Software also empowered networking ships, aircraft, sensors, and systems to an extent previously unseen.

In the 1990s, the Navy's undersea roster included the last boats of the Ohio-class. After 2000, the four oldest SSBN (*Ohio*, *Michigan*, *Georgia*, and *Florida*) underwent a conversion to guided-missile submarines, retaining their pennant numbers (SSGNs 726–729).[119] After the costly procurement of the *Seawolf*-class submarines (SSN 21 through SSN 23) – a product of the Cold War ultimately cut to only three units – the *Virginia*-class nuclear-powered fast attack submarines (SSN 774, etc.) entered service after 2001. They were a cheaper and timelier alternative to the *Seawolf*.[120] They followed (and will replace) the *Los-Angeles*-class fast attack submarines procured until the mid-1990s.

In the surface fleet, the *Whidbey Island*-class dock landing ships (LSD 41–49) sustained the vertical and horizontal insertion capabilities of the Marine Corps, providing well decks and deck space for the new tilt-rotor V-22 Osprey aircraft that appeared towards the end of the decade.[121] Much larger than the LSD (and to replace the older tank- and dock-landing vessels of the *Newport-*, *Austin-*, and *Anchorage*-classes) was the new *San-Antonio*-class (LPD 17) amphibious transport dock. The first four vessels of that 24,900-ton type were procured in FY 1996, 1999, and 2000 (two), respectively.[122] Dry cargo ships of the *Lewis-and-Clarke*-class (T-AKE 1 through T-AKE 14) were also procured, providing one platform for resupply of ammunition and combat stores previously on separate classes of auxiliary ships. The Navy emphasized fewer, more efficient ships to replace more numerous, less capable hulls.

Rapid technological innovation, sweeping military transformation, and contrasting ideas for the size and design of the twenty-first century fleet spurred debate about future platforms. The 1990s witnessed ambitious design and procurement plans for a new generation of warships. A new class of command ships, the JCC(X), was studied, but never built. The Surface Combatant for the Twenty-First Century (SC-21) program proposed three main ship types designed for naval gunfire support. This fell in line with the Navy's strategic and operational power projection into the littorals. The SC-21 study envisaged a future destroyer-like combatant for power projection ashore, a cruiser-like warship for ballistic missile defense and carrier battle group operations, and an arsenal ship. The latter, a completely new type of warship, was proposed to be much more cost-effective than the high-maintenance battleships. This combatant would have up to 500 VLS tubes for cruise missiles, ride low in the water, and have a drastically reduced crew. Deploying such a ship to a crisis area would, in the mind of the new platform's supporters, signal U.S. resolve without endangering many American lives (Federation of American Scientists, 1999). With cost overruns and conflicting ideas about the future force, all but one of the concepts was abandoned by the early 2000s. The DDG 1000, the single surviving concept, will remain a three-ship class of futuristic large destroyers to be used for extensive research and testing. The more feasible replacement of such drastic and perhaps all-too-innovative ideas came in the form of the SSGN conversions and, more importantly, new flights of *Arleigh-Burke*-class destroyers.

Naval aviation was modernizing as well. The new A-12 Avenger II carrier-based stealth aircraft was cancelled amidst dramatic cost overruns in 1991. Instead, the Navy picked the F/A-18 E/F Super Hornet to replace the A-6 Intruder and A-7 Corsair II attack planes, and the F-14 Tomcat fighter aircraft.[123] Meanwhile, new versions of Sikorsky's Seahawk MH-60 helicopter joined the fleet and replaced older models in missions such as transport, MCM, and ASuW.

During the 1990s, the U.S. Navy's conventional and nuclear forces declined in real numbers, tonnage, and construction/upkeep budgets. Smaller units were decommissioned more often than larger ones, yielding an imbalance in the fleet toward the capital units. It is ironic that the Navy, which would have been better suited for most Clinton-era policies than, for example, the Air Force or the Army, was disproportionally affected by the drawdown in numbers and capabilities. Still, with the fleet inventory and the investment into research of future platforms, the United States remained the world's dominant naval force.

Strategic and operational implementation: planned vs. actual

The Navy's high operational tempo in the 1990s rested expertise gained over the final years of the Cold War. The majority of combat operations were against shore targets, while warfare and, consequently, experience at sea were minimal.[124] The introduction of Tomahawk land attack cruise missiles through-out the fleet altered operations: during the Clinton years, the missile quickly emerged as the number-one weapon for strike operations, against Iraq, but also Sudan and Afghanistan in response to the U.S. embassy bombings in Africa in 1998, and in the Balkans.[125] The Gulf War marked the debut of these weapons, delivered from cruisers, destroyers, attack submarines, and even battleships.[126] As it was, TLAM became a strategic weapon used at the discretion of the President. Liberally used, it saved the president from making hard choices regarding the deployment of ground troops or air force bombers. Concurrently, there were now more expeditionary operations that the Navy had to cater.

Major U.S. naval operations[127]

On balance, there are at least four strategic naval operations characterizing the 1990s from a U.S. Navy perspective. American sea power was directed as a natural extension of U.S. grand strategic goals and postulations – sometimes powerful, often hesitantly and in measured doses. High seas control was uncontested, but the littoral zone mandated a conceptual and intellectual strategic shift in Navy thinking and operations. Consequently, the 1990s demanded a conscious appreciation of the fuller range of sea power measures across the entire spectrum.

The Persian Gulf (1990–2000)[128]

The Gulf War at the transition from the Cold War to the emerging new world (dis-)order was one of the largest U.S. Navy operations of the post-World War II era. The Navy fielded up to seven aircraft carrier groups and two battleships groups. The conflict essentially consisted of four phases.

- "Operation Desert Shield," a defense of Saudi-Arabia (August through October 1990) and
- Preparation for the offensive against Hussein's troops (November through mid-January 1991).
- "Operation Desert Storm" designated the push of Iraqi troops from Kuwait. It featured a four-week air campaign against Iraqi targets in Kuwait and Iraq that began on January 17, 1991, followed by a 100-hour ground war.
- The war's aftermath kept the U.S. disproportionally busy for the rest of the decade.[129]

The Persian Gulf, Red Sea, and eastern Mediterranean served as staging areas for the naval component of the broad international military coalition that the Bush Sr. administration assembled; naval supply routes ferried supplies into the theater.[130] Here was a robust U.S. political and military push-back of Iraqi aggression, although the Joint Staff initially was more inclined to safeguard Saudi-Arabia rather than to fight for Kuwaiti liberation.[131]

Within days of the Iraqi incursion into Kuwait, two U.S. Navy carrier battle groups centered on *Independence* (CV 62) and *Dwight D. Eisenhower* (CVN 69) which were on station in the Gulf of Oman and the Red Sea, respectively. The naval armada that assembled through early 1991 eventually consisted of more than 150 warships from 14 countries. The U.S. Navy contributed 108 of these, including the carriers *Midway* (CV 41), *Saratoga* (CV 60), *Ranger* (CV 61), *America* (CV 66), *John F. Kennedy* (CV 67), and *Theodore Roosevelt* (CVN 71).[132] Carrier aviation accounted for almost one-third of anti-Iraqi coalition air forces.[133] The aircraft carrier once again underlined its operational and strategic utility even as the geopolitical landscape was shifting from global superpower conflict to regional wars. Two battleships, 13 submarines, and a large amphibious force complemented the overwhelming display of American sea power.[134] Two-hundred and eighty-two naval cruise missiles were launched throughout the war.[135]

The Gulf War was the first major test of integrated planning, interoperability, and procurement laid out in the Goldwater-Nichols Act. The Navy's strategic culture of independence from the other services was severely tested during the military campaign. The coalition air component commander's Air Tasking Order (ATO), a flight operations management system to coordinate and integrate the air campaign, had to be flown out on paper to the carriers every day instead of being transmitted electronically. The Navy simply did not field the systems to process these orders automatically. In addition, the Navy's commander in theater preferred to be on his flagship instead of being at the U.S. HQ ashore. This issue amplified the Navy's joint organizational and operational problems in the modern combat environment (Schneller, 2007: 22). The swift military victory, "one of the most decisive victories in military history" (ibid: 30), overshadowed other subsidiary Navy-related concerns that occurred, such as the missile-boat threat[136] and the enduring challenge of mine warfare.[137]

Containment of Iraq remained at the forefront of U.S. strategic interests in the Persian Gulf throughout the 1990s, with naval forces as a major lever for that objective.[138] Throughout the 1990s, U.S. military aircraft enforced a no–fly zone over parts of Iraq ("Operation Northern Watch"/"Operation Southern Watch"). U.S. cruise missiles pounded Iraq in June 1993 and September 1996. From October to December 1994, U.S. forces were rushed into the region to hedge against another possible Iraqi assault on Kuwait. In December 1998, coordinated U.S. cruise missiles and air strikes codenamed "Operation Desert Fox" targeted infrastructure in response to the Iraqi regime's repeated failure to cooperate in the enforcement of the U.N. sanctions regime and to adhere to the no–fly zones.[139]

The Adriatic Sea (1993–1996, 1999)

In 1991, the disintegration of Yugoslavia and the ethnic conflicts that followed pitted newly independent states against each other in a civil war. The conflict, a result of the end of the Cold War and the demise of Yugoslav ruler Josip Broz Tito, required concerted international military engagement including naval assets. After the outbreak of hostilities, NATO and West European Union (WEU) member states began to provide assets to a U.N. force in the Republic of Bosnia and Herzegovina and to enforce a no–fly zone over Yugoslavia (now consisting of Serbia and Montenegro). When it became evident that Serbian aggression against its neighbors was not deterred and European nations by themselves would be unable to achieve a peaceful outcome of the conflict, a weapons embargo was imposed (Prince and Brett, 2013: 48–49).

On June 15, 1993, NATO and the WEU began a combined maritime mission in the Adriatic Sea called "Operation Sharp Guard." Its objective was to monitor and enforce sanctions and provide leverage for U.N. Security Council resolutions. "Operation Sharp Guard" was significant in that it constituted the alliance's first out-of-area mission. The mission drew forces from established multinational naval commands, namely Standing Naval Force Atlantic (STANAVFORLANT), Standing Naval Force Mediterranean (STANAVFORMED), and the Western European Union Contingency Maritime Force (WEUCONMARFOR). Airborne early warning aircraft such as NATO AWACS E-3A jets featuring multinational crews patrolled the skies and provided surveillance, command, control, and communication. Special arrangements overcame tensions between conflicting U.N. and NATO objectives for their respective Balkans missions. These measures also reduced the frictional loss among navies because of their differing rules of engagement (ROE).[140]

To U.S. naval planners and operators, "Operation Sharp Guard" provided a markedly different example of engagement in the Sixth Fleet AOR from the Cold War years. Over the operation, the U.S. Navy dispatched guided missile cruisers (such as *Dale* [CG 19] and *Monterey* [CG 61]), as well as destroyers (such as *Comte de Grasse* [DD 974]), frigates (e.g., *Boone* [FFG 28], *Nicolas* [FFG 47], and *Samuel B. Roberts* [FFG 58]),[141] and numerous P-3C maritime patrol aircraft to the area.[142] In its 43 months of activity before June 1996, "Operation Sharp Guard" and its preceding missions challenged 74,192 merchant vessels en route to Balkan ports and boarded over one-twelfth of them in search of contraband. More than 1,400 ships were diverted away for further inspection and six violators of U.N. sanctions were identified. Maritime patrol aircraft flew over 7,000 sorties. Occasionally, USN aircraft carriers supported the mission. Sharp Guard, NATO's first combat operation, was a large-scale and successful effort.[143]

In parallel, NATO and the United Nations conducted "Operation Deliberate Force" between August 30 and September 20, 1995 to guard U.N.-designated safe areas from attack by Bosnian Serbs. Four-hundred NATO aircraft participated in the operation, launching precision strikes against Serb positions and installations in Bosnia, serving C4ISR needs, and providing aerial refueling. The naval contributions to the operation included three aircraft carriers (the French *Foch* [R 99], the Royal Navy's *Invincible* [R 05], and the U.S. Navy's *America* [CV 66]) in the Adriatic Sea and Tomahawk cruise missile launches against Serbian targets. NATO forces were under the command of U.S. Navy Admiral Leighton Smith as Commander, Allied Forces South. Smith subsequently commanded the NATO-led Implementation Force (IFOR) for Bosnia (Stillwell interview with Smith, 2006/2010).[144]

U.S. and coalition forces returned to the Balkans in 1999 when the Kosovo War led NATO to conduct a sustained air campaign against Serbia. Here, the U.S. Navy's contribution to "Operation Allied Force" (March–June) and its follow-up peacekeeping "Operation Joint Guardian," a freestanding case of air power exclusively achieving political results, included the carriers *Enterprise* (CVN 65) and *Theodore Roosevelt* (CVN 71) CVBGs, as well as the *Kearsarge* (LHD 3) ARG. Carrier aviation provided significant military leverage against Serbian targets in the 78-day-long campaign. The presence of U.S. warships after the conclusion of hostilities deterred Serbia from attacking Kosovo again.[145] These operations underlined that continued U.S. engagement in European security affairs remained imperative because of the lack of organic European capabilities and, perhaps more importantly, domestic political will.[146]

Haiti (1994–1996)

In America's backyard, the early 1990s held yet another crisis for the Clinton administration. In Haiti, some 1,200 km from Florida, a *coup d'état* by the military ousted the democratically elected President Jean-Bertrand Aristide and placed a series of de-facto rulers in the leadership of the country. In 1994, the U.N. Security Council adopted a resolution authorizing the establishment of a multinational force (MNF). The United States planned for two military contingencies: a forced entry (codename "Operation Restore Democracy") and a permissive entry (codename "Operation Uphold Democracy") to reinstate Aristide's presidency. The Navy's role began in June 1993 when the international embargo against the regime in Port-au-Prince began enforcement. The Navy conducted maritime interception operations. In addition, the Navy and the Coast Guard supported the interdiction and processing of some 75,000 refugees who had attempted to flee the conflict-torn country, often on unseaworthy vessels.[147] U.N. Security Council Resolution 940 (July 31, 1994) allowed member states to make use of all necessary means for the removal of the military government and to re-establish order and legitimate rule.

On September 18, 1994, just hours before starting a military invasion, President Clinton dispatched a last-minute diplomatic task force headed by former president Jimmy Carter, (former Chairman of the Joint Chiefs of Staff) General (ret.) Colin Powell, and Senator Sam Nunn to Haiti. The effort was an eleventh-hour success (most of the paratrooper force was already headed to its drop areas when the solution came through) and the forced entry turned into a compliant intervention (the timetable prompted some to describe "Operation Uphold Democracy" as an "intervasion"). A potential reprisal of the Mogadishu events a year before was averted and the operation took on much more of a humanitarian, almost altruistic face (catering to the idealist strain of U.S. foreign-policy thinking). An exit plan, conforming to the Weinberger and Powell doctrines, provided a schedule for the reduction of U.S. forces and transition of peacekeeping functions within the MNF to the United Nations. The operation underlined that multi-mission capable naval forces could provide a range of options even in a joint, inter-agency, and coalition environment.[148]

Taiwan Strait (1994–1996)

Another series of highlighted U.S. naval operations occurred in the Western Pacific in 1995 and 1996 in the context of American-Chinese confrontations over Taiwan.[149] After the Chinese civil war, which took place between 1927 and 1949, the country divided unequally into two. The Communist-held mainland (the People's Republic of China) and the pro-Western island of Taiwan (the Republic of China) emerged as two de-facto states both laying claim to represent the legitimate government of China. U.S.-Chinese relations had bloomed cautiously in the late 1970s when diplomatic relations were first established. Subsequently, U.S. recognition shifted from Taiwan to China. When the Soviet Union disintegrated, China did not require as close a relationship with the United States, and began increasingly assertive actions against Taiwan and others. The massacre on Beijing's Tiananmen Square in June 1989, amidst the thawing Cold War in Europe, furthered the deterioration of Chinese standing in the region and the world. In the mid-1990s, Taiwan emerged as a free-market economy and a booming Asian economic powerhouse. A democratic leadership which openly discussed Taiwanese independence competed with Beijing's aim to reunite the nation on its terms. A visit by Taiwanese president Lee Tung-hui to the United States in May 1995 for a university commencement address tipped the situation over the edge. During July and August, the Chinese PLAN undertook missile launches and live firings less than 130 kilometers from Taiwan to inhibit the island's government and send a strong signal to the U.S. administration that it disapproved of Washington's de-facto recognition of Taiwanese independence.

That December, President Clinton ordered an aircraft carrier group led by *Nimitz* (CVN 68) through the strait separating Taiwan from China. In January 1996, the amphibious assault ship *Belleau Wood* (LHA 3) also transited. Both instances signaled to Beijing American intent to defend Taiwan's right of self-determination. Dispatching U.S. Air Force or Army units to achieve a similar effect would have been considerably more difficult than employing the naval assets forward-deployed in the area. However, China was hardly deterred and began a major exercise the next month. Beginning in February 1996, attack submarines, destroyers, frigates, patrol craft, and amphibious vessels from each of China's three fleets converged on the coast of Fujian Province across from Taiwan. Chinese troops numbering 150,000 were deployed, along with hundreds of capable fighters, bombers, and attack planes.[150]

In preparation for the Taiwanese presidential campaign in March of that year, the Chinese military conducted concerted large-scale exercises, some of which were barely outside of the island's waters. This time, the American response was considerably stronger. Days after diplomats condemned Chinese coercion, the aircraft carrier *Independence* (CV 62), the guided missile cruiser *Bunker Hill* (CG 52), the destroyers *Hewitt* (DD 966) and *O'Brien* (DD 975), and the frigate *McClusky* (FFG 41) had assumed station near Taiwan. A second carrier group – led by *Nimitz* and consisting of the guided missile cruiser *Port Royal* (CG 73), the destroyers *Oldendorf* (DD 972) and *Callaghan* (DD 994) as well as the frigate *Ford* (FFG 54), two attack submarines (*Columbus* [SSN 762] and *Bremerton* [SSN 698]), and support ships – was dispatched to the region 24 hours later. Although there is no indication that the carriers actually transited the Taiwan Strait, the U.S. naval commitment sent a strong signal that the leadership in Beijing had failed to anticipate.

However, cordial Chinese-American relations were soon restored, not least for economic reasons. Taiwan emerged from the crisis unscathed (and has begun to consider closer ties with mainland); the U.S. underlined its unambiguous commitment to Taiwan; and it brought closer ties between the U.S. and other Asian nations such as Singapore and Japan, the latter historically a competitor with China for regional influence. Forward-deployed naval power including the aircraft carrier in the Seventh Fleet AOR had sent a strong signal to the countries affected. They provided options that only sea power could offer.

Relationships to allies[151]

The Navy's relationship to its international partner services was tested repeatedly in the 1990s by real-world contingencies. As on the joint front, combined operations became increasingly common and integrated rather than merely coordinated. Naval action in the Persian Gulf in 1990/1991 set the tone, and other multinational naval operations such as in the Adriatic Sea – the first real-life NATO contingency since the Cold War – followed. Allies were increasingly interested in investing resources in technologies, sensors, and platforms developed by the United States.[152] In turn, the U.S. Navy also began to be interested in advanced allied systems such as air-independent propulsion submarines or high-speed catamarans.

Many European partners radically cut their defense budgets, often in the hope of re-distributing substantial Cold War military expenditures into more popular social welfare programs. Navies were obviously affected as well by these indiscriminate cuts. At the same time, the U.S. Navy continued to practice and engage with allied nations, most visibly in such long-standing exercises as BALTOPS in the Baltic Sea and RIMPAC in the Pacific. Remarkably, "… From the Sea" was cited in Australian, British, Canadian, and Indian capstone documents between 1997 and 2007,[153] indicating the quality and lasting impression it made in allied naval forces.

Significant organizational changes

To reflect the altered security environment, the 1990s witnessed wide-ranging changes to bureaucratic structures and processes. Most of these reflected the Goldwater-Nichols Act taking full effect. It shifted power from the service branches – i.e., the Navy – to OSD, the Joint Staff, and the CINCs. In essence, it reduced the purpose of the services to become force providers. In 1992, a major OPNAV reorganization and re-designation was implemented to reflect the expansion and vision of the Joint Staff. This substantial change resulted in the breaking of the previously powerful warfare community barons (surface, submarine, and aviation). Instead, programming offices gained substantial power. N8, the newly designated branch for strategic programming, subsumed 400 of the 1,200 personnel assigned to OPNAV,[154] dubbed "Super N8." Strategy took a back seat to writing the budget.

Admiral Kelso's changes were significant by implementing joint thinking into the Navy bureaucracy, with sweeping consequences. Instead of basing priorities on naval warfare areas (such as antisubmarine or strike warfare), they now focused on joint warfare capabilities. Program sponsors now had to justify their part of the budget across all seven of these joint mission areas.[155] Kelso's successors, CNOs Boorda and Johnson, fine-tuned many of the processes that kicked off in the early 1990s. While the changes in the Navy and OSD bureaucracy were significant in their own right, one of the more immediately visible innovations was the creation of the U.S. Fifth Fleet in 1995, a dedicated force responsible for the Arabian Sea, the Red Sea, the Persian Gulf, and the Strait of Hormuz. This was a direct lesson of the large-scale contingencies during the Gulf War, where U.S. Navy assets and organization were deemed unfit for handling a major operation in the region.[156]

Assessment: American sea power in a decade of uncertainty, 1989–2001

From a strategic point of view, the long 1990s were a challenging period for the Navy. Navy budgets shrank, ship and aircraft numbers went down, manpower was reduced drastically, and new warship procurement was cut significantly. At the same time, the fleet was in high operational demand. Crises in Yugoslavia, Iraq, Somalia, and Haiti were exactly the kind of brushfires that the Navy antici-pated after finally shelving "The Maritime Strategy." Only after dropping "The Maritime Strategy," was the Navy able to muster intellectual capital and time its drafting of the white paper, "… From the Sea". It was a lucid, strategic concept in Samuel Huntington's sense. The most important message in "… From the Sea" was that the Navy now concentrated on naval operations in the framework of a joint task force involved in a major regional contingency rather than engag-ing in a global conventional struggle as a semi-independent force.[157] "… From the Sea" also marked a departure from a classic naval strategy that concerned itself with blue-water events. Instead, it shifted the focus. Sea control was not an end in itself, but now should better enable land control, thereby broadening the Navy's naval scope to a more comprehensive, even maritime one (which assumed increasing jointness and combined arms operations).[158]

As a conceptual framework, it realigned unified efforts from the sea toward the land, emphasizing the focus on strike and littoral operations. Unlike many other documents of the 1990s, it also gave the Navy a sense of institutional rationality. Its lasting influence can be explained by the real innovation that it intellectually lent the service and by acknowledging that the Navy was increas-ingly silent – at least strategically – for the remainder of the decade. In a move reminiscent of its behavior in the years after World War II, the 1990s American defense establishment focused on how the military fought, not why.[159]

The Navy needed to balance high-end capabilities with low-end scenarios (which it correctly accomplished) and also square high-end capabilities with the need for numbers (which it did not achieve as a look at the decade's ship pro-curements will illustrate). Technology increasingly shaped traditional naval operations and missions, a relatively easy sale to Congress. Emphasizing pricey gear was a tactic that allowed the Navy to procrastinate on answering any more strategic ambitions, for example defining what its geopolitical roles and missions were, and how it could contribute to the political ends of sea power. In addi-tion, the very processes of formulating capstone documents in the 1990s for the Navy were often confusing, ineffective, repetitive, and erratic. Therefore, stra-tegic adjustment – in other words, the fundamental transformation of the service – rested principally on the institutionalization of ideas in the Navy itself.

This transformation was neither the inevitable consequence of changes in the international environment nor dictated by individuals or groups outside of the naval service.[160] The Navy solely satisfied its own intellectual needs.

At the same time, the sheer number of official naval strategic documents – eight – was a function of changes in leadership and associated (actual or anticipated) changes in priorities. In part, the collection reflects the desire by the Navy as well as by individual leaders to have their own defining statements.[161] To a degree, such measures are necessary when political administrations change, but they ran the risk of introducing entirely new vocabulary and different points of reference along the way, thus providing more confusion than clarity. A document's half-life can be severely curtailed under such circumstances.

Bush and Clinton began by enunciating foreign policies that contained interventionist notions. Both also put a priority on increasing diplomatic and economic engagement as tools for foreign and security policy ends. In theory, this would have put the Navy in the spotlight, given sea power's inherent opportunities (presence, maritime security, etc.) and that naval forces have the luxury of providing an inherently more diplomatic military tool which armies or air forces cannot afford.[162] The opportunity for transitioning to a truly maritime American grand strategy, which diplomatically would have allowed the U.S. to assume the role of an off-shore "balancer" and a "grand-facilitator,"[163] was missed. Ironically, both presidential administrations engaged in substantial across-the-board defense spending cuts, with the Navy disproportionally affected by them.

The lack of a template for American sea power in the 1990s let the Navy strictly manage itself instead of reflecting on what it was organized, trained, and equipped for in the first place. A systemic role for the Navy emerged only very slowly toward the end of the decade when the effects of globalization began to be felt. After all, the American-led liberal economic and political system had prevailed – "a system whose designers understood the notion that economic power is the father of military power."[164] For the time being, little was done to disseminate that observation and introduce such themes into its capstone documents or even national concepts, thereby making U.S. grand strategy for the 1990s truly maritime.

The Navy ended the decade with mixed morale. It was understandably proud of its operational record. Its intellectual focus on forward presence and emphasis of strike capabilities from different platforms invigorated the service. Shedding legacy platforms as part of the mandated reductions was a necessary but ultimately helpful exercise. The Navy was able to have the defense establishment accept and embrace the consensus that buttressed "…From the Sea," particularly on the primacy of power projection. However, there was a concern about waning ship numbers and the degree of readiness. ASW and ASuW capabilities were declining at a time when regional powers such as China or Iran began to develop A2AD measures to keep the U.S. Navy at bay.

After the 2000 attack on the USS *Cole*, force protection became a major concern for operators, emblematic of the Navy's overall focus on sub-strategic issues during the better part of the 1990s. That decade was replete with challenges related to military and political planning in the face of uncertainty. Those dynamics blocked the careful crafting of a truly maritime national strategy, and the Navy only occasionally achieved some success in its subordinate naval programs. The American *fin de siède* was characterized by scattered crises, conflicts, wars, and policy conditions at home which bore little resemblance to the Cold War days. This illustrates that strategy often emerges pragmatically. The art of strategy needs talent, and such talent needs grooming. If conditions are adverse, even the most motivated artist will eventually be discouraged.

Notes

1 For this chapter, it is helpful to understand the decade as "the long 1990s," framed by the pivotal events of the fall of the Berlin Wall on the one hand and the terrorist attacks on September 11, 2001 on the other. Both events serve to remind the analyst as well as the senior decision-maker of strategic uncertainty. For an expanded discussion of U.S. foreign and national security policy during that period, see Chollet and Goldgeier, 2008.

2 Hattendorf, 2006: 1.

3 Hattendorf, 2006: 1.

4 Bush, 1990a.

5 For a short introduction on the role of the United Nations in U.S. policy on Iraq in the run-up to the Gulf War 1990/1991, see Bruns, 2008: 37–74. For a general and worthwhile analysis of the role of the U.S. Navy in U.N. peace-keeping operations, see Allison, 1993.

6 Bush, 1990b.

7 Haynes, 2013: 66.

8 The U.S. retained the sea-borne submarine leg of its nuclear deterrence triad.

9 It should be noted that the nuclear threat did not disappear, but rather regionalized, replacing the global war scenario. Examples for regional nuclear aspirations in the 1990s can be found for North Korea, Pakistan, India, Iran, China, and some successor states of the former Soviet Union.

10 Gray, 1992: 290.

11 Lundesgaard, 2011: 6.

12 Krauthammer, 1990.

13 For a study on smaller-scale contingencies and the forces that shape the Navy, see Swartz and McGrady, 1998.

14 Rosenberg, 1993: 144–145.

15 Smith, 1999: 11.

16 Trost, 1990: 93.

17 This was also facilitated by the emerging, then towards the end of the decade rapidly expanding World Wide Web. The internet, originally developed with a military purpose in mind, dramatically affected people's lives – and, as the 2000s showed, not least military doctrines, people's security concerns, and warfare.

18 For the address, see Lake, 1993. An analysis of the foreign policy implications can be found in Keller, 2008.

19 Gormley, 2010: 177–184; Kan, 2014: 1–50.

20 Remarkable attacks include the 1993 bombing of the World Trade Center parking garage in New York City (six†, more than 1,000 injured), the 1995 bombing of a federal building in Oklahoma City by U.S. right-wing militants (168†, more than 600 injuries), and the Sarin nerve gas attack on the Tokyo

subway by the Aum Shinrikyo cult the same year (13†, more than 6,000 injured).

21 Pearl and O'Rourke, 2001: CRS-2. See also Kirk S. Lippold, *Front Burner. Al Qaeda'a Attack on the USS Cole.* New York, NY. Public Affairs Publisher, 2013.

22 The invasion of the Central American country was designed to unseat the ruling regime of General Manuel Noriega. "Operation Just Cause" contained limited military objectives (removal of Noriega and stability for the country which was of obvious strategic interest to the U.S. because of the Panama Canal). The Panama Canal Zone was principally U.S.-controlled territory. In 1977, the Carter administration agreed to relinquish control over the area adjacent to the Canal by 1999. The operation contained only some Navy/Marine Corps assets and rested primarily on the shoulders of the Army, Air Force, and Special Operation Forces (Phillips, 2004: 5–49).

23 The incident was part of the larger "Operation Gothic Serpent." More commonly, the events are also often referred to as the "Black Hawk Down" incident, named after the loss of two name-sake Sikorsky UH-60 helicopters. The battle was described in a 1999 book of the same name, and popularized through a commercially successful movie which was released in 2001. For a review of the operation from the U.S. Army's perspective, see Stewart, 2002.

24 Haynes, 2013: 133.

25 Liang and Xiangsui, 1999: n.p.

26 On Bush's comprehensive reflections of his tenure in the national security arena and the defense issues at stake, see Bush and Scowcroft, 1998. On foreign relations, the end of the Cold War, and the Bush presidency, also see Hurst, 2000, and Maynard, 2008.

27 Les Aspin, "On the Sea Change in the Security Environment," The *Officer* Magazine, February 1993, cited in Liang and Xiangsui 1999, n.p.

28 Hacke, 2005: 456–520. For the Secretary's own views on his tenure, see Baker, 2008.

29 The annual symposium of the "Tailhook Association", a fraternal non-profit group of naval aviators, held in Las Vegas (Nevada) in September 1991 was overshadowed by at least 90 cases of sexual harassment and physical abuse during the conference.

30 Vistica, 1997.

31 According to Haynes (2013: 53–54), however,

> Powell was among those that did not fully 'understand' or 'appreciate' the Navy's continuing role. Powell had an incomplete understanding of the Navy. […] Powell did not understand the nature of the Navy's thinking during the Cold War. He did not understand the reasons for the Navy's generic operational flexibility approach […].

32 The White House, 1994: 2.

33 The White House, 1999: 2.

34 Cited in Davis, 1993: 17.

35 Office of the Historian, Department of State, 2013.

36 Department of the Navy, 2000.

37 Haynes, 2013: 135.

38 A *Baltimore Sun* article on the occasion of Boorda's death insinuated the relationship between the service's culture and the admiral's personal problems (N.N., 1996).

39 Shenon, 1996.

40 Naval History and Heritage Command, 2008.

41 Swartz, 2012b: 20, slide 39 and 35, slide 70.

42 Vistica, 1997.

43 To complement top-level guidance, the White House submitted a steady stream of National Security Directives (NSD, Bush Sr.) or Presidential Decision Directives (PDD, Clinton), respectively. These national security memos were often used to clarify administration policies. In the national security and military realm specifically for the Navy (some were referenced in the capstone documents), the following directives are of note: NSD-49 (October 12, 1990) on freedom of navigation issues; NSD-74 (November 24, 1992) on peacekeeping and humanitarian relief policy; PDD-25 (May 6, 1994) on U.S. policy regarding multilateral peace operations; PDD-26 (June 9, 1994) on U.S. Arctic policy; PDD-32 (January 23, 1995) on freedom of navigation issues; PDD-56 (May 1997) on administration's policy on managing complex contingency operations; and PDD-60 (November 1997) on nuclear weapons employment policy. The full texts of the memos can be found at the website of the George Bush Presidential Library and Museum (http://bushlibrary.tamu.edu/research/nsd.php) and the William J. Clinton Presidential Library (www.clintonlibrary.gov).

44 See Joseph A. Gagliano, *Congressional Policymaking in Sino-US Relations during the Post-Cold War Era*, London. Routledge, 2015, 173–174.

45 Chairman of the Joint Chiefs of Staff, 1992: 17–25.

46 Swartz, 2012b: 27, slide 53.

47 For an in-depth discussion of the Base Force, see Larson *et al.*, 2001: 5–39.

48 Department of Defense, 1993. For an in-depth discussion of the Bottom-Up Review, see Larson *et al.*, 2001: 41–81.

49 Owens, 1993: 16–17.

50 Larson *et al.*, 2001: 46–48

51 Department of Defense, 1993: 13.

52 The established model of the spectrum of conflict for the military consists of notional phases in a serial chain. The pattern describes a conflict's dynamics and the role that the U.S. military intends to play. In its most common way, it consists of six phases. Phase Zero is known as the "Shape" phase in which prevention and contingency preparation are undertaken. Phase I, "Deterrence," is a defined crisis that needs to be met by capable actions and means. Phase II, the "Seize" part, contains the assurance of friendly freedom of action and access to a theater's infrastructure. Phase III, "Dominance," establishes powerful force capabilities to achieve full-spectrum superiority. Phase IV is the "Stabilize" round where security is established and pre-conflict services (such as governance, infrastructure, etc.) are restored. Phase V contains the transfer of responsibility to a civilian authority and the military's redeployment; it is known as "Enable Civil Authority."

53 Larson *et al.*, 2001: 59.

54 Bierling, 2003: 224–226.

55 Department of Defense, 1997. For an in-depth discussion of the Quadrennial Defense Review 1997, see Larson *et al.*, 2001: 83–120.

56 CJCS General John Shalikashvili came out with the report before the civilian leaders of OSD were able to influence it significantly. Secretary of Defense William Cohen had little leverage within the policy process (Larson *et al.*, 2001: 83–84).

57 Golightly, 1990: 33.

58 It was flanked by a notable increase in books from third parties on topics of American and world naval history including strategy, military innovation, and tactics (for a list, see Swartz, 2012b: 50–59). In part, this intellectual-academic influence strove to explain how the U.S. Navy had dealt with strategic change before, hoping to provide some template for the 1990s force- and strategic-planning communities.

59 Swartz, 2012b: 8, slide 16. A view epitomized in an article penned by the outgoing CNO titled "Maritime Strategy for the 1990s" (Trost, 1990).

60 Swartz, 2012a: 2, slide 3, 75, slide 149, 98, slide 195.
61 This paragraph is based on John Hattendorf's lucid description of the process (2006: 7–11).
62 Hattendorf, 2006: 11.
63 Garrett *et al.*, 1991, reprinted in Hattendorf, 2006: 24–26.
64 Haynes, 2013: 76.
65 Published shortly before the 1992 Presidential election but three years into the post-Cold War world, the "Navy Policy Book" (reprinted in Hattendorf, 2006: 39–86) was drafted in the CNO's office (Captain James Stark) and received input from the Navy's strategic branch, OP-603 (Captain Dick Diamond). In response to a number of bad press issues for the Navy – catastrophic technology failures, bribery, and sexual assault scandals mentioned before – it focused heavily on the Navy as an organization, its values, traditions, and heritage. As a guideline policy document, it sought to explain the Navy – to the Navy.
66 Hattendorf, 2006: 9, Haynes, 2013: 76–77.
67 Reprinted in Hattendorf, 2006: 30.
68 Swartz, 2012a: 14, slide 27. Swartz notes that "'The Way Ahead' was 'way ahead' of its time. [It was] A vision for the early 2000s, but not for the 1990s" (Swartz, 2012a: 19).
69 The name was a clear attempt to provide something that would stick, be marketable, with the ellipses and capital 'F' a deliberate play on readers' expectations. The initial product was designed to have different titles such as "Power from the Sea," "Diplomacy from the Sea," or "Engagement from the Sea." Based on suggestions of Admiral Kendall Pease, it also included warfare areas from the sea ("Naval aviation … from the Sea," "Amphibious warfare … from the Sea," "Submarine warfare … from the Sea") (Scott Truver interview, 2012, 00:53:11–00:53:50). According to Admiral Smith, it was he who realized one morning at breakfast upon glancing at his open briefcase which contained these drafts that

> it could be anything from the sea. So why don't I just put three dots down here: '… From the Sea.' You can fill in what you want. And I did it. […] I mean, the name just grabbed hold and everybody loved it.
> (Stillwell, Leighton W. Smith interview #9, March 13, 2006: 644)

70 For a list of participants of the NFCPE, see Hattendorf (2006: 88, footnote ★).
71 Haynes, 2013: 98.
72 Scott Truver noted that he came on as an outside contractor overseeing draft 19B, seeing it through draft 65C (interview 2012, 00:39:30–00:40:40). Admiral Smith's quotation stems from that discussion. See also Stillwell, 2006.
73 Kelso *et al.*, 1992, reprinted in Hattendorf, 2006: 87–99.
74 Swartz, 2012a: 32, slide 63. The signature of Bush's political appointee O'Keefe would not have helped. In fact, it would have conveyed a politicized impression to the incoming defense and national security staff. One of the contractors tasked with finishing the draft aptly called that process the act of "de-Bushifying" the document. The job after the election was to find out what Clinton had said about the Navy, a task that yielded few substantive results. As a candidate, Clinton had only made two speeches with Navy relevance, one in Charleston (South Carolina) and one in Groton (Connecticut) (Scott Truver interview, 2012: 00:44:15–00:45:05).
75 Truver recalls that the Navy was not pleased by the initial appearance of the publication. The version that had been sent out on September 30, 1992 was not proof-read very closely, and software issues complicated the format. A reworking produced a second version dated October 15, which was sent up the chain of

command for approval. The signatures of the Secretary of the Navy, the CNO, and the CMC were obtained by copy & paste from an earlier version (Truver interview, 2012, 00:41:45–00:44:10).

76 In his official portrait painting on display at the Pentagon, Secretary of the Navy O'Keefe – whose tenure was cut short to just a few months by the change from the Republican to the Democrat administration – is seen carrying the "… From the Sea" magazine, thus illustrating and embracing the document's thrust and scope.

77 Hattendorf, 2006: 97.

78 Ibid.: 14.

79 Swartz, 2012a: 45–46, slides 90–92.

80 The following other doctrinal publications were released: NDP 2 Naval Intelligence, NDP 4 Naval Logistics, NDP 5 Naval Planning, and NDP 6 Naval Command & Control. Most revealingly, NDP 3 Naval Operations was never published over disagreements regarding command relationships between Navy and Marine Corps (Swartz, 2012a: 63), a consequential event that undermined the other five volumes, the Naval Doctrine Command's status, and the expectation that the Navy could develop coherent doctrine (Haynes, 2013: 158).

81 Swartz, 2012a: 59, slide 117.

82 Haynes, 2013: 87.

83 Hattendorf, 2006: 101.

84 In U.S. terms these were: objective, mass, maneuver, offensive, economy of force, unity of command, simplicity, surprise, and security (Hattendorf, 2006: 128–130).

85 They included the conduct of contingency operations, noncombatant evacuation, combat of terrorism, aid to host nations through security assistance and foreign internal defense, assistance of other nations' defenses, enforcement of U.N. sanctions, participation in peace-support operations, interdiction of vessels engaged in illegal migration, disaster relief, humanitarian assistance, civil support operations, coordination of public health operations, and counter-drug operations (Hattendorf, 2006: 115–116).

86 Boorda *et al.*, 1994, reprinted in Hattendorf, 2006: 149–158.

87 Haynes (2013: 136) concedes that "(Secretary of the Navy, S.B.) Dalton's problem was straightforward" and citing Dalton's speechwriter, then-Lieutenant Commander Sam Tangredi, "Critics would say that 'Forward … From the Sea' was really no different than '… From the Sea' (except emphasizing forward presence). They were right. It was not meant to be different, it was meant to be signed."

88 As previously mentioned, the "Bottom–Up Review" replaced the "Base Force" concept of the Bush years which had outlined a future military that would wage two *simultaneous* regional conflicts at once. The "Bottom–Up Review" saw the military engaged in two *nearly simultaneous* conflicts.

89 The Revolution in Military Affairs (RMA) signaled another demand of a new way of thinking for the Navy and the other services. The mutual relationship between technology in military affairs and the means to apply it for warfare – or in other words, compelling doctrine – has been subject to increasing interest in the literature. Innovation in peacetime offers unique challenges and opportunities for military breakthroughs that are likely to take some time (Rosen, 1994). Historically, navies have often been less enthusiastic about adopting paradigm shifts in military technology that changed doctrine and organization of land warfare. This is rooted in their unique strategic culture and the established missions that were long considered unchanged and uninhibited by the latest fashion of armies (and later air forces). An exception to that observation is the advent of nuclear propulsion and the nuclear bomb, which from the 1940s for the first

time gave the Navy the ability to strike the adversary's center of gravity and thus decide global war (Tritten, 1995: 130). Parsed to enhance military effectiveness, the RMA was about embracing technologies of the information age and implanting them into the heart of joint doctrine. In other words, advanced technology was supposed to shape doctrine. The RMA's objective was to allow a smaller, but highly effective high-tech military to enable swift and decisive victory on the battlefield with comparatively few casualties. In general, the U.S. military in the 1990s experienced a bent towards reductionist warfare theories, jointness, and RMA. These big ideas drove defense thinking in the 1990s (Sloan, 2002; Fitschen, 2007). Inevitably, their advancement soon became an end in itself (Haynes, 2013: 151–152).

90 Department of the Navy, 1994.
91 Haynes, 2013: 140.
92 Interview 2012, 00:59:30–01:00:30.
93 Chief of Naval Information, 1997, reprinted in Hattendorf, 2006: 159–170.
94 Haynes, 2013: 162–166. "2020 Vision" translated Admiral Boorda's idea of an arsenal ship (yet to be designed and developed) into practice. The arsenal ship would have provided a massive barrage of sea-launched precision strikes against enemy command and control infrastructure and other targets. With it, the Navy would have again emphasized a shift in its focus from the littoral to a more regionally dispersed, blue-water approach (see Scott, 1995, Federation of American Scientists, 1999).
95 According to Scott Truver, the "2020 Vision" did make its way onto Johnson's desk eventually – through a backdoor. The draft was reworked slightly and incorporated into the annual Navy program guide "Vision, Presence, Power" (formerly "Force 2001") as its chapter on strategy and policy: "In effect, Johnson signed out Boorda's 'Vision 2020' [sic] and didn't know it" (Truver interview, 2012, 01:00:55–01:02:30).
96 Bouchard interview, 2012, 01:13:40–01:13:45.
97 Johnson, 1997, reprinted in Hattendorf, 2006: 171–176.
98 Swartz, 2012a: 131, slide 262.
99 General (USMC) Charles Krulak, Commandant of the Marine Corps from 1995 to 1999, introduced the "Three Block War" concept in an essay for the January 1999 issue of *Marines* Magazine. In conjunction with describing the realities which Marines faced, Krulak argued that leadership had to be organized lower and lower in the chain of command to better reflect the demands of a complex operational environment. Ultimately, the responsibility would land on the corporal, the lowest-ranking non-commissioned officer, whose leadership decisions would bestow upon him a strategic function, thus creating the notion of the "Strategic Corporal" (Krulak, 1999).
100 Haynes, 2013: 188.
101 The NSPG 1999 was classified because of its substantial intelligence section, making it the only secret Navy declaratory capstone document of the decade. The NSPG 2000 (Chief of Naval Information, 2000, reprinted in Hattendorf, 2006: 177–266) was unclassified to facilitate a broader discussion at home and abroad.
102 The White House, 1999.
103 Swartz, 2012a: 145, slide 290.
104 Ibid.: 144–146, slides 287–292.
105 Based on Forster, 2013: 21.
106 For more detail on this subject, see Amund Lundesgaard's recently published PhD dissertation, *Controlling the Sea and Projecting Power. U.S. Navy Strategy and Force Structure After the Cold War*. University of Oslo, 2016, pp. 218–335.
107 Haynes, 2013: 50.

108 Swartz, 2012b: 37, slide 73.
109 Trost, 1990: 94.
110 Haynes, 2013: 11.
111 Aspin, 1993: iii.
112 A 2000 Department of the Navy Shipbuilding Report slightly upped those numbers, partially in preparation for the next QDR due in 2001, to 50–66 SSN, 11–15 active carriers (nuclear/conventional), 116–133 surface combatants, and 36–42 amphibious ships (Swartz, 2012b: 37, slide 73).
113 For a forward-deployed, rotational force such as the U.S. Navy, for any ship that is on station, at least two more need to be available. A second unit returns from a deployment and is being refurbished, while a third unit parallel prepares for a deployment or undergoes major maintenance.
114 Evidently unmindful of Samuel Huntington's warning (1954) that

> A military service may at times, of course, perform functions unrelated to external security, such as internal policing, disaster relief, and citizenship training. These are, however, subordinate and collateral responsibilities. A military service does not exist to perform these functions; rather it performs these functions because it has already been called into existence to meet some threat to the national security.

115 Swartz, 2012b: 35–37, slides 70–73.
116 Navy History and Heritage Command, 2011.
117 Terzibaschitsch, 2002: 33.
118 Swartz, 2012b: 41, slide 81.
119 For more on this conversion, see O'Rourke (2008).
120 For more information on the Virginia-class attack submarines, see O'Rourke, 2014.
121 With its innovative and technologically complex design, the aircraft combines the functionality and V/STOL capability of a helicopter with the long range of a conventional turboprop airplane. Its tilt rotors allow a combination of both functions. The V-22 underwent an extended testing and training phase. To date, only the U.S. Air Force and the U.S. Marine Corps operate this model. The USMC makes heavy use of the multi-mission airframe. It will eventually replace the Corps' CH-46 Sea Knight twin-rotor helicopter. The Navy has not yet ordered V-22 aircraft although the service is looking for future replacement for its C-2 Greyhound carrier onboard delivery (COD) aircraft. Future Navy missions for an organic V-22 could also include SAR, ASW, and transport.
122 For more information on the program, see O'Rourke, 2011.
123 With the F/A-18 E/F, the Air Force-only F-22 Raptor, and the proposed F-35 Lightning II Joint Strike Fighter, the Department of Defense had no less than six tactical aircraft in design, production, and procurement during the 1990s. The F-35, built in three variants for the Air Force, the Marine Corps, and the Navy, emerged from plans in the early 1990s to develop a joint forces airplane (Gertler, 2014).
124 Swartz, 2012b: 38, slide 76.
125 TLAMs were the preferred weapon for strafing Iraq in the 1990s. Concerted cruise missiles strikes against Iraq were conducted in 1993, 1996, and 1998.
126 Friedman, 2006: 565–568.
127 Major naval operations understood as the sustained commitment of forces engaged in expeditionary operations against a shore or a fleet. On the problem of definitions, see Vego (2008: 7–39). In this chapter, these are selected naval operations designed to illustrate the real-world operations that the U.S. Navy conducted in the 1990s. For a chronological list of Navy-Marine Corps crisis response and combat actions in the period between January 1991 and 9/11, see the U.S. Navy's 2004 Program Guide, Department of the Navy, 2004: 169–173.

128 For a deeper discussion, see Edward Marolda and Robert Schneller, *Shield and Sword. The United States Navy and the Persian Gulf War*, Annapolis, MD. Naval Institute Press, 2001.

129 For an overview over U.S. Navy engagement with Saddam Hussein's regime post-Gulf War, see Schneller, 2007: 31–37, 59–62. For the U.S. Navy's role in sustained maritime interdiction operations (MIO) in the Arabian Gulf region in cooperation with allied navies between 1991 and 2003, see Barlow, 2013.

130 The logistics train that spanned from the U.S. into the Persian Gulf region carried over 2.3 million tons of equipment, more than 535,000 tons of supplies, and 4.3 million tons of petroleum products during the Desert Shield and Desert Storm phases of the conflict. The Military Sealift Command (MSC) fielded a total of 393 cargo ships to facilitate this (Schneller 2007: 23–24).

131 Rearden, 2012: 509–510.

132 The Navy used 10 of the 11 available aircraft carriers either in Desert Shield or as replacements for forward-deployed carriers (Love, 1992: 813).

133 Pemsel, 2006: 1287.

134 The other primary mission of U.S. naval forces in the Gulf – next to supporting the air war – was poising to stage an amphibious invasion on Iraq's southern flank, thus rendering a massing of Iraqi troops on the main battle line (Kuwait/Saudi-Arabia) impossible. The Marines were used for a deception operation in February 1991.

135 A comprehensive summary report of U.S. Navy in Desert Shield/Desert Storm including a chronology of events is the CNO's report (Office of the Chief of Naval Operations, 2014). Also see Love, 1992: 808–837.

136 Most Iraqi missile boats were neutralized (sunk or rendered unusable) in January 1991, effectively establishing uncontested U.S. sea control in the Northern Persian Gulf. Notably, the battleship *Missouri* (BB 63) and accompanying smaller units were targeted by an Iraqi land-based Silkworm missile on February 25, in the middle of the ground campaign to expel Hussein's forces from Kuwait. One of the missiles fell short while the other one was shot down by the British destroyer (HMS) *Gloucester* (D 96) (Schneller, 2007: 30).

137 On February 18, 1991, within three hours and just 10 nautical miles apart, the veteran amphibious assault ship *Tripoli* (LPH 10) and the two-year old AEGIS guided-missile cruiser *Princeton* (CG 59) struck mines while conducting operations in the northern Arabian Gulf. Both vessels sustained extensive damages, but no loss of life had to be reported. Coalition forces undertook substantial mine countermeasure operations throughout the war. The amphibious assault ship *New Orleans* (LPH 11) was used as a mine-countermeasures flagship (i.e., fielding MH-53E Super Stallion mine-clearing helicopters), degrading the flexibility and range of the Navy's amphibious component. As Brigadier General Peter Rowe, Commander, Fifth MEB, remarked (1992: 131), "I don't think the ripple effect of removing a ship from an amphibious task force is understood well enough, where it really matters."

138 See Robert Schneller, *Anchor of Resolve. A History of U.S. Naval Forces Central Command/Fifth Fleet*. Washington, D.C. Naval History and Heritage Center, 2007.

139 Ministry of Defense, 2009, 2–7.

140 See Randy Papadopoulos, The U.S. Navy's Contribution to Operation Sharp Guard, in Gary Weir/Sandra Doyle (ed.), *You Cannot Surge Trust. Combined Naval Operations of the Royal Australian Navy, Canadian Navy, Royal Navy, and United States Navy, 1991–2003*. Washington, D.C. USGPO, 81–100.

141 This frigate stands emblematic for the enormous versatility of U.S. Navy vessels and the broad range of missions that the service undertakes. The ship, known colloquially as "Sammy B," hit a mine on April 1988 14, while deployed in the Persian Gulf in support of the U.S. operations in the "Tanker War." The

warship returned to the Persian Gulf after repairs in time for participation in allied operations against Saddam Hussein as part of Operation Desert Storm (1991). Years later, it operated in the embargo operations in the Mediterranean described here. In 1996, this workhorse participated in joint interagency task force (JIATF) drug interdiction operations in the Caribbean, the Eastern and the South Pacific with a number of sister ships. It was decommissioned in 2015.

142 For a concise review of the U.S. Navy's contribution to "Operation Sharp Guard" and the context of joint and combined operations, see Papadopoulos (2013).

143 Papadopoulos, 2013: 95. A lessons-learned report (Reddy, 1997: 1) formulated with considerable foresight that,

> Operation Sharp Guard proved that NATO and WEU can work well together, at least on joint naval operations and under NATO command. However, until the EU matures and can present a common front on foreign policy issues with more regularity, the U.S. should not expect the WEU to take on an operational task and go it alone.

144 For an analysis of the operation, see Ripley (1999).

145 For a lessons-learned report, see U.S. Congress (2000), in particular testimony by Vice Admiral Daniel J. Murphy, Jr., Commander, U.S. Sixth Fleet and Striking and Support Forces, Southern Europe; Brigadier General Robert M. Flanagan, Deputy Commander, II Marine Expeditionary Force; and Vice Admiral James F. Amerault, Deputy Chief of Naval Operations (Logistics), excerpted at Naval History and Heritage Command 2004 (www.history.navy.mil/faqs/faq127-1. htm).

146 Hendrickson, 2006.

147 The main processing point ashore for refugees was the U.S. naval base at Guantanamo Bay, Cuba.

148 Siegel, 1996; Kretchik *et al.*, 1998.

149 This section substantially draws on Marolda's comprehensive and lucid description of the Taiwan Strait crisis (2012: 113–118).

150 Marolda, 2012: 115.

151 In contrast to the "The Maritime Strategy" of the 1980s, the various U.S. Navy strategies of the 1990s were less outspoken about global aspirations and often treated the integration of allies as secondary topics. In lieu of an analysis of every single Navy capstone document's relationship to U.S. allies, this section briefly outlines the most enduring trends across the decade.

152 Examples for the 1990s are the introduction of the U.S.-made Aegis system by the Japanese Self-Defense Maritime Force [JSDMF] in 1993 on their *Atago*- and *Kongo*-class destroyers (Kim, 1999: 18–45; Cole, 2013: 61–77), and later the South Korean, Spanish, and Norwegian navies.

153 Swartz, 2012a: 56, slide 111.

154 Swartz, 2012b: 43–45, slides 86–89.

155 Haynes, 2013: 124. These were Joint Strike, Joint Littoral Warfare, Joint Surveillance, Joint Space and Electronic Warfare/Intelligence, Strategic Deterrence, Strategic Sealift/Protection, and Presence.

156 The establishment of the Fifth Fleet complemented the 1983 installation of the U.S. Central Command and the subsidiary Naval Forces Central Command. Until the creation of its own numbered fleet, the naval part of USCENTCOM had relied on forces temporarily assigned to it. The Gulf War surge forces came from the U.S. home fleets and were Sixth/Seventh Fleet assets.

157 Tritten, 1995: 132.

158 Breemer (1994: 45–46) declared "… From the Sea" to be the end of *naval* strategy as the world knew it (emphasis added), although he was not quite sure

how final that end would really be given the inherent uncertainty that surrounds strategy (ibid: 48).
159 Haynes, 2013: 189.
160 Trubowitz and Rhodes, 1999: 8.
161 Hattendorf, 2006: 4.
162 Forster, 2013: 14.
163 Owens, 1993: 13.
164 Haynes, 2013: 2.

References

Allison, George. "The United States Navy and United Nations Peace-Keeping Operations." *Naval War College Review* 46(4) (1993): 22–35.

Aspin, Les. "Many Nations Profoundly Anti-American." *The Officer* 69(2) (1993): 26–30.

Baker, James, and Fiffer, Steve. *"Work Hard, Study … And Keep Out of Politics!"* Evanston, IL: Northwestern University Press, 2008.

Barlow, Jeffrey. "The U.S. Navy's Role in Coalition Maritime Interception Operations in the Arabian Gulf Region, 1991–2001." *You Cannot Surge Trust: Combined Naval Operations of the Royal Australian Navy, Canadian Navy, Royal Navy, and United States Navy, 1991–2003*, eds. G. Weir and S. Doyle Washington, D.C.: NHHC 2013, 23–43.

Boorda, Admiral Jeremy, Dalton, John, and Mundy, General Carl. "Forward … From the Sea." *U.S. Naval Institute Proceedings* 120(12) (1994).

Bouchard, Joseph, Captain, United States Navy (retired). Norfolk (Virginia), September 17, 2012, 02 hr 40 min.

Bierling, Stephan. *Geschichte der amerikanischen Außenpolitik. Von 1917 bis zur Gegenwart*. München: C.H. Beck, 2003.

Bruns, Sebastian. *Via New York nach Bagdad? Die Vereinten Nationen und die Irak-Politik der USA*. Tectum: Marburg, 2008.

Bush, George H.W. "Remarks at the Aspen Institute Symposium in Aspen, Colorado, 2 August 1990." 1990a.

Bush, George H.W. "Address before a Joint Session of the Congress on the Persian Gulf Crisis and the Federal Budget Deficit, 11 September 1990." 1990b.

Bush, George H.W., and Scowcroft, Brent. A *World Transformed*. New York, NY: Knopf, 1998.

Chairman of the Joint Chiefs of Staff. "The National Military Strategy of the United States of America." Washington, D.C.: Department of Defense (DOD), 1992.

Chief of Naval Information. "Naval Strategic Planning Guidance with Long-Range Planning Objectives, April 2000." Washington, D.C.: DON, 2000.

Chollet, Derek, and Goldgeier, James. *American between the Wars, 11/9 to 9/11. The Misunderstood Years between the Fall of the Berlin Wall and the Start of the War on Terror*. BBS Public Affairs: New York, NY, 2008.

Cole, Bernard. *Asian Maritime Strategies: Navigating Troubled Waters*. Annapolis, MD: NIP, 2013.

Davis, Jacquelyn. *Aircraft Carriers and the Role of Naval Power in the Twenty-First Century*. Cambridge, UK: Institute for Foreign Policy Analysis (= National Security Paper 13), 1993.

Department of Defense. "Report on the Bottom-Up Review. October 1993." Washington, D.C.: DOD, 1993.

Department of Defense. "Quadrennial Defense Review, May 1997." Washington, D.C.: DOD, 1997.

Department of the Navy. "Forward... From the Sea." Washington, D.C.: DON, 1994.

Department of the Navy. "Secretary of the Navy, the Honorable John H. Dalton. 1 June 2000." Washington, D.C.: The Pentagon, 2000.

Department of the Navy. "Vision. Presence. Power 2004: A Program Guide to the U.S. Navy." Washington, D.C.: DOD, 2004.

Federation of American Scientists, ed. "Arsenal Ship," Military Analysis Network, U.S. Navy Ships. 1999. www.fas.org/man/dod-101/sys/ship/arsenal_ship.htm.

Fitschen, Patrick. *Die Transformation der US-Streitkräfte: Die Neuausrichtung der Streitkräfte der Vereinigten Staaten zwischen 2001 und 2006.* Frankfurt am Main, Germany: Peter Lang (= Analysen zur Sicherheitspolitik, Vol. 1, Distributed by the Institut für Sicherheitspolitik an der Christian-Albrechts-Universität zu Kiel), 2007.

Forster, Larissa. "Trust Cannot Be Surged: Challenges to Naval Forward Presence." *Military Power Revue der Schweizer Armee,* no. 2/2011 (2011): 47–59. *Influence without Boots on the Ground: Seaborne Crisis Response.* Newport, RI: Naval War College Press, 2013.

Friedman, Norman. *The Naval Institute Guide to World Naval Weapon Systems,* 5th edition. Annapolis, MD: NIP, 2006.

Gagliano, Joseph A. *Congressional Policymaking in Sino-US Relations during the Post-Cold War Era,* London: Routledge, 2015.

Gertler, Jeremiah. *F-35 Joint Strike Fighter (JSF) Program.* CRS Report RL 30563. 55. Washington, D.C.: Congressional Research Service, 2014.

Golightly, Neil. "Correcting Three Strategic Mistakes." *U.S. Naval Institute Proceedings* 116(4) (1990).

Gormley, Dennis. *Missile Contagion: Cruise Missile Proliferation and the Threat to International Security.* Annapolis, MD: NIP, 2010.

Gray, Colin. *The Leverage of Sea Power: The Strategic Advantage of Navies in War.* New York: Macmillan, 1992.

Hacke, Christian. *Zur Weltmacht verdammt. Die amerikanische Außenpolitik von J.F. Kennedy bis G.W. Bush.* 3. Auflage, aktualisierte Neuausgabe, München: Ullstein, 2005.

Hattendorf, John, ed. *U.S. Naval Strategy in the 1990s.* Newport, RI: Naval War College Press, 2006.

Haynes, Peter. *American Naval Thinking in the Post-Cold War Era: The U.S. Navy and the Emergence of a Maritime Strategy, 1989–2007.* Dissertation, Naval Postgraduate School, Monterey, CA, 2013.

Hendrickson, Ryan. *Diplomacy and War at NATO: The Secretary General and Military Action After the Cold War.* Columbia, MO, and London: University of Missouri Press, 2006.

Kan, Shirley. *China and Proliferation of Weapons of Mass Destruction and Missiles: Policy Issues.* CRS Report 31555. 76. Washington, D.C.: Congressional Research Service, 2014.

Keller, Patrick. *Von der Eindämmung zur Erweiterung: Bill Clinton und die Neuorientierung der amerikanischen Außenpolitik.* Bonn: Bouvier, 2008.

Kim, Duk-Ki. *Naval Strategy in Northeast Asia: Geo-Strategic Goals, Policies and Prospects.* London and Portland, OR: Cass, 1999.

Krauthammer, Charles. "The Unipolar Moment." *Foreign Affairs* 70(1) (1990), 23–33.

Kretchik, Walter, Baumann, Robert, and Fishel, John. *Invasion, Intervention, 'Intervasion'. A Concise History of the U.S. Army in Operation Uphold Democracy.* Fort Leavenworth, Kansas: U.S. Army Command and General Staff College Press, 1998.

Krulak, Charles. "The Strategic Corporal: Leadership in the Three Block War." *Marine Corps Gazette* 83(1) (January 1999): 18–22.

Lake, Anthony. "'From Containment to Enlargement', Johns Hopkins University School of Advanced International Studies, Washington, D.C., 21 September 1993." 1993.

Larson, Eric, Orletsky, David, and Leuschner, Kristin. *Defense Planning in a Decade of Change. Lessons from the Base Force, Bottom-Up Review, and Quadrennial Defense Review.* Santa Monica, CA: Rand Corporation, 2001.

Liang, Qiao, and Xiangsui, Wang. *Unrestricted Warfare.* Beijing: PLA Literature and Arts Publishing House. Translated by the Foreign Broadcast Information Service, 1999.

Lippold, Kirk. *Front Burner. Al Qaeda'a Attack on the USS* Cole. New York, NY. Public Affairs Publisher, 2013.

Love, Robert. *History of the U.S. Navy, Volume II 1942-1991.* Mechanicsburg, PA: Stackpole, 1992.

Lundesgaard, Amund. "Controlling the Sea and Projecting Power: U.S. Navy Strategy and Force Structure After the Cold War." Dissertation, University of Oslo, Norway, 2016.

Lundesgaard, Amund. *US Navy Strategy and Force Structure After the Cold War* (IFS Insights No. 4, November 2011). Oslo, Norway: Institutt for Forsvarsstudier, 2011.

Marolda, Edward, and Schneller, Robert. *Shield and Sword – The United States Navy and the Persian Gulf War.* Annapolis, MD: NIP, 2001.

Marolda, Edward. *Ready Seapower. A History of the U.S. Seventh Fleet.* Washington, D.C.: NHHC, 2012.

Maynard, Christopher. *Out of the Shadows. George H.W. Bush and the End of the Cold War.* College Station, TX: Texas A&M University Press, 2008.

Naval History and Heritage Command (NHHC). "Kosovo: U.S. Naval Lessons Learned during Operation Allied Force, March–June 1999." Washington, D.C.: NHHC, 2004.

N.N./Anon. "Death of an admiral Mike Boorda: CNO's suicide illuminates personal and service's troubles." *The Baltimore Sun*, May 19, 1996.

Office of the Chief of Naval Operations. "The United States Navy in 'Desert Shield'/'Desert Storm', Ser OO/lU500179, 15 May 1991." Washington, D.C.: NHHC, 2014.

Office of the Historian, Department of State. "Milestones, 1993–2000: The War in Bosnia, 1992–1995." Washington, D.C.: Department of State, 2013.

O'Rourke, Ronald. "Navy Trident Submarine Conversion (SSGN) Program. Background and Issues for Congress." Washington, D.C., Congressional Research Service, 2008.

O'Rourke, Ronald. "Navy LPD-17 Amphibious Ship Procurement. Background, Issues, and Options for Congress." Washington, D.C., Congressional Research Service, 2011.

O'Rourke, Ronald. "Navy Virginia (SSN-774) Class Attack Submarine Procurement. Background and Issues for Congress." Washington, D.C., Congressional Research Service, 2014.

Owens, Mackubin. "Toward a Maritime Grand Strategy: Paradigm for a New Security Environment." Strategic Review (Spring 1993) (1993).

Papadopoulos, Sarandis. "U.S. Navy's Contribution to Sharp Guard." *You Cannot Surge Trust: Combined Naval Operations of the Royal Australian Navy, Canadian Navy, Royal Navy, and United States Navy, 1991–2003*, eds. G. Weir and S. Doyle. NHHC: Washington, D.C. 2013, 83–99.

Pemsel, Helmut. *Seeherrschaft (III). Seekriege und Seepolitik von 1914 bis 2006*. Wien/Graz, Austria: Neuer Wissenschaftlicher Verlag/Köhler 2006 (= Weltgeschichte der Seefahrt, Vol. 7).

Perl, Raphael, and O'Rourke, Ronald. *Terrorist Attack on USS* Cole: *Background and Issues for Congress* (CRS Report RS20721). Washington, D.C.: Congressional Research Service, 2001.

Phillips, R. Cody. *Operation Just Cause: The Incursion into Panama* (CMH Pub No. 70–85–1). Washington, D.C.: U.S. Army Center for Military History, 2004.

Rearden, Steven. *Council of War. A History of the Joint Chiefs of Staff, 1942–1991*. Washington, D.C.: NDU Press, 2012.

Reddy, Kathleen. *Operation Sharp Guard: Lessons Learned for the Policymaker and Commander*. Newport, RI: Naval War College Press, 1997.

Ripley, Tim. *Operation Deliberate Force: The UN and NATO Campaign in Bosnia, 1995*. Lancaster University: Centre for Defence and International Security Studies, 1999.

Rosen, Stephen. *Winning the Next War: Innovation and the Modern Military*. Ithaca, NY: Cornell University Press, 1994.

Rosenberg, David. "The Realities of Modern Naval Strategy." *Mahan Is Not Enough: The Proceedings of a Conference on the Works of Sir Julian Corbett and Admiral Sir Hugh Richmond*, eds. J. Goldrick and J. Hattendorf. Newport, RI: Naval War College Press 1993, 141–175.

Rowe, Peter J. "Interview with John Lehman." *U.S. Naval Institute Proceedings* 118(5) (May 1992): 128–131.

Schneller, Robert. *Anchor of Resolve: A History of U.S. Naval Force Central Command/Fifth Fleet*. Washington, D.C.: NHHC, 2007.

Scott, Richard. "Arsenal Ship Launched." *Jane's Navy International* 101(7) (1995), 5.

Siegel, Adam. *The Intervasion of Haiti* (CNA Professional Paper No. 539). Alexandria, VA: CNA, 1996.

Shenon, Philip. "Admiral, in Suicide Note, Apologized to 'My Sailors,'" *New York Times*, May 18, 1996.

Sloan, Elinor. *The Revolution in Military Affairs*. Montreal and London: Queen's University Press, 2002.

Smith, Edward A. "*… From the Sea*: The Process of Defining a New Role for Naval Forces in the Post–Cold War World." *The Politics of Strategic Adjustment: Ideas, Institutions, and Interests*, eds. P. Trubowitz, E. Goldman, and E. Rhodes. New York: Columbia University Press, 1999, pp. 267–303.

Stewart, Richard. *The United States Army in Somalia 1992–1994*. CMH Pub 70–81–1. Washington, D.C.: U.S. Army Center for Military History, 2002.

Stillwell, Paul. *Interview #9 with Leighton Smith Jr., Admiral, United States Navy (retired)*. Transcript. Annapolis, MD: U.S. Naval Institute, 2006/2010.

Swartz, Peter, and McGrady, E.D. *A Deep Legacy: Smaller-Scale Contingencies and the Forces that Shape the Navy* (CRM 98–95.10). Alexandria, VA: CNA, 1998.

Swartz, Peter, and Duggan, Karin. *U.S. Navy Capstone Strategies and Concepts (1991–2000): Strategy, Policy, Concept, and Vision Documents* (slideshow). Alexandria, VA: CNA, 2012a.

Swartz, Peter, and Duggan, Karin. *The U.S. Navy in the World (1991–2000): Context for U.S. Navy Capstone Strategies and Concepts* (slideshow). Alexandria, VA: CNA, 2012b.

Terzibaschitsch, Stefan. *Die Schiffe der U.S. Navy.* Hamburg, Germany: Koehler, 2002.

Tritten, James. "'Revolution in Military Affairs,' Paradigm Shifts, and Doctrine." *The Navies of United States, Great Britain, France, Italy, and Spain. A Doctrine Reader,* edited by J. Tritten/L. Donolo (= Newport Papers #9), Newport, RI: Naval War College Press, 1995, 125–51.

Trost, Carlisle. "Maritime Strategy for the 1990s." *U.S. Naval Institute Proceedings* 116(5) (May 1990): 92–100.

Truver, Scott. Washington Navy Yard, Washington, D.C., September 10, 2012, 01 hr 50 min.

U.S. Congress, House Committee on Armed Services, Military Readiness Subcommittee. "Operations in Kosovo: Problems Encountered, Lessons Learned and Reconstitution. 106th Cong., 1st sess., 26 October 1999, H.A.S.C. No. 106–27." Washington, D.C.: GPO, 2000.

Vego, Milan. *Major Naval Operations.* Newport, RI: Naval War College Press, 2008.

Vistica, Gregory. *Fall from Glory: The Men Who Sank the U.S. Navy.* New York, NY: Touchstone, 1997.

The White House. "A National Security Strategy of Engagement and Enlargement." Washington, D.C.: The White House, 1994.

The White House. "A National Security Strategy for A New Century. December 1999." Washington, D.C.: The White House, 1999.

6 A sea power rationale for the twenty-first century (2001–2008)

Prelude

For America and much of the rest of the world, the election of George W. Bush as 43rd President of the United States politically rang in the new decade. The chaotic course of the November 2000 election mean that the Bush team had substantially less time than previous administrations to transition into office. The administration at first focused its foreign policy attention on Russia and China,[1] on determining whether a Middle East peace settlement was on the cards, and on building a ballistic missile defense system.[2] Antagonists like Iraq were also discussed, not least because Saddam Hussein continued to be a nuisance (vast amounts of military resources were tied up enforcing the two no-fly zones as well as the sanctions program). It is not without a degree of irony that Bush's initial foreign and national security policy until September 11, 2001 bore little resemblance to the policies that followed the terrorist strikes. In fact, Bush was more domestically focused, even nationalist, than his predecessor. Much like all presidents, he was relatively cautious on the international scene.

Initially, no single dominant threat emerged for the Bush team. Radical Islam, for one, was not seen as a major challenge, and international terrorism was not perceived as a national security or defense issue per se. Instead, Bush saw an opportunity to implement an ambitious program of domestic military change driven by a sustained belief in modularity, precision–guided ammunition, information technology, high-tech weaponry, and stealth, in short: transformation. In essence, this concept tied together the promises of network–centric warfare to counter the range of state and non–state actors seen as having potential to undermine American security. It promised cost-effectiveness and to reduce the likelihood of the U.S. being dragged into murky wars and conflicts with substantial numbers of ground troops. As it progressed, military transformation was increasingly not evaluated by its contribution to political goals, but slowly morphed into becoming an end in itself. For a president who had underlined in his campaign that the military should not be used for nation-building, hailing the promise of transformation fit well into his idealistic outlook.[3]

U.S. Navy strategy 2001–2008: the macro-level

Global trends and challengers to U.S. security

September 11, 2001 effectively ended the first post–Cold War decade and, as some would have it, America's "holiday from history"[4] in the 1990s. Terrorism, however, was just one of a host of challenges to U.S. security that characterized the first decade of the twenty-first century.

More militarily subtle but nevertheless fundamental global issues became urgent throughout the 2000s: globalization, climate change and related natural disasters, extreme hunger and poverty, access to universal primary education, and combating major diseases emerged as transnational, indeed global risks. These reshaped the context for naval strategy.

With 9/11, terrorism – the first broad challenge – took center-stage. Prior to the attacks in New York and Washington, terrorism was primarily seen as a law-enforcement task. The attack on the guided-missile destroyer *Cole* (DDG 67) in Aden (Yemen) on October 12, 2000 began to change that perception for the Department of Defense, not least because this particular act of maritime terrorism was in retaliation to cruise missiles launched against Sudan in 1998, which in turn were ordered after al-Qaida embassy bombings in Kenya and Tanzania that year. Connecting these dots, however, did not yield palpable results before 9/11. Terrorism in its new form – unlike the first generation in Europe in the 1970s and 1980s, often centered on political representatives – targeted Americans per se, and was often motivated by frustration about perceived or actual backwardness in the Islamic world.[5]

In 2001 the high number of civilians killed in a single attack and the use of hijacked commercial airliners were fundamentally novel. It was quickly determined that al-Qaida leader Osama bin Laden and his organization were behind the attacks killing nearly 3,000 people.[6] Al-Qaida's sanctuary was Afghanistan; a Central Asian country ravaged by Soviet intervention and decades of costly civil war. The Taliban, a radical Islamic group ruling large parts of the country since 1996, provided al-Qaida with a safe haven. Even with this sanctuary routed, in early 2002 pockets and regional affiliates of the terrorist network spawned. In the process, al-Qaida utilized weak, failing, and failed states to establish regional terrorism organizations that participated in a religiously motivated global campaign against "the West." Examples of the latter included al-Qaida in the Maghreb, on the Arab peninsula, and loosely organized Islamic subsidiaries in several other regions of the world.[7] The number of transnational terrorist incidents (some of them maritime) climbed from 2001 and their lethality soared.[8] Initially, military planning remained state-centric and directed against foreign regimes not limited to failing countries in Central Asia. States such as Iran, North Korea, China, or Iraq could challenge U.S. primacy in some areas, and undermine strategic interests for the hegemon, for example access to natural resources, maritime transit, or alliances.

A second generational challenge related to globalization arose from the ascent of the BRICS, a loosely organized group consisting of Brazil, Russia, India, China, and South Africa. These rising or resurgent powers are considered as coming contenders in the markets of information technology, defense industry, and other vital areas. Their rapid ascension and world politics-shaping potential usually rests on dynamics inherent to these particular developing countries, including favorable demographics (with the exception of Russia), inexpensive labor, and centralized systems of government.[9] In recent years, the shaping power of this group of countries has considerably waned.[10]

The third challenge came with the proliferation of nuclear weapons (as well as biological and chemical agents, recalling the anthrax attacks in the U.S. in 2001). While the safety and security of the arsenal of established nuclear powers and signatories to the Nuclear Non-Proliferation Treaty (NPT) continued to be an objective, the first decade of the 2000s saw an increasingly worrisome trend of rogue states, renegade regimes, terrorist networks, and non-state actors attempting to obtain such ultimate weapons of mass destruction. The fear of proliferated nuclear, biological, or chemical weapons (or components thereof) drove the implementation of the Proliferation Security Initiative (PSI) in 2003. From an American point of view, it was the prospect of rogue regimes, organized criminals, or terrorists fielding a bomb – even if it was a crude ("dirty") one – against U.S. or allied targets.[11]

A fourth challenge to U.S. national security arose from overstretching America's financial resources, forces, and political capital in the wake of 9/11. A complex amalgam of the costly wars in Afghanistan and Iraq (both in capital and in human terms), the large investments in security and defense on the home front, a deep recession, and a rising unwillingness of domestic opinion to support the ground wars in Southwest Asia contributed to an overstretched and increasingly hollow American position. Before 9/11, the military was in somewhat of a holding pattern, waiting for something bad to happen and demonstrating, when the U.S. would intervene, the seemingly overwhelming successes of airpower (Kosovo War) or Tomahawk cruise missile strikes. While the U.S. retained military and economic primacy, it also learned the limits and legacies of costly, sustained military nation-building campaigns.[12]

These roughly sketched trends and the related challenges to U.S. security determined what kind of wars America wanted to fight and the types of conflicts it would contend with, and how it sought to direct naval power.

Conflicts, crises, and wars

I can hear you. The rest of the world hears you.

And the people who knocked these buildings down will hear all of us soon![13]

The armed conflicts characterizing the decade in the most fundamental geo-political and doctrinal terms were the U.S.-led interventions in Afghanistan and Iraq. After 9/11, the U.S. was determined to target regimes actively sup-porting or even harboring terrorists, even though strikes against elusive non-state adversaries would be significantly more difficult to conduct than would be going after their sponsors. Following that notion, and based on intelli-gence processed immediately after 9/11, the Taliban regime in Afghanistan was identified as providing al-Qaida with a safe haven. On October 7, 2001, the U.S. launched military strikes to unseat the regime in Kabul and rid the terrorist network of its major sanctuary. Under pressure from the resurgent violent Taliban movement, foreign extremists infiltrators, diverging and contradictory political and military objectives in the coalition and in civil-military affairs, ravaging corruption inside the Afghan government, and mounting costs and casualties for the International Stabilization and Assistance Force (ISAF), the comprehensive nation-building attempt came to a grinding halt. The international community remained increasingly bogged down in Afghanistan.[14]

By early 2003 the United States had already opened a second major front in its global campaign against terrorism. The Bush administration sought regime change in Iraq. Like his father, Bush enlisted the United Nations as a forum to obtain an international mandate for removing Hussein from power.[15] After the U.N. Security Council remained unconvinced of Hus-sein's alleged weapons of mass destruction plans and his connection to inter-national terrorism, the United States forfeited a legal mandate and assembled a "coalition of the willing" instead. The U.S.-led intervention dubbed "Operation Iraqi Freedom" (OIF) succeeded in quickly driving Hussein from power and routing Iraq's regular military forces.[16] In a speech aboard the air-craft carrier *Abraham Lincoln* (CVN 72) on May 1, 2003, a triumphant Pres-ident Bush declared major combat operations over. However, Iraq soon descended into a violent civil war.

The U.S. military and political leadership found itself unprepared for the unexpected insurgency that ensued. The transition from a large standing Cold War military to a smaller, agile, more flexible posture to address twenty-first century warfare demands was in full swing, but post-invasion planning and the nation-building challenges in both Afghanistan and Iraq remained largely unaccounted for in 2002 and 2003. Only after a concerted effort to revamp U.S. military thinking and operations – a process develop-ing a twenty-first century counterinsurgency doctrine between 2005 and 2007 – could the violence in Iraq be contained. A similar approach was attempted for Afghanistan, where the insurgency had substantially different characteristics.[17]

Notwithstanding the focus on Afghanistan and Iraq, the global nature of the war on terrorism remained in place. The number of al-Qaida-related ter-rorist incidents rose markedly after 2001.[18] The strategic landscape that formed the focal point of the Global War on Terrorism had colossal maritime and littoral dimensions. From East to West, it encompassed the world's most important maritime choke points (the Strait of Gibraltar, the Bosporus/ Dardanelles, the Suez Canal, the Gulf of Aden and Bab-el-Mandeb, the Strait of Hormuz, and the Straits of Malacca), major trading and transit routes, extensive coastlines, and a significant portion of the world's oil reserves. The concurrence of Islamist fundamentalism in areas indispensable to the global economy spelled a scenario in which isolated small-group terrorist actions and failing states could single-handedly curtail or even stop the flow of petroleum and throw the international system into chaos.[19] It appeared that national and systemic security – that is, national protection of the United States on the one hand, but also the systemic security of the international order that the U.S. underwrote by military might – were so subtly intertwined as to be indistinguishable in practice. This had consequences for policy planners and military leaders if the military's purpose should accordingly be viewed in relation to systemic requirements.[20]

Even as the war against terrorist networks and their sponsors as well as the two expeditionary campaigns in Iraq and Afghanistan notoriously dominated America's security concerns, more traditional dynamics of power play returned to center-stage. The short Russo-Georgian War (2008) saw a more assertive Russia in Eastern Europe routinely use military and economic coercion to attain political objectives. In Southeast Asia, where a devastating tsunami in December 2004 provided insight into the force and fallout of a natural disaster, China and North Korea demanded continued attention as their regional military aspirations fueled crises and concerns. The former increasingly fielded global power and influence and American-Chinese economic interdependence deepened significantly by 2008.[21] The country's military modernization drove sustained change in East Asia, with conflicts in the East and South China Seas poignant examples. While the U.S. Navy carefully eyed Chinese naval growth with a mixture of uncertainty and professional interest, Vietnam, Indonesia, and Singapore quickly began to modernize their military forces (in particular their navies) in the 2000s.[22]

Personalities, domestic conditions, and national security strategies

Presidents, secretaries, and policy/strategy leaders

The presidency of George W. Bush ('Bush 43' in the American terminology) drew on a number of seasoned individuals who had served in national security positions reaching back to the administrations of Richard Nixon, Gerald Ford, Ronald Reagan, and George H.W. Bush ('Bush 41'). As a foreign policy novice, 'Bush 43' relied heavily on his experienced team to offset his public image. His relatively casual managerial style at first fell in line with a more nationalist foreign policy plan echoing his election campaign in 2000. After 9/11, and in particular during the 2004 Presidential campaign, he pursued a very activist foreign and security policy underwritten by a Manichean philosophy, thereby fashioning himself as a wartime president.[23] Throughout his presidency, Bush left considerable leverage to his more experienced cabinet and staff.[24]

In particular, Vice President Richard "Dick" Cheney consolidated influence and considerably shaped Bush's foreign policy.[25] Cheney had been Secretary of Defense 1989–1993 for 'Bush 41' and in that capacity oversaw the end of the Cold War and "Operation Desert Storm" (Cheney had also been White House Chief of Staff during the Ford Presidency). Donald Rumsfeld joined the administration as Secretary of Defense (2001–2006) after having served in the same capacity (1975–1977) under President Ford.[26] Rumsfeld ardently supported the Revolution in Military Affairs, now rebranded as "Transformation," which promised a far leaner, more agile, and smaller military footprint in support of U.S. security and defense objectives. He was also highly motivated to re-assert civilian control over the Joint Staff and the military services. For Rumsfeld, military leaders could produce doctrine and vision statements and were encouraged to think in global terms, but they could not and should not do strategy. To him, service-written strategic concepts amounted to gross insubordination.[27] The Deputy Secretary of Defense was Paul Wolfowitz, a former Undersecretary of Defense for Policy for Bush Sr. At the State Department, Colin Powell – former Reagan National Security Advisor (1987–1989) and Chairman of the Joint Chiefs of Staff under Bush 41 (1989–1993) – took the helm. Richard Armitage (an Assistant Secretary of Defense under Reagan and a former naval officer in the evacuation of South Vietnam in April 1975) became Deputy Secretary of State.[28] As his National Security Advisor, George W. Bush picked Condoleezza Rice, former Political Science professor at Stanford University who as an NSC staffer had played a key role in managing the end of the Cold War and relations with the Soviet Union for Bush's father. In January 2005, she replaced Powell at the top of the State Department.[29]

In short, Bush 43 fundamentally relied on people whose outlook was shaped by their experiences during and toward the end of the Cold War. With a few notable exceptions such as Secretary Powell, many of these seasoned "Cold Warriors" were also part of a resurgent intellectual movement. These "neoconservatives" were an idealistic and missionary group whose ideas were rooted in disappointment with liberalism and protest against 1960s' counter-culture, and gave Bush's policy an intellectual underpinning.[30] Their central security-policy views included a push for a strong military, the call for unilateral U.S. interventionism to safeguard national interests, and criticism of international forums. Bush 43's foreign and security policy advisory circle (dubbed the "Vulcans" after a statue of the Roman god in Rice's Alabama hometown, Birmingham) found considerable overlap of their own career views and these intellectual currents. With problems looming large for the administration when the campaign in Iraq did not progress as envisioned, the administration's line-up changed during the second term. Most prominently, these included Rumsfeld's demission; he was replaced by Robert "Bob" Gates in December 2006. Gates, who previously had a career with the Central Intelligence Agency, remained in office until July 2011, serving Bush's successor Barack Obama. He thus became the first Secretary of Defense to serve successive Presidential administrations from opposing political parties.

On Capitol Hill, the Bush administration could count on a Republican majority in the Senate from 2003 to 2007 and the House of Representatives from 2001 to 2007. In the 110th Congress (2006–2008), the Democrats wrested control of both chambers from the Republicans and for two years, with newly elected Democratic President Obama in the White House, enjoyed a brief period of united government (through the 111th Congress, until 2010).

Back in the Pentagon, the Department of the Navy witnessed considerable continuity in the early 2000s. Gordon England, who had had a career in the defense industry, served as the 72nd and as the 73rd Secretary of the Navy (2001–2003, 2003–2006).[31] England's priorities were a focus on current operational demands (the war on terrorism, humanitarian assistance/disaster relief, and homeland security) and maintenance of a surge capability. Despite spending almost as much time as Secretary of the Navy as his Reagan-era predecessor John Lehman, England – who later became Deputy Secretary of Defense – was considerably less active in formulating the strategic importance of American sea power.[32] His successor at the top of the Navy Department was Donald Winter, a businessman who continued the focus on the ongoing wars in Afghanistan and Iraq and taking care of veterans and their families, building the future fleet of ships, and acquisition reform.[33] None of the capstone documents of that period bore Secretary Winter's signature.

Admiral Vern Clark served as CNO for the first half of the decade. From 2000–2005, Clark oversaw the wars in Afghanistan and Iraq, and the global campaign against terrorism. In contrast to many of his predecessors, Clark embraced jointness in that he did not see the Navy as responsible for developing its own strategic narrative. In addition, Clark wanted to carefully groom politically important relationships with the Pentagon leadership. In particular, he sought to optimize many of the Navy's business procedures to reduce inefficiencies. Although Clark's interest in a glossy strategy publication was limited, it occurred to him that he still needed a tool to broadcast his priorities. During his tenure, no less than five OPNAV offices worked on U.S. Navy strategic statements and similar projects simultaneously.[34] Clark co-signed major capstone documents such as "Sea Power 21" (2002), which concentrated on projection of sea power from the littorals ashore. The "Fleet Response Plan" (2003), which Clark also signed, altered the way the Navy deployed, by introducing the crisis surging of the fleet from its continental U.S. bases as a complementary measure to dogmatic forward naval presence. Under Clark's direction, the Navy introduced the concept of an Expeditionary

Strike Group (ESG). This concept built on the existing Amphibious Ready Group (ARG), now integrating amphibious warships and U.S. Marine Corps units with combat power delivered by guided-missile cruisers and destroyers, a frigate, and fast attack submarine. These improved operational formations complemented, and in some case compensated for, aircraft carrier groups (CSG) centered on big-deck carriers.

Clark's successor was Admiral Michael "Mike" Mullen (previously Commander, Allied Forces Europe, and Commander, Allied Joint Force Command Naples).[35] Another surface warfare officer, Mullen was a strategically sensitive CNO with an appreciation for integration of capabilities and resources. Mullen actively engaged and presided over the development of a new strategy that included a system-centric approach, one carried by the Navy, Marine Corps, and Coast Guard, and featuring new global initiatives under the umbrella of cooperation and common responsibility. Before submitting the strategy that became "A Cooperative Strategy for 21st Century Seapower" (or CS-21), Mullen was nominated as CJCS in 2007, the first such naval officer since the end of the Cold War.[36] Admiral Gary Roughead, who succeeded Mullen, built on his predecessor's ideas before submitting CS-21 (and other signature policies), and held the position as CNO between 2007 and 2011. Roughead, with experience as fleet commander in the Pacific and the Atlantic under his belt, was the third surface warfare office in a row to serve as Chief of Naval Operations. He was able to build on Mullen's previous work, although he made some significant alterations to his predecessor's initiatives, both in wording and substance.[37]

Mullen's nomination to CJCS was the most visible in a series of naval flag officers rising to elevated national security and combatant command positions. Others included the selection of Vice Admiral Mike McConnell as Director of National Intelligence (serving from 2007 to 2009), Admirals Eric Olson and William "Bill" McRaven as Commanders, Special Operations Command (2007–2014), Admiral William "Fox" Fallon as Commander, Central Command (its first naval leader, serving from 2007 to 2008), and Admiral Jim Stavridis as Commander, Southern Command and then European Command and Supreme Allied Commander, Europe (SACEUR) (serving from 2006 to 2013).[38]

Domestic conditions

A number of national security reviews after 9/11 revealed critical gaps in counter-terrorism policy and the security architecture. In response, the Department of Homeland Security was created in March 2003. It pooled many agencies for national disaster preparation and relief (in particular the U.S. Coast Guard, previously under the jurisdiction of the Department of Transportation). These measures reflected the momentary elevation of anti-terrorism to the top position of the U.S. national interest grid. The "War on Terrorism" became the desperate attempt to fight an idea and a tactic using military means.[39] Terrorism – or the perceived threat thereof to the homeland – was not the only domestic event of note that created a new sense of national security. Natural disasters also played a role in underlining the growing concern for homeland security. Two visible examples with distinct maritime dimensions were Hurricane 'Katrina' (August 2005) and the Deepwater Horizon oil spill (April–July 2010).

To fund the operations in Afghanistan, Iraq, and elsewhere, the defense budget nearly doubled, rising from $408 billion in 2001 to $713 billion by 2010 (Figure 6.1). Since 2003, the long-standing rule of thumb that the Army, the Air Force, and the Navy budgets would be roughly equal was set aside. The Army and the Marines were subject to increasing demands for their central role in the ground wars on terrorism abroad, and consequently they were allocated more money. With that came a substantially increased public and political focus on these two branches of the military. The Navy's story and its strategic place, in contrast, did not have the desired effect with the wider public, which increasingly began to grow accustomed to the Army and the Marines bearing the brunt of casualties in the "War on Terror." In losing public support, the Navy risked the undermining of two of the three elements of a military service, namely its purpose or role in implementing national policy, and the human and material resources it required to implement a strategic concept.[40]

Despite throwing more money at the problem, neither the troops nor their military or political leaders were prepared enough for the quagmires in

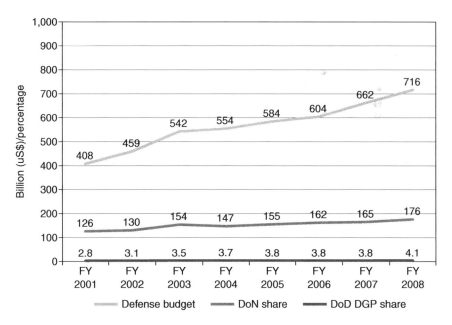

Figure 6.1 U.S. Defense Budget, Department of the Navy share, FY 2001–FY 2008, in FY 12 billion US-$; GDP DoD share in %.[41]

Southwest Asia. Discontent with the wars grew. Caring for "wounded war-riors" overwhelmed hospitals and other facilities. Extended tours for service-members put severe strains on many military families. It also appeared that the government bureaucracy (specifically, the Department of Veterans Affairs) was ill-prepared for the massive numbers of veterans returning from the battlefields.[42]

Selected U.S. national security policies, doctrines and capstone documents

When the Bush administration came into office, it proposed leaner, smaller, more agile military forces employing technological superiority to deter aggressors and quickly attain military ends in a future conflict. To the pres-ident, the military's purpose was not to engage in vague, aimless, and endless deployments. Instead, the future U.S. military would deter conflicts and win the wars it was unavoidably drawn into if deterrence failed.[43] After 9/11, Bush's rhetoric and many policies changed. Increasingly, a dialectical view, not unlike the one from the Cold War days, came to dominate politics. The threat this time was not the Soviet Union, but international terrorism admin-istered by the al-Qaida network. In his address before a joint session of Con-gress on September 20, just nine days after the attacks, Bush began to break down the new threat's complexities into a simplified rationalization.[44] The world consisted of two irreconcilable camps, who were either with the U.S. or with the terrorists; a military strike at al-Qaida was imminent. Infused with a high degree of public sympathy and international support, the swift and suc-cessful removal of the Taliban from power in Afghanistan seemed to vindi-cate the administration's approach. Empowered by the progress, American grand strategy post-9/11 changed to now include a stronger emphasis on regime change, preemptive warfare, and promotion of democracy abroad. Such "Wilsonianism in boots" underpinned global U.S. primacy.

Buttressed by increasing spending on military hardware and research, development, and testing of the next-generation materiel, U.S. primacy in the global commons – the sea, the air, space, and cyberspace – was declared the objective. This required a new mixture of conventional and unconven-tional warfare, and reliance on superior technology as well as unorthodox means. After all, transnational terrorist networks, the newly encountered enemy, were certainly hard to deter by nuclear force, although the latter obviously remained a pillar in the American policy arsenal.

The necessities of adapting to the new environment, however, came at an intellectual cost. Previously, in the early months of the Bush presidency, the focus of strategic thinking in the defense realm rested principally on the revolu-tion in military affairs. "Shock-and-awe" strikes, effects-based operations, will-ingness to accept operational risks, network-centric warfare, and precision-guided munitions were the cornerstones of this loosely defined post–Cold War force transformation. The 2001 Quadrennial Defense Review declared:

Transformation results from the exploitation of new approaches to operational concepts and capabilities, the use of old and new technologies, and new forms of organization that more effectively anticipate new or still emerging strategic and operational challenges and opportunities and that render previous methods of conducting war obsolete or subordinate.[45]

"Transformation mania,"[46] a post–1990 process amplified after 2001, swept through the Pentagon. Ill-defined in reality, it quickly became the singular yardstick by which all military services needed to demonstrate relevance on the battlefield of the future. By way of contrast, classic objectives of a global military such as forward deployment, power projection, control of vital sea lanes, and deterring nation-states became almost subordinate categories for thinkers inside Washington. In principle, this theme constituted yet another major challenge to the Navy's strategic narrative. It had to demonstrate its relevance (once again) to a public and politicians who increasingly held little appreciation for sea power means and ends.

The 2001 QDR, the second of its kind after 1997, was essentially driven by the RMA's transformation goal. A new strategic objective was introduced: dubbed the 1–4–2–1 approach, the U.S. military would be postured to defend the homeland (an aspect hastily introduced into the metric after 9/11), deter threats in four critical regions worldwide, be able to conduct two major combat operations (MCOs), and win in one of them. For the Navy, it included a requirement for 12 active aircraft carriers and a force level goal of 310 ships. In principle, this national capstone document remained rooted in pre-9/11 thinking, when much of it had already been written. Consequently, its influence was curtailed during the tumultuous times thereafter, and the emergence of a personality-focused policy over the course of 2002.[47]

The Bush Doctrine, emerging from his State of the Union address in January of 2002 and a speech at the U.S. Military Academy at West Point later that year, singled out three countries in particular: North Korea, Iran, and Iraq, which he characterized as an "axis of evil." This notion devised the crucial link between weapons of mass destruction and terrorist networks. Such grim rhetoric signaled a forceful, preemptive, and activist global policy underwritten by superior military force to deter and defeat such challengers. Those notions were codified in the 2002 National Security Strategy,[48] the third underpinning of the Bush Doctrine. The document identified the combination of terrorism, tyranny, and technology – that is weapons of mass destruction – as the key threat to U.S. security.[49] Implicitly, the American military, as part of the U.S. foreign policy toolkit, would be employed in time-consuming, long-lasting nation-building efforts which – in accordance with the preemptive and preventive war mantra – needed to be conducted swiftly.

The NSS 2002 propelled transnational terrorism to the top of the list of threats, a remarkable overreaction. In part motivated by their Cold War mindset, the Bush administration returned to a classic Reagan-era focus on nations as terrorism-sponsors. The thinking behind this approach was that a transnational terrorist organization could not sustain itself without the resources of a sponsoring government somewhere. More so, the Bush administration charged the previous Clinton administration with failing to control the behavior of other nations, which in its eyes resulted in the emergence of al-Qaida and terrorist threats in the first place.[50]

The National Military Strategy (NMS) 2004, produced by the Chairman of the Joint Chiefs of Staff and subsequent National Defense Strategy (NDS) 2005, issued by the Secretary of Defense, further elaborated on the NSS's goals, supporting the protection of the U.S. against external attacks and aggression, prevention of conflict and surprise attack, and prevailing against adversaries. In the face of the insurgency that began to plague Iraq in late 2003, the Bush Administration in March 2004 produced a major (and at the time classified) document called the Strategic Planning Guidance. It laid the foundation for the NDS 2005 by forcefully shifting American planning from transformation and reliance on expensive, advanced technology to the immediate task at hand, namely to win in Afghanistan and Iraq by conducting counterinsurgency campaigns.

This contradiction effectively undermined the goals of the RMA. In fact, the military underwent two transformations at the same time; the problem was they led in opposite directions. The top-down transformative demands triggered by the global war on terrorism mandated a reappraisal of counterinsurgency tactics and technology; these could include high-tech as much as low-tech assets on the murky ground, all seemingly long forgotten since Vietnam. The bottom-up transformative demands triggered by the revolution in military affairs (the original "transformation") hailed next-generation high tech and a lean, swift, stand-off force. Together, these approaches expressed the demands of a more complex environment where a 'one-size-fits-all' military was unsuitable. The early days of the wars in Afghanistan and Iraq seemingly validated the promises of the revolution in military affairs, but their later stages showed the flawed assumptions that senior military planners had fallen prey to. Pressed by realities on the ground, U.S. strategy needed to concentrate on asymmetric warfare at the expense of more established military roles.

Bush secured a second term as President. Against the background of a deteriorating security situation in Iraq and the ongoing global war on terrorism (including the hunt for Osama bin Laden), preparations for the next QDR went ahead. The Bush White House published its (second) National Security Strategy in mid-March 2006, a month and a half after the QDR.[51] Traditionally, while the QDR focuses on national defense in general and defense procurement issues in particular, the NSS takes a strategic perspective in the broadest of terms. It is thus remarkable that the overarching whole-of-government National Security Strategy was presented only *after* the Department of Defense document, when the causal and logical chain of events should have been the other way around. In the words of Deputy Secretary of Defense England, the QDR was designed to enable the Pentagon to "continue to move in the direction of speed, agility, precision and lethality in force posture, shifting emphasis farther away from the Cold War construct."[52] Strategy would follow.

The QDR 2006 was, at its core, a capstone document developed during wartime. Nevertheless, the QDR's new threat matrix of four challenges to U.S. security – irregular, catastrophic, traditional, and disruptive – committed the military to increase cooperative measures between services and develop and deepen partnerships with other militaries. It sought to better address the four major challenges of defeating terrorist networks, defending the homeland, shaping the actions of rising powers like China, and preventing state and non-state actors from gaining access to weapons of mass destruction.[53] In addition, the QDR proposed to increase forces in the Pacific, effectively anticipating the "rebalance to Asia" that filled many commentators' notepads in the 2010s.[54] The Navy planned to adjust its force posture and basing to provide at least six operationally available and sustainable CVNs, and 60 percent of its submarines, in the Pacific to support engagement, presence, and deterrence.[55]

The 2006 National Security Strategy reaffirmed the theme of a nation at war. The concepts of the 2002 National Security Strategy were reiterated and progress in selected areas was assessed. Significantly, the close link between the promotion of democracy and economic participation worldwide on the one hand, with U.S. security and well-being on the other, was underlined. Such emphases placed a premium on the systemic value of joint and inter-agency forces, that is those working to improve good governance in areas of interest and those – naval/maritime forces – that would secure and keep open maritime trade routes.[56] This overarching system was understood as one based on shared rules, and maritime and naval forces were consequently seen as most appropriate means to enforce these directions. The QDR and the NSS 2006 were the two last major grand strategic and national defense capstone documents of the Bush era.

Developing and promulgating USN strategy (2001–2011)

The Navy's first capstone document came out in the year after the assaults of 9/11. Over the course of the decade, the U.S. Navy published 14 capstone documents (nine during the Bush presidency) of strategic, declaratory intent (some remaining classified and thus unavailable for analysis), almost twice the number as in the 1990s. They were self-titled visions, concepts, strategic plans, strategic guidance, or just a simple plan. A list of these strategic documents (including their classification status) is given in Table 6.1.

The large number of these documents reflected the broad uncertainty that surrounded the Navy's role in coping with the political and military

Table 6.1 USN capstone documents 2001–2008[57]

Name	Self-titled format	Year	Status
Sea Power 21 & Global CONOPS	Vision	2002	Unclassified
Naval Power 21 … A Naval Vision	Vision	2002	Unclassified
Naval Operating Concept for Joint Operations	Concept	2003	Unclassified
Fleet Response Plan	Plan	2003	Unclassified
Navy Strategic Plan ISO POM 08	Strategic Plan	2006 2006	Secret Unclassified
Naval Operations Concept	Concept	2006	Unclassified
Navy Strategic Plan ISO POM 10	Strategic Plan	2007	Secret
A Cooperative Strategy for 21st Century Seapower	Strategy	2007	Unclassified
Navy Strategic Plan ISO POM 10 (Ch 1)	Strategic Plan	2007	Secret

consequences of 9/11, while attempting to develop a larger maritime but still naval-centric narrative regarding the use of sea power. Both aspects in part echoed divergent expectations in the Navy and the Pentagon about what the future of U.S. military engagements worldwide would look like. Put another way, the Navy struggled with arguing whether the United States needed to plan for a long, asymmetric, generational war against terrorists and other hybrid state/non-state actors, or whether the post-9/11 expeditionary operations reflected a departure from the norm of planning for state-on-state conflicts. The plurality of documents is thus also a function of the environment where Secretary Rumsfeld reasserted civilian management over the Joint Staff and the services. To CNO Clarke and many of his senior staff, strategy that went beyond the next budget submission (designed to defend the Navy's programs) was a lesser-included task at best. Consequently, Clark's selective actions in establishing strategic-thinking subordinate offices were erratic, and weakened strategic naval planning when it was arguably needed most in the years of the emerging Bush Doctrine. In addition to N51 (the Strategy and Policy Division itself) there were no fewer than four separate offices under the OPNAV umbrella working on five partially overlapping strategy projects during 2002 and 2003.[58] Consequently, confusion and bureaucratic rivalry ensued, and effective strategy-making was impoverished. Clarke's tenure was also characterized by a significant disparity between the number and quality of strategic planners in the Navy and their actual, lasting, and sustainable output.[59] Only after Rumsfeld's demission, and with CNO Mullen at the helm, was the Navy reenergized. Its products became better coordinated and streamlined. Processes were optimized, thus ending a period of strategic under-ambition and naval-strategic disarray.

Sea Power 21 and Global CONOPS

Evolution

The first concerted effort to create a strategy for the new century resulted in "Sea Power 21," a multi-volume series of articles including a global Concept of Naval Operations (CONOPS).[60] "Sea Power 21" was signed by CNO Clark and other admirals. It originated from the Strategic Action Group (N00K) and the Assessments Division (N81). As an unclassified vision, it appeared in the Navy's professional magazine, *Proceedings*, in back-to-back issues between October 2002 and January 2004.[61] In parallel, it was posted on the internet and published as a stand-alone pamphlet. By referencing the three most influential Navy strategies to date – "The Maritime Strategy" (1986), "... From the Sea" (1992), and "Forward ... From the Sea" (1994) – "Sea Power 21" forged a bridge to efficient declarations of naval intent and placed itself in a historical context. It was also tied to previous documents such as the "Naval Strategic Planning Guidance" (1999/2000).

With "Sea Power 21," the Navy presented itself as fully integrated into the joint force. It finally (at least on paper) embraced the mandate of the 1986 Goldwater-Nichols Act. The 375-ship goal that was the hallmark of CNO Clark's plan was never even neared. The tactical focus of "Sea Power 21" and its companion Global CONOPS was also subject to criticism. The recital of concepts and programs overshadowed the core messages of the capstone document (Haynes describes it as a "complex, sprawling, and multi-faceted beast"[62] and "Janus-faced"[63]). "Sea Power 21" nevertheless retained considerable influence within OPNAV and other Navy commands. It instigated internal frameworks and organizing templates within OPNAV for the rest of the decade. It was promoted by frequent reference to it in speeches and congressional testimony by senior Navy leaders throughout the 2000s. The concept was also relatively catchy and easy to remember; but in all of that, the document was much more influential inside the service than as an external statement of Navy vision.[64]

Strategic concept

"Sea Power 21" emphasized presence of naval forces in a given theater of operations, perhaps in part energized by the Navy's immediate role in the military response to 9/11. Within hours, naval assets had redeployed to provide the initial capabilities for the combat action that followed. The Navy was able to demonstrate to senior military leaders that their organic, carrier-borne strike warfare was just as good as that of the Air Force, yet had exceptional advantages in flexibility, sustainability, speed, and fewer diplomatic ramifications courtesy of naval power. Such joint assimilation dovetailed with the promotion and value of naval presence. It echoed concepts of the Cold War derived from the understanding that forward defense-in-depth as well as sea and area control required geographically oriented forward forces.

"Sea Power 21" represented a confirmation of the close affiliation between the Navy and the Marine Corps to command the littorals and project power ashore.[65] The return to focus on global joint operations signaled a farewell to the previous planning metric (just two "major" combat operations) and its more regional focus.[66] The Global CONOPS underwrote such developments publicly. Serving to implement the QDR 2001's planning metric; it emphasized global presence and dispersed combat striking power, while also downgrading the importance of forward hubs. This was a convenient explanation of the Navy's inability to maintain and the political leadership's unwillingness to fund three forward hubs as it did during the Cold War: the Mediterranean was the one to give way. The force repackaging with the integration of SSGN submarines and BMD surface ships provided flexible combat response capability.

"Sea Power 21" used the easily identifiably prefix "Sea" to convey its networked and integrated thinking. At sea, Sea Strike (power projection, ISR, information operations, force delivery/insertion), Sea Shield (sea-based theater and strategic defense, and homeland defense), and Sea Basing (enabler for Sea Strike and Sea Shield) were to be facilitated by FORCEnet (the only deliberate divergence from the prefix), which was understood as the information-age integrating glue that would bind the three former concepts together. Behind this fancy vocabulary lurked established naval missions: sea control, deterrence, power projection, forward presence (Admiral Turner's 'classic 4'), and sealift. Sea Warrior (the recruitment of the future force), Sea Trial (research, development, testing, and rapid fielding of superior equipment), and Sea Enterprise (streamlining the Navy's business practices to identify efficiencies in every part of the service) were designed as the ashore components at the bureaucratic home front.

"Sea Power 21" was an ambitious attempt to square a circle: it attempted to innovatively address both the strike warfare demands of combatant commanders in theater, and at the same time identify cost efficiencies to fund expanding the fleet. Its legacy is therefore more of a managerial, internal one.[67] Compared with previous Navy statements from the 1990s, it benefited from the higher degree of certainty regarding the threats that the U.S. faced: terrorism, failing states, conventional (asymmetric) warfare, A2AD, organized crime, and WMD, in direct relationship to (U.S.) homeland security were all encompassed in "Sea Power 21." The document represented an important step of the U.S. Navy toward becoming a "post-modern" force.[68] Such navies do not limit themselves to the classic roles of naval forces (i.e., protection of sea lanes, delivery of combat power ashore, etc.), but also guard the global maritime system and its underlying values. They do so by sea control, expeditionary operations, enforcing good order at sea, and a broad cooperative maintenance of the maritime consensus.[69] Precision-strike warfare, however, remained at the core of even this most post-modern of navies. This last point demonstrates that naval strategy is evolutionary, not revolutionary.

Naval Power 21 ... A Naval Vision

Evolution

The following capstone document, "Naval Power 21 ... A Naval Vision"[70] struck a similar note. The unclassified short pamphlet was distributed exclusively via the internet. In principle, this document sought to staple together the messages of the Navy's "Sea Power 21" and the Marine Corps' own "Strategy 21," and distinguish them with the Secretary's endorsement – who saw the benefit of promoting his own agenda. It was the first truly joint Navy-Marine Corps (naval) strategic capstone document since "Forward ... From the Sea" (1994). The six-page self-described vision was authored by OPNAV's "Deep Blue" think tank, securing contribution from OPNAV N513. Personalities involved included the Secretary of the Navy, Captain Will Dossel (N513), and Rear Admiral – later full admiral, Commander U.S. European Command (USEUCOM), and Supreme Allied Commander Europe (SACEUR) – James G. "Jim" Stavridis. The document, for lack of conceptual leverage, remained most remarkable for the involvement of these individuals and the signatures of the three Navy Department and service leaders.[71] Its influence proved limited.

Strategic concept

"Naval Power 21 ... A Naval Vision" (2002) fell far behind any strategic aspirations. Its limited impact inside and outside the Navy can be attributed to its unfortunate timing – it was simply overshadowed by other Navy-related capstone documents. In addition, Secretary England did little to rally consensus for his document. The cost-effectiveness measures the document proposed had little leverage in the big picture (and the proposed growth in fleet size by 25 percent never even closely materialized). More precisely, "Naval Power 21" worked with a force-planning metric which reiterated ideas found in preceding documents, but not strategic missions. Its 3/4/8 framework contained three fundamental pillars – assured access, fighting to win, and continuous transformation – as well as four "fundamental qualities of naval forces": decisiveness, sustainability, responsiveness, and agility. It also reiterated a number of distinct concepts that were already seen in "Seapower 21" (Sea Strike, Sea Shield, Sea Basing enabled by FORCEnet, and Sea Warrior, Sea Trial, and Sea Enterprise).[72] On balance, the impact of "Naval Power 21" on other Navy strategic capstone publications, the Navy, or the strategic community was minimal at best. It did initiate the next capstone document, however.

Naval operating concept for joint operations

Evolution

The development of a new operational concept was a task identified in "Naval Power 21" (2002). Consequently, a concept addressing the Navy's and the Marine Corps' joint operational contribution to national defense was signed in April 2003 by CNO Clark and the (new) CMC General Michael Hagee.[73] It was unclassified and published on the web shortly thereafter. The "Naval Operations Concept for Joint Operations" aimed to close the ranks of the Navy and the Marine Corps in that it was designed as the Navy Department's consensual contribution to the OSD-developed "Joint Operations Concepts" (JOC).[74] The naval operating concept aimed to provide a rationale for surge forces at home and forward presence, outlined near-term, mid-term, and long-term (to 2020) visions, discussed how to meet conventional and unconventional threats, and surveyed nation-state and non-state adversaries. The document cited and underscored the ideas proposed in "Sea Power 21" and the Global CONOPS. Not unlike "Naval Power 21," it had little lasting impact beyond the doctrinal offices. "Naval Power 21" and the "Naval Operating Concept for Joint Operations" were small pieces in a larger puzzle, namely how to generate more efficient and effective naval input for U.S. strategy; the documents did not speak to the larger political roles and goals of naval forces in peace, crisis, and war and thus remained limited in impact.

Strategic concept

The NOC outlined how the two naval services would operate across the spectrum of military operations through the year 2020. Whereas the document sought to meet the "1–4–2–1" metric mandated by broader strategic documents,[75] it drew criticism for its inability to set real priorities. As Swartz noted, the Navy and the Marine Corps covered nothing less than the whole playing field.[76] The document pitched a long-term temporal horizon, but its primary focus was the currently serving Navy and Marine Corps officers' corps. That internal audience, the reasoning went, needed to be brought onto the same page regarding their joint operations, not strategy (that could happen later). Such a technical, sea-*operational* paper sought to strengthen the Navy-Marine Corps consensus on issues like sea-basing but provided little in the sense of a larger sea-*strategic* concept; it simply reaffirmed what had been said before, providing little emotion and innovation (only the specific link to Special Operations Forces [SOF] concepts gave an exception that proved the rule). If anything, the "Naval Operating Concept for Joint Operations" advocated a more capability-based approach to counter generic state/non-state, conventional, and unconventional threats. This reprised the Navy's long-standing narrative, but lacked more comprehensive explanation of American sea power. Subsequently, the document foundered because it was hardly embraced by the Navy Department leadership. Seldom mentioned in successive speeches and testimony, it was eclipsed by larger strategic capstone documents such as "Sea Power 21."

Fleet Response Plan

Evolution

It became the "Fleet Response Plan" (FRP) role to address a looming short-coming connected to the Navy's traditional forward-deployed culture.[77] Prior to 2003 (from about 1986), the Navy dispatched its carrier groups on the predictable basis of the 18-month Inter-Deployment Training Cycle (IDTC). Mandated by the complexity of deploying overseas, the associated maintenance and work-up (including training, equipping, and manning) were calibrated to give a unit a relatively reliable planning schedule. Between six-month long tours on station, there was a total of 12 months scheduled for post-operational power-down, repairs, and preparation until the carrier (and its escorting ships) put to sea again.[78] On the one hand, this was sensible to reduce wear and tear on the machinery, and allow relatively reliable personnel planning. On the other hand, it appeared that the surge potential of the force was not being utilized. In the words of Bush-era Undersecretary of Defense for Personnel and Readiness David Chu, "There is in the Navy and Marine Corps a substantial portion of the structure that is unavailable to the president on short notice, short of heroic measures."[79]

The "Fleet Response Plan" was to modify this practice. Its focus on readiness and speed of response were planned to better align the Navy's culture and operational practices with the crisis response and anti-terror needs of the Bush administration. Preemptive military action was a hallmark of the 2002 National Security Strategy – much like Operation Iraqi Freedom (2003) – mandating a substantial surge capability by naval forces. In the minds of the planners, such actions hardly allowed a 12-month planning schedule. Instead, anticipation of more short-notice campaigns like OIF reigned. For that, the Navy needed to be ready and deployable. Consequently, OPNAV's "Deep Blue" cell developed – and later passed on to the Commander, Fleet Forces Command (then Admiral Robert Natter) for refinement – a concept to alter maintenance and deployment cycles. As a bonus, it would henceforth also be more difficult for American adversaries to pre-calculate U.S. carrier presence off their coasts. The "Fleet Response Plan" appeared in the spring of 2003 and included a metric for six carrier strike groups (CSG) deployable within 30 days (with an additional surge CSG within 90 days).[80] The new readiness mandate was accompanied by a public relations campaign and comprehensively tested in exercise Summer Pulse 04 which incorporated the near-simultaneous forward operation of seven CSGs around the world. In the exercises Valiant Shield 2006 and 2007 in the Pacific, three CSGs tested their simultaneous operating capabilities.

Strategic concept

By 2004 the Iraq War exposed and unraveled the American strategic approach to war-fighting. The U.S. military had for too long hailed its transformed, reductionist and even minimalist strike warfare rooted in information dominance. In the face of the mounting insurgency in Iraq, the U.S. military had to redefine the larger political purpose for which wars would be undertaken in the first place. Even though the NDS 2005 (with its focus on forward-deployed homeland defense, security of access, building and fostering of alliances, and setting favorable security conditions worldwide) presented the Navy with a chance to underline its inherent capabilities through orchestrating military, constabulary, and diplomatic roles, the service was unable to embrace it. On the strategic level, naval presence can be valuable for deterrence, coercion, and defense-in-depth policy. The leading role of naval forces in the early stages of OEF and OIF, respectively, had demonstrated that to U.S. policy-makers. But for the Navy, the regional commanders had already based their requirements for assets on the notion of combat-credible forward presence. Should presence become an end in itself, it risked being too predictable, detached from the larger strategic picture and taxing to the fleet.

More dramatically, the strategic shift that drove the NDS 2005 rendered the Navy's "Sea Power 21" focus on precision-strike power projection warfare unfashionable. Consequently, the service descended into its most fundamental institutional crisis since the 1970s.[81] To add insult to injury, the Navy also faced dramatic budget and shipbuilding cutbacks.[82] Shipbuilding had been low on Clark's list of priorities because he was more concerned with readiness and cost efficiencies.

Under a national policy requiring services to be better prepared for more surged deployments, and where one-third of overseas bases were slated for closure, the Navy's whole force structure was threatened. The president's strategic direction, meanwhile, did not address where a future enemy would fight, but how. Consequently, the "Fleet Response Plan" (2003) signaled an intellectual change from the Navy's cultural fixation on scheduled fleet forward presence towards emphasizing its surge capabilities. The plan's main thrust – presence – spoke for itself; larger strategic rationales were not discussed. It was too carrier-centric and hardly mentioned other components of the balanced fleet, whose routine deployments could bring about strategic effects as well; in short, it did not situate itself well into the broad American sea power narrative.[83]

Interregnum: the influx of fresh ideas[84]

It was up to Vice Admiral John Morgan Jr., from August 2004 on serving as the new Director of OPNAV's N3/N5 division (Plans, Policies, and Operations), to provide the Navy with a broader and fresher perspective on the strategic environment and, more importantly, the fundamental role played by American sea power. He became the key driver within OPNAV for a genuinely new maritime strategy that went beyond annual reports or budget requests. Morgan argued that the Navy needed a coherent, overarching strategy to place the service – and naval assets in the broadest sense – into the maritime overall context, which in turn buttressed U.S. military and grand strategy. He and his staff developed such a narrative to reach from the bottom end to the highest echelons.

In January 2005 Morgan and Rear Admiral Charles Martoglio (Director of OPNAV's Strategy and Policy Division, N51) briefed a new initiative to rearrange the Navy's joint capabilities. It became known as the "3/1 Strategy" (its accompanying slide reminded many of a feral limb, thus coining the more colloquial description of 'Bear Paw.' Although never beyond draft status, it served as a point of departure for the capstone documents that followed. The paper's fundamental innovation was that it reshaped the understanding of the Navy's principal missions. Along with the enduring need to be prepared for major combat operations, the new model described Homeland Security and Defense, Stability Operations, and the Global War on Terror as three distinct areas each demanding specialized capabilities. They could – and indeed should – no longer be understood as subsets of the pre-9/11 planning metric outlining two major regional conflicts/major theater wars as governing force-planning. Such a bold move emphasized that the Navy could succeed in traditional and non-traditional mission sets, but only when forward-deployed. Inside the Navy, such notions met some concerted resistance, by blue-water navy advocates who found the service had indeed adapted to use high-end capabilities for lesser tasks.

Under Admiral Mike Mullen, the new CNO from July 2005, the Navy gravitated toward a more formalized and structuralized process of drafting its capstone objectives. Once in office, Mullen aggressively pursued an analysis of the Navy's composition, fleet size, and resulting shipbuilding budget.[85] The Navy Strategic Plan ISO POM 08 (2006) was the first Mullen-sponsored document. Two signature initiatives, the "1,000–ship Navy" and "Global Fleet Stations" were developed at the time by CNO Mullen and his Deputy CNO Morgan. These departed from the strike focus and a fundamentally novel version of U.S. power projection.

The "1,000–ship Navy" drew on the understanding that maritime security was the responsibility of likeminded, international partners. In an environment holding vast complexity through the interdependencies created by globalization, the "1,000–ship Navy" was the tool to knit together navies, coast guards, and maritime constabulary units in a self-organizing and self-governing cooperative security network.[86] Together, this global force could secure ports and harbors, territorial waters, the high seas and the international straits from terrorists, pirates, illegal migration, human smuggling, drug trafficking, environmental abuse, and the proliferation of weapons of mass destruction.[87]

"Global Fleet Stations" (GFS), another theme shepherded by Vice Admiral Morgan, was a project to emerge from N00Z and N5's Strategy and Concepts office (N5SC) in OPNAV. In an unpublished draft White Paper,[88] it was described as a self-sustaining base of one of more large amphibious ships to (save for the occasional port visit) linger off a country's coast. There, they played host and coordinated the activities of U.S. small-craft and riverine boats, helicopters, trainers, engineers, explosive ordnance disposal (EOD) teams, salvage divers, medical teams, U.S. federal agencies, NGOs, and others. GFS were to cooperate with host nations and support ships and units of other nations working with the U.S. Navy regionally. For both ends, maritime domain awareness, or MDA (the pooling and sharing of intelligence from commercial maritime traffic such as automated identification systems [AIS]) was promoted to track ships at sea and significantly improve the situational picture. Knowing what happened at sea would drastically improve understanding and oversight. It also offered the opportunity to cooperate with likeminded navies and coast guards worldwide.

In principle, such an approach substantially limited the need for a costly and potentially politically contentious footprint ashore. Such support functions were now elevated to adapt to the demands of the early 2000s. That vocabulary and its underlying concepts – although the "1,000-ship Navy" was quickly changed into a less-unilateralist (and perhaps less-Reagan-era) sounding "Global Maritime Partnership" – resonated throughout the Navy and its capstone documents. Many foreign partners (some still troubled by the Iraq War) remained skeptical of the concept. It reminded them of American unilateralism, militarization of foreign and security policy, and gunboat diplomacy.

Navy Strategic Plan ISO POM 08

Evolution

The "Navy Strategic Plan" was designed to support the FY 2008 budget submission and the 2006 QDR, both due within a few weeks of one another.[89] That put a high degree of pressure on its drafters, a momentous task given the need for collaboration, coordination, management buy-in, and consensus-building in the complex bureaucracy of OPNAV. The plan's intellectual underpinning was the "3/1 strategy" (of Vice Admiral Morgan) from 2004/2005, which stated that the Navy's stability, anti-terrorism, and homeland defense missions were not merely lesser-included cases or subsets of major combat operations, but critical mission sets in their own right, demanding a dedicated force structure and strategic (as well as budgetary) attention.[90] That approach was not without critics. Led by Admiral John Nathman, Commander of the Navy's Fleet Forces Command (FFC), this group charged against what they saw as an unjustified focus on the low-end, asymmetric, systemic roles and missions of the Navy. They advocated looking beyond current operations (OEF, OIF) – in that, their view did not substantially differ from that of Vice Admiral Morgan and his team – arguing that concentrating on high-end competition against nation-states was the Navy's future. Despite a number of rewrites and pushback from Admiral Nathman and his command (which by all accounts engaged in constructive criticism), the position of the CNO and his deputies prevailed. A major support for Mullen's and Morgan's position came from the "National Strategy for Maritime Security," a collaborative effort by DOD and DHS signed by President Bush in September 2005. That document supported Mullen's and Morgan's arguments on the relationship among sea power, cooperative maritime security, and global systemic affluence.[91]

Strategic concept

As a reapplication of the "3/1 strategy," the "Navy Strategic Plan" was fundamentally a proclamation designed to inform investments. It also reflected the fundamental change in U.S. strategy brought about by the post-9/11 response. Leveraging off the QDR 2006, it picked up on the three mission sets that this overarching document proposed. These focus areas were the "Global War on Terror" and associated irregular warfare, homeland security and defense (e.g., the Navy's role in the war on drugs, border security, and natural disasters), and conventional campaign missions. The Navy document emphasized the systemic value of the liberalist, hegemonic sea power that served the international system. It also provided audiences – principally U.S. Navy program and planning officers – with three maritime focus areas for the future force. These were the Western Pacific (in particular Southeast Asia), the Middle East and Southwest Asia, and the Mediterranean (the increasing responsibility of NATO in that area, it was noted, freed up U.S. assets for operations elsewhere).[92]

This tied together what the Navy did and where it did it, a means and ends relationship. It provided a rationale for its 313-ship force level goal. At the same time, the paper called for using significantly smaller force packages (such as SEALs and independent Marine Corps, Coast Guard, or Navy expeditionary teams operating on ships and submarines), again reflecting the operational realities of OEF and OIF. These forces were to be used in regions of secondary strategic importance such as Africa, the Indian Ocean, and the Eastern Pacific. The Navy now recognized that it need not only move into the littorals, but also into coastal and internal, green- and brown-water areas. The document's focus on stability operations (constabulary sea power, such as anti-piracy operations, sanctions, embargo enforcement, peacekeeping, counter-drug, counter-terrorism, and others) briefly overshadowed conventional deterrence and war-fighting missions. The paper did succeed in making a case for the merits of naval forces in shaping the environment, providing leverage which air forces or armies could not. At the same time, in relating U.S. military force to larger and more systemic goals (something the NSS 2006 had also argued) it helped a more population-centric view inside the Navy gain traction. The "Strategic Plan" document provided the "means" as another declaratory statement of strategic intent named the "Naval Operations Concept" – the "ways" – was already under way.[93]

Naval Operations Concept (2006)

Evolution

The Naval Operations Concept (NOC) was first drafted as a single-service Navy document in December 2005. It sought to match the determining principles at the core of contemporary naval operations with those overarching strategic demands that senior civilian leaders in OSD and the White House set. The paper was overseen by senior Navy and Marine Corps flag officers. However, for the Navy, responsibilities shifted throughout, and while USN–USMC relationships were relatively smooth, there was some friction within the Navy over ownership of it.[94]

Strategic concept

Although the "Naval Operations Concept" focused on long-standing areas of U.S. naval force engagement (the Mediterranean, the Arabian Sea, the Western Pacific) and three emerging areas of operations (the Gulf of Guinea, East Africa's littorals, and Latin American waters) as the "Naval Strategic Plan ISO POM 08," it broadened its ambitions considerably. It also referred to the traditional, irregular, catastrophic, and disruptive challenges to American national security identified in Rumsfeld's National Military Strategy (2005). By citing three guiding principles from the "National Strategy for Maritime Security" (2005) (freedom of the seas, free movement of seaborne goods, and cross-U.S.-border situational awareness), it discussed the mission set construct of the 2006 QDR (homeland defense, war on terror/irregular warfare, conventional campaigns). The authors of the paper thus sought to demonstrate that the Navy understood and embraced the geostrategic, military, and operational realities of the twenty-first century. It was thus integrative and broad in scope, reflecting established common denominators with the national defense leadership.

The downside was the document overreached. It identified no fewer than 13 missions for the Navy and the Marine Corps.[95] It also named nine permanent naval principles.[96] On top of that, it noted four foundations of its narrative (including global maritime and littoral domain awareness), nine methods (including globally networked operations, adaptive force-packaging, aggregation and disaggregation, sea-basing, and cultural awareness), and five strategic objectives/outcomes (winning wars, establishing favorable security conditions, securing strategic access and retaining global freedom of action, strengthening alliances and partnerships, and securing the U.S. from attack). The capstone document encompassed, for the first time, maritime security operations as a distinct and genuine mission area. It recognized globalization as a driving force of global change, and briefly mentioned hybrid forms of conflict and warfare.[97] However, the document is notably vague regarding which countries or non-state actors were included in this large scope. The

NOC 2006 is also mute on such other important naval issues as mine warfare, convoy and blockade operations, and strategic sealift.[98]

While the document's scope is laudable, its mention of strategic objectives demonstrates a broader consideration of the naval services' effects, and its elevation of the Navy's constabulary role in relation to its military and diplomatic ones was remarkable.[99] But its methodology produced too many lists to remember and use, let alone understand. Consequentially, for the time being it had limited influence outside of the Navy. The NOC 2006 embraced the changing nature of sea power from combat at and from the sea to include the littorals. In this, the document partially reflected the intellectual shift the Navy had undertaken, albeit with some detours and occasional hesitance, since the end of the Cold War.

Navy Strategic Plan ISO POM 10 (September 2007)

Evolution

Before publication of CS-21, another document was slated to appear: the secret, single-service "Navy Strategic Plan ISO POM 10."[100] Just like its predecessor (2006), it was to inform the Department of the Navy's leadership, programmers, and budget staff about the future direction of the service. The memo for the "Navy Strategic Plan ISO POM 08" had directed that the process of drafting a strategic plan, once established, was to be repeated at least biennially. The 2007 version happened to be the first Navy capstone document finalized after Robert Gates succeeded Donald Rumsfeld as Secretary of Defense. Gates' initial objectives focused on providing the troops in Afghanistan and Iraq with the right material and political support; he was not a strategic aspirant. At the time, both irregular warfare and the more conventional security challenges signaled a murky and challenging environment for the application of military force. The process of writing the plan was overseen by those in N3/N5 (such as Vice Admiral Morgan), with considerable input from N81 (the programming division). Through the end, it remained a Navy-only concept. It appeared before the (public) unveiling of CS-21, therefore lingering in between more publicized documents. Its signing was rushed, as Admiral Mullen stepped down as CNO prior to become the 17th Chairman of the Joint Chiefs of Staff.

Strategic concept

The document was to "translate national strategic guidance into USN guidance; translate new concurrently drafted maritime strategy into a plan to inform Navy investments; [and] continue to build consensus in Navy around new strategic ideas."[101] It was intended to bridge "A Cooperative Strategy for 21st Century Seapower" (2007) and the "Naval Operations Concept" (2006). Unfortunately, its classified status prohibited any distribution and discussion of strategic effects. The document's far-reaching assessment of the strategic context confronting the Navy remains unavailable, so it must be omitted here.

A Cooperative Strategy for 21st Century Seapower

Evolution

During the summer of 2006, at the annual Current Strategy Forum at the Naval War College in Rhode Island, Admiral Mullen called for the development of a new maritime strategy for all sea services. Not just a Navy effort, this comprehensive maritime (Navy, Marine Corps, and Coast Guard) document made a clear nod to "The Maritime Strategy" of the 1980s. More so, "it was to be highly collaborative and inclusive, consisting of a number of 'forums' that would feed ideas and research" into Admiral Morgan's staff.[102] Together with action officers from the Marine Corps and the Coast Guard,[103] Commander Bryan McGrath as the lead author fleshed out the strategy over the course of one-and-a-half years. The sea services, it was hoped, could develop a narrative for Congress, the White House, and the American people to support the Navy's energetic and assertive ideas.

The Naval War College led one of the forums. After the ground rules were made clear (most importantly, any discussion of force structure was outlawed), several workshops gathered naval and grand strategy professionals at Newport, Rhode Island and Annapolis, Maryland (the U.S. Naval Academy) to produce options for N3N5. The team wargamed various approaches to grand strategy (primacy, selective engagement, cooperative security, and offshore balancing) and five strategic challengers (China, Iran, Pakistan, North Korea, and radical Salafists).[104]

Based on the results of the wargame, the 150 faculty and staff of the USNWC came up with the following options for the new maritime strategy.

- "Winning Combat Power Forward," which stemmed from the primacy approach and centered on East Asia and the Middle East;
- "Surge Force," rooted in offshore balancing where the Navy and the Marine Corps would be on station with minimum forces at two hubs with the balance poised in home waters;[105]
- "Trimodal Force" was championed by Prof. Waynes Hughes of the Navan Postgraduate School and consisted of a sea denial force of submarines, missile boats, low-end maritime security forces, and legacy power-projection forces;
- "Sea Control", championed by USNWC Dean Robert "Barney" Rubel, which maintained sea command capabilities in the blue-water and sea denial in the littoral;
- "Prevent War," based on the realization that great-power conflict was the most fundamentally disruptive event to the global system.[106]

From these, McGrath and his team created a hybrid.[107] This utilized the big, system-centric idea (which only the United States could secure), integrated the primacy idea (for the Far East and the Arabian Sea), and combined them with sea control and partnerships. These ideas were fleshed out by vetting through chains of command, enlisting feeder articles, and testing them in executive seminars, conferences, and other public forums. In the third stage, the core team (the "Strategic Action Group" in OPNAV N3/N5) eventually became the writing team and set out to finalize the strategy between June and October 2007.

The title chosen for the document could speak volumes on its scope. Even the spelling and capitalization in it could be interpreted as deliberate references to the institutional, systemic dimension of sea power; the ultimate tie-in of functional, geographic, and institutional dimensions of naval power. Even if such reasoning was sound, the position taken by the strategy's lead author regarding Seapower is equally compelling: "[I] Deliberately [used] one word, deliberately capitalized [it]. I am unaware of a distinction between the concepts of a one word or two word version, I just liked one better."[108]

As the third member of the family of documents which NOC 2006 and the "Navy Strategic Plan" had begun, CS-21 was able to draw from them as frames of reference to structure its own ambitions. Only once nearing completion in the summer of 2007 was Secretary of the Navy Winter briefed. Eventually, the new strategy was signed by the CNO, Admiral Gary Roughead, CMC General James Conway (USMC), and the Commandant of the U.S. Coast Guard, Admiral Thad Allen in October 2007.[109] The same month, the strategy was unveiled publicly (although the process had been unclassified and inclusive from the start) at the Naval War College. The final product, at its heart a 16-page booklet available on the Navy's website, was disseminated widely.[110] This included articles in professional magazines and journals, CNO testimony before Congress, brochures, downloadable posters, a video clip,[111] and – utilizing an increasingly important medium – military blogs.[112]

Strategic concept

The strategy emphasized the significance of the international global system for trade and security. CS-21 reflected the innovative conceptual framework Vice Admiral Morgan sought to implement to reverse the existing process of strategy-making. Before him, programmatic decisions derived from the annual Navy budget submissions dictated the service's strategy; Morgan wanted to turn around that causality. Recognition of interdependencies, of energy demands, and the unhindered exchange of goods and information in the global system was the central enabler for CS-21. By tying itself directly to American grand strategy and the systemic notion of international security and stability (in which the U.S. had a fundamental interest and at the same time fielded the capabilities to orchestrate its protection), the Navy as an institution attempted to rise above the Southwest Asian ground wars and the annual budget submissions that dominated much of the strategic debates at the time.[113] It also sought to broaden the nation's view again, arguing that there was more to American hegemony than messy and obscure counterinsurgency wars. The Navy wanted to provide military and political leaders with a compelling strategic concept that offered an alternative to unwinnable ground wars.

In highlighting the Navy's role in guarding the liberal international system, sustained American sea power was linked to global prosperity and the advancement of democratic principles. In its deliberately benign characterization of American power, the strategy dovetailed with the popular American understanding of its role in the world as a benevolent hegemon. CS-21 moved enthusiastically beyond the merely military role of naval forces, as well as elevating constabulary and diplomatic uses of the sea. With that last step, it discarded the counter-societal and counter-military visions long dominant in the understanding of the strategic effects navies could have.

Strategically, CS-21 linked key naval tasks to strategic imperatives. These included regionally concentrated credible combat power in the Western Pacific, the Arabian Gulf, and the Indian Ocean to deter major-power war, win those armed conflicts that the U.S. did have to fight, and contain regional wars. However, the authors of the document did not name names, that is possible antagonists, to uphold the inclusive spirit of the document.

Additionally, the strategy recommended globally distributed and tailored forces with a focus on Africa and the Western Hemisphere. The hindrance of local disruptions, the contribution of the sea services to homeland defense-in-depth, and the imperative for sustained cooperation were also highlighted. For that, the strategy extrapolated six core capabilities for the sea services, namely forward presence, deterrence, sea control, power projection (these were Admiral Turner's original naval missions) as well as maritime security and humanitarian assistance and disaster relief (HA/DR) missions along a descending level of violence.[114] In elevating the last two soft power missions to strategic importance, the strategy sought to generate more resources and visibility for these aspects.

The Navy, the Marine Corps, and the Coast Guard fashioned themselves as essential guardians of the system which underpinned globalization. Critics charged that a specific threat (a country or non-state actor) was deliberately missing and that the strategy's key assumptions were simplistic.[115] Many traditional naval warfare missions were only implied and some operating areas notably absent from the strategy.[116] The document's explanatory narrative sidelined all Navy strategic conceptual efforts since "The Maritime Strategy," causing some irritation, but did not provide a compelling force level planning, programming, and budgeting link. Instead, cooperation and trust were emphasized, undertaking a long view was encouraged, and war prevention was elevated to the same importance as winning wars.[117] This gave the Navy both a tie to the systemic dimension of international relations and a linkage to the population-centric roles and missions of the military fashionable at the time. (FM 3–24) Admiral Mullen was able to shepherd the document's main points through his tenure as CJCS and aspects of CS-21 were echoed in the top-level strategic documents of the Obama administration.[118]

The naval missions that the documents outlined to achieve strategic goals are shown in Table 6.2. Only three of these capstone documents identified naval missions.

Force structure

At the turn of the century, the quantitative decline in U.S. Navy forces continued slowly but steadily. This led to a scaled down version of the Cold War fleet, but with individually more capable ships that were still grouped around the nuclear-powered aircraft carriers.[119] The carriers were again validated as they provided the first wave of attacks against Taliban strongholds in Afghanistan. However, trouble was brewing for the Navy's force structure. To fund the U.S. military's unexpectedly higher expenses in the ground campaigns in Afghanistan and later in Iraq, the Navy shipbuilding budget accounts were drained. Carriers, submarines, and destroyer programs suffered.[120] In addition, legacy platforms that had joined the fleet since the late 1970s and early 1980s were decommissioned in increasingly large numbers. Their maintenance was deemed too costly against the background of the pressing demands of the

Table 6.2 2000s capstone documents and Navy sea–strategic concepts[121]

Name	Year	Missions identified
Sea Power 21 & Global CONOPS	2002	Five enduring missions ("classic 4" plus sealift)
Naval Power 21 … A Naval Vision	2002	
Naval Operations Concept for Joint Operations	2003	
Fleet Response Plan	2003	
Navy Strategic Plan ISO POM 08	2006/2007	
Naval Operations Concept	2006	13 naval missions, including "classic 4" (no mention of sealift)
Navy Strategic Plan ISO POM 10	2007	
A Cooperative Strategy for 21st Century Seapower	2007	Six expanded core capabilities ("classic 4" plus maritime security operations, humanitarian assistance/disaster relief; no mention of sealift)
Navy Strategic Plan ISO POM 10 (Ch 1)	2007	

current wars. With the beginning of the withdrawal of the *Oliver-Hazard-Perry*-class frigates from service and the decommissioning of the five oldest *Ticonderoga*-class guided-missile cruisers, the Navy lost one-fifth of its cruiser and frigate inventories between FY 1999 and FY 2009.

The Global CONOPS (2002) had included new force package labels in an attempt to better utilize the flexibility of naval forces, maximize combat capability, and provide intellectual backing for the 375-ship battle fleet goal. By rearranging and re-labeling carrier and expeditionary groups, establishing surface action groups, and adding the four converted Ohio-class SSGN (capable of carrying 154 Tomahawk cruise missiles each), the Navy went from 24 formal strike groups to 37 – although that was based on the assertion that expeditionary strike groups (ESG), surface action groups (SAG), or guided-missile submarines (SSGN) could somehow replace a carrier strike group (CSG).[122]

By the early 2000s, the introduction of newer ships was imminent. On November 1, 2001, the Navy announced its Future Surface Combatant Program. This family of next-generation surface warships included three classes of ships: a destroyer program dubbed DD(X) (later DDG-1000) for long-range strike and naval gunfire support missions, a cruiser program called CG(X) for fleet air and ballistic missile defense, and a whole new platform called the littoral combat ship (LCS).[123] In contrast to the other, multi-mission-capable ships of the Navy, the LCS was designed to be fitted with specific modules which are interchangeable, allowing a tailored employment in mine warfare, anti-submarine warfare, or surface warfare missions.[124] Although the design stemmed from the time before the September 11 attacks and the assault on the destroyer *Cole* in Yemen (2000), the LCS promised a suitable and efficient response to the challenges of asymmetry that emerged with the long war against terrorism as well. Presumably it would be easier, more effective, and more efficient to send a littoral combat ship, rather than an expensive cruiser or a valued destroyer, into the murky and dangerous littorals of the twenty-first century. As such, the LCS enjoyed strong support by CNO Clark.

However, the next-generation surface combatant suffered epochal blows. The CG(X) program was terminated in 2010 for cost, and never got beyond the initial design phase. The DDG-1000 program, rooted in early 1990s' designs for a twenty-first-century destroyer, was reduced to just three (from 32) units in 2009. The Navy instead opted to procure more optimized destroyers of the *Arleigh-Burke*-class to fill the widening capability gap. The LCS program, built to both a conventional mono hull and futuristic trimaran designs, was capped at 32 units as recently as 2014 in favor of an agile, more versatile, and larger frigate-type ship that is yet to be constructed.[125]

The debate about the right mix for U.S. naval force structure reflected the different schools of thought on the subject. Conducting humanitarian assistance, maritime security, and disaster relief missions (a notion echoing Samuel Huntington's 1954 similar warning) risked eroding the service life of the expensive fleet. These lesser-included missions were of little overall value and thus should not be elevated to strategic importance. On the other hand, those like CNO Admiral Mullen and Vice Admiral Morgan lobbied for a broader, less militarized understanding of sea power, which needed to be reflected better in force structure.[126] The Navy's force structure decisions for the time being also muted the smoldering argument between the proponents of flexible, multi-mission warships and the fans of specialized platforms for niche missions. Even more fundamentally, this debate echoed the "high-low" force structure discussions of the 1970s. Mullen and Morgan's argument that a trade-off was unnecessary appealed to much of the Navy and Congress. It reflected the desire for a balanced fleet of high- and low-end assets, able to be forward-deployed as well as surge-capable, to address the whole range of imaginable threats. This energetic approach could not conceal that Navy force structure is a very conservative business and cannot be turned around within a few years.

The next-generation surface warships were not the only shipbuilding programs hit by cost overruns, procurement delays, and design flaws. The 24,900-ton amphibious transport docks of the *San-Antonio*-class (LPD 17) were commissioned beginning in 2006 (to date, nine are in service and two more are under construction) but numerous mechanical failures and a doubling of the price for each yielded bad press, spinning the program out of control.[127] The Navy of the twenty-first century, despite all its lip-service to irregular warfare and asymmetric threats by proponents of the long war against terrorism and the cheerleaders for small vessels, remained grouped around aircraft carriers. The nuclear-powered *Ronald Reagan* (CVN 76) and *George H.W. Bush* (CVN 77) were procured.[128] Large-deck flat-tops were also added with the *Iwo Jima* (LHD 7 and *Makin Island* (LHD 8).[129] Many classes retained constant numbers. Others, like all 12 *Osprey*-class minesweepers, were decommissioned between 2006 and 2007 (further degrading the Navy's organic, sea-frame MCM capabilities). Mid-decade decreases in other classes, for example, in the destroyer category (the *Spruance*-class warships were decommissioned and disposed) were offset with the purchase of newer *Arleigh Burke*s. The first LCS warships at sea and new joint high-speed catamarans for Army/Navy intra-theater lift (JHSV) in the building yards foreshadowed new ship designs and capabilities. On balance, the Navy remained a big-ship navy in still further reduced numbers.

Table 6.3 breaks down the total numbers of the actual ship inventory.

With the debate between the balance of high-seas, blue-water options with a littoral, green- and brown-water orientation carried over from the 1990s and reflected in the declaratory documents of the time, force composition became an increasingly popular subject of study. The proposed forces would continue to be structured around aircraft carriers. Table 6.4 lists suggestions of some of the major reports and studies. The table is reprinted here to illustrate the range and scope of force level plans with which the Navy was faced in various reports.

Table 6.3 U.S. Navy active ship force levels, 2001–2008[130]

Date	9/01	9/02	9/03	9/04	9/04	9/06	9/07	9/08
Carriers	12	12	12	12	12	12	11	11
Cruisers	27	27	27	25	23	22	22	22
Destroyers	53	55	49	48	46	50	52	54
Frigates	35	33	30	30	30	30	30	30
LCS	–	–	–	–	–	–	–	1
Submarines	55	54	54	54	54	54	53	53
SSBNs	18	18	16	14	14	14	14	14
SSGNs	0	0	2	4	4	4	4	4
Mine warfare	18	17	17	17	17	16	14	14
Amphibious	41	41	38	37	37	35	33	34
Auxiliary	57	56	52	51	45	44	46	45
Surface total	127	127	118	115	111	114	115	118
Total active	316	313	297	292	282	281	278	282

Note
To clarify the ship numbers included in this table, the year 2000 entries include active commissioned ships, those in the Naval Reserve Force (NRF) and ships operated by the Military Sealift Command (MSC). Row entries are self-explanatory, with the auxiliary category including combat logistic ships (such as oilers, ammunition, and combat store ships), mobile logistics ships (such as submarine tenders) and support ships (such as command, salvage, tugs, and research ships). Command ships have been subsumed into that category and the separate line entry removed. A new row has been added for guided missile submarines (SSGN) and for the Littoral Combat Ships (LCS). The battleship category has been removed.

Table 6.4 2000s USN force level goals;[131] the various 30-year shipbuilding plans are omitted from this table

Report: Ship type:	2000 Shipbuilding Report	2001 QDR (Navy View)	2002 USN Global CONOPS	2005 USN Interim Long-range plan (range of numbers)	2006 DON plan
Total battle force ships	305–360	310	375	260–325	313
Attack submarines	50–66	55	55	37–41	48
Aircraft carriers	11–15	12	12	10–11	11
Surface combatants	116–133	116	160	130–174	143
Amphibious ships	36–42	36	37	17–24	31

Despite occasional lobbying efforts to reverse the quantitative attrition of the fleet and a host of studies that analyzed current and future fleet design, the Navy's force structure degraded over the 2000s. Most of the decade was a headwind period for the service in terms of budget and national standing.

With CS-21, the service wanted to gain momentum to change that dynamic and develop a narrative supporting force growth. However, CS-21 was not a shipbuilding strategy; it was a deliberately declaratory document. Designed as a growth strategy, it recognized that 313 ships were too low a number to account for all the missions the Navy was tasked to do (and asserted through its strategy). The final tally would have been more in the vicinity of 342 warships, including 38 amphibious ships. However, a force-structure plan that was to follow within six months of CS-21 never materialized. Such a document would likely have been more interesting to Congress; as things stood, "CS-21" was pretty readily dismissed and the focus remained on current shipbuilding plans and associated problems.[132] Figure 6.2 shows how force levels decreased.

The graph illustrates that declaratory force level goals, with the exception of the first year, were never met. The Navy routinely fell short of that goal by 30 ships or more. In 2005, when a force level goal of somewhere between 260 and 325 ships was postulated, the inventory would have been made to fit. Given the conservative structure of a Navy and the long-term dynamics of warship design, construction, procurement, and service life, a significant rebalancing in the force structure (a decrease of force levels notwithstanding) is still not observable.

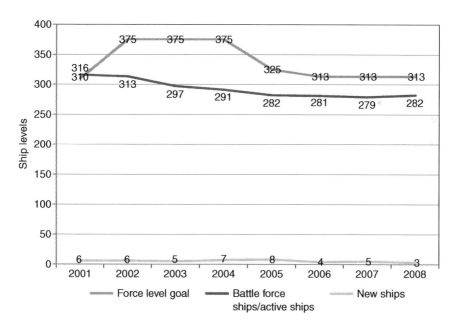

Figure 6.2 USN 2000s ship levels;[133] in 2005, the force level goal was between 260 and 325; in 2010, the landing zone was between 313 and 323. The CRS and NHHC numbers on the battle force and the active ships levels, respectively, align.

Strategic and operational implementation: planned vs. actual

The intertwining of U.S. naval strategy and operations remained as relevant in the twenty-first century as it did during any other time covered in this study. Operational experiences influenced the making of strategy as commanders rotated into OPNAV billets. The fleet, in turn, set out to operationalize documents handed down to them. Simultaneously, the Navy worked hard to provide forces when called to serve American foreign policy interests and ends. It followed that the Navy's operational tempo was high. This busyness brought larger operating and manpower costs but also provided the service with considerable expertise and experience. In the following section, three major naval operations will be discussed briefly to illustrate the real-world circumstances shaping Navy thinking and conduct after 2001.

Major U.S. naval operations[134]

Horn of Africa/Operation Enduring Freedom (since 2002)

In response to the terrorist attacks of 9/11, the U.S. orchestrated military strikes against targets in Afghanistan starting on October 7, 2001. With neither the patience of senior U.S. leaders available, nor the infrastructure in the region in place to reprise Gulf-War-style invasion plans, a more unconventional CIA-developed plan was adopted. Using proxy tribal armed forces of a loose anti-Taliban alliance, managed and paid by the agency's operatives and aided by small numbers of SOF, U.S. naval air power (together with the USAF and allied air forces) provided the bulk of the initial combat thrust against Afghanistan.[135] The carrier *Kitty Hawk* (CV 63) served as an improvised afloat forward base for SOF helicopters.

OEF has since merged into a larger concept encompassing several subordinate operations that span from the Caribbean to the Horn of Africa, Afghanistan, and the Philippines. The war in Afghanistan accounted for the overwhelming majority of OEF operations and, despite the landlocked character of the operating area, the Navy is involved in joint operations there. It provided (and in many cases still does) C4ISR, strike and special operations, Seabee engineers, and Navy specialists from a wide range of disciplines (e.g., intelligence, medical, supply, explosive ordnance disposal, legal, personnel, information dominance, and law enforcement) for the range of tasks that come with working in the irregular warfare environment. In addition, the Marine Corps was increasingly engaged in the ground war around the country.[136]

The most visible naval subordinate operation is the OEF component at the Horn of Africa (HOA). Just as in Afghanistan operations, OEF-HOA falls under responsibility of U.S. Central Command. Its main objectives, covering the whole western Indian Ocean, are the physical protection of maritime traffic from terrorist attacks, force protection, and providing stability against re-grouping terrorist networks. Al-Qaida was very active in the Horn of Africa region in the 1990s and U.S. leaders considered that area a likely destination for terrorists fleeing from combat in Afghanistan. Navy operations typically involved maritime monitoring, boarding, search and seizure of suspect ships and dhows. This work helped gather intelligence, inhibit terrorism, curb armed robbery, and limit smuggling.[137] As with the war in Afghanistan, the naval presence in the Arabian Sea was also multinational in nature. Many countries contributed to both, obviously restricted by their respective capabilities, rules of engagement, and U.S. requirements. Participants at the Horn of Africa included long-time NATO partners, other allies, and recently-arrived countries that joined the U.S. effort in the "Global War on Terror."[138] Beyond the operations already mentioned, OEF-HOA forces also engaged in humanitarian assistance, counter-proliferation, and counter-piracy efforts.[139]

Piracy began to affect maritime security in the region in earnest beginning in 2008, after having plagued African coasts and Southeast Asia, although qualitatively different in the Strait of Malacca, for many years prior to then.[140] Consequently, separate EU, NATO, and Combined Maritime Forces (CMF) counterpiracy missions have protected shipping and fight piracy off the Horn of Africa. After high points in 2009 and 2010, the quantity and quality of piracy incidents has decreased remarkably because of a combination of naval force presence, shipping industry best-management practices, and anti-piracy operations ashore.

In addition to the immediate curbing of piracy, the host of naval platforms in the area provides geostrategic results: naval presence matters in ways that armies and air forces cannot fulfill. While taxing navies' resources, the operational cooperation is an example of a global maritime partnership in action.[141]

Arabian Gulf and Operation Iraqi Freedom (2003–2011)

After the U.S. decision to attack Iraq, operational plans for the Arabian Gulf region needed to be revamped.[142] The premise of a "Desert Storm II" plan approved in 1998 consisted of a six-month build-up of 400,000 troops, which was not viewed favorably by Rumsfeld, who wanted something faster and much leaner. Iraqi forces had degraded since their defeat in the first Gulf War a decade earlier, but to the "coalition of the willing" assembled for this operation it was still a formidable opponent (on land). On the naval side, five carrier strike groups, two amphibious ready groups, two amphibious task forces, and a Royal Navy amphibious task group were assigned to CENTCOM[143] at the outset of the Iraq campaign. The surge of half of the Navy's operational carriers and 10 expeditionary strike groups (a remarkable demonstration of U.S. sea power) was a function of the emerging "Fleet Response Plan" (2003) and an overwhelming and intimidating display. Sealift moved cargo, fuel, and equipment to the troops and did so with even less opposition than in 1990/1991. Early in the war, Navy Special Forces seized Iraqi oil fields and terminals, and thwarted the covert sowing of mines. Joint operations against Iraq were, in marked contrast to 1990/1991, relatively smooth because the Navy had practiced and learned to interoperate with the other military branches during the long decade of enforcing no-fly zones over Iraq. Naval aviation (especially the F/A-18 workhorses) flew 65 percent of the strike, reconnaissance, and power-projection sorties over Iraq and 35 allied warships fired more than 750 Tomahawk missiles against targets ashore (Schneller, 2007: 96). Although the Army and the Marine Corps bore the brunt of the ground onslaught, Navy and Coast Guard (e.g., EOD teams, MCM personnel, Seabee battalions, riverine forces, etc.) became drawn into the deteriorating security situation and the quagmire that was left behind. The emerging counterinsurgency doctrine required much intellectual flexibility from the Marine Corps and, to a much lesser degree, the Navy.[144]

Tsunami Relief (2004/2005)

In the middle of the two major U.S. ground wars in Afghanistan and Iraq, a natural disaster in Southeast Asia demonstrated the humanitarian assistance and disaster relief capabilities of naval forces. On December 26, 2004, a 9.1-magnitude earthquake northwest of the Indonesian island of Sumatra resulted in a massive tsunami that swept through the whole Indian Ocean littoral. More than 230,000 people (165,000 in Indonesia alone) died, and upwards of one million inhabitants were left homeless. The international community responded swiftly and dispatched substantial goods and personnel into the worst-affected regions.[145] Military forces, particularly navies, of many countries played an indispensable role in providing medical help in floating hospitals, offering command centers, and providing much-needed water-purification facilities. The military also provided vital security in the devastated areas ashore. In "Operation Unified Assistance," the U.S. Navy's response included the *Abraham Lincoln* (CVN 72) carrier strike group and the *Bonhomme Richard* (LHD 6) expeditionary strike group (later relieved by *Essex* [LHD 2]). One of the most important parts of this disaster response was the deployment of the hospital ship *Mercy* (T-AH 19), a converted oil tanker commissioned in 1986 (the U.S. Navy operates two such ships). Combined, more than 100,000 patients were treated. The U.S. Navy's contribution to the relief operation amounted to more than 25 ships in 2004/2005. The Navy adopted these successful operations and increasingly conducted proactive humanitarian assistance deployments. Hospital ships or LHD helicopter carriers were dispatched increasingly to support Pacific and Latin American countries. This practice (which also improved the U.S. reputation in the affected regions) was later codified in the "Global Fleet Stations" concepts that were integral to "CS-21."[146]

Relationships to allies

9/11 and the "Global War on Terrorism" sparked an unprecedented degree of multilateral naval cooperation. These were no longer limited to traditional alliances; instead, the U.S. Navy increasingly also relied on coalitions of the willing and other non-binding partnerships (at sea, navies historically have frequently trained and interoperated with each other). This was less instrumental in support of the ground wars in Afghanistan and Iraq where coalitions by-and-large worked. Cooperation was all the more significant in the global littorals and at sea. CNO Admiral Mullen's "1,000-ship Navy" concept to engage maritime forces around the world had two focal points.

- "Global Fleet Stations" to engage local and regional navies, coast guards, harbor police, NGOs, and local government entities to facilitate capacity-building in the naval realm and enhance U.S. (and by implication, Western) standing in a given region.[147]
- Combined operations and exercises, information-sharing, and technology transfer between the U.S. Navy and its allies continued. The anti-terror "Operation Active Endeavour" (OAE)[148] in the Mediterranean (since 2001), Proliferation Security Initiative (since 2003) operations, and the multilateral anti-piracy operations off the Horn of Africa (since 2008) provided an unparalleled degree of naval cooperation and operational integration.

In 2007, the fleet balance shifted from the Atlantic to the Pacific. More ships were now operating in Asian waters than in European and African waters, combined. Established USN-led maneuvers and exercises continued (e.g., BALTOPS in the Baltic Sea, MALABAR exercises in the Indian Ocean, CARAT in Southeast Asia, UNITAS in the Americas, and RIMPAC in the Pacific) just as new forums were developed and implemented (e.g., Valiant Shield in the Pacific since 2006). Yet, it was CS-21 which courted other navies, gave them a sense of ownership and participation in U.S. naval power, and provided a sense of political top cover to engage with the U.S. Navy.[149]

Assessment: American sea power and U.S. Navy strategy in a time of challenges and innovation, 2001–2008

After the shock of 9/11 and marginalization by the ground wars in Afghanistan and Iraq, the sea service was energized by the trifecta of strategic capstone documents.[150] This deliberately connected group of writing replaced the single line of documents of the 1980s and the more erratic, often isolated works which characterized Navy strategy-making in the 1990s. Throughout the 2000s, Navy budgets increased and the battle fleet inventory started to recover after years of reductions.

At the beginning of the decade, 9/11 fundamentally changed the security perception of Americans. The terrorist attacks heralded a decade dominated largely by ground wars in Afghanistan and Iraq as well as a global campaign against illicit actors. Non-state actors and those providing them safe havens increasingly moved into the focus of security policy. As in the past, the Navy occasionally but ultimately unsuccessfully pushed back against the view of land-power focused "continentalists," who saw the generation-long war against international terrorism as emblematic for future U.S. military action. Along that narrative, the U.S. was never fully at war nor fully at peace.

Navy thinkers rediscovered that the service had always operated across the spectrum of operations and, if made aware of these conceptual roots, was well suited to provide the senior civilian leaders with a range of options. The Navy needed to align better with grand strategy and if possible translate such knowledge into policy contributions for the Bush administration. Sea power theorists and practitioners needed to grasp that trend and reverse it in their favor, managing to do so by developing the idea of defending the system of globalization (but not its advancement) underwritten by maritime power.[151]

Cornered by both public and political focus on the ground wars, and burdened by the growing demands of ongoing missions and naval operations, the Navy looked toward regaining the conceptual initiative. First, naval planners remembered and restated the naval missions that had been codified by Admiral Turner in the 1970s and arguably, Samuel Huntington in the 1950s. Second, these same officers returned to the realization that forward-deployed navies have always had a very distinct position to play in shaping conditions ashore and in the littorals, thereby uniquely influencing events and strategic outcomes. Animated by the top-cover of Navy leadership, revitalized by input from formal and informal study groups, think tanks, and other discussion forums, and sensing momentum, CS-21 emerged as genuinely new maritime (not just a naval) strategy. It fashioned the Navy as a post-modern force to defend the global system. Strikingly, its development ran against prevailing currents of military and political planning. Mullen and his collaborators managed to design a document at once in line with the overarching grand-strategic demands of the Bush administration (even if Bush 43's foreign policy was perceived by some as increasingly belligerent and unilateral) and fashioned a concerted, forward-looking, and systemic approach at the same time. In fact, the selection of the strategy's title proved a revelation. In proposing a seapower (one word) strategy for this century, CS-21 forged a bridge between the universal and institutional meaning of the concept (since the globalized world is so interconnected and integrated that it can indeed be understood as one system – or more precisely, a system of systems) and the physical political, diplomatic, constabulary, and military exercise of sea power (two words).

CS-21 also helped to overcome the previous, rather limited focus on operations and budget submissions, or the unfettered belief in the promises of transformation and the revolution in military affairs. The paper was a politically safe way to rationalize the service to a Congress very concerned with war-fighting and weapons systems, but otherwise lacking a vision which earlier strategic documents had partially offered. As surface warfare officers, Vice Admiral Morgan and Admiral Mullen were better able to identify and embrace a more population-centric role of sea power. Given the indisputable facts that Kabul and Baghdad were inland cities, making Afghanistan's and Iraq's sea power marginal, the Navy needed to develop something different and novel. Conceptually, CS-21 refocused the understanding of sea power's value for foreign-policy ends and elevated it. For much of the post–Cold War time, the Navy (usually for a lack of ambition, institutional coherence, or intellectual vigor) had conveniently concentrated on operational, doctrinal, and tactical aspects of naval warfare.

Shortly after the publication of the 2007 CS-21, the U.S. stock market plunged. One of the main implicit assumptions of the strategy (continuous mutual prosperity) faded away. In Washington, the assumption of rising defense budgets turned out to be incorrect as the U.S. economy went into a downward spiral. The global financial crisis deeply shocked the world economy and international trade nearly collapsed. China began to challenge the United States in the Pacific and by extension in the South and East China Sea. Russia's 2008 war against Georgia foreshadowed Moscow's resurrected geopolitical ambitions. The nuclear programs of North Korea and Iran continued unabatedly despite sanctions and political-military pressure. These are fundamental, considerably more violent shocks to the global system that CS-21 outlined.

With CS-21, the Navy built momentum to develop upward pressure and fashion a national, systemic, and truly maritime strategy. The subsequent failure to develop the idea further and implement the document – because of economic events, a changed administration more focused on domestic politics and generally shy of strategic and military ideas, political gridlock in Washington, more immediate concerns about the ground wars in Afghanistan and Iraq, and an ever-shifting geopolitical situation – is regrettable. Nonetheless, these twenty-first century documents underlined that only a strategy addressing political ends in naval warfare can be assured some impact. These missions are a common theme over more than four decades and are a link to what the future may hold for U.S. Navy strategy and the exercise of American sea power around the world.

Notes

1 In an incident in April 2001, a U.S. Navy EP-3 reconnaissance plane and a Chinese F-8 jet collided in international airspace over the South China Sea. The Navy airplane made an emergency landing on the Chinese Hainan Island, where the crew of 24 was detained by Chinese authorities for 11 days. The bilateral crisis was eventually defused through negotiations. See Kan *et al.*, 2001 for details.
2 Leffler, 2011.

3 Cf. Bush (1999), A Period of Consequences.
4 Charles Krauthammer, "Paying for Our Holiday from History," The (Houston, TX) Chronicle, February 15, 2003.
5 Hacke, 2005: 635.
6 When American Airlines flight 77 crashed into the Pentagon that day taking the lives of 184 victims aboard and on the ground, it also significantly decimated the Navy's Strategic Concepts Group (N513). That OPNAV branch's office spaces were located in the D-Ring portion of the building where the jet impacted. For details, see Goldberg *et al.*, 2007. For an analyses of the events leading up to the 9/11 attacks and the circumstances under which they happened, see the *Final Report of the National Commission on Terrorist Attacks upon the United States*, 2004.
7 Krause, 2014: 21–24.
8 National Consortium for the Study of Terrorism and Responses to Terrorism, University of Maryland (2014). Despite wide-reaching expectations to the contrary, maritime terrorism has been a rather rare occurrence. Only a fraction of all terrorist attacks happen at sea or against a maritime/naval target. See Murphy, 2009: 183–375, and Lehr, 2013, for detailed and convincing discussions.
9 Looney, 2014.
10 Khuzwayo, 2016, *Clouds loom over BRICS power.*
11 Medalia, 2011.
12 Bilmes, 2013; Katz, 2014.
13 President George W. Bush speaking to rescue workers on September 14, 2001 at 'Ground Zero,' New York City.
14 Dale, 2014.
15 For the utilization of the U.N. for Bush's policies, see Bruns, 2008: 81–122.
16 Weapons of mass destruction, the principal justification for removing Hussein from power, were not found. Saddam Hussein was arrested by U.S. troops on December 13, 2003 near his home town Tikrit. A Iraqi special tribunal found him guilty and he was executed on December 30, 2006 in Baghdad.
17 The development of counterinsurgency doctrine in light of the events in Iraq and Afghanistan is a key study in how military is forced to adapt to changing strategic, operational, and tactical parameters. This process occurred in the middle of sweeping changes to post-Cold War force structure, technology, and thinking. The push for modernized, or transformed, military force heavily relying on network-centric warfare while U.S. forces on the ground were bitterly fighting an asymmetric war therefore pitted against each other very contrasting threads and understandings of how the next war would be fought (and won). On the genesis of counterinsurgency doctrine from the hard lessons in Iraq, see Ricks, 2006, West, 2008, and Crane, 2010. On the development of that doctrine in the view of one key participant, see Nagl, 2015. ISAF's strategic restart in light of previous mistakes is described by Schroeder, 2014.
18 For an authoritative overview of the development of terrorism from the views of successive U.S. administrations, see the annual U.S. State Department's Country Reports on Terrorism (since 2004, previously named Patterns of Global Terrorism, 2001–2003).
19 Murphy, 2009: 183–375.
20 Haynes, 2013: 283.
21 China served as the second largest trading partner for the U.S. and its largest source of imports; for the U.S., China was the largest holder of U.S. public debt and the third-largest U.S. export market. In turn, the U.S. was China's largest single trading partner, its fourth largest source of imports, and its largest export market (Swartz, 2011a: 20, slide 39).
22 Till and Chan, 2013.
23 Carla Marinucci, "Bush defends record: 'I'm a war president'/He takes the

offensive in Oval Office interview," The San Francisco Chronicle, February 9, 2004.

24 Woodward, 2002, 2004; Mann, 2004.

25 On Cheney's tenure, see Barton Gellman and Jo Becker, "Angler. The Cheney Vice Presidency," *Washington Post*, June 24–27, 2007.

26 Rumsfeld was arguably the senior administration official to be directly affected by the terrorist attacks of 9/11: he was in the Pentagon on September 11, when the building was attacked. His office and those of other senior military leaders (save for the Navy Command Center) were spared, but Rumsfeld helped survivors at the crash site (Goldberg *et al.*, 2007).

27 Haynes, 2013: 227.

28 A critical acclaimed study of that mission led by the *Knox*-class frigate *Kirk* (FF 1087) is Jan Herman's *The Lucky Few* (2013).

29 Rice, 2011.

30 Cf. Keller, *Neokonservatismus und amerikanische Außenpolitik* (2008), pp. 168–169. On Bush's war cabinet, see Mann, 2004.

31 His tenure was interrupted by an eight-month period in 2003 when England became the first Deputy Secretary of Homeland Security, the new department established in the wake of the terrorist attacks of 9/11.

32 "Naval Power 21 ... A Naval Vision" (2002) was the only Navy strategic capstone document that England co-signed.

33 Department of Defense, 2009.

34 Swartz, 2011a: 4, slides 7–8.

35 A tour that was crucial to Mullen's take on the military, as Haynes, 2013: 278, states:

> Mullen blossomed intellectually during his tour as commander of U.S. Naval Forces Europe. Given that he basically had no shops to command, he had to find more nuanced ways to advance U.S. security policy. He grew to appreciate [...] 'soft power' [...] through personal relationships [...] with officials from other nations, U.S. federal agencies, and international organizations, governmental and non-governmental alike.

36 General Richard Myers (USAF) held the top military position as Chairman of the Joint Chiefs from 2001 to 2005. He had relieved General Hugh Shelton (USA), who served as CJCS from 1997 to 2001. Myers was tasked with the initial planning and execution of the operations in Afghanistan and against Iraq, in which the Air Force played a pivotal role. Myers' successor was General Peter Pace (USMC), the first Marine to hold the position of Chairman in the history of the Joint Chiefs. Pace officiated from 2005 to 2007. After one term, he was – unexpectedly to many observers at the time – replaced. Pace's comments over the progress of the Iraq War cost him the second nomination. There were also grave concerns that the confirmation hearings in the Senate would have turned into a tribunal by the Democrats to attack the Republican foreign and security policy under Bush 43 (Gates, 2014: 64–66).

37 Fellman, 2011.

38 These tenures were not always free of confrontation with senior leadership. Mullen had complained in public that the war in Iraq drew necessary resources from the war in Afghanistan, Fallon had urged not to go to war with Iran, and McConnell gave an interview for *The New Yorker* in which he characterized the controversial interrogation tactic of water boarding as torture, all of which did not fare well with President Bush (and prompting the president to ask his Secretary of Defense, 'What is it with these admirals?') (Gates, 2014: 187).

39 For a list of 40 foiled terrorism plots on American soil since September 11, 2001, see Carafagno and Zuckerman, 2011.

40 Huntington, 1954.
41 Swartz, 2011a: 28, slide 56 and 57, slide 113.
42 Gates, 2014: 135–142.
43 Faiz Shakir, "Bush Administration's Pre-9/11 Focus Was Missile Defense, Not Terrorism" (2006).
44 Bush, 2001.
45 Department of Defense, 2001: 29.
46 Haynes, 2013: 223.
47 For a discussion of the objectives that were to be represented in the 2001 QDR, see Flournoy, 2001.
48 The White House, 2002.
49 Haine and Lindström, 2002.
50 Captain (ret.) Joe Bouchard characterized this as "the most bizarre, strategically inept conclusion [...] since Pearl Harbor" (interview 2012, 02:10:20–02:11:00).
51 The White House, 2006; Department of Defense, 2006b.
52 Department of Defense, 2006a: 3.
53 Gunzinger, 2013: 10.
54 The Department of Defense's Global Defense Posture Review from 2002 to 2004 had already mandated an increase in Pacific bases while conducting a draw-down in European bases. It also demanded a more adaptive and flexible network of operating locations (Swartz, 2011a: 43, slide 86).
55 Department of Defense, 2006b: 47.
56 On September 20, 2005, the Bush administration released its first "National Strategy for Maritime Security" (the only such document to date) (The White House, 2005). That document signaled the development of eight individual plans on key areas of maritime security. The National Strategy for Maritime Security is not a Navy capstone document per definition because it lacked the sustained involvement of the Navy Department's strategy shop and the signature of the CNO or the Secretary of the Navy. Its level of ambition is different from that of the capstone documents discussed here.
57 Swartz, 2011a: 2, slide 3, 77, slide 153, and 140, slide 280.
58 These were "Deep Blue," the Navy's former QDR cell, which was expanded after 9/11 to evolve into a distinct operationally focused multi-purpose think tank; N00Z, the code for the Strategic Actions Group, which like "Deep Blue" also reported directly to the CNO and which took over a number of tasks from the CNO's Executive Panel, code-named N00K; N00K itself, which retained some strategy-making projects; the Strategy and Concepts branch (N513), which was still tasked with the big picture of connecting strategy and operations; and N81, the Assessments Division that held the important access to integrated program planning (Haynes, 2013: 225–226).
59 Haynes, 2013: 225–226.
60 Clark, 2002.
61 Clark, 2002; Corbett and Goulding, 2002; Bucchi and Mullen, 2002; Dawson and Nathman, 2002; Moore and Hanlon, 2003; Mayo and Nathman, 2003; Mullen, 2003; Harms *et al.*, 2003; Natter, 2003; Mullen, 2004.
62 Haynes, 2013: 233.
63 Ibid.: 239.
64 Swartz, 2011a: 27–30, slides 53–60.
65 One of the key assets to this was the USMC-backed Maritime Prepositioning Force (Future) – or MPF(F) – concept. It argued for the construction of tailored vessels to continue the strategic forward-stationing of materiel around the globe in regions of U.S. interest. In some Navy circles, making sea basing a pillar of the Navy's capstone document represented an unwarranted concession to the USMC (Swartz, 2011a: 26, slide 51).

66 Swartz, 2011a: 18, slide 36.
67 This is not necessarily a negative verdict keeping in mind that the promulgation of strategy must go hand-in-hand with its implementation, or in other words: making strategy and executing it are two sides of the same coin.
68 Lundesgaard, 2011: 18.
69 Till, 2009: 7.
70 England *et al.*, 2002.
71 Swartz, 2011a: 33, slide 65.
72 Swartz, 2011a: 38, slide 75.
73 Department of the Navy, 2003a.
74 The JOC was published by Secretary Rumsfeld in November 2003. It outlined how the U.S. military intended to operate in the coming 15 to 20 years, proposing to link the larger strategic guidance of the Bush administration to the integrated application of military capabilities. As such, it presented itself as the conceptual framework and guidance for future joint operations and across-the-board concept development and experimentation. This would include "the development and acquisition of new capabilities through changes in doctrine, organization, training, materiel, leadership and education, personnel and facilities (DOTMLPF)" (Department of Defense, 2003: 4).
75 QDR, 2001; NSS, 2002.
76 Swartz, 2011a: 51, slide 102.
77 Department of the Navy, 2003b.
78 This schedule explains the demand for three warships of a certain class/type if one unit is to be operational and deployed at any given time; the second unit is on post-deployment stand-down while the third warship is on pre-deployment work-up.
79 Cited in Swartz, 2011a: 64, slide 128.
80 From 2007, it included three CSG on deployment, three more deployable within a month's notice, and one deployable within 90 days. The same year, the rigorous scheme was somewhat relaxed for the carriers as the "Fleet Response Plan" was extended to the Expeditionary Strike Groups and the total number of Navy carriers fell from 12 to 11 between 2004 and 2007. *John F. Kennedy* (CV 67), although in commission, did not deploy (Swartz, 2011a: 68, slides 135–136).
81 Haynes, 2013, 262–263.
82 Papadopoulos, 2016, 271.
83 Still, the Navy's program was well-received with senior policy-makers such as the Secretary of Defense. Consecutive naval leaders would also return to the "Fleet Response Plan" in their own speeches, testimonies, and documents (especially the surge portion) for the remainder of the decade although it has yet to be fully endorsed and implemented as a national policy, part of the joint force (Swartz, 2011a: 75, slide 149).
84 Based on Peter Haynes, *Toward a New Maritime Strategy: American Naval Thinking in the Post-Cold War Era*, Annapolis, MD: US Naval Institute Press, 2015.
85 He also discharged Vice Admiral Joe Sestak, Deputy CNO for Warfare Requirements and Programs (N6/N7), a protégé of Mullen's predecessor CNO Clark.
86 "Admiral Mullen attended the International Seapower Symposium in October [of 2005], and there seemed to achieve a kind of epiphany that each region of the world had similar maritime security problems" (Robert "Barney" Rubel, Development of A Cooperative Strategy for 21st Century Seapower, e-mail to author, July 14, 2015.)
87 Morgan and Martoglio, 2005: 14. The challenge of how to respond if the new cooperative concept drew out navies that were not exactly allies, such as the Chinese, was not openly addressed. On particular challenges of building and maintaining the "1,000-ship navy" capabilities, see Ratcliff, 2007, and Reveron, 2007.

88 Cited in Haynes, 2013: 297.
89 Department of Defense, 2006a.
90 Swartz, 2011a: 91, slide 181.
91 Haynes, 2013: 298.
92 Swartz, 2011a: 95, slide 189–190. Although the creation of U.S. African Command in 2006 signaled the increasing importance of the continent, the African seas were not identified as a premier maritime focus area – save for the anti-piracy and capacity-building efforts on the East African and West African coasts, this has remained the case in terms of the USN's operational reality.
93 This trifecta sequence was established only in hindsight with the drafting of the 2007 "Cooperative Strategy for 21st Century Seapower" (= "the ends"). In November 2007, VADM Morgan (quoted in Swartz, 2011a: 142, slide 284) admitted that the logical chain had been turned on its head before, "We knew we were doing the process [of formulating strategy, S.B.] in a backwards way. [...] Now ... we want the strategy to lead." The characterization of the "Navy Strategic Plan," the "Naval Operations Concept," and "CS-21" as sequential integrals to overall U.S. naval strategy is also used by Haynes, 2013: 307–315.
94 Swartz, 2011a: 115, slides 229–230. The paper itself fed from the USMC's own "Marine Corps Operating Concepts for a Changing Security Environment (MOC)," published in March 2006; a corresponding Navy-only operating concept was debated, but was never drafted.
95 In addition to the "classic 4" from Vice Admiral Turner (forward naval presence, power projection, sea control, and strategic deterrence), it called for crisis response, maritime security operations, security cooperation, civil-military operations, counterinsurgency, counterterrorism, counter-proliferation, air and missile defense, and information operations. Notably absent from the list was one of the three key missions of "The Maritime Strategy": sealift. Some of these were long-standing tasks that the Navy had considerable experience in; others reflected the emerging security environment of the 1990s and in particular the Navy and Marine Corps' operations after 9/11.
96 These were: agility, adaptive force packaging, coordinated global influence, precision, ability to deploy and employ forces, speed, interoperability, a persistent presence, and unpredictability for adversaries (as well as reliability for allies).
97 See Frank Hoffman, *Conflict in the 21st Century: The Rise of Hybrid Wars*, Arlington, VA, Potomac Institute, 2007.
98 Swartz, 2011a: 120–121, slides 239–242.
99 Haynes, 2013: 314–315.
100 The discussion of this particular document's procedural evolution and its strategic scope is based on the open information provided by Swartz, 2011a: 126–140, slides 252–279.
101 Swartz, 2011a: 128, slide 256.
102 Robert "Barney" Rubel, Development of A Cooperative Strategy for 21st Century Seapower, e-mail to author, July 14, 2015, p. 1.
103 Colonel Doug King (USMC) and Captain Sam Neill (USCG) were the principle drafters for their services, respectively.
104 Robert "Barney" Rubel, Development of A Cooperative Strategy for 21st Century Seapower, e-mail to author, July 14, 2015, p. 2.
105 In briefing the results to a panel of three-star officers, this option was dismissed and discontinued.
106 Robert "Barney" Rubel, Development of A Cooperative Strategy for 21st Century Seapower, e-mail to author, July 14, 2015, p. 3.
107 According to McGrath (2007) and Haynes (2013: 325–333), the process differed slightly. They recount the core group considered a primacist strategy which focused on particular areas of interest, a Corbettian sea control strategy to

counter adversary naval forces and commerce and protect the sea lines, a global systems strategy (which highlighted the cooperative safeguarding of global integrated trade and security), a high-low mix strategy built around Admiral Zumwalt's 1970s idea using legacy forces to stiffen the high-end and low-end capabilities, and a minimalist, offshore-balancing strategy (which limited standing U.S. naval deployments to the Arabian Gulf with the rest of the fleet maintained in readiness and surged as the situation required and the senior leaders directed). The final document emerged as a hybrid of the first three.

108 Bryan McGrath, e-mail to author, July 22, 2014.

109 It was thus the first capstone document signed by all three service chiefs, and the first unified strategy since "The Maritime Strategy."

110 U.S. Navy, U.S. Marine Corps, U.S. Coast Guard, 2007.

111 "The Seapower Video," https://youtu.be/ffaPxrZFkkY (February 28, 2017).

112 This broad distribution in turn led to a large number of subsequent analyses and articles in across all media. For a selection, see Swartz (2011a: 180–182, slides 360–364).

113 Not least, the Navy as the driver behind CS-21 pushed for a document to counter the dominating Army/Marine Corps Field Manual 3–24 (the COIN doctrine), released in 2006.

114 The link to Admiral Turner's missions is remarkably close: Zumwalt and Turner discussed sea control and presence in reaction to Vietnam War power-projection focus; CS-21 discussed sea control and presence in reaction to 1990s power projection focus (Swartz, 2011a: 179, slide 358).

115 Pendley, 2008.

116 Work and van Tol, 2008.

117 This is illustrated by the notion in the strategy that, contrary to military force and materiel, trust could not be surged.

118 The White House, 2010; Department of Defense, 2010.

119 Lundesgaard, 2011: 24.

120 Papadopoulos, 2016: 277.

121 Forster, 2013: 21.

122 Robert Work, *The US Navy. Charting a Course for Tomorrow's Fleet.* Washington, D.C. Center for Strategic and Budgetary Assessment, 2008.

123 For more details on these shipbuilding programs, see the comprehensive CRS reports on CG(X) (O'Rourke, 2010), DDG-1000 (O'Rourke, 2014a), and the LCS (O'Rourke, 2014b).

124 The LCS evolved from the "Streetfighter" concept (1999). These inexpensive, small, but agile and capable warships were designed with their expendability in mind (a concept that fundamentally challenged the foundations of naval strategic culture). In other words, these ships could go into harm's way near an enemy coast without risking the deployment of a larger, more expensive vessel. It rested on the conviction that to make a strategic difference, the Navy had to forcefully embrace littoral warfare and accept all the challenges (and opportunities) that came with it.

125 If the original plans for the LCS had gone through, that class of ships would have accounted for one-sixth of the total Navy battle fleet inventory, signaling a focus on the littorals but deemphasizing blue-water capabilities of the U.S. Navy.

126 The "3/1 strategy" draft from 2006 declared that the Navy could no longer allow the inefficiency that came with utilizing high-end platforms for lesser-included missions. Counter-piracy, -narcotics, and -terrorism operations wore the fleet out and peacekeeping, disaster response, and humanitarian assistance took their toll as well. However, the "3/1 strategy" asserted that these missions were now significant for prevailing in the global, generational, long-war. Consequently, they needed to be dealt with in a coherent and fitting way that was represented in strategic plans, shipbuilding, and the budget.

127 The next-generation amphibious ship, designed to replace the aging *Whidbey-Island*-class/*Harpers-Ferry*-class from the 2020s, is already in planning. For the program dubbed LX(R), see O'Rourke, 2014c.

128 For an overview of other aircraft carrier missions and leveraging their potential, see Gordon IV *et al.*, 2006.

129 On a related note, the inventory of naval aviation was also modernized. Whereas the last F-14 "Tomcat" fighters were decommissioned and the last S-3 "Viking" ASW aircraft paid off during the decade, 369 new F/A-18E/F "Super Hornet" multipurpose carrier-based jets, 78 EA-18G "Growler" EW aircraft, and 300 MH-60R/S multipurpose "Sea Hawk" helicopters were added (Swartz, 2011b: 65, slide 126). The F-35 Joint Strike Fighter, the fifth-generation multirole aircraft, began design and production in the mid-2000s. The program, which will deliver variants to USAF (conventional), USN (carrier), and USMC (V/STOL), remains under pressure from cost overruns and technological challenges.

130 Naval History and Heritage Command, 2011.

131 Swartz, 2011a: 58, slide 116.

132 The Navy's 30-year-shipbuilding plan has in recent years been a central subject of deliberations on Capitol Hill, for example in the House of Representatives Armed Services Committee and its appropriate subcommittee, the Seapower and Projection Forces Subcommittee. In many discourses, numbers have replaced any strategic reasoning in that regard.

133 Swartz, 2011a: 57–58, slides 113–115.

134 Major naval operations understood as the sustained commitment of forces engaged in expeditionary operations against a shore or a fleet. On the problem of definitions, see Vego, 2008: 7–39. In this chapter, these are selected naval operations designed to illustrate the real-world operations that the U.S. Navy conducted in the 2000s.

135 Haynes, 2013: 222.

136 For a description of the USMC's operations against Afghanistan 2001–2002 from the sea, see Lowrey, 2011.

137 Schneller, 2007: 100–101.

138 A picture from September 14, 2001 made considerable headlines on the brotherhood in arms after 9/11: the U.S. guided-missile destroyer *Winston Churchill* (DDG 81) and the German Charles-F.-Adams-class guided-missile destroyer *Lütjens* (D 185) met on the Atlantic. The crew of the (U.S.-manufactured) German warship manned the rails and presented a banner that read "We stand by you." Germany participated on the naval side of OEF at the Horn of Africa with destroyers, frigates, fast-patrol boats, submarines, tenders, and MPA between 2002 and 2010 (Bundeswehr, 2014).

139 For a discussion of the particulars of piracy and maritime terrorism, in particular an analysis against confounding the two phenomena in designing suitable counter-strategies, see Murphy, 2008, and Chalk, 2008.

140 One of the most notable piracy events at the Horn of Africa with U.S. involvement was the hijacking of the container ship M/V *Maersk Alabama* in April 2009. The ship was subsequently released and the pirates made off with the master towards the Somali coast. *Bainbridge* (DDG 96), *Halyburton* (FFG 40), *Boxer* (LHD 4), a SEAL team, and a P-3C Orion MPA were dispatched to end the hostage-taking. Eventually, three pirates were killed, two more were arrested, and Captain Phillips was released.

141 Bruns, 2009.

142 Ricks, 2006; Cheney, 2011.

143 Schneller, 2007: 92.

144 A good introduction to the Marine Corps' embrace of operational aspects of counterinsurgency is Hoffman, 2010. The Navy conducted counterinsurgency

during in Vietnam, which by virtue of its geography provided a much more suitable terrain than Iraq or Afghanistan ever could. For an introduction on the naval support to counterinsurgency, see Murphy, 2010.

145 Margesson, 2005; Elleman, 2007.

146 U.S. Navy, U.S. Marine Corps, U.S. Coast Guard, 2007; Sohn, 2009. The response to the Haiti earthquake in January 2010 reiterated the Navy's disaster response role: the Navy surged 112 ship task force grouped around aircraft carriers, helicopter carriers, and amphibious assault ships. That operation underlined the themes of cooperation and trust that "CS-21" articulated.

147 In 2008, Robert Work suggested seven of these global fleet stations (Work, 2008: 64). For an analysis of the strategy, see Sohn, 2009, and for short assessments of those GFS already in place (African Partnership Station, APS; Southern Partnership Station, SPS; and Pacific Partnership, PP), see Bruns, 2010, 2013: 10–13.

148 OAE was one of the first military responses to the invocation of Article 5 North Atlantic Treaty after the 9/11 attacks.

149 Robert "Barney" Rubel, Development of A Cooperative Strategy for 21st Century Seapower, e-mail to author, July 14, 2015, pp. 2–4.

150 These were the "Naval Operations Concept," the "Navy Strategic Plan," and "A Cooperative Strategy for 21st Century Seapower." The new spirit was characterized by the Navy's advertisement slogan for the 2000s, "A Global Force for Good" (www.navy.com/about/gffg.html).

151 Robert "Barney" Rubel, Development of A Cooperative Strategy for 21st Century Seapower, e-mail to author, July 14, 2015, pp. 3, and Rubel, *Navies and Economic Prosperity – the New Logic of Sea Power*, 2012.

References

Bilmes, Linda. *The Financial Legacy of Iraq and Afghanistan: How Wartime Spending Decisions Will Constrain Future National Security Budgets*. Faculty Research Working Paper Series RWP 13–006. Harvard Kennedy School of Government, 2013.

Bruns, Sebastian. *Via New York nach Bagdad? Die Vereinten Nationen und die Irak-Politik der USA*. Tectum: Marburg, 2008.

Bruns, Sebastian. "Multipolarity Under the Magnifying-Glass." *Security+Peace (Sicherheit+Frieden)* 27(3) (2009): 174–179.

Bruns, Sebastian "African Partnership Station: From Global War on Terrorism to Grass-Roots Maritime Security." *Strategic Insights by Risk Intelligence. Global Maritime Security Analysis* 25 (2010): 18–23.

Bruns, Sebastian."Beyond the Aircraft Carrier? Non-Traditional Security Threats and the Future of U.S. Navy Sea-asing." *Strategic Insights by Risk Intelligence. Global Maritime Security Analysis* 46 (2013): 9–13.

Bouchard, Joseph, Captain, United States Navy (retired). Norfolk (Virginia), September 17, 2012, 02 hr 40 min.

Bucchi, Mike, and Mike Mullen. "Sea Shield: Projecting Global Defensive Assurance." *U.S. Naval Institute Proceedings* 128(11) (2002): 56–8.

Bush, George W. "'A Period of Consequences,' The Citadel, South Carolina. 23 September 1999." 1999.

Bush, George W. "Address to the Joint Session of the 107th Congress," Capitol Hill, Washington, D.C., 20 September 2001." 2001.

Bush, George W. "Address before a Joint Session of Congress on the State of the Union", 29 January 2002." The White House, Washington, DC, 2002.

Carafagno, James, and Zuckerman, Jessica. *40 Terror Plots Foiled Since 9/11. Combating Complacency in the Long War on Terror.* (= Backgrounder #2604, 7 September 2011). Washington, D.C: The Heritage Foundation, 2011.

Chalk, Peter. *The Maritime Dimension of International Security: Terrorism, Piracy, and Challenges for the United States.* Santa Monica, CA: RAND Corporation, 2008.

Cheney, Dick. *In My Time. A Personal and Political Memoir.* New York, NY: Threshold, 2011.

Clark, Vern. "Sea Power 21. Projecting Decisive Joint Capabilities." *U.S. Naval Institute Proceedings* 128(10) (2002), 33–41.

Corbett, Art, and Goudling, Vince. "Sea Basing: What's New?" *U.S. Naval Institute Proceedings* 128(11) (2002): 34–6.

Crane, Conrad. "United States Doctrine." *Understanding Counterinsurgency. Doctrine, Operations, and Challenges*, eds. T. Rid and T. Keaney. London/New York, NY: Routledge 2010, 59–72.

Dale, Catherine. "The 2014 Quadrennial Defense Review (QDR) and Defense Strategy: Issues for Congress," *CRS 7–5700*, February 24, 2014.

Dawson, Cutler, and Nathman, John. "Sea Strike: Projecting Persistent, Responsive, and Precise Power." *U.S. Naval Institute Proceedings* 128(12) (2002): 54–8.

Department of Defense."Quadrennial Defense Review Report, September 30, 2001." Washington, D.C.: DOD, 2001.

Department of Defense. "Joint Operations Concept. November 2003." Washington, D.C.: The Pentagon, 2003.

Department of Defense. "Quadrennial Defense Review Report. 6 February 2006." Washington, D.C.: DOD, 2006a.

Department of Defense."Navy Strategic Plan in Support of Program Objective Memorandum 08." Washington, D.C.: DOD, 2006b.

Department of Defense. "Navy Secretary Departs Office", Release No: 167–09, March 13. Washington, D.C.: DOD, 2009.

Department of Defense. "Quadrennial Defense Review Report. February 2010." Washington, D.C.: DOD, 2010.

Department of the Navy. "Fleet Response Plan." Washington, D.C.: DON, 2003a.

Department of the Navy. "Naval Operating Concept for Joint Operations." Washington, D.C.: DON, 2003b.

Department of the Navy. "Biography of The Honorable Gordon R. England, Secretary of the Navy 1/10/2003-28 December 2005." Washington, D.C.: The Pentagon, 2009.

Deutsche Bundeswehr. "Kampf gegen den internationalen Terrorismus – OEF (Operation ENDURING FREEDOM)." Berlin: MOD, 2014.

England, Gordon, Clark, Vern, and Jones, James. "Naval Power 21: A Naval Vision." Washington, D.C.: DON, 2002.

Elleman, Bruce. *Waves of Hope: The U.S. Navy's Response to the Tsunami in Northern Indonesia.* Newport, RI: Naval War College Press, 2007.

Fellman, Sam. "Greenert takes over for retiring CNO Roughead," *Navy Times*, September 23, 2011.

Flournoy, Michèle (ed.). *QDR 2001. Strategy-Driven Choices for America's Security.* Washington, D.C.: NDU Press, 2001.

Forster, Larissa. "Trust Cannot Be Surged: Challenges to Naval Forward Presence." Military Power Revue der Schweizer Armee, no. 2/2011 (2011):47–59. *Influence without Boots on the Ground: Seaborne Crisis Response.* Newport, RI: Naval War College Press, 2013.

Gates, Robert. *Duty: Memoirs of a Secretary at War*. New York, London: Random House, 2014.

Gellman, Barton, and Becker, Jo. "Angler. The Cheney Vice Presidency," *Washington Post*, June 24–27, 2007.

Goldberg, Alfred, Papadopoulos, Sarandis, and Putney, Diane. *Pentagon 9/11*. Historical Office, Office of the Secretary of Defense: Washington, D.C., 2007.

Gordon IV, John, Wilson, Peter, Birkler, John, Boraz, Steven, and Lee, Gordon. *Leveraging America's Aircraft Carrier Capabilities: Exploring New Combat and Noncombat Roles and Missions for the U.S. Carrier Fleet*. Santa Monica, CA: RAND Corporation, 2006.

Gunzinger, Mark. *Shaping America's Future Military: Toward a New Force Planning Construct*. Washington, D.C.: Center for Strategic and Budgetary Assessments, 2013.

Hacke, Christian. *Zur Weltmacht verdammt. Die amerikanische Außenpolitik von J.F. Kennedy bis G.W. Bush*. 3. Auflage, aktualisierte Neuausgabe, München: Ullstein, 2005.

Haine, Jean-Yves, and Lindström, Gustav. *An analysis of The National Security Strategy of the United States of America* (= European Union Institute for Strategic Studies Analysis, 18 September 2002), Brussels: EUISS, 2002.

Harms, Alfred, Hoewing, Gerald, and Totushek, John. "Sea Warrior: Maximizing Human Capital." *U.S. Naval Institute Proceedings* 129(6) (June 2003): 48–54.

Haynes, Peter. *American Naval Thinking in the Post- Cold War Era: The U.S. Navy and the Emergence of a Maritime Strategy, 1989–2007* (dissertation, Naval Postgraduate School, Monterey, CA, 2013).

Herman, Jan. *The Lucky Few. The Fall of Saigon and the Rescue Mission of the USS* Kirk. Annapolis, MD: Naval Institute Press, 2013.

Hoffman, Frank. *Conflict in the 21st Century: The Rise of Hybrid Wars*. Arlington, VA: Potomac Institute, 2007.

Hoffman, Frank. "Marine Corps Operational Aspects." *Understanding Counterinsurgency. Doctrine, Operations, and Challenges*, eds. T. Rid and T. Keaney. London and New York: Routledge, 2010, 87–99.

Huntington, Samuel. "National Policy and the Transoceanic Navy." *U.S. Naval Institute Proceedings* 80(5) (May 1954): 483–493.

Kan, Shirley *et al. China–U.S. Aircraft Collision Incident of April 2001: Assessments and Policy Implications* (CRS Report RL 30946 10 October 2001). Washington, D.C.: Congressional Research Service, 2001.

Katz, Mark. *Implications of America Withdrawing from Iraq and Afghanistan. War on Terror in Perspective*. Washington, D.C.: Middle East Policy Council, 2014.

Keller, Patrick. *Neokonservatismus und amerikanische Außenpolitik. Ideen, Krieg und Strategie von Ronald Reagan bis George W. Bush*. Paderborn: Schöningh, 2008.

Khuzwayo Wiseman. "Clouds loom over BRICS power." *Independent Online*. July 11, 2016.

Krauthammer, Charles. "Paying for Our Holiday from History." *The (Houston, TX) Chronicle*, February 15, 2003. Commission Report. Washington, D.C., Government Printing Office (GPO), 2004.

Krause, Joachim. "Kooperative Sicherheit und die Rolle von Streitkräften." *Maritime Sicherheit im 21. Jahrhundert*, ed. H.D. Jopp. Baden-Baden: Nomos (2014): 134–162

Leffler, Melvyn. "September 11 in Retrospect. George W. Bush's Grand Strategy, Reconsidered." *Foreign Affairs* 90(5) (2011), online/s.p.

Lehr, Peter. "Maritimer Terrorismus." *Maritime Sicherheit*, eds. S. Bruns, K. Petretto, and D. Petrovic. Wiesbaden, Germany: VS Verlag für Sozialwissenschaften, 2013: 115–127.

Looney, Robert (ed.). *Handbook of Emerging Economies*. London: Routledge, 2014.

Lowrey, Nathan. *From the Sea – U.S. Marines in Afghanistan 2001–2002, U.S. Marines in the Global War on Terrorism*. Washington, D.C.: History Division, United States Marine Corps, 2011.

Lundesgaard, Amund. *US Navy Strategy and Force Structure After the Cold War* (IFS Insights No. 4, November 2011). Oslo, Norway: Institutt for Forsvarsstudier, 2011.

McGrath, Bryan. "Maritime Strategy 2007, The Team Leader Speaks." *Steeljaw Scribe*. October 21, 2007.

Mann, James. *Rise of the Vulcans. The History of Bush's War Cabinet*. London *et al.*: Penguin, 2004.

Marinucci, Carla. "Bush defends record: 'I'm a war president'/He takes the offensive in Oval Office interview." *San Francisco Chronicle*, February 9, 2004.

Margesson, Rhoda. *Indian Ocean Earthquake and Tsunami: Humanitarian Assistance and Relief Operations* (CRS Report 32715, updated February 10). Washington, D.C.: Congressional Research Service, 2005.

Mayo, Richard, Nathman, John. "ForceNet: Turning Information into Power." *U.S. Naval Institute Proceedings* 129(2) (2003): 42.

Medalia, Jonathan. *'Dirty Bombs.' Technical Background, Attack, Prevention and Response, Issues for Congress*. CRS Report R 41890. 88 Washington, D.C.: Congressional Research Service, 2011.

Moore, C. W., and Hanlon, Edward. "Sea Basing: Operational Independence for a New Century." *U.S. Naval Institute Proceedings* 129(1) (January 2003): 80–85.

Morgan, John, and Martoglio, Charles. "The 1,000-ship Navy Global Maritime Network." *U.S. Naval Institute Proceedings* 131(11) (2005): 14–17.

Mullen, Mike. "Global Concept of Operations." *U.S. Naval Institute Proceedings* 129(4) (April 2003): 66.

Mullen, Mike. "Sea Enterprise: Resourcing Tomorrow's Fleet." *U.S. Naval Institute Proceedings* 130(1) (2004), s.p.

Murphy, Martin. *Small Boats, Weak States, Dirty Money: Piracy and Maritime Terrorism in the Modern World*. London: C. Hurst & Co., 2009.

Murphy, Martin. "Naval Support." *Understanding Counterinsurgency: Doctrine, Operations, and Challenges*, ed. T. Rid and T. Keaney. Routledge: New York and London: Routledge, 2010, 114–127.

Nagl, John. "The Evolution and Importance of Army/Marine Corps Field Manual 3–24, Counterinsurgency." *Stabilisierungseinsätze als gesamtstaatliche Aufgabe. Erfahrungen und Lehren aus dem deutschen Afghanistaneinsatz zwischen Staatsaufbau und Aufstandsbewältigung (COIN)*, eds. R. Schroeder/S. Hansen. Erfahrungen und Lehren aus dem deutschen Afghanistaneinsatz. Nomos: Baden-Baden, 2015, 127–132.

National Commission on Terrorist Attacks Upon the United States. "The 9/11 National Consortium for the Study of Terrorism and Responses to Terrorism," University of Maryland: Global Terrorism Database, 2009.

Natter, Robert. "Sea Trial: Enabler for a Transformed Fleet." *U.S. Naval Institute Proceedings* 129(11) (November 2003): 62–68.

Naval History and Heritage Command (NHHC). "U.S. Navy Active Ship Force Levels." Washington, D.C.: NHHC, 2011–2016.

O'Rourke, Ronald. "Navy CG(X) Cruiser Program: Background for Congress." CRS Report RS34179. Washington, D.C., Congressional Research Service, 2010.

O'Rourke, Ronald. "Navy DDG-51 and DDG-1000 Destroyer Programs: Background and Issues for Congress." Washington, D.C., Congressional Research Service, 2014a.

O'Rourke, Ronald. "Navy Littoral Combat Ship (LCS) Program: Background and Issues for Congress." Washington, D.C., Congressional Research Service, 2014b.

O'Rourke, Ronald. "Navy LX(R) Amphibious Ship Program: Background and Issues for Congress." Washington, D.C., Congressional Research Service, 2014c.

Papadopoulos, Sarandis. "Having to 'make do': U.S. Navy and Marine Corps strategic options in the twenty-first century." *The Routledge Handbook of Naval Strategy and Security*, eds. Joachim Krause and Sebastian Bruns. London: Routledge, 2016, pp. 268–282.

Pendley, William. "The New Maritime Strategy: A Lost Opportunity." *Naval War College Review* 61 (Spring 2008): 61–68.

Ratcliff, Ronald. "Building Partners' Capacities: The Thousand-Ship Navy." *Naval War College Review* 60(4) (October 2007): 45–58.

Reveron, Derek. "Research and Debate: How Many Countries Does It Take to Make a Thousand-Ship Navy?" *Naval War College Review* 60(4) (October 2007): 135–137.

Rice, Condoleezza. *No Higher Honor. A Memoir of My Years in Washington*. New York, NY: Crown, 2011.

Ricks, Thomas. *Fiasco. The American Military Adventure in Iraq*. London *et al.*: Penguin Books, 2006.

Rubel, Robert ("Barney"). *Navies and Economic Prosperity – The New Logic of Sea Power* (Corbett Centre for Maritime Policy Paper No. 11). London, Corbett Centre for Maritime Policy, 2012.

Schneller, Robert. *Anchor of Resolve: A History of U.S. Naval Force Central Command/ Fifth Fleet*. Washington, D.C.: NHHC, 2007.

Sohn, Kathi. "The Global Fleet Station: A Powerful Tool for Preventing Conflict." *Naval War College Review* 62(1) (January 2009): 45–58.

Shakir, Faiz. "Bush Administration's Pre-9/11 Focus Was Missile Defense, Not Terrorism", *Center for American Progress*, September 26, 2006.

Schroeder, Robin. "Not too little, but too late. ISAF's Strategic Restart of 2010 in light of the coalition's previous mistakes." *Afghanistan, Pakistan and Strategic Change. Adjusting Western Regional Policy*, eds. J. Krause/C. King Mallory, IV. New York, NY/London: Routledge, 2014, pp. 19–69.

Swartz, Peter, and Duggan, Karin. *The U.S. Navy in the World (2001–2010): Context for U.S. Navy Capstone Strategies and Concepts* (slideshow). Alexandria, VA: CNA, 2011a.

Swartz, Peter, and Duggan, Karin. *U.S. Navy – U.S. Air Force Relationships 1970–2010* (slideshow). Alexandria, VA: CNA, 2011b.

Till, Geoffrey, and Chan, Jane (eds.) *Naval Modernization in South East Asia – Nature, Causes, and Consequences*. London: Routledge, 2013.

Till, Geoffrey. *Seapower. A Guide for the 21st Century*, 2nd edition. London: Routledge, 2009.

U.S. Navy/U.S. Marine Corps/U.S. Coast Guard. "A Cooperative Strategy for 21st Century Seapower." Washington, D.C.: DON, 2007.

Vego, Milan. *Major Naval Operations*. Newport, RI: Naval War College Press, 2008.

West, Bing. *The Strongest Tribe. War, Politics, and the Endgame in Iraq*. Random House: New York, NY, 2008.

The White House. "The National Security Strategy of the United States of America. September 2002." Washington, D.C.: The White House, 2002.

The White House. "National Strategy for Maritime Security." Washington, D.C.: The White House, 2005.

The White House."The National Security Strategy of the United States of America."
Washington, D.C., The White House, 2006.

The White House. "National Security Strategy. May 2010." The White House:
Washington, D.C., 2010.

Woodward, Bob. *Bush at War.* New York, NY: Simon & Shuster, 2002.

Woodward, Bob. *Plan of Attack.* New York, NY: Simon & Shuster, 2004.

Work, Robert. *The U.S. Navy: Charting a Course for Tomorrow's Fleet.* Washington,
D.C.: Center for Strategic and Budgetary Assessments, 2008.

Work, Robert, and van Tol, Jan. *A Cooperative Strategy for 21st Century Seapower: An
Assessment* (CSBA Backgrounder). Washington, D.C.: Center for Strategic and
Budgetary Assessments, 2008.

7   Sea Change

American national security and U.S. seapower in an increasingly chaotic world (2009–2016)

Prelude

Barack Obama, a Democrat from Illinois, became 44th President of the United States in 2009. His campaign promised a different political spirit and a less militaristic foreign-policy tone which aimed to restore national and international faith in the presidency after the Bush years. Obama sought to complement this at home with a drive to unify Democrats and Republicans, as well as a divided country. Buoyed by a campaign that emphasized change and a can-do spirit, he invested considerable political capital in the establishment of a general healthcare system in the United States. In the wake of a range of deadly shootings at schools and other public places, he pushed for stronger gun legislation. With an increasing number of race-related problems, ethnic polarization of the United States became a center issue for the president. All of this ate away at the time and energy to be spent on foreign policy. Ironically, the president pursued similarly idealist, almost utopian goals in the international arena. Obama – a novice to foreign and defense policy like so many of his predecessors – promised, among other things, closing the terrorist detention facility in Guantanamo Bay, ending the U.S. military involvement in Iraq, extending an outstretched hand to the Arab world, an effort to dismantle all nuclear weapons worldwide ("Global Zero"), and a re-set in U.S.–Russian relations.[1] The simple aspiration of all of this earned him the Nobel Peace Prize in 2009, the year that he took office.[2]

Despite a number of policy breakthroughs at home and abroad such as the liberalization of same-sex marriage in the U.S., healthcare reform, opening relations with Cuba, negotiating a deal with Iran, and pushing for comprehensive climate change policies, Obama's presidential record remains mixed. The Obama presidency can also be characterized as a series of domestic and foreign policy crises that it had to cope with. While it is too soon to evaluate the President's record and take a comprehensive look at his legacy as it relates to national security decisions and their defense and naval implications, a few broad strands do emerge.

Macro level

Obama's presidency was marked by the desire to end the U.S. military engagement in Iraq and bring the war in Afghanistan to an amicable outcome. Obama's objective to get out of the land wars in Southwest and Central Asia was also driven by the rise of other key powers in the international system, such as China or Russia, and a diversification of national security challenges in the face of a disintegrating Middle East. Aware of the overstretched nature of U.S. forces, Obama sought to consolidate American engagement and re-establish an overarching reasoning for the deployment of U.S. military force beyond his predecessor's catch-phrase of "Global War on Terrorism."

Global trends and challenges to U.S. security

When Obama came into office, the effects of the financial crisis of 2007/2008 were in full swing. What began as U.S. consumers and banks overleveraged on shaky credit and asset valuations, especially in housing, soon evolved into a global financial and economic crisis, which required government intervention into the private sector to save certain sectors (like the banking or car manufacturing branches) from defaulting. Worldwide, fiscal deficits rose and threatened the stability and well-being of countries like Greece, Italy, Spain, or Portugal. The effects of the crisis also drew the European Union into policy action to guarantee some member states' bonds and re-assure financial markets. These regulatory efforts to contain – but not resolve – the crisis diverted much energy and time from other foreign policy developments.

The dominating challenges in foreign policy during the first Obama administration were rooted in the military commitments in Central Asia as part of the 'Global War on Terrorism' and the strain this put on U.S. troops, the defense budget, and morale. In Afghanistan, a troop surge entwined with a training program for local forces was put into place by the international coalition that had come together to rid the country of its fate. As of 2014, the nation has 350,000 trained and equipped security forces, coalition forces were withdrawn by schedule, and the economic and social conditions under which Afghans grow up have markedly improved, even if narco-trafficking and the influence of the Taliban continued to be a persistent threat to the country.[3] Across the border, Pakistan moved increasingly into Washington's focus by 2011. The difficult relationship between Pakistan and the United States was exemplified by Osama bin Laden spending the last years of his life under cover in a house in the Abbottabad in North Eastern Pakistan. He was killed in a night raid conducted by a Navy Special Warfare unit in "Operation Neptune's Spear" in the morning hours of May 2, 2011.[4] Any hope that the United States and its allies would be afforded a calmer Middle East were quickly shaken by the 'Arab Spring' which unfolded simultaneously in early 2011. From North Africa to Central Asia, uprisings swept through many of the authoritarian regimes and thrust countries such as Egypt, Libya, and Syria into an ongoing mélange of unrest, civil war, and instability. Other countries in the region such as the U.S. ally Saudi-Arabia tightened their grip on possible opposition forces to consolidate their power. The 'Arab Spring' demonstrated the fragility of the Arab world and the powerful dynamics of demographics and the potential of Islamist influence in the new regional order.[5]

On the far side of the Persian Gulf, Iran, a traditional competitor with Saudi-Arabia over regional hegemony and a benefactor of the turmoil caused in Iraq in the wake of the U.S.-led military invasion, demanded attention from Obama. With its nuclear program, its missile program, the quest for biological and chemical weapons, and its asymmetric warfare capabilities, Iran doubled as a strategic threat to the United States as well.[6]

In one of his earliest foreign policy initiatives, President Obama sought to 'reset' relations with Russia to help steer the bilateral relationship into calmer waters. Russia's willingness to intimidate its neighbors through hybrid warfare means and the factual annexation of territory has demonstrated Moscow's willingness to exploit an inconsequential administration. Washington's persuasiveness, it appears, is severely curtailed. In fact, Russian disinformation campaigns have tried to drive a wedge among NATO member states, furthermore underlining that the Western model of democracy is under pressure.[7] The disillusioned West was dealt insult to injury when Russia gave political asylum to U.S. intelligence community defector Edward Snowden. Snowden's revelations about U.S. eavesdropping on key allies such as Germany have weakened the transatlantic normative cause. Finally, during Obama's presidency, China was a challenge. Relations to the world's most populous country can be characterized as mixed at best, given the very close economic and financial ties on the one hand, and the military aspects pertaining to China's further rise on the other hand.[8]

Finally, ballistic missile defense (BMD) has emerged as a capital-intensive key policy problem for Obama. It has governed relations with Russia, which is vividly opposed to European BMD, and informed a significant degree of force posture in the European perimeter – indeed with a naval component, four forward-based *Arleigh-Burke*-class guided missile destroyers in Rota, Spain. In contrast to other contemporary security challenges, BMD with its focus on deterrence of state actors appeared almost anachronistic in an era of non-state, hybrid, transnational, and asymmetric threats.[9]

Conflicts, crises, and wars

If one was to group the global national security challenges for the United States during the Obama era, three geographic clusters emerge: Central Asia, North Africa/the Middle East, and the European periphery as it pertained to Russia's increasingly adventurous foreign policy.

First, the land wars of Central Asia begun in response to the terrorist attacks of September 11, 2001 dominated Obama's agenda during his first two years in office. Acknowledging that both wars were different in nature and that there were different degrees of motivation of the international community and the coalitions of the willing to intervene in the first place, respectively, the United States grew increasingly frustrated with both conflicts. They also had significant impact on U.S. force structure and morale on the home front.[10] Eventually, the U.S. withdrew its forces at the end of 2011, increasingly frustrated with the lackluster Iraqi government. In Afghanistan, Obama directed a surge of troops of 30,000 own forces complemented by NATO allies.[11]

Second, from early 2011 the so-called 'Arab Spring' led to uprisings in Tunisia and Egypt. Where regime changes occurred, the United States had to carefully navigate the prospects of the new leadership given how stable and reliable relations had been even with previous autocratic rulers.[12] Another civil war erupted in Libya, where Muammar Gaddafi was still in power in 2011. On the face of it, Gaddafi had changed from the terrorism sponsor of the 1980s to a more cordial autocrat, sensing momentum after the attacks of 9/11 to avoid being targeted for actual or possible ownership of weapons of mass destruction. When his forces threatened to quell the opposition, the West – led by France and Italy, supported by the U.S. – intervened militarily. Using a combination of naval and air forces in the U.S.-led "Operation Odyssey Dawn" and later as the NATO-led "Operation Unified Protector," the operation demonstrated some fundamental shortcomings in the naval power of the U.S. and its allies.[13] It also demonstrated how Obama, who fashioned himself as a post-partisan president,[14] oscillated between intervention, leading from behind, and being pressured by the Republican-controlled House of Representatives in national security matters.

Just as the alliance had intervened in North Africa, the civil war in Syria erupted. In contrast to the intervention in Libya, the United States and NATO did not engage with a similar operation in the Levant, both for geopolitical and operational reasons. For one, the situation in Syria was vastly more complicated than in Libya with its relatively clear military geography. In addition, in contrast to the limited humanitarian intervention in Libya, the West risked being drawn into the Syrian war with ground troops. Moreover, it emerged that Syria had very powerful quasi-allies in Iran and Russia that Obama and the West had to reckon with. In fact, Russia emerged as a de-facto military *Schutzmacht* for Syria's ruler, Bashar Assad, and his war against any opposition force. The vicious infighting in Syria has drawn neighbor states into the conflict in various ways. It has displaced 100,000s and cost the lives of many 100,000s more as the country descended into chaos with the rise of the barbarian terrorist organization of the Islamic State (IS).

Russia's reach extended to Syria, but the roots of Russian policy decisions led back to the European perimeter at the fault lines among NATO, Eastern and Southeastern Europe, and Russia itself. Despite an initial easing of relations between the U.S. and Russia early in Obama's presidency, such as the 2010 START agreement, and Russian access-granting for U.S. troop deployments into Afghanistan from the North, aspects of a soured relationship soon came to light. Growing militancy over perceived motifs and actual policy decisions has soured the connection between the former and the current world power. From Russia's seizing of Crimea in early 2014 to its defying involvement in the Ukraine civil war ever since,[15] from intimidation of neighboring states and NATO allies,[16] to Russia's military modernization in particular at sea,[17] little common ground appears to be available. The West's inability to meet the Russian hybrid challenge, and Russia's masterful testing of the West's political will, has created a challenge of its own, namely alliance cohesion. From land- and sea-based BMD plans to its support of the Ukrainian democratization movement, from military assurance measures for Baltic member states to the future of the disintegrating Middle East, there is a profound lack of Western counter-narratives and frankly, ideas. Mutual hostility between Russia and the West is not restricted to political elites, but is evident at the societal level, too.[18] A sense of disappointment prevails.[19] A return of a great-power conflict appears more likely than ever.[20]

Personalities, domestic conditions, and national security strategies

President, secretary, policy/strategy leaders

As has been noted, President Obama, the constitutional lawyer, came into office on a platform that aimed at reconciliation both at home and abroad. Consequently, his security policy team thus included Secretary of Defense Gates and Chairman of the Joint Chiefs of Staff, Admiral Mullen (both were carried over from Bush 43). Gates was eventually succeeded by former Director of the CIA, Leon Panetta (2011–2013), who in turn handed the baton to former Republican Senator Chuck Hagel in 2013. Hillary Clinton, Obama's presidential primary rival, served as Secretary of State during Obama's first term.

With such a seasoned staff, the president aimed to offset his foreign policy inexperience and create a bipartisan thrust to tackle the strategic and military challenges that the U.S. faced. Early on, he hoped to create momentum that supported his decision to send 30,000 more troops to Afghanistan by mid-2010. As such, Obama sought to equilibrate his new ideas with the enduring political, military, and strategic demands of a nation that at the time had also been at war for the better part of the decade. This balancing act strained the Obama presidency as the crisis of the U.S. economy deepened. Obama's foreign policy until 2011 was seen as increasingly unenforceable and considered lacking in direction and traction. That was exacerbated by a White House team that was perceived by senior military leaders to be too young, isolated, inexperienced, and distrustful of a military altogether, which to make things worse it increasingly sought to micro-manage.[21]

On the other end of Pennsylvania Avenue, on Capitol Hill, Congress was an increasingly important force that the president had to reckon with. While the Democrats held the majority in the House of Representatives and the Senate in the 111th Congress (2008–2010), a Republican landslide victory switched the majority in the lower chamber for the 112th Congress (2010–2012). A major driver behind that event was the ascendency of the so-called Tea Party, a conglomerate of libertarian and conservative interest groups that sought to roll back government influence, taxation, and social welfare program spending. Often vigorously opposed to President Obama as an individual and welcomed by a Republican Party that sought to obstruct presidential initiatives, it began to dominate many Republican primaries and the political day-to-day discourse.[22] Concurrently, a number of seasoned Democrats with naval ties lost their seats in the 2010 election, among them Rep. Gene Taylor (Mississippi), Rep. Ike Skelton (Missouri), and Rear Admiral (ret.) Joe Sestak (Pennsylvania), a former influential Navy strategist.[23] The next shakeup occurred with the 114th Congress (2014–2016), where Republicans also wrestled control of the Senate from the Democrats. Obama, in short, enjoyed just two years of a unified government and an instrumental legislative branch.

Back at the Department of Defense, Ray Mabus became Secretary of the Navy in 2009. The 75th Secretary of the Navy, a former junior naval officer, governor of Mississippi, and U.S. ambassador to Saudi-Arabia, was the longest serving official in that position since World War I when he retired in 2017. His two undersecretaries were Robert O. Work, a retired Marine Corps colonel and highly regarded defense intellectual, and Janine A. Davidson, a former Air Force pilot and international affairs scholar. For the three, the leading issues would be shipbuilding, changing department use of energy, realizing personnel changes, especially with regard to sexual assault, and incorporating unmanned systems.

No less than three admirals served as Chiefs of Naval Operations during the Obama presidency. Gary Roughead, a surface warfare officer, had replaced Admiral Mike Mullen in 2007 when the latter was picked to serve as Chairman of the Joint Chiefs of Staff. As a flag officer, he commanded Cruiser Destroyer Group 2, the *George Washington* Battle Group; and U.S. Second Fleet/NATO Striking Fleet Atlantic and Naval Forces North Fleet East. Ashore, he served as Commandant, United States Naval Academy, the Department of the Navy's Chief of Legislative Affairs, and as Deputy Commander, U.S. Pacific Command. These unique experiences (a career not unlike that of his predecessor as CNO, Admiral Mike Mullen) helped provide the global outlook that appealed to the incoming administration's foreign policy objectives. Admiral Roughead oversaw the execution and implementation of CS-21, the groundbreaking document that could only emerge after a number of implausible events such as the shock of an impending U.S. defeat in Iraq 2004–2007, two costly irregular ground campaigns that called into question the relevance of the U.S. Navy and its strike-warfare focus, the systemic threat of a global terrorist network threatening sea lanes and trade, and new institutional experiences after 9/11.[24]

Roughead's successor as Chief of Naval Operations was Admiral Jonathan Greenert, who served from September 2011 to September 2015. The 30th CNO, the first submariner since Admiral Frank Kelso to rise to the highest position in the U.S. Navy, had previously served in the Pacific. This made him well-suited for the emerging "Pacific Century" – or "Pivot to the Pacific," a foreign-policy term devised by Secretary of State Hillary Clinton and publically expressed in a 2011 piece on the website of *Foreign Policy*.[25] After all, which military service could better underpin the transformative momentum devised in Washington than the U.S. Navy, notwithstanding that the majority of warships had already been on the U.S. West Coast and in the Pacific theater for many years? As a service leader, however, Greenert faced a more daunting task, namely the adaptation of CS-21 to the political challenges at home and abroad of the early 2010s. A focus on innovation and dealing with related flaws and delays with new platforms and weapons (DDG-1000, littoral combat ships, railgun, etc.) characterized his tenure. In particular, the increasing operational tempo strained the fleet and its sailors as more and more ship days with a smaller number of ships proposed a fundamental conundrum for combatant commanders, the service, and the defense-policy world. At least as visible and with far-reaching strategic ramifications, the People's Republic of China finally came out with its maritime and naval ambitions during Greenert's tenure.[26] In fact, the CNO sought to embrace China's navy politically as it rises from a coastal defense force to what appears to be a determined regional power-projection blue-water navy. Still, Greenert faced much political criticism, not least from U.S. Congress, about the real strategic investments into the Navy and the way the service would be headed.[27] Towards the end of CNO Greenert's time in office, the Navy published a revised version of "A Cooperative Strategy for 21st Century Seapower," subtitled "Forward, Engaged, Ready" and usually shortened to CS-21R.

The implementation of that new strategic document fell to Greenert's successor, Admiral John Richardson, another submariner, who began to serve as 31st Chief of Naval Operations in September 2015. Richardson previously worked as Head of the Naval Nuclear Propulsion Program, a hybrid organization of the Department of the Navy and the Department of Energy. This program's unique position is a legacy of Admiral Hyman G. Rickover, the imperator of the Navy's nuclear propulsion from the 1950s to the early 1980s. Rickover's principal idea was that everyone who operated in the nuclear field as a naval officer would also be trained as a nuclear engineer. The high degree of specialization meant that typical career paths and the shift between billets ashore and at sea would be ruled out, which in turn should foster focus on the nuclear issues to avoid catastrophic incidents to the nuclear fleet. Richardson's nomination was unique in that he was the first naval officer from this career path to ascend to the Navy's top position, effectively eclipsing Rickover's legacy and adding the Naval Nuclear Propulsion Program to the host of career paths which for any given naval officer could theoretically lead to nomination as CNO.

Domestic conditions

For the purpose of this book, it must suffice to note that during the period under consideration here, the polarization in U.S. politics has increased sharply. The divided, and sometimes fundamentally obstructionist government is but one indication of a larger erosion of the national security consensus and a debate about America's future role.[28] As faith in the American ability to benevolently shape the liberal world order dwindled and the tremendous costs of the two lengthy ground wars in Southwest and Central Asia bore down on the American people, the effects of the financial crisis 2007/2008 have added insult to injury for many citizens. As a nation, the United States is facing many centrifugal demographic challenges at once, which can further strain societal dynamics.[29] The heated debate about the right direction for the country magnified in issues as diverse as general health care, gun laws, race relations, and minority rights has consumed much policy and public attention. At the same time, cooperation between the major political parties in Washington and in fact the very faith in the federal government's ability to compromise has dropped significantly.[30]

Concurrently, trust in Congress and the President has been at record-low levels.[31] A remarkable low-point was reached with the shutdown of government and federal agencies in the unresolved debate about the federal budget.[32] The national security consensus, traditionally a field where both political parties would find much room for compromises and collaboration, was also deeply affected. The Budget Control Act of 2011 enacted wide-ranging spending caps (see Figure 7.1). The process called sequestration mandates across-the-board spending cuts in the military with little to no flexibility for senior leaders and future programs.[33]

Such developments required to be reflected accordingly in the overarching national security policies and capstone documents.

Selected U.S. national security policies, doctrines, and capstone documents

The major national capstone documents of the new Obama administration included the National Security Strategy and Quadrennial Defense Review that were issued in 2010. The Defense Strategic Guidance of 2012 and another Quadrennial Defense Review in 2014 also need to be noted supporting what has been characterized as an emerging Obama Doctrine.

The NSS 2010 struck a markedly more somber, less ambitious tone than Bush's documents had. As Obama's first such work, it tried "to blend the idealism of Mr. Obama's campaign promises with the realities of his

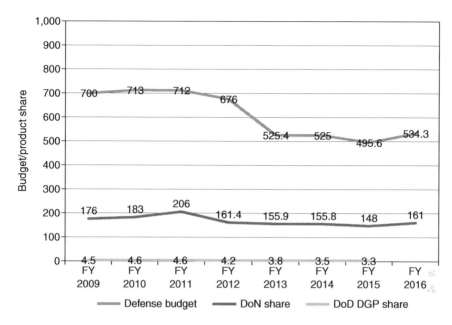

Figure 7.1 FY 2009–2016 defense budget, not including overseas contingency operations (OCO) budget, Department of the Navy portion, and overall gross
domestic product share.[34]

confrontations with a fractious and threatening world,"[35] The independent,
but related QDR of the same year was the sixth full-scale post–Cold War
force review. It reflected an ongoing evolution of strategic thinking which
led away from planning for smaller Cold War-style conventional conflicts
not unlike the 1991 Gulf War, and toward planning to cope with much
more diverse challenges. As one analyst pointed out on the occasion of the
QDR's publication,

> One premise is that no future adversary is likely to confront U.S. conven-
> tional, Cold War-era military capabilities directly. Instead, any foe, ranging
> from violent, radical non-state terrorist groups to a technologically
> advanced near-peer competitor, will try to exploit weaknesses in U.S.
> defenses through asymmetric means. A related premise is that the notion of
> a spectrum of conflict, ranging from unsophisticated insurgents or terrorists
> at the low end to sophisticated national armies at the high end, is becoming
> blurred, with 'low-end' terrorist groups using advanced technologies and
> near-peer competitors likely to use indirect means of attack.[36]

In naval terms, this suggested that the major pundits – usually grouped around
those advocating aircraft carriers and those grouped around the idea of smaller

surface combatants – needed to sharpen their arguments for the future role of naval forces for U.S. naval security once again.

The 2010 QDR's objectives included recalibrating U.S. defense priorities to support the ongoing campaigns in Southwest Asia, while trying to strike a balance between the established two–aggressor standard that had been used as a force-sizing measure and a strategic approach. The force review outlined four national security objectives – prevailing in the current armed conflicts, prevention and deterrence of conflict, preparation to defeat any possible adversaries in a wide range of contingencies, and preservation and enhancement of an all-volunteer force. Regarding the Navy, the QDR described a force size for the fiscal years 2011–2015 of 255 to 289 surface combatants complemented by strategic ballistic missile submarines, ships with prepositioning equipment, and 51 strategic sealift vessels.[37]

The QDR, as well as the Defense Strategic Guidance of 2012, outlined reduced budgets but did not yet operate under the assumption that massive cuts triggered by sequestration would and could in fact be in line. The Defense Strategic Guidance was announced by President Obama, a highly unusual, top-cover move in the first place, but also a signal that he was serious about the rebalancing of U.S. security policy focus to Asia. By taking ownership of the "Pivot," a step that built on administration statements and policy guidance from 2011, the president committed himself to undertaking massive rebuilding efforts of the U.S. military's focus and, in effect, America's role in the world. The Guidance shifted the focus of military planning to the Asia-Pacific area, called for significant and deep reductions of U.S. Army and Marine Corps ground forces in favor of air and naval forces, abandoned the "2-war" capability concept, and bid farewell to nation-building and counter-insurgency operations.[38]

However, it was up to the QDR of 2014, the seventh full-scale U.S. defense review in the quarter of a century since the end of the Cold War, to address how the U.S. saw the world and acted upon it under the conditions of the grave budgetary constraints.[39] The QDR, acknowledging planning for uncertainty, called for reduced personnel costs to free up resources for key technology and military modernization. The Army bore the brunt of these cuts.[40] Still, the QDR expressed a sense that the U.S. should still play a leadership role in the world, but it remained vague and conflicted in the ways and means to be employed to that end. As Congressional Research Service analyst Catherine Dale has pointed out,

> Most U.S. strategic guidance documents underscore the need for U.S. 'leadership' on the world stage. But leadership can be used toward a great variety of different ends, and exercised in a great variety of ways—none are givens, and all require choices. Further, in practice, approaches toward exercising leadership are generally predicated, explicitly or otherwise, on some theory of how power operates in the global arena. Yet leading experts disagree vehemently about the respective importance of

personalities, perceptions, military capabilities, economic strength, norms, and other factors.[41]

Dale unwittingly sketched the challenges of an emerging "Obama Doctrine," as *The Atlantic* characterized it in its April 2016 issue.[42] Although there is no capstone document to it, this issue deserves some attention at this stage for its shaping of U.S. leadership, both perceived and actual, in the period under consideration.[43] As has been noted, Obama was propelled into the presidency on a message of "Hope" and "Change," which raised the highest of expectations in the electorate and the world.[44] When it came to American national security, however, Obama was not much of a believer in Manichaen rhetoric. In fact, as Jeffrey Goldberg recalls, "Obama, unlike liberal interventionists, is an admirer of foreign-policy realism of President George H.W. Bush and, in particular, of Bush's national-security advisor, Brent Scowcroft."[45] Obama by and large practiced a non-hysterical policy-style using a deliberate, non-threatening, and diplomacy-based approach to foreign relations. In his first term as President, he found that the 'Washington Playbook,' which can be understood as the established code of conduct in the capital when it came to threats to American national security credibility, established a logic that often led to the use of military force abroad. This had been practiced for almost a quarter of a century since the end of the Cold War, and the U.S. Navy with its stand-off capabilities such as Tomahawk cruise missiles or carrier air strikes had often been the instrument of choice for a president. When it came to a potential military intervention in the Syrian civil war,[46] five *Arleigh-Burke-*class guided missile destroyers had already taken position in the Eastern Mediterranean. Obama had second thoughts and felt jammed into war by his own cabinet and national security apparatus. His infamous 'red line' about the employment of chemical weapons by the Syrian regime was not enforced. Even if Obama's consequential decision haunts Syrians and the international community until today, it liberated the president from the logic that governed Washington: "The moment Obama decided not to enforce his red line and bomb Syria, he broke with what he calls, derisively, 'The Washington Playbook.' This was his liberation day."[47] U.S.–Russian cooperation to remove these weapons from Syria was set up (again with a strong naval component), but it certainly did not mark the end of the devastating civil war on the Levant.

> History may record August 30, 2013, as the day Obama prevents the U.S. from entering yet another disastrous Muslim civil war, and the day he removed the threat of a chemical attack on Israel, Turkey, or Jordan. Or it could be remembered as the day he let the Middle East slip from America's grasp, into the hands of Russia, Iran, and ISIS.[48]

The rise of the Islamic State and the Russian military intervention into the war on Bashar Assad's side significantly complicated Middle East policy for

Obama, whose main challenge as President included having to distinguish the merely urgent from the truly important problems on the globe, and to focus on the important ones first and foremost. According to the profile in *The Atlantic*, Obama, unlike his own Secretary of State John Kerry, in fact did not regard terrorism as a direct threat to the United States. Instead, climate change, Asia, Africa, and Latin America deserved more attention because the president saw these issues and focus areas as more integral to America's future than the Middle East.[49]

The consequences of Obama's policies will be felt down the road as this century unfolds, but this is neither the time nor the place to speculate about that. Instead, this chapter now returns to U.S. naval strategy and operations during the Obama years.

Developing and promulgating USN strategy 2009–2016

When Obama entered office, "A Cooperative Strategy for 21st Century Seapower" (CS-21) was fresh in place. CS-21 had articulated six core naval missions, ranging from overseas presence to deterrence, sea control, power projection, maritime security and freedom of the seas, and humanitarian assistance/disaster relief. The president showed little aspiration of overhauling it or amplifying it to a truly national maritime strategy as he focused on other policy reforms and "fresh starts" both domestically and abroad after the George W. Bush years.

Building on "CS-21": Navy Strategic Plans and Guidance, Naval Operations Concept (2010), Naval Doctrine Pub 1 – Naval Warfare

Naturally, the development of capstone documents and the formulation of Navy contributions to U.S. strategy did not stop with the publication of CS-21. There were in fact several Navy capstone documents to round out the decade, in particular the "Navy Strategic Plan ISO POM 10 (Ch 1)" (Roughead's revision of outgoing Mullen's strategic plan of the same name [2007]), the "Navy Strategic Guidance ISO PR 11" (2009), the "Navy Strategic Plan ISO POM 12" (2009), the pertinent "Naval Operations Concept" (2010), the equally important "Naval Doctrine Pub 1: Naval Warfare" (2010), and the "Navy Strategic Plan ISO POM 13" (2010) (Table 7.1).

The "Navy Strategic Guidance" document (2009) remains classified. What little is publically available underlines the notion that this document reiterated the strategic imperatives that CS-21 had formulated and linked them to Navy core capabilities, thus sharpening the Navy's arguments on what maritime missions such as sea control, deterrence, power projection, forward presence, maritime security operations, and HA/DR could provide. The document also mentioned a number of additional naval objectives and capabilities, namely using the sea as a staging area (sea basing), superiority in the space and cyber domains, global domain awareness, maritime BMD, and expeditionary logistics. As a programming support tool for the incoming administration, it laid out the larger objectives of Secretary of Defense Gates and CNO Roughead. The "Navy Strategic Plans" (2009/2010) were in principle, much like the "Navy Strategic Guidance," directed internally (hence their classification). They continued the by then routine output of such specialized documents, which were increasingly aligned with other budgetary and programming cycles so that they could have more leverage. These documents used the constructs that CS-21 established and thus increasingly provided some much-needed intellectual cohesion and continuity.[50]

To provide the "ways" for the "ends" that the "Cooperative Strategy for 21st Century Seapower" described, an updated and expanded "Naval Operations Concept" (NOC) to implement the new strategy was issued in May 2010 (it was signed by the same three service chiefs as "CS-21").[51] Again, the process of drafting and implementing the concept was also a tri-service effort of the Navy, the Marine Corps, and the Coast Guard. Whereas the larger strategic aspirations and objectives of these sea services were comparatively easy to align, the NOC needed to address all of the diverse current operations of the three sea services. Essentially, this entailed the whole spectrum of challenges and missions, from global sea-based nuclear deterrence and power projection on the high end, to counter-drug operations on the low (irregular) end, and a plethora of conventional and hybrid challenges in between. This yielded an extended drafting process and a lengthy final, unclassified product (at 102 pages, it was larger than all previous NOC combined). At least three major sets of pressures affected the drafting process:

- First, it proved to be challenging to define and articulate how sailors, marines, and coast guardsmen actually fought.
- Second, the authors needed to provide fodder for the development of future joint/Navy concepts and doctrines.
- Third, it needed to explain the linkage between "CS-21" and the Navy's force-level goals (i.e., "the means") to Congress and defense policy analysts (an effort to publish a force-structure plan that built on "CS-21" had been abandoned earlier).[52]

In describing how naval forces contributed to U.S. national security in a range of operations, the document aimed to reiterate primarily to itself (although Congress, the Obama administration, and the American public were certainly secondary audiences) that the Navy was not just about blue-water operations, the Marine Corps did not simply constitute a second land army, and the Coast Guard was not simply a coastal gendarmerie but a true military partner. Integrated and orchestrated, all of them could embrace all uses of the sea according to their relative leanings.

Dozens of drafts circulated among a large number of stakeholders in the services, and it was nowhere as inclusive as CS-21. The incoming administration and their capstone documents complicated the process and delayed the completion. Operationally, the document accentuated the sea as a maneuver space for all three services. It employed the six core capabilities of CS-21 (forward presence, maritime security, HA/DR, sea control, power projection, and deterrence) and related them to the various classes of naval vessels to describe each ship's place and role in the overall picture. Critics charged that the end product was too simplistic and obvious, a doctrinal instead of a conceptual project, bore little Navy ownership, and did not include risks and trade-offs.[53] As a document, it always was in the shadow of CS-21. The NOC's influence was further curtailed in that it was too voluminous and took too long to roll out.

Just three months after the publication of the NOC, another Navy capstone document was issued. "NDP 1: Naval Warfare" (a doctrine aimed at the men and women in uniform, naval service civilians, and the policy community) superseded the first such pamphlet by the same name issued in 1994 (and in fact, NDP 1 through NDP 6).[54] The 2010 version included the contribution of the Coast Guard and subsequently bore the signature of its service chief, too. The pamphlet made heavy reference to joint documents as well as Navy and Marine Corps warfare publications. Eventually, NDP 1's drafting dragged on for more than 18 months. Its public release was deliberately held back so that the Naval Operations Concept (NOC) could be issued first. NDP 1 included sections on the very general nature of naval service, the employment of its forces, and the conduct of naval operations (in addition, it provided service core values, mentioned the levels of war, and included some naval history). Given the Navy's aversion to written doctrine, the document's influence remained as limited as that of its 16-year-old predecessor, not least because it failed to speak to the political role of naval forces and to future force structure.[55]

A Cooperative Strategy for 21st Century Seapower – Forward, Engaged, Ready (CS-21R)

In the spring of 2015 (a Friday, March 13, to be more precise, but without an astrological interpretation of this here), the U.S. Navy, the U.S. Marine Corps, and the U.S. Coast Guard published a revised volume of "A Cooperative Strategy." It was aptly amended by three adjectives, forward, engaged, and ready. As Robert Rubel pointed out,

> The title suggests that it is an update of the 2007 document [...]. However, the two documents share little except their title. Their purposes as well as intended audience are entirely different, reflecting the strategic needs of the Navy as well as the professional outlook of the Chief of Naval Operations (CNO), Admiral Jonathan Greenert.[56]

Calls for a revision of the original CS-21 had been voiced as early as 2009, including by individuals such as Bryan McGrath, lead author of that 2007 version of American maritime strategy.[57] The domestic and international policy environment, but not the strategic framework which in principal still mandated global maritime security cooperation, had evolved since 2007. President Obama's far-reaching policy shifts, albeit still more in rhetoric than in substance, gradually changed the prospective role of the Navy in support of U.S. national security interests. In addition, the new CNO shared some of the concerns that critics of CS-21 had voiced earlier, such as the lack of a force level or the absence of warfighting first as a core USN mission.

CS-21R still breathed a cooperative spirit, but it mentioned China as a coming peer competitor and thus signaled a significant shift from CS-21, a document that had abstained from naming names. The new force level was set for more than 300 ships to account for the demands of forward-presence, which should include inter alia 11 nuclear-powered aircraft carriers and 33 amphibious vessels. In a marked difference to 2007, the new document was supplemented with a supporting surface warfare strategy ("Distributed Lethality"), a Secretary of the Navy's Innovation Vision, and a series of Congressional hearings. In comparison to 2007, it emphasized warfighting and did not overly concentrate on peacetime missions. It was clearly aimed at an increasingly partisan U.S. Congress, not so much the Navy itself, or the American public. Consequently, the grander maritime, idealist motifs of former strategies were muted. In sum, this led one analyst to grudgingly concede that "[t]his is what a twenty-first century U.S. naval strategy looks like."[58]

A design for maintaining maritime superiority

To complement CS-21R and in part to make their own mark, the new Chief of Naval Operations, Admiral John Richardson and his staff have been busy with publishing supplementary documents to enhance this capstone document.[59] One example is "A Design for Maintaining Maritime Superiority," a handy 10-page pamphlet presented in January of 2016, just a few weeks after Richardson took office. Along with its sister publications, the document aims,

Table 7.1 Navy capstone documents 2009–2016

Name	Year
Navy Strategic Plan ISO POM 10 (Ch 1)	2007
Navy Strategic Guidance ISO PR 11	2009
Navy Strategic Plan ISO POM 12	2009
Naval Operations Concept	2010
Naval Doctrine Pub 1: Naval Warfare	2010
Navy Strategic Plan ISO POM 13	2010
A Cooperative Strategy for 21st Century Seapower Revised (CS-21R)	2015
A Design for Maintaining Maritime Superiority	2016

if not explicitly, to make sense of an ever-shrinking fleet, emphasize the need for forward-presence and deep cooperation with the U.S. Marine Corps, and direct innovation and experimentation to new levels. One U.S. defense analyst was blunt in his assessment, stating "warfighting and deterrence have trumped peacetime presence, capability has trumped capacity, and quality has trumped quantity. This isn't just a change in terminology. It signals a change in course, one with strategic and budgetary ramifications."[60] Once again, these ramifications will need to be measured against time, although they are in the end little more than functions of different, competing schools of naval and maritime thought.[61]

Force structure

Force structure numbers (see Table 7.2) did gain some prominence when they were briefly debated in the 2012 Presidential Debates between incumbent Barack Obama and his Republican Party challenger, Mitt Romney.[62] Unfortunately, this exchange was not followed up by a more focused (logical, but perhaps politically inopportune at the time) discussion on just what kind of Navy would be desirable and what such a well-balanced fleet for the U.S. would look like.

The debate about force structure continued for the rest of the decade and is ongoing.[63] In 2009 and 2010, alternative U.S. Navy force level goals emerged to complement, or rival, the CNO's opinion of 313 ships as a floor. A "Report to Congress on Annual Long-Range Plan for Construction of

Table 7.2 U.S. Navy active ship force levels, 2009–2015[64]

Date	9/09	9/10	9/11	9/12	9/13	9/14	9/15	9/16
Carriers	11	11	11	11	10	10	10	10
Cruisers	22	22	22	22	22	22	22	22
Destroyers	57	59	61	62	62	62	62	63[1]
Frigates	30	29	26	23	17	10	–	–
LCS	1	2	2	3	4	4	5	8
Submarines	53	53	53	54	54	55	54	52
SSBNs	14	14	14	14	14	14	14	14
SSGNs	4	4	4	4	4	4	4	4
Mine warfare	14	14	14	14	13	8	11	11
Amphibious	33	33	31	29	30	31	30	35
Auxiliary	46	47	47	52	55	59	59	58
Surface total	121	123	122	121	115	118	99	103
Total active	285	288	285	288	285	289[2]	271	275

Notes
1 Including one of the planned three new destroyers DDG-1000, the USS *Zumwalt*, at 14,800 tons.
2 Patrol craft of the *Cyclone*-class (10 units) were factored in that year. They do not appear in the table. See text for discussion.

Naval Vessels for FY 2011" (the 30-year Navy Shipbuilding plan) floated the number 292 battle force ships by FY 2016, 304 battle force ships by FY 2028, and 301 battle force ships by FY 2040. The 2010 QDR projected a number of 255–289 ships for FY 2011-FY 2015 plus an according number of SSBNs, prepositioning vessels, and 51 ships for strategic lift. Secretary of Defense Gates in August 2010 derived from the QDR his 313–323 battle force goal noted in Figure 7.2 (Swartz, 2011a: 59, slide 118). Other alternatives were pitched in various publications by the Center for Strategic and Budgetary Assessments (CSBA) (2008) – 326 ships; the Center for New American Security (CNAS) (2008) – 300 ships; the Sustainable Defense Task Force (SDTF) (2010) – 230 ships; the QDR Independent Panel (QDRIP) (2010) – 346 ships; and the CATO Institute (2010) – 241 ships.[65]

Perhaps the most visible change in the force structure occurred with the retirement of the last of the *Oliver Hazard Perry*-class frigates built for the U.S. Navy between 1977 and 1989. These sturdy warships, a late Cold War backbone to the U.S. Navy and part of the original hi-low mix proposed by CNO Admiral Elmo Zumwalt in the early 1970s, were decommissioned by September 2015. It robbed the Navy of a tested and trained platform that had been quite useful in its original ASW and escort role and, after the end of the Cold War, also provided valuable presence in areas as diverse as the Caribbean (where it engaged, among other things, in counter-narcotics operations)

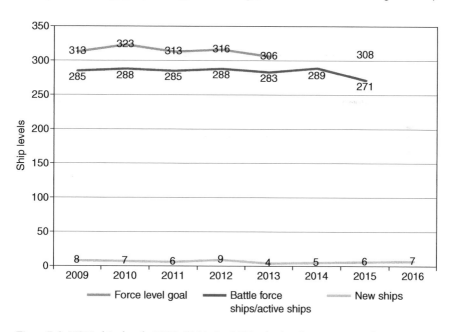

Figure 7.2 USN ship levels 2009–2016. In 2010, the landing zone was between 313 and 323. In 2012, the landing zone was between 313 and 316 ships. FY 2011–FY 2016 new U.S. Navy ships derived from www.shipbuilding history.com.

or the Baltic Sea (where *Perry*-class frigates participated in exercises such as BALTOPS). The frigates' proposed successors, the Littoral Combat Ships of the *Freedom-* and *Independence*-classes, have hardly filled that role properly, and a new frigate program is on the way at the time of writing this book.

A significant, if highly politically charged debate ensued from March 2014 on. In a letter to Congress, Secretary of the Navy Mabus announced changes in the ship counting mechanisms. The measure effectively introduced a different metric to counting ships of the battle fleet by including auxiliary vessels such as hospital ships, expeditionary fast transport catamarans of the incoming *Spearhead*-class, and the *Cyclone*-class patrol boats into the total. It was in particular Republican lawmakers who criticized this move as a thinly veiled attempt to grow fleet numbers.[66] Despite the political points to score, such debates are hardly new, although they can be very confusing and the analyst cannot help but wonder if this is a mere straw man debate conducted in lieu of a more nuanced and sincere strategic debate.[67] A look at the recent "paper trail" of fleet design and force structure studies demonstrates the amount of intellectual investment that is instilled in this debate in U.S. defense circles.[68]

Strategic and operational implementation: planned vs. actual

Perhaps the most telling aspect of the U.S. Navy's role in American national security during the presidency of Barack Obama is its increasing ops tempo rather than "the one large" event. This is demonstrated in part by some significantly longer ship deployments. For instance, aircraft carriers were deployed for as much as 10 months at a time, a remarkable change from six-month tours just a decade earlier. Recently, the Navy has attempted to shorten such lengthy and costly deployments to eight months.[69] While these measures are draining naval resources and professional patience of military professionals first and foremost, there were also more visible naval operations, among them in wars in Libya, Syria, and in numerous smaller show of force/presence missions in the European periphery and in the Indo-Pacific region.

Major U.S. naval operations

Libya

The war was the first test for NATO's Allied Maritime Strategy, which had emphasized crisis management, military operations other than war, and cooperative security.[70]

The military upshots were manifold. Naval forces closed the sea lines of communication for the Libyan regime, thus effectively imposing a blockade. They provided access by deploying overwhelming force, such as through eliminating strategic enemy air defense in the first two nights of "Operation Odyssey Dawn" with Tomahawk missiles. This helped enable the no-fly zone. Through maritime presence closest to the area of operations, naval assets supported the civilian protection mission with Harrier aircraft from USS *Kearsarge* (LHD 3), naval gun-fire support especially from U.K. and French surface warships, and light helicopter attacks later in the conflict. Other key naval roles included maritime surveillance (ISR), electronic warfare, combat search and rescue, and command and control such as from USS *Mount Whitney* (LCC 20). Moreover, the Naval Air Station in Sigonella (Italy) became a significant basing asset for NATO air power.[71]

Syria / Iraq / Counter-Daesh

While a direct U.S. military intervention against the Assad regime did not come to fruition despite the "red line" invoked (see above), the U.S. Navy has played an important role since. First, together with allied navies, the U.S. safeguarded the removal and disposal of chemical weapons from Syria in Operation RecSyr in 2014. Interestingly enough, the Chinese PLAN and the Russian Navy were also part of that truly multinational group of navies, a strong testament to the diplomatic and operational opportunities of sea power.

With the rise of the self-proclaimed Islamic State in Iraq and Syria (ISIS), also known as Daesh, the international military intervention that began in earnest in June 2014 (including an on-going proxy conflict with Russia and Iran) continues to be supported by dedicated maritime assets. The U.S. Navy, for instance, used carrier-based airpower to supplement allied air forces which flew sorties on targets in ISIS strongholds.[72]

Continuous demand in Europe

Beyond the increasing turmoil and unrest around the southern and western Mediterranean, the U.S. Navy was also in continuously high demand in other European areas of concern. From the Black Sea to the High North, European allies saw a significantly higher degree of U.S. naval involvement. It ranged from joint exercises to training missions and from classic naval diplomacy to reassurance measures of NATO partners on the Eastern flank. The increasing threat of terrorism as manifested in attacks in Europe and one of its root causes, the disintegration of large parts of NATO's Southern flank, tied together various theaters and security challenges, signaling an increasingly complex and chaotic security environment. At the same time, where CS-21R emphasized warfighting missions, in Europe partnerships with allies gained significant importance in the thinking of naval strategy leaders.[73] Coinciden-tally, relations with an aspiring Russia at sea also intensified. Russian aircraft "buzzing" U.S. warships occurred in both the Black Sea and the Baltic. The U.S. Navy and its allies were also hard at work re-learning to counter estab-lished naval threats and missions which had been largely abandoned in the post-sea control era since 1990, for example antisubmarine warfare.[74]

Relationship to allies

In this security environment, relations to allies waxed and waned. Allied relationships were often burdened by national security and defense priorities, such as the postulated American "pivot" to the Pacific, which raised concerns in parts of Europe that the U.S. would all but abandon the old continent. Concurrently, European governments were to a large degree self-absorbed with managing the conflagration of domestic and financial crises on the continent, which often left little room for more robust military and defense considerations. In addition, allied military actions such as the (land forces centric) war in Afghanistan contributed to a fatigue. The growing frustration on both sides of the Atlantic could be observed by then-Secretary of Defense Robert Gates' harsh criticism directed at European NATO allies on his "farewell tour" in Europe; a message that has been voiced much more strongly by the new U.S. President and Obama's successor, Donald J. Trump, and his senior staff.[75]

Despite these tendencies, both NATO and the European Union issued capstone documents for the maritime security domain. In 2011, the Alliance published its Alliance Maritime Strategy, a 20-point plan that addressed the maritime security environment, the maritime contributions to NATO security, deterrence and collective defense in the maritime domain, crises management, cooperative security (thus echoing the key tenet of the U.S. Navy's CS-21 strategy), maritime security, the maritime aspects of the comprehensive approach, and the role of alliance transformation.[76] The Alliance Maritime Strategy was the first post-Cold War document to address the maritime (and naval) implications of NATO transformation and although some parts of it have been taken over by recent events, the document is quite important for the future of the alliance. In fact, a more formal reiteration of its key principles will be a worthwhile endeavor.

Three years later, in 2014, the European Union followed suit and published its own strategy, albeit less vocal and more maritime than naval in nature.[77] The European Union Maritime Security Strategy was adopted in the summer of that year and contained selected maritime security interests of the EU, its member states, and its citizens, risks and threats, and a host of bureaucratic implementation measures. In addition, an action plan was also submitted.[78]

While the integration of allied and U.S. naval forces continued unabated (e.g., with German frigates in U.S. carrier strike groups, German air-independent submarines training with U.S. forces, and the usual large-scale exercises in the Indo-Pacific), the U.S. Navy's introduction of CS-21R reinvigorated allied interest in the U.S. Navy's trajectory.[79]

Assessment

At the time of writing, it is much too early to arrive at an assessment of the Obama presidency through a seapower lens. Given the trajectory of world affairs, the policies of his successors, and the many variables and parameters which shape a sound review, this is not necessarily a bad thing for navalists who are taking the long view that is inherent to seapower and strategy.[80] If, for instance, Obama's covert grand strategy of disentangling the United States from the Middle East through a series of concerted measures and seemingly unconnected policy decisions is successful, he might well go down in history as a great American president (although others may, as a principle, disagree). On the other hand, Obama's tenure might be seen as inconsequential in times of a changing world order and significantly eroding trust in America, both by its people and its allies.

Notes

1 See Miller Center of Public Affairs. "Barack Obama: Foreign Affairs."
2 "The Nobel Peace Prize for 2009 to President Barack Obama – Press Release". *Nobelprize.org*. Nobel Media AB 2014.
3 Stavridis, 2014: 48–49.
4 Bergen, 2012; Owen and Maurer, 2012.
5 See Paul Danahar, *The New Middle East: The World After the Arab Spring* (2015) for a detailed analysis.
6 Cf. Katzmann, 2016: 18–30.
7 Neil MacFarQuhar, "A Powerful Russian Weapon: The Spread of False Stories." *New York Times*, August 28, 2016.
8 See Morrison, *China–U.S. Trade Issues*, 2015; O'Rourke, *Maritime Territorial and Exclusive Economic Zone (EEZ) Disputes Involving China: Issues for Congress*, 2016a; O'Rourke, *China Naval Modernization: Implications for U.S. Navy Capabilities— Background and Issues for Congress*, 2016a; and Office of Naval Intelligence, 2015a, for representative analyses. On the future of China's Navy, see Sarah Kirchberger's excellent study (and interesting methodology to analyze naval forces), also from 2015.
9 Seidler, 2015: 210.
10 Bruns, 2012b: 339–340.
11 Stavridis, 2014: 42.
12 This was especially important in the case of Egypt, an important country in the Middle East and guardian of the Suez Canal, one of the world's most important maritime choke points. On U.S.–Egyptian relations and military ties, see Sharp, 2015. Egypt made headlines when the country purchased the two French *Mistral*-class amphibious assault ships ordered by Russia in 2009 but not delivered by France in 2014 in the wake of EU sanctions against Moscow.
13 See McGrath, 2013, and Smith-Windsor, 2013, for details.
14 Cf. Bruns, 2012b: 341.
15 Russia's support of Ukrainian rebels and active participation of unmarked Russian ground forces without patches in a series of hybrid campaigns had one of its terrifying low points in the shooting down of a civilian aircraft over Ukraine on July 17, 2014 with the loss of all 298 lives, using a Buk antiaircraft missile.
16 Cf. Posener, 2016; Withnall, 2015.
17 Office of Naval Intelligence, 2015b.
18 Lo, 2015: 168–179.
19 Stavridis, 2014: 97.
20 Krause, 2014: 144–151.
21 Gates, 2014: 222.

22 Jacobson, 2011: 2–3.
23 Sestak served on the staff of the Chief of Naval Operations as Head of the Strategy and Concepts Branch and Director of the Strategy and Policy Division. He was then the Director of the Navy Quadrennial Defense Review, after which he became the first Director of the Navy Operations Group ("Deep Blue"). He also served in the Office of the President of the United States as the Director for Defense Policy on the National Security Council staff at the White House; as Director, Assessment Division/Capability Analysis Group (N81/N00X); and as Deputy Chief of Naval Operations for Warfare Requirements and Programs (N6/N7) on the staff of the Chief of Naval Operations. Vice Adm. Sestak's last assignment was as Special Assistant to the Vice Chief of Naval Operations, where he was removed by incoming Chief of Naval Operations Adm. Mike Mullen as one of the CNO's first administrative actions (Phucas, "Sestak command raises questions," April 5, 2006).
24 Haynes, 2015: 238.
25 Clinton, 2011. That policy shift was soon embraced by statements by the President and his senior national security staff, cf. "Remarks by President Obama to the Australian Parliament – As Prepared for Delivery," November 17, 2011; "Remarks by National Security Advisor Tom Donilon – As Prepared for Delivery," November 15, 2012. The term would later be refashioned as a rebalancing rather than a pivot, chiefly because the latter characterization was felt to have unnecessarily roused China and left the European allies and the Middle East to their own devices.
26 O'Rourke, 2016b; Kirchberger, 2015: 255–318.
27 "Letter to Admiral Jonathan Greenert, 28 July 2014," Rep. Randy Forbes.
28 Both major political parties saw long-lasting candidates in their respective primary nominations. These individuals ran on platforms that would dramatically alter the way the United States would shape the world. Senator Ron Paul (2008, 2012) and his quest for a Republican nomination come to mind as well as Senator Bernie Sanders for the Democrat ticket in the 2016, and the Republican candidate Donald Trump in the same race.
29 D'Vera Cohn and Andrea Caumont, "10 demographic trends that are shaping the U.S. and the world," Pew Research Center, March 31, 2016.
30 See Bruns, "A Window Seat on American Politics: Reflections on the GMFUS/APSA Congressional Fellowship," in *PS: Political Science and Politics*, Vol. 45, No. 2 (April 2012a), pp. 343–345.
31 "Americans' Confidence in Institutions Stays Low," Gallup Poll, June 13, 2016.
32 From October 1 through 16, 2013, the United States federal government entered a shutdown and truncated the majority of routine operations. Neither legislation appropriating funds for fiscal year (FY) 2014 nor a continuing resolution for the provisional authorization of appropriations for FY 2014 was passed in time.
33 John Grady, "Expert: Sequestration Spending Caps Will be Major Challenge for Next Administration," *USNI News*, August 2, 2016.
34 Congress failed to pass the budget for the FY 2011 (October 2010–September 2011) by the deadline (September 30, 2010) and the federal government operated on a series of continuing resolutions which kept spending at or near FY 2010 levels. The legislative deadlock cumulated in the threat of a government shutdown, but the budget bill was eventually enacted on April 15, 2011.
35 Sanger and Baker, 2010.
36 Daggett, 2010: 2.
37 Swartz, 2011b: 43, slide 85.
38 Cobb, 2012.
39 The Budgetary Control Act (2011) mandated cuts of U.S.-$487 billion across a decade as well as an additional sequester of U.S.-$50 billion per year over the same period of time should Congress fail to consolidate the national budget.

40 Marco Overhaus, "Quadrennial Defense Review 2014. Entwicklungstrends US-amerikanischer Verteidigungspolitik und Konsequenzen für die Nato," SWP Aktuell 12/März 2014, pp. 1–2.
41 Dale, 2014: 6.
42 The following paragraph is based on Goldberg, 2016: 70–90.
43 This is especially timely given much of the uncertainty regarding grand strategy, the national security and foreign policies of the 45th President of the United States of America, Donald J. Trump. This manuscript was submitted in March 2017, a mere six weeks into the presidency.
44 Friedersdorf, 2014.
45 Goldberg, 2016: 73.
46 John Kerry, "Statement on Syria," August 30, 2013.
47 Goldberg, 2016: 75.
48 Ibid., 76.
49 Ibid., 81.
50 For an overview of the information that is publically available on "Navy Strategic Guidance ISO PR 11," see Swartz, 2011a: 203–219, slides 406–437. For an overview of the information that is publically available on "Navy Strategic Plan ISO POM 12," see Swartz, 2011a: 219–234, slides 438–468; for "Navy Strategic Plan ISO POM 13," see Swartz, 2011a: 300–315, slides 600–630.
51 Department of the Navy, 2010a.
52 Swartz, 2011a: 237, slide 437.
53 Swartz, 2011a: 269, slides 537–538.
54 Department of the Navy, 2010b.
55 Swartz, 2011a: 296–297, slides 592–593.
56 Robert C. Rubel, e-mail to author, July 19, 2015.
57 McGrath, 2009.
58 Robert A. Newson, "This Is What a Twenty-First Century U.S. Naval Strategy Looks Like," Council on Foreign Relations, May 13, 2015. The eventual successes and shortcomings of this capstone document will need to be measured against these intents, a task far beyond this study.
59 CNO Greenert did not sit idly and wait for CS-21R to come out. In fact, he asked N00Z to publish out "a series of short, easy to understand papers, signed by him, labelled 'Sailing Directions', 'Navigation Plan', and 'Position Report', annually updated, that served as the Navy's 'capstone documents' until CS21R came out" (Peter Swartz, e-mail to author, August 28, 2015).
60 Freedberg, 2016.
61 Thus, R.B. Watts' 2016 book "American Sea Power and the Obsolescence of Capital Ship Theory" (McFarland: Jefferson, NC) might have to be reviewed if reprinted for a second or third edition.
62 George, 2013: 221.
63 For a pertinent study on U.S. Navy force structure, see the very recent PhD dissertation by Amund Lundesgaard, *Controlling the Sea and Projecting Power. U.S . Navy Strategy and Force Structure After the Cold War*, University of Oslo 2016.
64 Naval History and Heritage Command, 2011–2016.
65 Swartz, 2011b: 60, slide 119–120. A force structure assessment in December 2016 recommended a Navy of 355 ships. In 2017, shortly after Donald Trump was sworn in, three distinct studies once again raised broader attention to U.S. Navy force structure and shipbuilding. The Center for Strategic and Budgetary Assessments' "Restoring American Seapower: A New Fleet Architecture for the United States Navy" (written by Bryan Clark, Peter Haynes, Timothy Walton, Bryan McGrath, Jesse Sloman, and Craig Hopper, Washington, D.C., February 9, 2017) argued for a new strategic approach, innovative operating concepts, new deployment patterns and force packages, and a U.S. Navy of up to 382 ships. Alternatively, a U.S. Navy

study group's own report advocated 457 ships and 1,220 aircraft (Navy Project Team, "Report to Congress. Alternative Future Fleet Platform Architecture Study," October 27, 2016) and MITRE, a think tank, offered a 414-ship goal in their "Navy Future Fleet Platform Architecture Study, 1 July 2016" report sponsored by the Department of the Navy (it was in particular Senator John McCain, Chairman of the Senate Armed Services Committee and a staunch supporter of a strong U.S. military, who advocated on behalf of these various reports).

66 LaGrone, 2014.
67 Eckstein, 2015.
68 For recent samples, see Robert Work, "Winning the Race: A Naval Fleet Platform Architecture for Enduring Maritime Supremacy," Center for Strategic and Budgetary Assessments, March 1, 2005; Stuart E. Johnson and Arthur K. Cebrowski, "Alternative Fleet Architecture Design," Center for Technology and National Security Policy at the National Defense University, August 2005; Congressional Budgetary Office, "Options for the Navy's Future Fleet," May 2006; Ron O'Rourke, "Navy Force Structure: Alternative Force Structure Studies of 2005 – Background for Congress," Congressional Research Service Report RL33955, April 9, 2007.
69 McGarry, 2014.
70 Seidler, 2015: 203.
71 John D. Sherwood, e-mail to author, August 4, 2016. For a maritime strategy review of the campaign from a NATO perspective, see Brooke Smith-Windsor, "NATO's Maritime Strategy and the Libya Crisis as Seen from the Sea," NATO Defense College Research Paper No. 90, March 2013.
72 The nuclear-powered aircraft carriers USS *George H.W. Bush* (June–October 2014), USS *Carl Vinson* (October 2014–March 2015), USS *Theodore Roosevelt* (March–October 2015), USS *Harry Truman* (December 2015–July 2016), and USS *Dwight D. Eisenhower* (June–December 2016) provided a near-continuous presence in the Eastern Mediterranean/Persian Gulf. The lone French aircraft carrier in service, Charles de Gaulle, was also dispatched to the region to allow continuous attacks on the militia's positions and assets. Allied navies (such as the Royal Navy and the German Navy) are also participating in the naval mission. Even Russia has dispatched its single aircraft carrier, the aging conventionally powered *Admiral Kusnetsov*, to the Levante to bolster the Assad regime and send a powerful message to the home front – while the operational value of that particular deployment is more than questionable.
73 Cf. James Foggo III and Eric Thomson, "Implementing the Design for 'Maintaining Maritime Superiority' in Europe and Africa," PRISM 6, No. 2 (July 25, 2016a), pp. 70–81.
74 Cf. James Foggo III and Alarik Fritz, "The Fourth Battle of the Atlantic," USNI Proceedings Vol. 142/6/1360 (June 2016b), pp. 18–22.
75 MacAskill, 2017.
76 North Atlantic Treaty Organization, "Alliance Maritime Strategy," March 18, 2011.
77 Council of the European Union, "European Union Maritime Security Strategy," June 24, 2014.
78 Among other things, NATO AMS and EU MSS have spawned nations such as Germany to draft naval strategic documents which align with both of these strategies as well as with the U.S. Navy's own strategic enterprise. This author was a part of the German CNO's strategic advisory group 2014–2016 and drafted a capstone document, yet unpublished, "We shape the sea. Together. Responsibly" (the author holds a copy). For a broad overview of the key elements of German naval strategy, see Bruns, "Some elements of 21st century German naval strategy," in: Joachim Krause and Sebastian Bruns (eds.), *Routledge Handbook of Naval Strategy and Security*, London: Routledge 2016b, pp. 283–295.

79 For a view from Germany on CS-21R and its predecessor, see Sebastian Bruns, "The 'Cooperative Strategy' (CS-21/CS-21R): A View from Germany," Center for International Maritime Security, May 27, 2015. For implications of U.S. naval trends, see "Seemacht und Geopolitik: Wandel in der US-Marinepräsenz birgt neue Betätigungsfelder für die Marinen der europäischen Staaten," in: *Sicherheit + Frieden* 3–2014, 32. Jahrgang, pp. 176–181.
80 Recently, interest in the academic and policy-focused study of the U.S. Navy is expanding with more and more books, book chapters, and wide-ranging essays. See, among others, Papadopoulos, 2016, Swartz, 2016, and Bruns, 2017.

References

Bergen, Peter. *Manhunt. The Ten-Year Hunt for Bin Laden from 9/11 to Abbottabad.* New York, NY: Crown, 2012.

Bruns, Sebastian. "A Window Seat on American Politics: Reflections on the GMFUS/APSA Congressional Fellowship." *PS: Political Science & Politics* 45 (2012a), 343–345.

Bruns, Sebastian. "'In Search of Monsters to Destroy?' Die USA nach einem Jahrzehnt Anti-Terrorkampf." *Jahrbuch Terrorismus 2011,* ed. J. Krause and S. Hansen. Opladen/Farmington Hills: Budrich (2012b), 337–352.

Bruns, Sebastian. "Some elements of 21st century German naval strategy," eds. Joachim Krause and Sebastian Bruns, *Routledge Handbook of Naval Strategy and Security,* London: Routledge, 2016b, 283–295.

Bruns, Sebastian. "Seemacht und Geopolitik: Wandel in der US-Marinepräsenz birgt neue Betätigungsfelder für die Marinen der europäischen Staaten." *Sicherheit + Frieden* 3–2014 32 (March 2013): 176–181.

Bruns, Sebastian. *The U.S. Navy's Role in National Strategy, Especially Between 1980 and Today.* Washington, D.C.: NHHC, 2017.

Clark, Bryan, Haynes, Peter, Walton, Timothy, McGrath, Bryan, Sloman, Jesse, and Hopper, Craig. "Restoring American Seapower: A New Fleet Architecture for the United States Navy." Washington, D.C., *Center for Strategic and Budgetary Assessments,* February 9, 2017.

Clinton, Hillary. "America's Pacific Century." *Foreign Policy,* October 11, 2011, n.p. Accessed July 14, 2017. http://foreignpolicy.com/2011/10/11/americas-pacific-century.

Cobb, Ty. "The Defense Strategic Guidance: What's New? What is the Focus? Is it Realistic?" *Harvard Law School National Security Journal,* January 8, 2012.

Council of the European Union, "European Union Maritime Security Strategy", June 24, 2014.

Daggett, Stephen. "Quadrennial Defense Review 2010: Overview and Implications for National Security Planning," Washington, D.C.: Congressional Research Service, 2010.

Danahar, Paul. *The New Middle East: The World After the Arab Spring.* London, Bloomsbury UK, 2015.

Dale, Catherine. "The 2014 Quadrennial Defense Review (QDR) and Defense Strategy: Issues for Congress," *CRS 7–5700,* February 24, 2014.

Department of the Navy. "Naval Operations Concept 2010: Implementing the Maritime Strategy." Washington, D.C.: DON, 2010a.

Department of the Navy. "Naval Doctrine Publication (NDP 1)." Washington, D.C.:DON, 2010b.

Department of the Navy. "MITRE Navy Future Fleet Platform Architecture Study, 1 July 2016." Washington, D.C., DON, 2016.

Eckstein, Mega. "Battle Over How to Count Navy Ships is Confusing, But Not New," USNI News, March 16, 2015.

Freedberg, Sidney. "CNO: Warfighting Trumps Presence; ORP, EW Win; LCS Likely Loser," *Breaking Defense*, January 5, 2016.

Friedersdorf, Conor. "The Decline and Fall of Hope and Change," *The Atlantic*, January 30, 2014.

Forbes, Randy. "Letter to Admiral Jonathan Greenert, 28 July 2014."

Foggo, James, and Thomson, Eric. "Implementing the Design for 'Maintaining Maritime Superiority' in Europe and Africa." *PRISM* 6(2) (25 July 2016a): 70–81.

Foggo, James III, and Alarik, Fritz. "The Fourth Battle of the Atlantic." *USNI Proceedings* 142/6/1360 (June 2016b): 18–22.

Gates, Robert. *Duty: Memoirs of a Secretary at War*. New York, London: Random House, 2014.

George, Rose. *Ninety Percent of Everything. Inside Shipping, the Invisible Industry that puts Clothes on your Back, Gas in your Car, and Food on Your Plate*. New York, NY. Picador, 2013.

Goldberg, Jeffrey. "The Obama Doctrine. The President explains his hardest decisions about American's role in the world." *The Atlantic*, April 2016.

Grady, John. "Expert: Sequestration Spending Caps Will be Major Challenge for Next Administration", USNI News, August 2, 2016.

Haynes, Peter. *Toward a New Maritime Strategy: American Naval Thinking in the Post-Cold War Era*. Annapolis, MD: NIP, 2015.

Jacobson, Gary. "The President, the Tea Party, and Voting Behavior in 2010: Insights from the Cooperative Congressional Election Study." *SSRN Electronic Journal*, 2011.

Johnson, Stuart E., and Cebrowski, Arthur K. "Alternative Fleet Architecture Design." Washington, D.C., Center for Technology and National Security Policy at the National Defense University, August 2005.

Katzmann, Kenneth. *Iran: Politics, Gulf Security, and U.S. Policy*. Washington, D.C.: Congressional Research Service, 2016.

Kirchberger, Sarah. *Assessing China's Naval Power: Technological Innovation, Economic Constraints, and Strategic Implications*. Wiesbaden: Springer, 2015.

Krause, Joachim."Kooperative Sicherheit und die Rolle von Streitkräften." *Maritime Sicherheit im 21. Jahrhundert*, ed. H.D. Jopp. Baden-Baden: Nomos (2014), pp. 134–162.

LaGrone, Sam. "Navy's New 'Battle Force' Tally to Include Hospital Ships and Small Patrol Craft," USNI News, March 11, 2014.

Lo, Bobot. *Russia and the New World Disorder*. Washington, D.C.: Brookings Institution, 2015.

Lundesgaard, Amund. "Controlling the Sea and Projecting Power: U.S. Navy Strategy and Force Structure After the Cold War." Dissertation, University of Oslo, Norway, 2016.

MacAskill, Ewen. "Mattis threatens Nato with reduced US support over defence spending. Donald Trump's defence secretary warns US will no longer 'carry disproportionate share of defence of western values.'" *Guardian*, February 15, 2017.

MacFarQuhar, Neil. "A Powerful Russian Weapon: The Spread of False Stories." *New York Times*, August 28, 2016.

McGarry, Brendan. "Navy to Begin 8-Month Carrier Deployments." Military.com, January 24, 2014.

McGrath, Bryan. "Scrap the Maritime Strategy." *Information Dissemination*, December 4, 2009.

McGrath, Bryan. *NATO at Sea: Trends in Allied Naval Power* (AEI National Security Outlook No. 3). Washington, D.C.: American Enterprise Institute, 2013.

Miller Center of Public Affairs, University of Virginia. "Barack Obama: Foreign Affairs." Accessed February 21, 2017. http://millercenter.org/president/biography/obama-foreign-affairs.

Morrison, Wayne. *China–U.S. Trade Issues*. Washington, D.C.: Congressional Research Service, 2015.

Naval History and Heritage Command (NHHC). "U.S. Navy Active Ship Force Levels." Washington, D.C.: NHHC, 2011–2016.

Navy Project Team. "Report to Congress. Alternative Future Fleet Platform Architecture Study." Washington, D.C., DON, October 27, 2016.

Newson, Robert. "This Is What a Twenty-First Century U.S. Naval Strategy Looks Like," Council on Foreign Relations, May 13, 2015.

Noble Media AB. "The Nobel Peace Prize for 2009 to President Barack Obama – Press Release". Nobelprize.org, February 21, 2017.

North Atlantic Treaty Organization (NATO). "Alliance Maritime Strategy." Brussels: NATO, 2011.

Office of Naval Intelligence (ed.). *The PLA Navy: New Capabilities and Missions for the 21st Century*. Washington, D.C., ONI, 2015a.

Office of Naval Intelligence (ed.). *The Russian Navy. A Historic Transition*. Washington, D.C.: ONI, 2015b.

O'Rourke, Ronald. "Navy Force Structure: Alternative Force Structure Studies of 2005 – Background for Congress." Washington, D.C., Congressional Research Service, April 9, 2007.

O'Rourke, Ronald. "Maritime Territorial and Exclusive Economic Zone (EEZ) Disputes Involving China: Issues for Congress." Washington, D.C., Congressional Research Service, 2016a.

O'Rourke, Ronald. "China Naval Modernization: Implications for U.S. Navy Capabilities—Background and Issues for Congress." Washington, D.C., Congressional Research Service, 2016b.

Owen, Mark, and Maurer, Kevin. *No Easy Day. The Autobiography of a Navy Seal: The Firsthand Account of the Mission That Killed Osama Bin Laden*. New York: Dutton, 2012.

Overhaus, Marco. "Quadrennial Defense Review 2014. Entwicklungstrends US-amerikanischer Verteidigungspolitik und Konsequenzen für die Nato," Berlin, Stiftung Wissenschaft und Politik, 2014.

Papadopoulos, Sarandis ."Having to 'make do': U.S. Navy and Marine Corps strategic options in the twenty-first century." *The Routledge Handbook of Naval Strategy and Security*, eds. Joachim Krause and Sebastian Bruns. London: Routledge, 2016, pp. 268–282.

Phucas, Keith. "Sestak command raises questions," *The Times Herald*, April 5, 2006.

Posener, Alan. "In Defense of the Baltics." Carnegie Europe, August 4, 2016, last retrieved September 5, 2016.

Sanger, David, and Baker, Peter. "New U.S. Strategy Focuses on Managing Threats," *New York Times*, May 27, 2010.

Seidler, Felix. *Maritime Herausforderung der NATO. Strategische Auswirkungen und die Effektivität des Handelns.* Frankfurt *et al.*: Peter Lang, 2015.

Sharp, Jeremy. "Egypt. Background and US Relations." Washington, D.C.: Congressional Research Service, 2015.

Smith-Windsor, Brooke. *NATO's Maritime Strategy and the Libya Crisis as Seen from the Sea* (NDC Research Paper No. 90). Rome, Italy: NATO Defense College, 2013.

Stavridis, James. *The Accidental Admiral. A Sailor Takes Command at NATO.* Annapolis, MD: NIP, 2014.

Swartz, Peter. "American naval policy, strategy, plans, and operations in the second decade of the twenty-first century." *The Routledge Handbook of Naval Strategy and Security.* eds. Joachim Krause and Sebastian Bruns., London: Routledge, 2016, pp. 229–267.

Swartz, Peter, and Duggan, Karin. *U.S. Navy Capstone Strategies and Concepts (2001–2010): Strategy, Policy, Concept, and Vision Documents* (Slideshow). Alexandria, VA: CNA, 2011a.

Swartz, Peter, and Duggan, Karin. *The U.S. Navy in the World (2001–2010): Context for U.S. Navy Capstone Strategies and Concepts* (slideshow). Alexandria, VA: CNA, 2011b.

Withnall, Adam. "Russia threatens Denmark with nuclear weapons if it tries to join Nato defence shield," *Independent*, March 22, 2015.

Work, Robert. "Winning the Race: A Naval Fleet Platform Architecture for Enduring Maritime Supremacy", Washington, D.C., Center for Strategic and Budgetary Assessments, March 1, 2005.

8 Conclusion

This book has analyzed the evolution of U.S. Navy strategy and American sea power over the course of three decades as framed by major Navy capstone documents. To arrive at a more nuanced understanding of the concepts involved, it first discussed the relationship between seapower and sea power, the political and military uses of the sea, relevant theory, and the links between different levels of strategy, naval missions, and some particular contexts of the maritime domain which guide formulation of naval and maritime strategy. The analysis also showed the intimate relationship among strategy, planning, and force structure.

The role of navies in foreign policy and as strategic tools of security policy is underappreciated and widely unexplored in practical policy as well as in academic circles. The reasons for this remain tentative; perhaps it is because of the service's specialized strategic culture or its operations at sea, and thus out of sight, often making it appear inaccessible to outsiders. However, the military and political effects of navies and naval power are ultimately felt ashore. Strategic planners must take this into account, and analysts are well-served to conceptualize this, at least. Such importance warrants more study of modern seapower and sea power. At the very least, the U.S. government's commitment to be the world's pre-eminent sea power for over 75 years demands examination. Ken Booth's work of 1979 deserves to be dusted off.

More than just a semantic chicken-and-egg dance, one must carefully tease apart the different meanings of the concepts at hand. An assessment of the role (and relative value) of a navy in the national security construct of a state requires a consistent methodology and a careful differentiation. Terminology does not always help: after all, what exactly constitutes U.S. Navy strategy in the first place? What can be subsumed under the umbrella of "sea power?" The terms involved are so comprehensive they can easily mean something entirely different to anyone. To hedge against such confusion, this work breaks down the concept into seapower (one word) as an institutional and geographical quality of a nation and sea power (two words) as a universal, comprehensive, and conscious political choice in the application of military power.

There are some general aspects. Sea power includes diplomatic, constabulary, and military roles. These require a balanced fleet of different but multimission capable ships. To rationalize a balanced fleet, a navy must produce declaratory statements for various internal and external audiences such as policy and military leaders, legislators, programmers, the public, officers and enlisted men and women, allies, and even competitors. These declaratory capstone documents are the hinges which connect the frame of seapower to the door of sea power. For the researcher, the strategic concepts offer a unique prism through which intellectual, fiscal, geostrategic, technological, programming, personnel, and domestic political currents can be assessed. These aspects govern the effectiveness and efficiency of sea power. In turn, a look at how these declaratory documents played out in the real world – in force structure, naval operations, public support, relationship to allies, etc. – is also justified to arrive at the better placement of strategy into its context.

A causal relation between strategies (general or naval), their practical employment, and whether a strategy was a success, is difficult to trace much less to verify. Decision-making processes and institutional learning rarely conform to theoretical models. Instead, they are subject to diverse internal dynamics and external influences of a political nature. In short, they are contingent on changing world conditions, national policies, and personalities.[1] Moreover, the strategic orientation of a navy, its roles, missions, and force structure are never determined in a political vacuum. They hardly adhere to orderly hierarchical processes in which strategy follows from an articulation of national interests, an identification of threats, establishment of political-military objectives, matching of goals with available resources, and corresponding operations. Although strategy is the attempt to control events, in reality, making strategy is more often a complicated and even chaotic process.[2] Naval strategy and its underlying policies are both a product of and a factor in the competitions, interactions, and ambiguities of statecraft; they are simultaneously an input and a product. Individuals, events, or adverse decisions can interpose even in the most rational and theoretical logic of these processes; as former British Prime Minister Harold MacMillan apocryphally said of what can derail grand plans, "Events, dear boy, events."[3] Naval strategies can thus often only approximately align with overarching strategies. At best, they offer narratives which are compelling and adequately substantiated to exert upward political pressure, enhance service cohesion, and provide a comprehensive and optimistic general marching order. A study of naval strategy must reflect these limitations and dynamics or else render itself meaningless.

American seapower

America boasts the determinants of functional (geographic) as well as horizontal (institutional) seapower. "From Sea to Shining Sea," as the famous hymn "America, the Beautiful" declares, makes America an island nation with extended coastlines to the East and West, some of the world's largest and best-served ports, and a potent maritime industrial base. Although the quality and quantity of American shipbuilding is waning compared with many other nations, the domestic maritime industry supports nearly 500,000 jobs and almost $100 billion in annual economic output.[4] The United States' division of the world into areas of military responsibility is unique, but it is a function of the island nation, reflecting the established practice of forward presence.

Institutionally, there are a number of actors that make, as well as factors shaping, the constitution of American seapower and, by implication, statements of strategic quality and intent. The President, Congress, the Joint Chiefs of Staff (and its Chairman), the Secretary of Defense, and the regional and functional military commanders all matter. As principally laid out in the U.S. Constitution and Title 10, U.S. Code, they have codified responsibilities and obligations, continually exercised to shifting degrees, while facing interpersonal dynamics and influences. The president is important for overarching leadership and direction for where he wants the nation to go. The U.S. Senate and the House of Representatives are in charge of modifying presidential politics although historically they have been more interested in people and equipment which they are asked to fund, and less so in the larger strategic designs of the Navy.[5]

In a world where the military is thinking and acting progressively more jointly (and single-service strategies and programs are increasingly frowned upon), the Chairmen of the Joint Chiefs have a central role in the formulation of military strategy and in advising the president on security and defense policy matters (although the chain of command now essentially bypasses them). American unified combatant commanders also have an important role, as requirements for forces are based on their assessments. Even if these requests are more geared toward fulfilling current needs, they can exert upward pressure on thinking as well as resources through the chain of command.

The Secretary of Defense is important in coordinating the programming efforts of the services and departments. OPNAV and the Department of the Navy are the cores where service strategies (Navy capstone documents) originate, at least in the overwhelming majority of instances. Such projects are naturally subject to available budgets, specializations, individual and collective ambition, classification, and many more influences. It follows – and a look at the history of the documents proves – that in terms of strategy-making and defining institutional seapower, Chiefs of Naval Operations usually matter a lot, whereas the Secretaries of the Navy only matter sometimes.[6]

In any discussion of American seapower, a host of other shapers must be considered as secondary influences, although they neither have the constitutional nor legal rights and obligations to shape U.S. Navy strategy. It also behooves us to consider the unique qualities and capabilities that the other military services bring to bear. Where service strategies previously wrestled with influence and thrust, in an increasingly joint environment a service can now better attempt to shape coming legislation and even joint policy and strategy by deliberately finding partners. This must be taken into account in any analysis. Interest groups and the media are further aspects that can – however briefly – interpose. Although they often merely focus on individual issues or events far below the strategic level, their actions influence policy-makers to eventually make strategically relevant choices. This, in turn, can affect program planning and the crafting of strategy.

The underlying ideas and ideals that frame grand, security, and military strategy are those most interesting to the political scientist. These range from overarching, great visions (e.g., why does America go to war, to what ends, and against which targets does it direct political-military force) to more practical, but long-established naval missions (e.g., what and how does the Navy do at sea to contribute effectively and efficiently to foreign-policy objectives). Ideally, the former and the latter types of thought both factor equally for an analyst. The current practice in strategy-making as well as in its analyses, however, appears to be more about missions than about visions.

This is where the overlap between seapower theory and sea power theory is greatest. Seapower is a fundamental national security quality with sea power as its indispensable instrument. These general hypotheses have evolved since the writings of Alfred Thayer Mahan, Julian Corbett, or Stansfield Turner. Despite the advent of technology and the fundamental complexities of the modern age, there are a number of patterns that help understand and explain the enduring value of sea power for a seapower like the United States. Given such context, it follows that naval strategy is not revolutionary, but evolutionary. Technologically advanced, well-equipped, flexible and forward-present naval forces can serve the nation across a spectrum ranging from alliance-building and humanitarian assistance to surveillance and from economic coercion, show of force to limited and larger wars in ways that other military and diplomatic tools do not offer. Obviously, such a wide array of opportunities must be embedded in political and military guidance. In fact, the effects of a navy were seldom a problem for such a high-tech force; the determination of where to reach out and touch, and whether that makes a difference, is the supreme challenge.

U.S. Navy strategy and American sea power in perspective

The evolution of U.S. Navy strategy is deeply rooted in the normative and political history of the country, and its role and place in the world. After the Spanish-American War of 1898, the United States emerged as a truly global power. For the country, World War I and World War II were inherently maritime and naval in nature; in Washington, entanglement in both conflicts was signaled by events at or from the sea. After 1945, nuclear weapons began to dominate strategic thinking. In the absence of a capable sea control challenger, the Navy made its focus deterrence. Strategic bombing and massive retaliation became central to the political and military vocabulary even as real-world events showed that limited, non-nuclear armed conflicts remained a real possibility. The end of the U.S. monopoly on nuclear weapons and long-range aircraft, and the introduction of missile technology and nuclear propulsion, guided the development of a sea-based strategic deterrent. That SSBN force supplanted aircraft carriers in their nuclear strike role which became a milestone in the revival of a conventional naval strategy. This timely development occurred against the backdrop of the Vietnam War where the Navy's mission was reduced to power projection at the expense of its sea control capabilities. Emerging Soviet high seas power then required a re-concentration on giving the Navy a broader mission set just as the nation licked its wounds from defeat in Southeast Asia and the fallout of Watergate. The renaissance of a comprehensive sea power strategy slowly began inside the Navy but for the time being faced countercurrents from a generally anti-naval Carter administration.

With the presidency of Ronald Reagan and the top cover of Secretary of the Navy John Lehman, "The Maritime Strategy" eventually unfolded. It was a timely reaction to meet increasing Soviet confidence and came amidst deteriorating superpower relations in the 'Second Cold War' of 1979–1985. Buoyed by rising defense spending and fervent presidential rhetoric, the new strategy and the accompanying 600-ship force structure energized the Navy. The coming war, in the words of Admiral Jim Stavridis (who as a young lieutenant helped draft the strategy),

> was all about fighting the Soviet Union, it was about the Greenland-Iceland-United Kingdom gap [...], it was about the 'Hunt for Red October', the great undersea battle that would transpire. It was a very, very large, almost galactic struggle across the Atlantic and really around the world.[7]

Reagan's second presidential term saw eased relations with the Soviet Union. Defense reorganization and acquisition reforms changed how the military went about its business. In short, "The Maritime Strategy" was a meaningful piece of U.S. overall strategy, even if it ran the risk of unbalancing the Soviets through offensive carrier and attack submarine operations in the vicinity of Moscow's strategic SSBN preserves. "The Maritime Strategy" tracked with the President, Congress, the Navy, and – after the documents were unclassified – with the public and American allies. The U.S. Navy was also very busy with limited conflicts throughout the 1980s, which underlined naval roles across the spectrum of conflict, consistent with the presence-crisis-war continuum "The Maritime Strategy" described.

After the end of the Cold War, dramatically shrinking defense budgets put significant pressure on the service and the global existential threat of the Cold War was replaced by more nuanced, but vague regional scenarios (in the words of President George H.W. Bush, a new world order). This uncertain environment yielded an abundance of overarching strategies and policies from senior political and military leaders, in particular during the presidency of Bill Clinton, who tried to manage and grapple with the different era. The Navy sought to react accordingly. It produced a host of (usually unclassified) strategic concepts and documents with different names to influence the debate. With "… From the Sea" (1992) and "Forward … From the Sea" (1994), the Navy accepted power projection and refocused from the high seas to the littorals, while retaining a blue-water fleet. At the same time, the United States enjoyed uncontested maritime supremacy and rushed to draw down its Cold-War force (for the Navy consistently larger than strategic documents requested) rationally. Some of the substantial intellectual gains of "… From the Sea" and "Forward … From the Sea" unfortunately were eclipsed by contemporary scandals that unsettled the Navy. The Navy's capstone documents of the second half of the decade must therefore be understood as low-key efforts to right the service's culture and to provide it with doctrinal and operational consolidation instead of grander strategic and political–military visions.

The operations of the 1990s (with increasing integration of allies) reaffirmed the versatility of naval forces as adaptable instruments in the foreign policy toolkit. From mere peacetime presence to limited armed conflict, the Navy was engaged in many short wars and incidents. These operations were buttressed by significant advancements in technology, computerization, and shipbuilding.

After the terrorist attacks of 9/11, the Navy once again adapted and adjusted, having just recently submitted its "Seapower 21" capstone document. Homeland security and counter-terrorism now became a yardstick justifying many programs and approaches. Throughout this decade, the Navy's force level goals were higher than its ship inventory. From the confined waters of the Persian Gulf or the open seaways of the Arabian Sea, the U.S. Navy backed ground, air, and counterinsurgency operations in Afghanistan and Iraq with close air support, long-range strike, reconnaissance, surveillance, and intelligence collection. The Navy also forward-deployed thousands of troops on the ground for explosive ordnance disposal, communications, security, training, special operations, and additional missions in conjunction with other military branches, allies, and partners. The U.S. military was in the middle of its bottom-up transformation process when the demands of the asymmetric, hybrid war against terrorism mandated yet another change in posture and thinking, another transformative shock. This affected the Army and the Marine Corps most, which bore the brunt of the campaigns in Southwest Asia.

Despite rising defense budgets and the Navy's quest to identify inefficiencies, the service benefited comparatively little from the militarization under President George W. Bush. Cost and schedule overruns plagued the modernization of the fleet. In response, by the mid-2000s the Navy came up with a concept built around the dynamics and implications of globalization, while repudiating the popular and prevailing assumption of a generational war against irregular fighters. Implicitly, the strategic focus also shifted to near-peer competitors like China. Creating the resulting family of related documents included participation by the Marines and Coast Guard.

Much of the Navy's strategic outlook survived the transition to President Barack Obama although the future, as always, remained uncertain. Since 2009, geopolitical shifts, an ongoing, comprehensive economic and financial crisis, an erosion of American/EU political leadership and amicable trans-atlantic ties, political gridlock in Washington, and an increasingly worn president have weighed down on American drive and will to lead the world.

This book has described several enduring tensions in writing and using naval strategy. Unawareness of what navies can do, and how, must be overcome. Pressures to get budgets written and balanced will always challenge those trying to think through, write, and communicate a Navy strategy. The joint world needs to understand both the maritime environment and how navies work to make the best use of sea power. All these points suggest that maritime and naval strategy deserves consideration by those using and critiquing seapower. Despite these tensions, when the U.S. Navy got its strategy "right" either in the 1980s or, in a more attenuated way, after 2007, the service successfully overcame the friction they imposed. The victories of sea power are often silent. The exceptional flexibility of sea power has played an important role for the United States of America, but the appreciation for the Navy in the White House, on Capitol Hill, in the Pentagon leadership, and in the public has waxed and waned. This condition is especially true for the balance tilting in favor of continental and land-based conflicts America encountered since the end of the Cold War.[8]

The Navy carries its share of responsibility for this challenge. In short, it has a difficult time crafting strategy. Problems along the way of creating, crafting, and implementing such issues range from the pressures of jointness, a lack of appreciation for policy dynamics and terminology, the Navy's inherent tactical and operational focus, internal and bureaucratic problems, a fear of debate and discussion, budgetary concerns, Navy-Marine Corps issues, classification, or the lack of senior leader involvement.[9] Other issues include timing and alignment with joint planning circles and documents like the Quadrennial Defense Review, National Security Strategy, National Defense Strategy, and the National Military Strategy. The Navy's documents can never satisfy all audiences. Hence, the service can do naval strategy (like "… From the Sea" and "Sea Power 21"), but a maritime strategy (like "The Maritime Strategy" or CS-21) is more difficult to develop.

Most important of all, real-world actions usually interpose and undermine the attempt of strategy-makers to control the course of events. This means that only process is a viable key to comprehending U.S. Navy strategy and understanding American sea power, even if academically unsatisfying. The quality and assertiveness of naval strategic thought fluctuates. It requires constant grooming, consciousness of best practices, and a harkening back to traditional virtues. Enduring naval missions offer insights into what the future might hold for the U.S. Navy and the prospective exercise of American naval power around the world in the years to come. But the lesson is also clearer that a well-formulated strategy, combined with receptive political and public audiences, will build success for the U.S. Navy.

While naval missions result from the objectives assigned to naval forces (that eventually contribute to Grand Strategy objectives and general foreign policy goals), "naval strategy and doctrine are the way, or methods by which naval forces accomplish strategic and operational objectives."[10] Hence, naval strategy is the method[11] that allows analysts to assess how larger navies attempt to contribute to broader ends. Moreover, grasping this method can also help authors tasked with crafting naval strategy, as well as policy decision-makers, to better understand what seapower is and in which broad strands and lines it works.

Notes

1 Swartz, 2009: 18.
2 Hattendorf, 2004: viii.
3 https://en.wikiquote.org/wiki/Harold_Macmillan, accessed 15 January 2017.
4 Hunter and Scalise, 2014.
5 Swartz, 2009: 70.
6 Swartz, 2011: 84, slides 167–168.
7 Interview, 2012: 00:09:45–00:12:20.
8 Cropsey, 2013: 94.
9 Swartz, 2009: 32.
10 Rexrode, 2004: 9.
11 Germond, 2015: 46.

References

Cropsey, Seth. *Mayday: The Decline of American Naval Supremacy.* New York, London: Overlook Duckworth, 2013.

Germond, Basil. *The Maritime Dimension of European Security. Seapower and the European Union.* Basingstoke, Palgrave, 2015.

Hattendorf, John, ed. *The Evolution of the U.S. Navy's Maritime Strategy, 1977–1986.* Newport, RI: Naval War College Press, 2004.

Hunter, Duncan, and Scalise, Steve. "Making Headway with America's Maritime Industry. U.S. Shipping Contributes Billions to National Economy," *Washington Times,* March 25, 2014.

Rexrode, Tim. *Building Corbett's Navy: The Principles of Maritime Strategy and the Functions of the Navy in Naval Policy.* United States Marine Corps Command and Staff College, Quantico, VA, 2004.

Stavridis, James, Admiral United States Navy (Commander, U.S. European Command; Supreme Allied Commander, Europe). Mons (Belgium), June 15, 2012, 00 hr 25 min.

Swartz, Peter. *U.S. Navy Capstone Strategy, Policy, Vision and Concept Documents: What to consider before you write one* (slideshow). Alexandria, VA: CNA, 2009.

Swartz, Peter, and Duggan, Karin. *U.S. Navy Capstone Strategy and Concepts: Introduction, Background and Analyses* (slideshow). Alexandria, VA: CNA, 2011.

https://en.wikiquote.org/wiki/Harold_Macmillan, accessed January 15, 2017.

Index

Page numbers in *italics* denote tables, those in **bold** denote figures.